Reason and Republicanism

Reason and Republicanism

Thomas Jefferson's
Legacy of Liberty

EDITED BY
GARY L. MCDOWELL AND SHARON L. NOBLE

ROWMAN & LITTLEFIELD PUBLISHERS, INC.
Lanham • Boulder • New York • Oxford

ROWMAN & LITTLEFIELD PUBLISHERS, INC.

Published in the United States of America
by Rowman & Littlefield Publishers, Inc.
4720 Boston Way, Lanham, Maryland 20706

12 Hid's Copse Road
Cummor Hill, Oxford OX2 9JJ, England

British Library Cataloguing in Publication Information Available

Library of Congress Cataloging-in-Publication Data

Reason and republicanism : Thomas Jefferson's legacy of liberty / edited by Gary L.
    McDowell and Sharon L. Noble.
      p. cm.
      "From a conference held in November 1993 at the Institute of United States
Studies in the University of London"—Acknowledgments.
      Includes bibliographical references and index.
      ISBN 0–8476–8520–9 (alk. paper).—ISBN 0–8476–8521–7 (alk. paper)
      1. Jefferson, Thomas, 1743–1826—Political and social views—Congresses.
2. Political science—United States—History—18th century—Congresses. 3. Political
science—United States—History—19th century—Congresses. 4. Jefferson, Thomas,
1743–1826—Influence—Congresses. 5. United States—Politics and government—
1783–1865—Congresses. 6. Equality—United States—Congresses. I. McDowell,
Gary L., 1949– . II. Noble, L. Sharon, 1960– .

  E332.2R43   1997
  973.4′6′092—dc21   97-8235
                                                         CIP
ISBN 0-8476-8520-9 (cloth : alk. paper)
ISBN 0-8476-8521-7 (pbk. : alk. paper)

Printed in the United States of America

⊚™ The paper used in this publication meets the minimum requirements of American National Standard for Information Sciences—Permanence of Paper for Printed
Library Materials, ANSI Z39.48-1984.

To
Brenda McDowell and Howard Noble
for always being there

Contents

Acknowledgments

This book grew from a conference held in November 1993 at the Institute of United States Studies in the University of London. That conference on "Thomas Jefferson's Legacy of Liberty" was held as part of the international celebration of the 250th anniversary of Jefferson's birth organized in collaboration with the Smithsonian Institution in Washington, D.C. The idea sprang from early conversations with Wilton S. Dillon and A. E. Dick Howard, without whose guidance the program would not have been possible. We are deeply indebted to them.

The original conference was made possible by the generous support of the John M. Olin Foundation. This was not the first time, nor was it the last, that the Olin Foundation has supported the work of the Institute of United States Studies. We are most grateful for the moral as well as the financial support of this project celebrating Thomas Jefferson.

As in the preparation of any book, this project has accumulated a great many other debts along the way. To the staff and students of the Institute of United States Studies who lent a hand at various points, we are truly grateful. In particular, the assistance of Anna Brooke, from the planning and execution of the conference to making certain the manuscript was in the mail by the due date, was simply essential. So, too, was the splendid editorial assistance provided by Françoise Humphrey without whom the final touches could never have been made in so timely a manner.

Finally, this book is dedicated to the two who matter most.

Introduction

Gary L. McDowell

Thomas Jefferson: there has never been anyone quite like him in American politics. Author of the Declaration of Independence, governor of Virginia, minister to France, secretary of state, vice president and then twice president of the United States, founder of a political party that endures to this day, architect, farmer, scientist, lawyer, inventor, and musician, he was a man who could "calculate an eclipse, survey an estate, tie an artery, plan an edifice, try a cause, break a horse, dance a minuet, and play a violin."[1] As one of his most gifted biographers has said, the "tributaries of his mind ran in all directions."[2]

By the age of forty, Jefferson was already a citizen of the world. The intellectual vitality of the man and his cultured interests were clearly reflected in the esteem in which he was held by so many of those who came into contact with him. Despite his rhetoric extolling agrarian virtues, Jefferson was very much a city man, urbane of manners and sophisticated in his tastes. The opportunities to experience the theater, opera, art, and architecture he found during his years in Europe, for example, fulfilled his cultural longings and took him beyond the narrow confines of politics. From his first sojourn to England (with which he was not terribly impressed) through his treks around France, Germany, the Netherlands, and northern Italy, this man of boundless intellectual energy and insatiable curiosity sought the best Europe had to offer, becoming in the process America's first

1

connoisseur of the arts. Jefferson returned to the United States the "greatest apostle of European culture."[3]

The seemingly disparate strands of Jefferson's interests, from architecture to music to natural history to politics, ultimately were united in his abiding faith in human reason. Jefferson was, first and foremost, a student of the Enlightenment; his confidence in man's ability to better himself through his rational gifts never faltered. The great accomplishments in the arts and architecture that so captivated Jefferson during his tour of Europe, as well as the shortfalls of the old political orders he witnessed, only reaffirmed his most basic faith in mankind. But more, his time in Europe only bolstered his belief that America was an exception to the wretchedness and corruption that characterized the Old World.[4]

For Jefferson, the great European empires of the past were nothing compared to what the mind of man, freed from its shackles of past tyrannies, could create. To the very last, he maintained that the age in which he had been fortunate enough to live would prove to be the turning point in human affairs; it was truly the Age of Reason.

In the last letter he ever wrote, sending his regrets that he would not be able to travel to Washington, D.C., to participate in the Golden Jubilee of the Declaration of Independence being planned for July 4, 1826, Jefferson recalled with pride that document he had written half a century before:

> May it be to the world, what I believe it will be, (to some parts sooner, to others later, but finally to all,) the signal of arousing men to burst the chains under which monkish ignorance and superstition had persuaded them to bind themselves, and to assume the blessings and security of self-government. . . . All eyes are opened, or opening, to the rights of man. The general spread of the light of science has already laid open to every view the palpable truth, that the mass of mankind has not been born with saddles on their backs, nor a favored few booted and spurred, ready to ride them legitimately, by the grace of God.[5]

This was the essence of Thomas Jefferson. The idea that "the unbounded exercise of reason and freedom of opinion" was a natural right to which all men were entitled gave both shape and direction to Jefferson's political thought and remained the motivating force of his long public life. For the five decades that exactly separated the signing of the Declaration of Independence on July 4, 1776, and his death on July 4, 1826, Jefferson was a moral force in American politics, constantly defending the right of the people to self-government.

Jefferson's Great Collaboration

There is no better record of Jefferson's lifelong commitment to constructing an empire of liberty on the foundation of reason than his friendship with James Madison, an association that spanned the same fifty years between the Declaration of Independence and his death and one that was captured in their carefully preserved correspondence. They first met in 1776, a few months after the Declaration was signed; Madison was twenty-five years old, Jefferson was only thirty-three. They began working closely in 1779 when Jefferson became Governor of Virginia and Madison was a member of the Executive Council. It was an acquaintance that deepened quickly to friendship and finally flowered into a full and robust political partnership. Neither man ever had a better or more trusted friend.

They were unrestrained in their mutual admiration. To Madison, Jefferson was "one of the most learned men of the age";[6] in Jefferson's estimation, his friend was simply "the greatest man in the world," possessed of "a luminous and discriminating mind."[7] Their affection spawned a friendship, as Madison would write, that was "for life, and . . . was never interrupted in the slightest degree for a single moment."[8] As Jefferson entered his last year, with, as he put it, "one foot in the grave, and the other uplifted to follow it," he wrote to Madison that "you have been a pillar of support through life" and assured his oldest friend "that I shall leave with you my last affections."[9]

What had given the great vitality to their "friendly communion" was that the virtues of the one complemented those of the other perfectly. One observer notes that while Jefferson's intellect was "the most brilliant," Madison's was "the most profound"; yet another concludes that while Jefferson was a man of vibrant imagination, Madison "excelled perhaps in judgement." John Quincy Adams marveled that "the mutual influence of these two mighty minds upon each other is a phenomenon, like the invisible and mysterious movements of the magnet in the physical world."[10] And each received as much as he gave. As Merrill Peterson has said, "the account balanced."[11]

The nature of how Jefferson and Madison complemented each other was to be of immense importance to the founding and early development of the American Republic. Benjamin Henry Latrobe described Jefferson "as a man out of a book," while Madison was "more a man of the world."[12] Ever the idealist, Jefferson was constantly given to philosophical flights of fancy, while the patiently realistic Madison was always there as his sober second thought.

Between them, with Jefferson's tendency toward the abstract countered by Madison's anchor in the concrete realities of life, they produced a body of political thinking that was remarkably consistent in its devotion to the republican principles that shaped their political lives.

Nothing better captures the two sides of this "great collaboration," as Adrienne Koch so aptly dubs it, than the two documents with which their names will be forever linked.[13] Jefferson's Declaration of Independence, with its powerful invocation of the laws of nature and of nature's God, set out the philosophical premises of modern constitutionalism: that all men are by nature endowed with certain inalienable rights and that to secure these rights, governments are instituted among men, deriving their just powers from the consent of the governed. Eleven years later, Madison's Constitution put those principles into practice. Where the Declaration spoke of self-evident truths, natural rights, and political legitimacy, the Constitution spoke of the powers to fix weights and measures and to establish post offices and post roads, and other mundane matters such as terms of office. The intellectual relationship of Jefferson to Madison is reflected in the political relationship of the Declaration to the Constitution.

Jefferson was an idealistic democrat, Madison was a cautious republican. Where Jefferson saw danger in the powers of government, Madison feared the licentiousness of the people. When Jefferson argued for a frequent appeal to the people to resolve constitutional conflicts, Madison feared any such plan would only inflame public passion at the expense of public peace. When Jefferson, during the heady days of the French Revolution, wrote to Madison from Paris "that no society can make a perpetual constitution, or even a perpetual law. The earth belongs always to the living generation," Madison quickly pointed out how utterly impractical such a notion would be to good government. While it might be a fascinating glimmer "in the eye of the philosophical Legislator," Madison wrote back, "a government so often revised [would] become too mutable to retain those prejudices in its favor which antiquity inspires, and which are perhaps a salutary aid to the most rational government in the most enlightened age."[14]

Jefferson was not simply shaped by his friend's opinions; he, too, could persuade. When he finally saw the new Constitution of 1787, Jefferson thought it ill advised not to include a bill of rights. "Let me add," he wrote in December 1787, "that a bill of rights is what the people are entitled to against every government on earth, general or particular, & what no just government should refuse, or rest on inferences."[15] By October 1788, Madison had come around to favor a bill of rights because, as he saw it, "it might be of use, and, if properly executed, could not be of disservice." In particular, he thought such "political truths declared in that solemn manner [could] acquire by degrees the character of fundamental maxims of free government" and thereby, if some future danger arise from a tyrannical government, serve as "a good ground for an appeal to the sense of the community." In the end, it was for Madison less a matter of fundamental rights than political prudence: "Should this danger exist at all, it is prudent to guard against it, especially when the precaution can do no injury."[16] The Bill of Rights that was eventually appended to the Constitution, of course, bore far more the marks of Madison's republican sobriety than Jefferson's democratic passion.

Despite occasional differences, the strength of their shared assumptions and common political faith connected them at both the personal and the political level. Much of the correspondence between Jefferson and Madison addressed the most pressing issues of their day, from taxes to treaties to protective tariffs and trade wars. And it was by their efforts in the nuts and bolts of policy that the two Virginians found themselves confronted by formidable political enemies who, to say the least, did not share their strict views of the Constitution and the nature and limits of political power under it. Within five years of the adjournment of the Federal Convention, confrontations with Alexander Hamilton over what Jefferson and Madison saw as the tendency of his policies to increase the powers of the national government at the expense of the states led to Jefferson's founding the Republican Party to do battle with Hamilton's Federalists. Through it all, Jefferson fought for what he believed to be the simple truths of republican government.

The bedrock of Jefferson's republicanism was the idea of equality; the essence of his dedication to equality was an unfaltering commitment to individual liberty and confidence in the ability of each person "to judge for himself what will secure or endanger his freedom."[17] Thus were the ideals of liberty and equality inextricably linked to education. "If a nation expects to be ignorant and free, in a state of civilization," Jefferson argued, "it expects what never was and never will be."[18] Republicanism presupposed the people understanding the stakes involved in policy decisions their governments would make.

The essence of his battles with Hamilton and the Federalists was not simply over the size and reach of the national government; it was also over what the other side presumed were the legitimate functions of that national government. The perceived tension between commerce and freedom was an integral part of Jefferson's republicanism. Debt, public and private, could undermine republican liberties. As Jefferson wrote to Madison as early as 1789, public debt, "the contagious and ruinous errors" of Europe, had "armed despots with means, not sanctioned by nature, for binding in chains their fellow men."[19] Thus could he demand in *Notes on the State of Virginia* that America should let its "work-shops remain in Europe." Jefferson put his faith in the farmers whom he saw as nothing less than "the chosen people of God . . . whose breasts he has made his peculiar deposit for substantial and genuine virtue." Credit and debt led to corruption and degeneracy, which in turn undermined the "manners and spirit of a people which preserve a republic."[20] The preservation of republics takes work.

Upon completing his second term as president in 1809, Jefferson retired to his beloved Monticello and there began his last great project dedicated to the support of republicanism, the founding of the University of Virginia. Once Madison was released from what Jefferson described as the "incessant labors, corroding anxieties, active enemies and interested friends" of his own presidency, he joined Jefferson's plan to establish an "academical village."[21] It was a fitting collaboration. Madison thought, as did Jefferson, that there could be no "spectacle . . . more edifying or more seasonable than that of liberty and learning, each leaning on the other for their mutual and surest support."[22]

The University of Virginia would shore up the rational foundations of Jefferson's great empire of liberty: "this institution will be based on the illimitable freedom of the human mind. For here we are not afraid to follow the truth wherever it may lead, nor to tolerate any error so long as reason is left free to combat it."[23] But the shoring up could not simply be left to chance. Much of Madison's and Jefferson's work on the university went beyond architecture and funding; they sought to fashion a curriculum by which "the true doctrines of liberty, as exemplified in our political system, should be inculcated in those who are to sustain and may administer it." It was essential to find books that would be "both guides and guards" of the proper principles of republicanism.[24] Such care was necessary, Jefferson thought, if "that vestal flame is to be kept alive."[25]

Toward the end of Madison's life, ten years after Jefferson died, there were distressing clouds looming on the horizon; ill winds of factionalism threatened to blow out that flame of freedom and republicanism. The doctrines of "interposition" and "nullification" that Madison and Jefferson respectively had created in their Virginia and Kentucky Resolutions against the Alien and Sedition Acts of 1798 were coming back to haunt them. Wrenched from their earlier context, such doctrines were being embraced as a means of destroying the Union to which Jefferson and Madison had devoted their lives. States rights advocates such as John C. Calhoun were attempting to legitimate their views on nullification of federal law and even secession from the Union by appeals to Jefferson and Madison.

Madison's last years were spent seeking to protect Jefferson's reputation from those who would invoke his authority on behalf of such "preposterous and anarchical" theories as that of nullification.[26] To the end, he strove to honor Jefferson's plea to take care of him when dead and to secure his image in the American mind as "the apostle of republicanism."[27] Thus was Madison's final piece of political advice, written in 1836 but not published until 1850 ("from the tomb" as he put it), "that the Union of States be cherished and perpetuated."[28] But it was too late; Madison's "Advice to My Country" could not stop the slide into the abyss of civil war.

Ultimately, of course, it was a dedication to the principles of Jefferson that preserved the Union. Twenty-five years after Madison died, a lawyer from Illinois took up the natural rights philosophy of Jefferson in order to maintain the Constitution and its republic against seemingly overwhelming odds. "All honor to Jefferson," Abraham Lincoln wrote,

> to the man who, in the concrete pressure of a struggle for national independence by a single people, had the coolness, forecast, and capacity to introduce into a merely revolutionary document, an abstract truth, applicable to all men and all times, and so to embalm it there, that today, and in all coming days, it shall be a rebuke and a stumbling block to the very harbingers of reappearing tyranny and oppression.[29]

It would be hard to think of a sentiment that would have pleased Jefferson more.

The Jeffersonian Legacy

Jefferson's legacy did not end with the Civil War and Lincoln's use of his principles; it has proved to be a lasting legacy, one that still informs and inspires not only American politics but political thinking around the world. The reason, of course, is that Jefferson's thought was not a child of its times; it was universal, based as it was on the belief that it is by nature that all people are created equal.

As John Zvesper shows in the lead essay in this collection, Jefferson's commitment to natural rights was a liberal vision of human nature, a vision that would prove very durable. His was a "Machiavellian moment," as Paul Rahe puts it, decidedly republican. His most fundamental principles he held to be scientific, as Robert Faulkner argues; his heroes were Isaac Newton, Francis Bacon, and John Locke for a reason. Yet, as scientific as he aspired to be, as deeply liberal as was his vision of natural rights, Jefferson was unable to reconcile the self-evident truths he had so magisterially proclaimed in the Declaration of Independence with the cruel reality of chattel slavery. Indeed, as Howard Temperley provocatively suggests, Jefferson failed to reconcile his grand public pronouncements with his own personal notions about black slaves. But in his defense, it must be said that Jefferson always understood that the deep division over the question of slavery was nothing less than a "firebell in the night," just possibly sounding "the knell of the union."[30] It was never lost on him that chattel slavery in the midst of a nation conceived in liberty and dedicated to the proposition that all men are created equal posed an irreconcilable moral contradiction, whatever the practical political considerations and obstacles surrounding it.

Too often, Thomas Jefferson is swept away by a tide of philosophic enthusiasm generated by his authorship of the Declaration. What gets lost is his grounding in the law. Trained by George Wythe in Williamsburg, Jefferson was by training and inclination a lawyer. As Raoul Berger shows in his perceptive essay, the law guided and encouraged Jefferson the theorist and statesman. The common law tradition to which he subscribed, that of the old-fashioned Sir Edward Coke as opposed to that of the Tory Sir William Blackstone, was a body of learning that took tradition seriously, as James Stoner argues. And it was that tradition of the law, steeped as it was in the English experience, that came to fruition in Jefferson's arguments for the addition of a bill of rights to the Constitution of 1787. He understood very well, as Robert Rutland shows, that liberty was possible only through law.

Jefferson's most enduring legacy, of course, is as the foremost advocate of the idea of the natural equality of mankind. That fundamental principle from the time of the Declaration onward has been the moral core of the American political experience. How that principle can be rendered secure in practice is what gives Jeffersonianism its lasting power and purpose. As Colin Bonwick points out, Jefferson was not a simple proponent of states rights as is often thought; he was an ardent nationalist in that he understood the importance of the Union to the ultimate objectives of the constitutional order. It is that principled commitment that has allowed Jefferson to remain a source of influence, sometimes directly and sometimes indirectly, to all subsequent eras of American history, from the Civil War as Peter Parish explains to the Progressive Era examined by Jeffrey Sedgwick to the New Deal of Franklin D. Roosevelt as described by Morton Frisch. And Jefferson's intellectual influence echoes still.

The pursuit of equality in American history, as J. R. Pole points out, has been a movement not always smooth; there have been fits and starts. The curious relationship between Jefferson and the leaders of the Civil Rights movement in the 1950s and 1960s, as Richard King demonstrates, is but one case in point. The quest for equal treatment for women under the law has been no smoother, nor has it been any easier, as is made clear in Elizabeth Fox-Genovese's probing essay. The intellectual tensions implicit in the principle of human equality as a political end have been kept constantly on the surface throughout the broad sweep of American history. Yet even in its failures, that quest has been ennobling. Never has there been a nation more committed to abstract truths of universal applicability than the United States; the great rights of man from Jefferson's time to the present have remained the object of that quest, a quest Thomas Jefferson himself would undoubtedly applaud, however imperfect the results.

The quest for equality, with all its shortfalls, as Jefferson knew so well, was the result of nothing less intractable than human nature. The constant battle between man's unruly passions and selfish interests on the one side and his moral sense and reason on the other could allow nothing else. Yet, as Jean Yarbrough shows, it was Jefferson's abiding faith in that moral sense and in the power of human reason to transcend the lower impulses of man's nature that shored up the foundation of his philosophic confidence in republican government. For ultimately, in Jefferson's view, reason and republicanism were inseparable.

Notes

This introduction draws upon Gary L. McDowell, "The Great Collaboration," *Times Literary Supplement*, June 9, 1995.

1. James Parton, as quoted in Merrill Peterson, *Thomas Jefferson and the New Nation* (New York: Oxford University Press, 1970), 31; hereinafter cited as *New Nation*.

2. Ibid., viii.

3. George Green Shackelford, *Thomas Jefferson's Travels in Europe, 1784–1789* (Baltimore: Johns Hopkins University Press, 1995), 167.

4. See *New Nation*, 297–389.

5. Jefferson to Roger C. Weightman, June 24, 1826, in *The Writings of Thomas Jefferson*, Andrew A. Lipscomb and Albert E. Bergh, eds., 20 vols. (Washington, DC: Thomas Jefferson Memorial Association, 1904–1905), 16:181–82; hereinafter cited as *Jefferson Writings*. See also Douglass Adair, "Rumbold's Dying Speech, 1685, and Jefferson's Last Words on Democracy, 1826," *William and Mary Quarterly*, 3d ser., 9 (1952): 521–31, for the origins of Jefferson's language.

6. Madison to Samuel Harrison Smith, November 4, 1826, in *Letters and Other Writings of James Madison*, 4 vols. (Philadelphia: J. P. Lippincott, 1865), 3:534; hereinafter cited as *Letters and Other Writings*.

7. James Morton Smith, ed., *The Republic of Letters: The Correspondence of Thomas Jefferson and James Madison, 1776–1826*, 3 vols. (New York: W. W. Norton, 1995), 1:13, hereinafter cited as *Republic of Letters*; and Thomas Jefferson, "Autobiography," in *Jefferson Writings*, 1:61.

8. Madison to Smith, November 4, 1826, in *Letters and Other Writings*, 3:534.

9. Jefferson to Frances Wright, August 7, 1825, in *Jefferson Writings*, 16:119; and Jefferson to Madison, February 17, 1826, in *Republic of Letters*, 3:1964-1966.

10. As quoted in *Republic of Letters*, 1:10–13, 1–2.

11. Merrill Peterson, *James Madison: A Biography in His Own Words* (New York: Newsweek, 1974), 266.

12. As quoted in *Republic of Letters*, 1:12.

13. Adrienne Koch, *Jefferson and Madison: The Great Collaboration* (New York: Alfred A. Knopf, 1950).

14. Jefferson to Madison, September 6, 1789, and Madison to Jefferson, February 4, 1790, in *Republic of Letters*, 1:631–36, 650–53.

15. Jefferson to Madison, December 20, 1787, in *Republic of Letters*, 1:513.

16. Madison to Jefferson, October 17, 1788, in *Republic of Letters*, 1:565.

17. Jefferson to John Tyler, May 26, 1810, in *Jefferson Writings*, 12:393.

18. Jefferson to Colonel Charles Yancey, January 6, 1816, in *Jefferson Writings*, 14:384.

19. Jefferson to Madison, September 6, 1789, in *Republic of Letters*, 1:635.

20. Thomas Jefferson, *Notes on the State of Virginia*, William Peden, ed. (Chapel Hill: University of North Carolina Press, 1955), 164–65.

21. Jefferson to Madison, April 15, 1817, in *Republic of Letters*, 3:1785.

22. Madison to W. T. Barry, August 4, 1822, in *Letters and Other Writings*, 3:279.

23. Jefferson to W. Roscoe, December 27, 1820, in *Jefferson Writings*, 15:303.

24. Madison to Jefferson, February 8, 1825, in *Republic of Letters*, 3:1924.

25. Jefferson to Madison, February 17, 1826, in *Republic of Letters*, 3:1965.

26. Madison to Nicholas P. Trist, December 1831, in *Letters and Other Writings*, 4:206.

27. James Madison, "Notes on Nullification," as quoted in *Republic of Letters*, 3:2001.

28. Adrienne Koch, ed., *James Madison's "Advice to My Country"* (Princeton, NJ: Princeton University Press, 1966).

29. Abraham Lincoln to Henry Pierce and others, April 6, 1859, in *The Collected Works of Abraham Lincoln*, Roy P. Basler, ed., 9 vols. (New Brunswick, NJ: Rutgers University Press, 1953–1955), 3:376.

30. Letter to John Holmes, April 22, 1820, in *Jefferson Writings*, 15:249.

Part I

Thomas Jefferson and the
Politics of Philosophy

1

Jefferson on Liberal Natural Rights

John Zvesper

Our Physiphobia and Its Consequences

For much of the twentieth century, the idea of natural rights has been intellectually suspect and politically dormant. Partly for this reason, historians tend to treat Thomas Jefferson as an inhabitant of a "lost world" that has little to teach us, even if they allow that we can—with great imaginative effort—visit that world as outside observers, mere historical tourists. For their part, political theorists, even those who "take rights seriously," seem frightened to take *natural* rights seriously, because they suspect that the idea of natural rights entails a dogmatic, illiberal kind of politics. Weird parties claiming to have natural law on their side reinforce that suspicion. Current liberal theorists therefore search for more "neutral," less controversial foundations for liberal politics. Talking about rights that are both liberal and natural seems to be talking dangerous nonsense.

This is clearly very different from Jefferson's way of thinking. His world may not be completely lost, but it has been deserted. For Jefferson, liberal politics—the politics of free human beings—would be unintelligible without the idea of natural rights. Even Jefferson's most progressive thinking—for example, his thinking about the necessity of all laws, even constitutions, being changeable—was based on the idea, as he put it in one of his letters, that "Nothing . . . is unchangeable but the inherent and unalienable rights of man."[1] With-

15

out that unchanging truth, one would not be able to judge which legal and constitutional changes were needed. Two weeks after he wrote the above line, in what was to be his last letter—regretfully declining an invitation to travel to Washington to celebrate the fiftieth anniversary of the Fourth of July (which was to be the day he died)—Jefferson confessed his belief that the Declaration of Independence (his most famous statement of natural rights) would eventually have a global impact, "arousing men to burst the chains under which monkish ignorance and superstition had persuaded them to bind themselves, and to assume the blessings and security of self-government. . . . All eyes are opened, or opening, to the rights of man."[2] Did Jefferson expect too much of natural rights? Or do we expect too little?

One reason that we distance ourselves from Jefferson's thinking about natural rights is that we suffer more than he did from physiphobia—an unreasonable fear of nature, especially of the ethical and political implications of human nature. This physiphobia has been encouraged by a long line of radical modern thinkers going back to Niccolò Machiavelli, who have made much of the distance between nature and humanity and have insisted that we see human and political life as an escape from, rather than a culmination of, natural conditions. In the twentieth century—in the wake of that first "friend of the earth," Friedrich Nietzsche—we have witnessed a reaction to physiphobia in various shades of "green" politics, but even that countermovement has largely accepted the obsolescence of human rights in order to emphasize the claims of and dangers to the natural world more generally.

One of the latter turns of this general distrust of nature in modern thinking has been an attack on natural rights thinking. During the nineteenth and twentieth centuries, appeals to natural rights have often seemed less plausible, less necessary, or less effective than they seemed to Jefferson and many of his political and philosophical allies. With what Jefferson would probably judge to be unwarranted and reckless complacency, critics of natural rights thinking, beginning with David Hume in the 1740s (about the time of Jefferson's birth), have argued that even if it is plausible to understand free political societies as originating in social contracts based on recognition of natural rights, it is not plausible to understand political authority in any large society as resting on consent by individuals aware of their natural rights. Once a free society is started, liberal practices supported by the conformist pressure of public opinion—what Hume called "moral sense"—is a more adequate sociological explanation of how such a society functions. Hume—followed in this by Edmund Burke and most other post–French Revolution conservatists—would add that reliance on a historically developed set of liberal social conventions and practices (as opposed to appeals to an abstract liberal "creed" of universal natural rights) is a sufficient, or at any rate the only safe, guarantee that the society will remain free, that political authority will be used in a liberal manner. In the early nineteenth century, Jeremy Bentham's famous denunciation of natural rights as "simple nonsense" (and "natural and imprescriptible rights" as "rhetorical nonsense, nonsense upon stilts")[3] pursued this same line of thinking, as did those self-consciously "realistic" founding fathers of modern political science in the early twentieth century who celebrated their liberation from "the idea that men possess inherent and inalienable rights . . . which are independent of the state."[4]

These utilitarian and conservative cases against natural rights have been supplemented by Marxist and social democratic arguments. Natural rights are squeezed from the left as well as from the right. While conservatives say natural rights theory goes too far, failing to appreciate the need for concrete growths and embodiments of rights in particular communities and leading to catastrophes such as the tyrannical phases of the French Revolution, critics on the left say natural rights theory does not go far enough. Marxists charge that natural rights ideas are not universal, but are simply the ideas of a certain ruling class at a certain moment of economic history. From this point of view, natural rights talk is mere window dressing for regimes in which rich capitalists exploit poor workers. To social democrats, natural rights talk is at best an inadequate assertion of what is needed for a truly democratic society, with little or no reference to the full range of economic and social rights that such a society would recognize and promote. In the latter half of the nineteenth century especially, many liberal thinkers (and judges in American courts) did seem to be more interested in using ideas about natural liberty to defend the property rights of the rich than in thinking through the full implications of natural rights. So the left-wing rejection of natural rights thinking was largely the rejection of a very narrow version of that thinking. It was no less emphatic for that reason.

In spite of all these doubts about natural rights sown in the last 250 years, today there are good reasons for wondering if the idea has been too readily discarded. For one thing, the philosophical arguments against natural rights are (to say the least) not conclusive. For another, some of the practical consequences of our physiphobia should make us take natural rights more seriously. For example, in American domestic politics, the rise of extreme claims about the

rights of groups, and the desperation of the struggle to understand how liberalism might respond to the challenge of "multicul-
turalism," can be traced in part to the reluctance of liberals to think
about the natural rights of individual human beings and citizens. In
American foreign policy, the same reluctance is at work, making
doubtful even the idea of holding up the American regime as an
example for the world to follow, to say nothing of the idea of "ex-
porting democracy" more forcefully. These crises of confidence in
contemporary liberal politics should make us ask ourselves if we
might want to visit the lost world of Jefferson with more than a
merely touristic interest.

Revolution, Nations, and Government

One of the most obvious advantages of Jefferson's political thinking over the currently dominant liberal political theories is that he
has no difficulty in providing us with a theory of liberal revolution.
The liberal revolutions of the 1970s and 1980s have not been well
served by the liberal political theory dominant in those years. Trans-
ported to our time, Jefferson would be astonished to find fashion-
able liberal political theories without a well-developed justification
for revolution. Because of the current liberal distrust of natural rights,
liberal revolution is more difficult to justify. If one's rights come only
from the state, it is difficult to justify challenging the state. If one's
rights really belong only to one's nation, it is difficult to urge that
nation's government to respect the rights and choices of individuals.

Although the Declaration of Independence is Jefferson's most famous statement both of natural rights and of the justification of revolution, it is also worth studying the arguments of his somewhat
earlier statement *A Summary View of the Rights of British America*
(1774). This was Jefferson's suggested draft of instructions for the
Virginia delegates to the First Continental Congress. Although it was
thought to be too radical to be adopted by the Virginia delegates, it
was published (attributed to "a native of Virginia") as a pamphlet
in Williamsburg and reprinted in Philadelphia and London. The
Summary View proposed to give George III one last chance to heed
the complaints of British Americans. As claimed in the last paragraph
of the *Summary View,* Jefferson's analysis states the American grievances:

> With that freedom of language and sentiment which becomes a
> free people claiming their rights, as derived from the laws of na-

ture, and not as the gift of their chief magistrate: Let those flatter who fear; it is not an American art. To give praise which is not due might be well from the venal, but would ill beseem those who are asserting the rights of human nature.[5]

In order to lay out fully the rights in question, and the invasions of them, Jefferson sets out "a view of them from the origin and first settlement of these countries."[6] In other words, Jefferson does not here go back to a primitive state of nature in order to establish "the rights of human nature" and the origins and ends of civil society; however, that kind of theory is clearly assumed by Jefferson, and what he does here is to indicate certain conclusions to be drawn from that theory about the individual and collective rights of "a free people."

He first reminds the king that the British emigration to America was parallel to the Saxon emigration to Britain, which established no "claim of superiority or dependence" over the Saxon emigrants by their "mother country"; analogously, British Americans

> before their emigration to America, were the free inhabitants of the British dominions in Europe, and possessed a right which nature has given to all men, of departing from the country in which chance, not choice, has placed them, of going in quest of new habitations, and of there establishing new societies, under such laws and regulations as to them shall seem most likely to promote public happiness.[7]

By nature, it is choice, not chance, that is the decisive element in establishing any particular political society. What is crucial is not being socialized into a particular nation or culture, but choosing to be part of a society. "Peoples" or nations—like other groups of human beings—have rights only because individual human beings have rights. Choosing to remain where one is, or choosing to set up elsewhere, is a right held by individuals, the exercise of which creates peoples. In the absence of choice—for example, when a citizen lacks the power to emigrate—the claims of a country to that citizen's loyalty become dubious.

The basic natural political right that peoples have is to choose their own government, "such . . . as to them shall seem most likely to promote public happiness." Jefferson thus explains the greater degree of connection between the Americans and their mother country, as distinguished from the Saxons and theirs, as a matter of choice, not of obligation:

the emigrants thought proper to adopt that system of laws under which they had hitherto lived in the mother country, and to continue their union with her by submitting themselves to the same common sovereign, who was thereby made the central link, connecting the several parts of the empire thus newly multiplied.[8]

Parliament's decision to assist the British Americans against France ("an enemy, who would fain have drawn to herself the benefits of their commerce, to the great aggrandizement of herself, and danger of Great Britain")[9] was clearly not a purely disinterested act, and in any case, it no more established Parliamentary sovereignty over the colonies than similar assistance that Parliament "had often before given to Portugal and other allied states" established parliamentary sovereignty over those states. Jefferson's thesis is that, since the British Parliament was never given any right to exercise authority over the colonists, all of the unwise and unjust acts of Parliament that were leading to the rupture with America were void.

Although Parliament is the first target of the *Summary View* (which was to have been addressed to the king, pleading with him to correct his errant legislators), Jefferson has almost as much to say against the king's and royal governors' "deviations from the line of duty" as the valid holders of "the executive powers of the laws of these states."[10] Notable among these deviations is the wrongdoings also perpetrated by Parliament: both Parliament and the king denied British Americans "the sovereign powers of legislation," which "[f]rom the nature of things, every society must at all times, possess within itself"[11]—Parliament by passing an act to suspend the legislature of New York, and the King both by refusing to confirm or to annul laws passed by American legislative assemblies and by dissolving some of these assemblies and refusing to call others to replace them.

Jefferson's revolutionary writings thus clearly cannot be characterized by Bentham's phrase "anarchical fallacies." Nor is there such tension as some have imagined between these writings and the Constitution-making activities that took place after the American Revolution. In these writings, Jefferson is as realistic a revolutionary as one could ask for. It is as clear from the Declaration of Independence as it is from the *Summary View* that the first and most important act of a people in declaring their independence from one government must be to choose another. Natural freedom is valuable only because it is the freedom to form a people by establishing a government. Jefferson complains that Parliament, in suspending the New York legislature, pretends to have the right to "reduce" the people of that state "to a state of nature,"[12] not an attractive state in which to live for long; anarchy is not choiceworthy. Jefferson's complaint against the king's dissolution of state legislatures is based on the same reasoning: "The feelings of human nature revolt against the supposition of a state so situated as that it may not in any emergency provide against dangers which perhaps threaten immediate ruin."[13] Government is so necessary for human safety and happiness that one of the worst things that a government (or part of a government) can do is to interfere with properly constituted governmental actions. Therefore, as Jefferson's *Summary View* does not hesitate to warn the king, properly constituted legislative power frustrated by being dissolved by the executive actually becomes more dangerous to the executive, because it "reverts to the people," who might well (and rightly) choose to set up irregular legislative bodies to fulfill the natural need for and natural right to government.[14] (This practice was becoming normal in America at the time Jefferson was composing his complaints.) In the Declaration of Independence, the first nine of the eighteen paragraphs specifying the king's "repeated injuries and usurpations" against the American states concern his actions or inactions that have obstructed these states' legislatures. Neither the *Summary View* nor the Declaration is an antigovernment document.

There is one other notably realistic character of Jefferson's thinking about natural rights and liberal political revolution. Both the *Summary View* and the Declaration are written with a clear understanding that the natural right to revolution is quite likely to involve war, or at least the credible threat of war. The Declaration of Independence is, among other things, a statement of the reasons for going to war. Already in the *Summary View* Jefferson would warn George III (*"as yet* the only mediatory power between the several states of the British empire"[15]—that is, between British America and Britain) that heeding the advice of his "great American council" might well be necessary for his "felicity and future fame, and the preservation of that harmony which alone can continue both to Great Britain and America the reciprocal advantages of their connection."[16] If he failed to heed the advice, as he did, the "mediatory power" might become, as it did, war. As John Locke had taught Americans, where there is no common judge on earth, one can appeal only to heaven—that is, to the gods of battle.[17] Judging when to exercise the right to revolution therefore requires not only knowledge of one's rights, but also prudent judgment of one's opportunities and powers. A passage in Jefferson's draft of the Declaration of Independence, omitted by Congress from the final version, reflects a consciousness of this fact: Americans and Britons, he notes, might have been

> a free and a great people together; but a communication of grandeur and of freedom, it seems, is below [the Briton's] dignity. Be it so, since they will have it. *The road to happiness and to glory is open to us, too.* We will tread it apart from them.[18]

If British Americans had not been able to see their way down the road to independence, they would have been well advised not to declare so boldly their awareness of their natural rights to independence.

Equality, Liberty, Justice, and Consent

In the famous second paragraph of the Declaration of Independence is Jefferson's concise statement of the natural rights premises that had been assumed and alluded to but not elaborated in the *Summary View*. In the Declaration, Jefferson, as Abraham Lincoln commented, "had the coolness, forecast, and capacity to introduce into a merely revolutionary document, an abstract truth, applicable to all men and all times."[19] Lincoln was referring to what Jefferson called the "self-evident" truth that "all men are created equal." Jefferson connected certain other self-evident truths with that first one:

> that they are endowed by their Creator with certain inalienable rights; that among these are life, liberty, and the pursuit of happiness; that to secure these rights, governments are instituted among men, deriving their just powers from the consent of the governed; that whenever any form of government becomes destructive of these ends, it is the right of the people to alter or to abolish it, and to institute new government, laying its foundation on such principles, and organizing its powers in such form, as to them shall seem most likely to effect their safety and happiness.

Like Locke in his *Second Treatise*, Jefferson derives strong ethical and political views from the fact that humans are by nature free and equal,

> there being nothing more evident, than that Creatures of the same species and rank promiscuously born to all the same advantages of Nature, and the use of the same faculties, should also be equal one amongst another without Subordination or Subjection.[20]

This truth is self-evident because it is contained within the definition of what it is to be human. Being human means (among other things) having no natural (or supernatural) ruler among one's fellow humans. No human beings have a godlike superiority over others, nor are any human beings to be governed as beasts. As Jefferson more pithily put it in his last letter fifty years later, "the mass of mankind has not been born with saddles on their backs, nor a favored few booted and spurred, ready to ride them legitimately, by the grace of God."[21] Ruling, or government (which, as we have already seen, is nevertheless necessary) therefore can be legitimately "instituted" and operated only by "consent," there being no other way in which humans can rightly be ruled.

It is well known that Jefferson was what some today would call an elitist: he did not think human beings were equal in all important respects. In a letter to John Adams, he spoke of "a natural aristocracy," based on "virtue and talents,"[22] and his proposed educational scheme described in his *Notes on the State of Virginia* was designed so that "the best geniusses will be raked from the rubbish annually, and be instructed, at the public expence."[23] But the natural *political* equality of human beings remains: government is still to be instituted and operated only with the consent of the governed. Jefferson (more optimistically than Adams) thought the best way of ensuring that the truly virtuous and talented, rather than the "artificial aristocracy" based on wealth and family connections, were those who ended up in positions of authority was "to leave to the citizens the free election and separation of the aristoi from the pseudo-aristoi, of the wheat from the chaff."[24] In contrast to the ancient Roman republic, with its "heavy-handed unfeeling aristocracy, over a people ferocious, and rendered desperate by poverty and wretchedness," the modern American republic had the benefit of "a people, mild in their dispositions . . . and affectionate to their leaders."[25] Such a people could be trusted to consent to be ruled by the true *aristoi* and did not need to be awed into submission.

Natural human equality implies not only the reason why government must be by consent, but also the limited purposes of government. The purpose of government is not (as "monkish ignorance and superstition" would have it) to embody some natural or divine hierarchy of human souls, but simply to help secure humans' equal natural rights—rights that cannot be well secured without government. Another way of saying that human beings are equal (that is, that there are no naturally-determined ruling relations among them) is to say that each of them has rights to "life, liberty, and the pursuit of happiness." Given the truth of this observation, government must

be understood to be directed toward securing these rights (a diffi-
cult-enough goal), rather than toward some more aspiring purpose.
If the goal of political society is justice, then justice means the securing of these rights for those who are members of the society.

The truth about human nature thus provides not only some strong
guidelines to constructing and conducting legitimate politics, it also
provides the deepest *problem* for liberal democratic politics: how to
reconcile justice—the securing of all citizens' equal rights—with consent, that is, with public opinion. Natural human equality demands
both equally: justice without consent is as great a denial of human
equality as is consent to unjust government. One of the greatest tasks
of liberal democratic statespeople is making this problem a vital tension rather than a morbid contradiction of liberal politics.

The politics of slavery was the greatest example of this characteristic liberal democratic problem in the new American republic.
Slavery was clearly a violation of naturally equal human rights. Jefferson included both in the *Summary View* and in his draft Declaration strong condemnations of slavery, as a violation of "the rights of
human nature."[26] He recognized that slaves had the natural right to
liberate themselves, if necessary by the "extirpation" of their masters.[27] Yet he also saw that if emancipation of the slaves was perceived to be a serious threat to the self-preservation of the masters,
then their consent to emancipation could be withheld, by the natural right of self-preservation: "we have the wolf by the ears, and
can neither hold him, nor safely let him go."[28] He gradually lost his
early hope that the masters were becoming less despotic, and the
slaves less slavish, preparing the way for an emancipation "with the
consent of the masters, rather than by their extirpation."[29] And he
was always pessimistic about the viability of an American polity with
citizens composed of former slaves and former slaveholders.[30] But
he never abandoned his belief that the only just resolution of the
problem would involve the education of both masters and slaves in
the ways of freedom—helped along by a popular religious "conviction" that God's "justice cannot sleep forever"[31]—so that the slaves
could rightly claim justice, and the masters consent to it. Slavery and
race relations were a difficult problem for Jefferson, because he took
seriously the twin but often conflicting demands of equal human
rights: the demands for justice and for consent.

Jefferson would have said that the firm public establishment of
certain basic political truths (as in his bill for "establishing" religious
freedom), rather than the search for some morally "neutral" basis
for liberal politics, carries the better hope of reconciling those two
demands. He would have criticized the utilitarian views of Hume

and Bentham with the same argument: what is to keep a liberal society from drifting off into illiberal ways, if public opinion is not firmly anchored in a "creed" of equal natural rights?

A Natural Liberal Constitution

In the second paragraph of the Declaration quoted above, Jefferson notes that it is the natural right of people instituting government to organize "its powers in such form, as to them shall seem most likely to effect their safety and happiness." What does the fact of natural rights imply about the forms of government to which people can or should consent? One of the meanings of natural human equality is that humans are all in-between beings, neither beasts nor gods. If all humans were perfectly rational and dispassionate, government might be unnecessary. If some humans were perfectly rational and dispassionate, they could be trusted to govern as natural rulers, without becoming a threat to the rights that governments are instituted to secure; the right to revolutionary resistance to tyranny would be less important, as would be the organizational form of government. So one thing that our acknowledgment of human equality and natural rights implies is that great care must be taken in choosing a form of government and that government, once instituted, must be watched by a vigilant public. This is not an antigovernment sentiment, it is simply a form of prudence. Similar good advice can be found in ancient political writings.[32] In this sense, Jefferson's modern emphasis on the equal natural rights of human beings simply underlines the wisdom of the efforts of ancient and previous modern political science in seeking devices that take account of the fact that those who govern are fallible and self-interested. Yet Jefferson also goes beyond ancient political science, and goes at least as far as Locke, by making active consent of the people (through representative institutions) a sine qua non of legitimate government.

It has been noticed that God appears in three ways in the Declaration of Independence (in the final version, not in Jefferson's draft):[33] as legislator (of "the laws of nature" appealed to in the first sentence), as judge, and as executive ("the supreme judge of the world" and the "divine providence" appealed to and relied on at the end). God can safely be all three and rightly rule over the universe as a benevolent despot (in the same way that humans can rule over beasts). But because humans are not gods, to place the legislative, executive, and judicial powers in the same human hands is an invitation to tyranny. The principle of constitutionally separating powers, if not absolutely required by natural rights, is clearly advisable. In his *Notes on the State of Virginia*, Jefferson (who had by then experienced the difficulties of being governor of that state) complained that the Virginia Constitution in effect left all three powers of government in the legislative body; he remarked that "concentrating these in the same hands is precisely the definition of despotic government," since human beings "soon learn to make interested uses of every right and power which they possess, or may assume."[34]

Similar reflections lead to the proposition that legitimate government must be representative government, with regular legislative assemblies of deputies chosen by the people. This is clear from Jefferson's *Summary View* as well as from the Declaration. In the former, Jefferson infers the "right of representation" (which had been violated by royal and parliamentary interference with American legislatures) from the natural fact of human equality, the fact that "kings are the servants, not the proprietors of the people," who cannot rightly be treated as "the absolute slaves" of their king's "sovereign will."[35] Jefferson would have the Congress remind George III that "he is no more than the chief officer of the people, appointed by the laws, and circumscribed with definite powers, to assist in working the great machine of government, erected for their use, and consequently subject to their superintendance."[36] It also follows from equal natural rights and from "the nature and purpose of civil institutions" that property can be "taxed or regulated" only by the relevant representative body.[37] Jefferson would call on George III to embrace this "liberal and expanded thought," lest his name become "a blot in the page of history."[38] In the Declaration, Jefferson adds to the list of tyrannical acts of the king and Parliament (among other things): interference with the independence of judges, subordination of the civil power of the military, maintenance of standing armies in peacetime without the consent of the relevant legislatures, and abolition of the right of trial by jury—all signs of "a tyrant . . . unfit to be the ruler of a free people."[39] In other words, he condemns all violations of the constitutional arrangements that should and would be chosen by a free people, aware of their natural rights, and that had been chosen by British Americans, "a people fostered and fixed in principles of freedom."[40]

Of course, Jefferson recognized that all these constitutional devices that were suitable to a liberal polity (and perhaps others yet to be discovered by political science) depended as much for their realization as for their suitability on the existence of an enlightened people, whose "eyes are opened . . . to the rights of man." For the people safely to participate in government by electing their leaders (a participation necessary to keep government safe), "their minds must be improved to a certain degree."[41] People's eyes can be slightly open or wide open. Progressive stages in people's enlightenment will justify further steps in the liberalization of their constitution and greater security for their natural rights:

> laws and institutions must go hand in hand with the progress of the human mind. As that becomes more developed, more enlightened, as new discoveries are made, new truths disclosed, and manners and opinions change with the change of circumstances, institutions must advance also, and keep pace with the times.[42]

Natural rights—the ends of government—are unchangeable; however, the forms of government best suited to help people secure those ends have to be determined by prudence, taking changing circumstances into account, especially the progress of popular enlightenment.

This progressive view can be applied to policies as well as to institutions, as twentieth-century social democratic liberals demand. But Jefferson would insist that it is erroneous to treat all desirable means to human welfare as rights that governments must try to secure. He would observe that human life can be made safer, but not absolutely safe, and that governments are not the only and not always the best means for human beings to make their lives and liberties more secure.

Jefferson usually optimistically believed that progress up the ladder toward the most "liberal and expanded" political understanding and institutions was inevitable, if properly encouraged by enlightened reformers like himself. However, even near the top of that ladder, Jefferson came to recognize that liberal partisanship might be necessary, because of the persistence of illiberal political partisans. Like James Madison, who by 1792 began talking about "natural" parties of republicans and antirepublicans, with the latter pessimistically directing policies "less to the reason of the many than to their weaknesses,"[43] Jefferson, during and after his experience as leader of the Republican Party, spoke of "natural" parties of Whigs and Tories, with the former optimistically addressing government "to the reason of the people, and not to their weaknesses."[44] Jefferson's Whigs, like Madison's republicans, were those who had more faith in the people and in the branches of government closest to the people; his "Tories," like Madison's antirepublicans, were those who were persuaded that the less popular branches of government needed to be strengthened: "The sickly, weakly, timid man, fears the people, and is a Tory by nature. The healthy, strong and bold, cherishes them, and is formed a Whig by nature."[45]

Human nature, it seems, must be acknowledged to contain a politically pessimistic side that, in a free political system, will inevitably be expressed and, if it gets out of hand, will therefore have to be opposed by the more optimistic side in partisan battles. One of the advantages of the more advanced stages of constitutional theory and practice, such as that reached by Americans with their Constitution of 1787, was that the more optimistic side was allowed more room for maneuver in these battles, even while the more pessimistic side still retained its own representative institutions.

Notes

1. Jefferson to Major John Cartwright, June 5, 1824, in *The Writings of Thomas Jefferson*, Andrew A. Lipscomb and Albert E. Bergh, eds., 20 vols. (Washington, DC: Thomas Jefferson Memorial Association, 1904-1905), 16:48; hereinafter cited as *Jefferson Writings*.

2. Jefferson to Roger C. Weightman, June 24, 1826, in *Jefferson Writings*, 16:182.

3. Bhikhu Parekh, ed., *Bentham's Political Thought* (New York: Barnes and Noble, 1973), 269.

4. Charles Edward Merriam, *A History of American Political Theories* (New York: Macmillan, 1931), 310.

5. Thomas Jefferson, "A Summary View of the Rights of British America," in *Writings*, Merrill D. Peterson, ed. (New York: Library of America, 1984), 120–121; hereinafter cited as *Writings*.

6. Ibid., 105.

7. Ibid., 105–106.

8. Ibid., 107.

9. Ibid., 106.

10. Ibid., 115.

11. Ibid., 118.

12. Ibid., 111.

13. Ibid., 118.

14. Ibid. The Declaration of Independence employs the same argument: the king's refusal to reestablish representative houses means that "the legislative powers, incapable of annihilation, have returned to the people at large for their exercise," and "it is their right, it is their duty . . . to provide new guards for their future security."

15. Ibid., 115; emphasis added.

16. Ibid., 121.

17. John Locke, *Two Treatises of Government: A Critical Edition with an Introduction and Apparatus Criticus*, 2d ed., Peter Laslett, ed. (Cambridge, England: Cambridge University Press, 1970), II.iii.21, xvi.176, and xix.242.

18. Thomas Jefferson, "Autobiography," in *Jefferson Writings*, 1:36–37; emphasis added. Jefferson made other efforts to convey this message to Britain; see his letter to John Randolph, August 25, 1775, in *The Papers of Thomas Jefferson*, Julian P. Boyd, ed., 25 vols. to date (Princeton, NJ: Princeton University Press, 1950–), 1:240–243; hereinafter cited as *The Jefferson Papers*.

19. Abraham Lincoln to Henry L. Pierce and others, April 6, 1859, in *The Collected Works of Abraham Lincoln*, Roy P. Basler, ed., 9 vols. (New Brunswick, NJ: Rutgers University Press, 1953–1955), 3:376; hereinafter cited as *Collected Works*.

20. Locke, *Two Treatises*, II.ii.4; see also ii.5: natural human equality is "evident in it self, and beyond all question."

21. Jefferson to Roger C. Weightman, June 24, 1826, in *Jefferson Writings*, 16:182.

22. Jefferson to John Adams, October 28, 1813, in *The Adams-Jefferson Letters: The Complete Correspondence Between Thomas Jefferson and Abigail and John Adams*, Lester J. Cappon, ed., 2 vols. (Chapel Hill: University of North Carolina Press, 1959), 2:387–392; hereinafter cited as *Adams-Jefferson Letters*.

23. Thomas Jefferson, *Notes on the State of Virginia*, William Peden, ed. (Chapel Hill: University of North Carolina Press, 1955), 146.

24. Jefferson to John Adams, October 28, 1813, in *Adams-Jefferson Letters*, 2:388.

25. Jefferson, *Notes on the State of Virginia*, 128–129.

26. *Writings*, 116.

27. Jefferson, *Notes on the State of Virginia*, 163.

28. Jefferson to John Holmes, April 22, 1820, in *Jefferson Writings*, 15:249.

29. Jefferson, *Notes on the State of Virginia*, 163.

30. "Deep rooted prejudices entertained by the whites; ten thousand recollections, by the blacks, of the injuries they have sustained; new provocations; the real distinctions which nature has made; and many other circumstances, will divide us into parties, and produce convulsions which will probably never end but in the extermination of the one or the other race" (Jefferson, *Notes on the State of Virginia*, 138).

31. Jefferson, *Notes on the State of Virginia*, 163.

32. See, for example, Aristotle, *Politics*, H. Rackham, trans. (London: William Heinemann Ltd., 1972), 1287a16–b35, 1318b38–40.

33. George Anastaplo, "The Declaration of Independence," *St. Louis University Law Journal* 9 (Spring 1965), 390.

34. Jefferson, *Notes on the State of Virginia*, 120, 121. See also James Madison's formulation in *The Federalist*, no. 47: "The accumulation of all powers, legislative, executive, and judiciary, in the same hands . . . may justly be pronounced the very definition of tyranny" (*The Federalist*, Jacob C. Cooke, ed., [Middletown, CT: Wesleyan University Press, 1961], 324).

35. *Writings*, 117, 121.

36. Ibid., 105.

37. Ibid., 119, 122.

38. Ibid., 121.

39. Jefferson, "Autobiography," in *Jefferson Writings*, 1:32–33, 35.

40. This phrase comes from Jefferson's draft of the Declaration in a portion deleted from the final version (*Jefferson Writings*, 1:35).

41. Jefferson, *Notes on the State of Virginia*, 148.

42. Jefferson to Samuel Kercheval, July 12, 1816, in *Jefferson Writings*, 15:41.

43. "A Candid State of Parties," published (anonymously) in *National Gazette*, September 26, 1792; cited in John Zvesper, *Political Philosophy and Rhetoric: A Study of the Origins of American Party Politics* (Cambridge, England: Cambridge University Press, 1977), 116–118.

44. Jefferson to T. M. Randolph, January 7, 1793, in *The Jefferson Papers*, 25:30.

45. Jefferson to the Marquis de Lafayette, November 4, 1823, in *Jefferson Writings*, 15:492; see also Jefferson's letter to Abigail Adams, September 11, 1804, in *Adams-Jefferson Letters*, 1:280; to John Adams, June 27, 1813, in *Adams-Jefferson Letters*, 2:335–336; and to Henry Lee, August 10, 1824, in *Jefferson Writings*, 16:73–74; and the discussion by Harvey C. Mansfield Jr., "Introduction," in *Thomas Jefferson: Selected Writings*, Harvey C. Mansfield, Jr., ed. (Arlington Heights, IL: AHM Publishing, 1979), xxxii–xli.

2

Jefferson and the Enlightened Science of Liberty

Robert K. Faulkner

Thomas Jefferson could seem merely a partisan, even in his principles. To his many enemies at home and abroad, he appeared a party man devoted to his country, his political sect, and to the popular following that sustained him. If in a spirit of inquiry we entertain the outlook of the British ministries of the time, or even of many Britons since, it will seem strange to attempt to learn from Thomas Jefferson and his teachings on liberty. This Jefferson helped tear away the then-jewel of the British Empire, was principal author of the Declaration of Independence from that empire, and rejected as "heresy" the supposition that British mixed government could be a model for republican America.

Such reservations should be confronted, for Jefferson's reputation can survive free inquiry. It was, after all, Jefferson who helped found the immense liberal democracy in the New World that during the twentieth century's world wars, sustained the liberal democracies of the Old, not least against ideological enemies. His defense of liberty was of a universal liberty, of natural rights and not just of American rights. If a party project, it was for the party of humanity. Also, it was not merely an ideal or a cause; Jefferson's project led to power as well as liberty. He planned an "empire of liberty" over the whole North American continent. His was a variation on a comprehensive intellectual plan for powerful nation-states, at once democratically

31

republican and expanding in wealth, population, and technology, that went back at least to John Locke. This immense plan has brought its partisans and followers to much liberty and to domination over most of the globe. To question Jeffersonianism one must go beyond charges of zealotry to question the immense means and the humanitarian ends.

We will not go wrong in calling this vast project "the Enlightenment," and we must acknowledge that questions now abound among the vanguard of contemporary progressive intellectuals. Enlightened liberalism is in marked decay and under fierce attack. The Enlightenment may have won a world-historical victory. It may have achieved the political-intellectual conquest that Francis Bacon, René Descartes, John Locke, and its other philosophic fathers intended. But now the very name Enlightenment is an object of obloquy in advanced circles and, "as an enterprise for linking the progress of truth and the history of liberty," a project to be not only dissected but surpassed.[1] The project for progress has turned on itself. What philosophers once thought philosophic light they now treat as a tunnel, as a new dark age of "Western rationalism." They say that a calculating and utilitarian science, social as well as technological, represses authentic human autonomy.

Paradoxically, this challenge makes especially necessary a philosophic and political reconsideration of the original counsels. Reflecting on modern rationalism helps to make clear how we got into our present fix—and whether we really are in a fix. Is "progress" so problematic at its root? Whatever the deeper issues, in any event, we can learn from a political science as comprehensive as Jefferson's. Jeffersonian liberalism, after all, instructs us in taking practical care of modern peoples. The critical thinking that now dogs it cannot. So-called postmodern thinking is inherently disabled in a crucial political respect: it is disabled from constructive thinking because it is obsessed with critical thinking.

The political science of liberty is the topic here. One could call it the intellectual background of Jefferson's politics, except that, for Jefferson, the plan is in the foreground. Much of Jeffersonian politics is aimed at converting peoples to the new faith. In this sense, Jefferson can be called a partisan of liberty and a partisan of science, and his Republican Party was meant not chiefly for officeholders but for success in the job of conversion. But Jefferson was more than a partisan; he was a propagandist for liberty and science, and he believed what he propagated.

No one among the founders of the United States thought liberty more important than did Jefferson. No one else, with the possible exception of Benjamin Franklin, put such a premium on science. Certainly, no one else expected so much for each, and for the whole future of humanity, from the relation of the two together. In a letter written some ten days before the fiftieth anniversary of the Declaration of Independence, the day on which he died, Jefferson said that the document was "pregnant with our own [fate] and [that] of the world." It was a signal "arousing men to burst the chains under which monkish ignorance and superstition had persuaded them to bind themselves, and to assume the blessings and security of self-government." Jefferson's attack is as much on government by grace over the mind as on more political hierarchies, and the call for self-government in both respects is irretrievably linked to the new rational science. "The general spread of the light of science has already laid open to every view the palpable truth, that the mass of mankind has not been born with saddles on their backs, nor a favored few booted and spurred, ready to ride them legitimately, by the grace of God."[2]

It would be a mistake to think this vivid proclamation of liberty and rational enlightenment an exceptional outburst. These were the poles about which revolved all of Jefferson's otherwise rather flexible thoughts. When he selected the three accomplishments to be memorialized on his tomb, two, the Declaration of Independence and the Virginia Statute for Religious Freedom, had to do with providing for liberty, and one, the founding of the University of Virginia, with learning.

In such views, Jefferson differed notably from the actual framers of the American constitutional government. He dwelt on governance of opinion and by opinion, rather than the energetic government that was advanced by, say, the authors of *The Federalist*. Government in the usual sense and executive energy, in particular, were secondary among Jefferson's priorities. They were secondary even among his more obviously political priorities. Jefferson certainly acknowledged that liberty required the establishment of organized peoples who could provide for their liberty. He acknowledged also that government (by consent) had to be the gist of their organization and provision, and in the United States he favored the establishment of a federal government. But he did not lead in making the federal government, he inclined to fear its strength (not, as did the Federalists, its weakness), and he promoted the "states-rights" party. More to the point, Jefferson always wrestled with an underlying conviction that government in general was a questionable imposition on natural liberty. To be sure, there were the many backslidings in practice toward executive decisiveness and governmental discretion, the paradoxical recurrences to Federalist doctrine that Henry Adams chronicles in his *History of the United States during the Administrations of Thomas Jefferson*. These no doubt show inconsistencies and difficulties in Jefferson's political principles. In his principles, nevertheless, Jefferson seemed mostly concerned for popular self-government and personal self-government. While he was brought to approve the Constitution of 1787, and to administer as president its institutions, he sought from the start to modify the new arrangement out of fear of the few and of executive power. He sought a bill of rights to secure freedom of religion, speech, and person, as well as trial by jury. He would weaken the scope of the government's authority and the power of its more energetic and authoritative branches (courts and Senate as well as presidency). He built a popular party to rein in the institutional government and its management by the few. And he rejected the view of some Federalists that the Constitution should be venerated as a sacred authority. While the fundamental law should not be changed lightly, he wrote, it like all "laws and institutions must go hand in hand with the progress of the human mind."[3]

Jefferson's politics turned especially on enlightening the public mind. "Consciousness-raising" may be the latest and liberated version, with its propagation of the equal dignity of those said to be hitherto repressed by the Western tradition, but from its start the Enlightenment called for a new and total republican faith. This involved grave transformations in custom and society, transformations more powerfully rooted than in schools and book learning. For example, Jefferson wanted a rather democratic farming economy that itself fostered a republican moral education. This was to be an education not in gentlemanly virtue, nor in the civic or citizen virtue now much celebrated by scholars of republicanism, but principally in self-reliance. Jefferson encouraged "agricultural virtue." This is an ability to provide for, and stand up for, oneself. It included industry and frugality, indeed, but also more than these economic virtues. Jealousy of those put above one, vigilance for dangers to one's rights—these, too, are bred by individual labor in the soil, away from the agricultural villages that might encourage a dependent peasantry.

While Jefferson celebrated a self-governing people, he despised and feared city mobs and, in general, the unenlightened. Schools and books were not to play the only part, but they were to play a big part, bigger than for any other statesman of the founding generation. Jefferson's draft of an education act proposed an educational qualification, literacy, for the suffrage. In districts rural and urban, enlightenment of the public mind was to be a primary political task.

The famous Jeffersonian plans for public education made education democratically general but also aristocratically hierarchical. All males would be admitted free to the first grades of public schools, but only a selected few to the free higher schools and only a "few geniuses raked from the rubbish" annually to a public university. Others might enter by paying their way, which afforded entry to the wealthy without compelling them. In general, Jefferson sought a natural aristocracy of enlightened talent as well as a democracy enlightened to be a republican citizenry. The mixture shows the extent to which an orientation by useful truth, and the prominence of its propagators and bearers, made Jeffersonian liberal democracy in important ways liberal but undemocratic. It is a political lesson that our present loose complacency about democracy and our more democratic liberalism make us neglect.[4]

Still, Jefferson himself blurred the issue, for he seemed to think that public enlightenment would lead the public to willingly follow the enlightened partisans of truth. "No experiment can be more interesting than that we are now trying," he wrote to Judge John Tyler in 1804, "and which we trust will end in establishing the fact, that man may be governed by reason and truth." By electing Jefferson and the Republicans, the American people have shown "that they may safely be trusted to hear everything true and false, and to form a correct judgment between them." Still, such trust in the people's appraisals could be given only to a people that had "avenues" to the truth about public affairs. "The most effectual hitherto found, is the freedom of the press."[5] Newspapers are a crucial way of mixing enlightened policy with popular power. It must be said that Jefferson's later experiences of the "depravity of taste in the popular press," especially its taste for "slander" and "defamation," gave vent to almost despairing sentiments.[6] Here is another practical problem. In principle, however, the "basis of our governments being the opinion of the people, the first object" is to "keep that right," and if Jefferson had to have "government without newspapers, or newspapers without a government," he would not hesitate, at least in 1787, to select the latter.[7]

The breadth of this enlightenment went far beyond politics in the usual sense. Energetic or not, governments make but a secondary contribution to human happiness. The "greatest service" that can be given any country is "a useful plant, especially a bread grain," and "the queen of the sciences, is agriculture."[8] The great relievers of human necessity are the useful sciences. When Jefferson listed the three "greatest men that have ever lived" for a group portrait that he commissioned from John Trumbull, they were not lawgivers or statesmen; they were the philosophers who have "laid the foundation of those superstructures which have been raised in the Physical and Moral sciences."[9] Two of the three (Francis Bacon and Isaac Newton) are known principally for works in physical science; John Locke alone is known in large part as a lawgiver to lawgivers, that is, for works on government. For Jefferson, the discoveries of physical science were the key to a vision of progress—and if not to government, then to the governance of the minds of men that would permit limited government.

Jefferson the *philosophe* followed his philosophic predecessors in promoting the sciences, like scientific agriculture and scientific medicine, that would relieve suffering and contribute to prosperity. The new experimental science was a search for the causes in nature that might prove useful to many—hence the profound involvement of enlightened physics with enlightened moral science. Moral science clarifies our natural moral sense by finding that "nature has constituted *utility* to man, the standard and test of virtue."[10] It follows that physics as Jefferson understands it, is subordinate to moral science as he understands it, and it is to play its place within the political-humanitarian plan for progress.

If Jefferson's attributions are correct, in short, his vast plan is owing to the first and most hopeful outburst of enlightened philosophy, the enormous project for progress on earth through the mastery of nature and the liberation of man. Jefferson seemed to think Bacon, the first great advocate of experimentation and useful knowledge, the philosophic founder most responsible. It is not merely that Jefferson had the painter Trumbull put Bacon "on top," and "Locke next; then Newton," for that order might reflect mere chronology. But he elsewhere calls Bacon responsible for "the first germs of so many branches of science," and he presumes that the Baconian plan for the advancement of learning would still supply, for the new University of Virginia, "the foundation" for selecting the sciences "useful to us."[11] This may be contrasted with his reliance upon Newton for particular practicalities, upon Newtonian calculations for aid in fixing the coinage, for example, and upon Newtonian laws of the pendulum as an aid to establishing reliable weights and measures.[12]

It is true, nevertheless, that there are other and later currents of modern thought mixed into Jefferson's often paradoxical outlook. Some might be summed up as a diluted Rousseauism; others, as a peculiarly optimistic scientism. Compared to the political views of Bacon and Locke, Jefferson's are more occupied with natural liberty, are a trifle less calculating and appeal to a moral sense or sympathy, are skeptical of European civilization and its commerce and inequalities, treat the people and not the government as sovereign, are more democratic, more humanitarian, and certainly more optimistic as to the historical progress of enlightenment. They are more concerned with republicanism and less with the harsh necessities of government. Jefferson was vastly surprised at the appearance of Napoleon; Locke had thought such despots a likely and eternal possibility.

To take a key example of Jefferson's variation on original liberalism, his interpretation of the "right to pursue happiness" differs interestingly from Locke's right to acquire property. Certainly, Jefferson did not dispute the contribution of industry, or of property as an incentive to industry. "The labor of man would make a paradise of the whole earth," and government was not to "take from the mouth of labor the bread it has earned." But he nevertheless explicitly queried the inclusion of a right to property in Lafayette's draft of the rights of man and appears to have urged Lafayette to substitute the phrase *la recherche du bonheur*.[13] Locke (and Federalists such as John Marshall) had thought protection of the acquiring faculty an indispensable means to overcome scarcity and to build up great power for national security. "That Prince who shall be so wise and godlike," Locke wrote, "as by established laws of liberty to secure protection and encouragement to the honest industry of Mankind against the oppression of power and narrowness of Party will quickly be too hard for his neighbours."[14] Jefferson was more sanguine about peaceableness and the self-reliance of sturdy farmers and less sanguine about the benefits of even the blandly economic Lockean version of Machiavellian principality. He emphasized less the right to acquire the means to an easier and secure life and more the equal right to the end, happiness. He was distinctly willing to limit the acquisitions of the few in order to ameliorate the little man's suffering. Jefferson erased primogeniture and entail from Virginia (in itself a Lockean reform), and he advocated laws dividing inheritances equally among children and taxing property progressively.[15]

Although in 1790 Jefferson praised "Locke's little book on Government" as "perfect as far as it goes," he said that it should be supplemented in application by *The Federalist* and in political economy by Adam Smith's *Wealth of Nations*. Smith's works themselves had looked somewhat to moral sentiment and supposed the inevitability of rational civilization. In later years, Jefferson would add works of Algernon Sidney and Joseph Priestley to his recommendation of Locke's, and of Joseph Say and Destutt de Tracy to Smith's.[16]

He eventually gave extravagant praise to *philosophes* such as

Priestley (the chemist, Unitarian, and democratizing liberal who was driven from Britain for his public defense of the French Revolution), de Tracy, and de Tracy's teacher, P. J. G. Cabanis. Jefferson went so far in 1818 as to commend de Tracy's *Review of Montesquieu* as "the elementary book of instruction" in civil government and his *Treatise on Political Economy* as the same for political economy. His remarks occur in a dedicatory epistle written for the English edition of the *Political Economy*; Jefferson himself did the translation and arranged for the publication. He thus provided the first publication of a work that had remained unpublished in de Tracy's native France, for reasons not the least of which was its thoroughgoing democratic, anti-aristocratic, and antireligious sentiments. Politics ought to attend above all to those with the least, it contended: "The laws should always endeavour to protect weakness; while too frequently they incline to favour power; . . . Of all interests, those of the poor should always be the most consulted, and most constantly respected." In the United States of 1818, Jefferson hoped to spread the *Political Economy*'s "sound principles" to "protect the public industry from the parasite institutions now consuming it."[17]

In 1812, Jefferson had called Cabanis's *Relation of the Physical Constitution and Morals* the "most profound of all human compositions."[18] The profundity evidently consisted in founding moral science on bodily motions and in a critique of other and allegedly higher sources of morality. Cabanis traced ethics to physics, that is, the pleasure of sympathy with others' emotions to the physiology, and in particular, to the sensations of man.[19] "The greatest and most useful revolution in philosophy," Cabanis proclaimed, is the establishment of the fundamental axiom that "ALL IDEAS COME THROUGH THE SENSES," or are "THE PRODUCT OF SENSATIONS."[20] "Ideas" are but "signs," that is, created symbols of sensations. Thus moral ideas, the "laws of ethics," derive from "the mutual and necessary relations of men in society, and these relations derive from their needs."

One should note some difficulties that later became conspicuous. Is not social utility a basis separable from natural need, and is it a basis dependent upon calculations of utility separable from interest and physiology? And what of the judgments ("value judgments," as later skeptics called them) involved in moving from appetite to "need," or from a necessity to a right? Be that as it may, Cabanis was fully confident that physiology finally provides "a solid basis for the moral sciences." The implications are political as well as epistemological. Indeed, they are chiefly political. The new theoretical basis destroys the old separation of the physical from some allegedly superior realm of the intellectual, moral, or spiritual. It is the

key to "the liberation of the human species." The fundamental revolution is then political-intellectual, or rather humanitarian. The power behind the political and industrial powers of popular nations is
the power of a new epistemology and a new method, which together discipline humankind to concentrate on providing for its real and
common necessities. Cabanis attributes the decisive revolution to
Locke, although it was prefigured by Thomas Hobbes and "the immortal Bacon." But he is far more optimistic than either Bacon or
Locke about popular enlightenment, that is, about, the propagation
of such a reductionist science among the people generally.[21]

Jefferson's mixture of a science of power with a science of liberty,
it has been contended, is an example of the main currents of
Enlightenment thought, somewhat varied. This explanation is now
much disputed.

There is the occasional scholar who attributes Jefferson's conservative revolutionizing to his background among the Virginia gentry.
But the natural *aristoi* of talent and virtue that Jefferson advocated
was quite different from any conventional aristocracy of inherited
property and title. Jefferson attacked the Virginia gentry's property
arrangements, its Anglican establishment in religion, and its prerogatives of rule in legislature and county courts. Government was not
to be by prerogative and grace, but by consent and election.

Some other scholars attribute Jefferson's democratizing revolutionizing to the crucible of the American Revolution, which at once
expressed and transformed the American people. This ignores the
liberal and enlightened principles of the revolutionary ferment and
of its leading figures. The Revolution surely ended with a nation for
"ordinary" people, as Gordon Wood argues, and surely had much to
do with a basically middle-class populace.[22] But its radicalism was
from the start linked to doctrines that went to the roots—to natural
rights of all and to reliable foundations for society and government.
"New democratic adhesives" there were, but they involved a limited and special democratizing. The power of the people and the accompanying hunger for equalizing were limited by private rights,
constitutional government, an economy of free enterprise, and the
new prominence of a technological natural science and its practitioners. Both of these explanations miss the distinctive and disputed
character of the "progress of the human mind" under way, with
the special contribution of propagandists such as Tom Paine, of
liberal statesmen such as Hamilton and Madison, and of liberal
statesmen-scientists-propagandists such as Benjamin Franklin and
Jefferson himself.

Most scholars acknowledge the influence of some traditions of belief, including the rationalism of the Enlightenment, but they suppose that the decisive force on the public mind was something else. The leading candidates just now are a "libertarian" or "oppositionist" republicanism derived from the English Civil War and Commonwealth period, a doctrine of rights derived from medieval natural law and representation, classical republicanism, and a repressive tradition of Western rationalism dating right back to Socrates.

In general, these four explanations neglect the fact that Jefferson, the leading theoretician of the Revolution and of the postfounded democratic Republic, slights or denies each of them. Bernard Bailyn may dwell upon the appearance in pre-Revolutionary pamphlets of John Trenchard and Thomas Gordon's *Cato's Letters* and *Independent Whig*, or of Algernon Sidney, John Milton, Robert Molesworth, Henry Neville, James Harrington, Benjamin Hoadley, Henry St. John (Viscount Bolingbroke), and Joseph Priestley, but Jefferson did not.[23] Most of these oppositionist or libertarian pamphleteers are never mentioned in all of Jefferson's voluminous public or private papers and letters (if—a big if—one can trust the analytical index to Lipscomb and Bergh's edition of the *Writings*). Those mentioned (Sidney, Milton, the *Independent Whig*, Bolingbroke, Priestley) are mentioned only once, except for Priestley and, perfunctorily, Lord Bolingbroke (to whom Jefferson gives high honor in reply to a query from Adams). Jefferson praises Priestley as a partisan of liberty, but Priestley, being more or less of Jefferson's generation (he was born ten years earlier), is hardly a republican from some old civil war period. It is Priestley the chemist and the reformer of Christianity whom Jefferson praises—and whom he tries to inveigle into planning his new university and especially into his pet project of revamping Christianity so as to portray Christ as not a God-man but a humane man: a teacher of humanitarian morals. Enlightened liberty and enlightened progress in useful knowledge are the dominating priorities.

The core of the scholarly turn to the English republicans contains a flaw now well known. The earlier oppositionist republicans cannot be separated from the modern individualist doctrines of liberty and republican empire, be they the acquisitive and imperial teachings of Machiavelli and the English Machiavellians or the doctrines of natural rights and acquisitive society of Hobbes and Locke.[24] After all, Locke's teaching of natural freedom is the root of modern libertarianism. His subtle teaching of a right of rebellion breeds unequivocal opposition, even "revolution," against every order in the world except those—to come—that will be modeled on his own plan for majority rule and representative republican government.[25] In the guise of rebellion against injustice and unrepresentative government, Locke would overturn virtually all existing orders and establish the new liberal justice and the new popular governments. It has been wisely said that those who deprecate Locke's influence often show little grasp of his full teaching.

One need say little about the argument that attributes liberalism to medieval natural law, except to repeat that fundamental rights are not the same as fundamental duties and that the right to provide for oneself on earth by industry and a man-made constitution is far from the duty to abide by moral law, and in particular, God's law. "The labor of men would make a paradise of the whole earth," Jefferson said, were it not for "misgovernment" and the "selfish interests of kings, nobles, and priests."[26] This was the only paradise seriously preached in the immense array of speeches and letters with which Jefferson sought to propagate the new faith. Various Locke works had revamped Christianity toward a liberal religion that put religious toleration ahead of religious truth. That plan for religious freedom guided Jefferson's more radical version, much of Priestley's work, and a host of other followers. The ultimate object of Jefferson in particular seemed to be a transitional creed that would "in time, it is to be hoped, effect a quiet euthanasia of the heresies of bigotry and fanaticism which have so long triumphed over human reason."[27] To miss this is to miss the modern propaganda of secularism and the Enlightenment's many-leveled war against Christianity and against the biblical God altogether.

Is Jefferson's thought, then, a variant on pagan republicanism? It is almost enough here to note his dismissal of *the* work of classical republicanism and classical political science, Aristotle's *Politics*. Jefferson did not care whether an accurate translation of the *Politics* existed, he wrote to a correspondent, or, indeed, whether "the political writings of Aristotle, or any other ancient" had ever been recovered. Those old writers may have understood "personal liberty," but they had no understanding "at all of the structure of government best calculated to preserve it," in particular, the separation of legislative from executive power. The introduction of the "principle of representative democracy," Jefferson concluded, has made "useless almost everything written before" on the topic.[28]

Aristotle's republicanism is about rule, not representation. It is principally about better and worse forms of rule. Aristotle gives a qualified primacy in politics to good character and, indeed, to the good life, which is not identical to good character. Jefferson gives primacy to a universal provision for human needs and thus to the universal right to secure the conditions of happiness as the individual defines it. Not the good life but the pursuit of happiness is his theme. In its final books, the *Politics* recommends rule by gentlemen in a small city where rulers can know the ruled. But the work also displays grave doubts about practicability. Regimes must vary with circumstances, and in typical circumstances, genuine gentlemen are a rare and endangered species caught between the multitude, the rich, and the despotic. In typical circumstances, the very best that can be expected is a democratic republic with a large middle class. By contrast, Jefferson can plan, not merely counsel. He can plan for a great democratic nation of private individuals who are protected by a government that is their agent. The plan can be not only definite, but also a future-oriented and universal project to improve the world. For its politics and science of basic needs can be expected to attract most people, and it can also reconcile them to superiors who seem but representatives and experts in service to the public or to humanity at large.

Perhaps the utilitarian improvement of the world is the fruit of Platonic or Socratic rationalism, as various descendants of Friedrich Nietzsche and Martin Heidegger seem to think. But it is perfectly clear that Jefferson did not so think. Socrates engages in inquiry through dialogue, not through experimentation or planning; and he begins his questioning with opinions held to be true or good, not with a foundation in necessity. Also, Socratic inquiries typically end in uncertainties, the propounding of myths, or suggestions for further inquiry. All this murky indefiniteness infuriated Jefferson, who treated Plato as an obscurantist enemy of modern enlightenment. "No writer, ancient or modern, has bewildered the world with more *ignis fatui*, than this renowned philosopher, in Ethics, Politics, and Physics." In old age Jefferson tried to study the *Republic*, but concluded that it is full of "whimsies, . . . puerilities, and unintelligible jargon." His chief question was how such a "foggy mind," clouded by interminable nit-picking, could have obtained such influence. He adopts Bacon's answer. Plato is simply one among the "genuine sophists." That is, he is a fraud, but an ingenious one who managed doctrines to obtain "immortality of fame and reverence."[29] If the aim was glory, the effect was to help rivet a vast tyranny upon the human mind. Plato's "mysticisms" had been "used to mythologize Christianity." Despite such Jeffersonian remarks, someone will no doubt point out that Jefferson excuses Socrates' "true wisdom" from Plato's mystifications, just as he distinguishes Christ's humane morality from Christianity's divinizing and theologizing of Christ. But Jefferson never celebrates or investigates Socratic wisdom, whatever it is.

Jefferson does praise a classical philosopher or two. The doctrines of the hedonist and materialist Epicurus, for example, contain "everything rational in moral philosophy which Greece and Rome have left us."[30] So much for such political philosophers as Plato, Aristotle, and Cicero. But even the philosophic hedonism of Epicurus is not very important to Jefferson. There is little or no reference in Jefferson's writings to Lucretius, the expounder of Epicurean materialism, and Jefferson tends to manage the apolitical Epicurean doctrines as ingenious weapons against apolitical Christian doctrines (Bacon had used Epicurus similarly). While Jefferson speaks of retiring to the consolation of "classic literature" and loves his Greek and Latin, this seems at least as much a consolation for loss of powers and activities as a serious occupation. About science, Jefferson is unequivocally serious. Serious science for Jefferson is not Socratic dialectic, at sea on the waves of opinion, but neither is it the speculative and resigned materialism of an Epicurus. It is useful and active materialism. The "business of life is with matter, that gives us tangible results," as Jefferson once put it. "Handling that, we arrive at knowledge of the axe, the plough, the steam-boat, and everything useful in life, but from metaphysical speculations, I have never seen one useful result."[31] Not Plato's philosophizing, but Dr. Franklin's Baconian science is the way to go, "because he always endeavored to direct it to something useful in private life."[32]

Supposing, then, that Enlightenment philosophers are decisive for Jefferson's peculiarly doctrinal but secular politics, what can be learned from them about its core? In particular, what do they say about liberty and science (the poles of Jeffersonianism) and the relations between them? The gist of the answer is this: there is a rational liberty that accords with what is useful to man and, accordingly, with the science of useful powers. The result is a liberty planned so as to provide for useful power; hence, such rights as those to life, liberty, and the pursuit of happiness. That is, enlightened liberty frees people to provide for their basic necessities, and thus it empowers them (to use a revealing contemporary formulation). It liberates both the energy of the passions and the force of ingenuity. It frees fear of death and the desire to acquire from moral or religious scruple and frees also utilitarian rationality: the rationality that devises useful arts and more tangible inventions. Enlightened liberty, then, is useful liberty. Political liberty and the rights to acquire property and exercise the mind can be fitted together. Together they contribute to securing a state that relieves human beings from the scarcity, war, and despotism that is all too natural. The crucial political effects of the new state are orderly and prospering republican nation-states and the progressive state of mind that is scientific civilization.

How can this vast articulation of science and liberty be clarified? Of the founders that Jefferson mentions, Francis Bacon is best known for the method of mastering nature and John Locke for the political science of liberty. One might suppose a certain division of labor, with Bacon supplying the physical science and Locke, the political. There is some truth in this, at least with respect to the special liberal doctrines of natural rights and representative government. Whatever the dark connections between the Hobbes whom Jefferson despised and the Locke he followed, it is Locke who presents the expanded account of natural rights that we associate with liberalism in its prime. He includes not only a right to life, but also rights to acquire property and to liberty, political and intellectual. Locke quietly moves toward holding only a "republic" legitimate; Hobbes had favored monarchy. Also, Locke thinks out a representative government of divided powers to be fixed in a fundamental "constitution." He thinks out, also, other and lesser liberal doctrines, such as religious toleration in the name of "civil interests" and a free market left more or less to the laws of supply and demand.

Still, a strict division into Baconian physics and Lockean politics will not do. For Locke's politics is a variation on a certain politics of rights, industry, and republicanism that is quietly present in germ and more than germ in Bacon's political works, notably in the *Essays* and some of the legal treatises. More generally, from the start, the Baconian (and Cartesian) advancement of learning encompasses a new moral and political science. The moral and political science is decisive. The famous methods of useful knowledge are governed by comprehensive judgments as to what is useful. Thus the mastery of nature is first and foremost the mastery of human nature. That is what the experimental method effects: the disciplining of the intellect and the senses. It is also what the critique of traditional morals and the introduction of a work ethic is about. The result of such a mixture of industry and art will be a state of future-oriented prosperity, production, and research. It is the vision of progress with which Bacon's *New Atlantis* would replace the biblical visions of Mosaic law, Solomonic wisdom, and Christ's heaven of milk and honey.

To put the relation more plainly, one can say both that Bacon moves in the direction of Locke's politics and that Locke in his *Essay concerning Human Understanding* develops and defends Bacon's methods of critique and invention. Bacon's "civil science" propounds a jurisprudence of private rights, a politics of popular republicanism modified by an administrative state (Bacon dwells upon judicial administration), and a middle-class civil society of enterprise and the work ethic.[33] Alternatively, Locke praises Lord Bacon's new way of "advancing" learning and shares its fundamentals, although he endeavors to fortify it. The new epistemology consists of critique and construction, and it rests on a new foundation. Both philosophers criticize allegedly natural ways of knowing (such as intuition of the true or good, dialectic, and divination). Both seek a reliable method that concentrates upon inventing knowledge of real use. Both suppose they have found a solid foundation for knowing what is useful in the directedness of the passions—the passions, that is, freed by critique from illusory beliefs and judgments of quality. Locke's *Essay concerning Human Understanding* goes to great lengths to deny the possibility of "inherent ideas" of morality, of divinity, and, indeed, of nature itself. The extended critique of morality is perhaps its most original critical argument, and the whole critique is a fortification of Bacon's attack on "primary notions" in the *Great Instauration* and *New Organon*. The *Essay* then interprets reason as essentially "judgment," which proves to be a faculty of invention (and a variation on Bacon's similar "ingenuity"). It is especially an ability to invent symbols that, when put together, comprise "maxims." Maxims are intermediate between the "idea" or effect that the mind wants and the ideas or properties in material things outside the mind.[34] One might call them the formulas for causing the effects people need or want. They are real means of production. Lockean knowledge, like Baconian knowledge, is power.

Finally, Locke in his politics and probably in his whole philosophy, like Bacon in his politics and probably his whole philosophy, finds much of his orientation in the fear of death. All that belongs to a man, Locke summarizes, is his property. The right of property, he tells us just after the middle of the *First Treatise of Government*, originates in the "first and strong desire God planted in man," the "strong desire of self-preservation."[35] In light of such a "principle of action," we may assume that we follow God's will in supposing that man has "a right to make use of those Creatures, which by his Reason or Senses he could discover would be serviceable thereunto."[36] It is a decisive contention, and it resembles the primacy in Bacon's thought of "enduring" or "continuance."[37]

Such a principle had led Bacon to doctrines of jurisprudence very much like Locke's later doctrines of rights and government. Universal private rights may be derived from a ground (*firmamentum*) in necessary private want, according to the first aphorism of Bacon's *Treatise on Universal Justice*. The title to government is by the consent of the people, according to Bacon's *Aphorisms on the Greater Law of Nations and the Fountains of Justice and Law*. Bacon, too, makes the basic law popular rather than divine or aristocratic: "*salus populi, suprema lex*"; "the safety of the people is most rightly said to be the supreme law." It is a doctrine removed from God's law, but one close to the fundamental Lockean law of reason that counsels the preserving of mankind. In fact, at a crucial point, Locke quotes just this Latin formulation. He justifies an enlightened executive, who attacks aristocratic influence in a legislature, despite the constitutional subordination of executive to legislative.[38]

Still, Locke's liberalism is distinctive. These Baconian doctrines are not quite the same, even in their foundation. The key difference is this: whereas Locke's doctrine of rights is rooted in nature, Bacon's is instrumental. There is no serious teaching as to justice in Bacon's thought. Bacon may speak of universal rights, but it is in the context of political expediency. His doctrine of rights is but a useful doctrine for encouraging immigration and mobilizing the people into a great power "fit for empire."[39] Such a one as Michel Foucault might see this as a disciplining of peoples by a science of law that leads by serving. It is an insinuating discipline that maximizes power while minimizing the need for visible coercion. That was, in fact, Bacon's intention.[40]

While Bacon also planned to spread the cause of human liberty,[41] his thought does not show Locke's concentration on spreading the cause of equal rights. The difference is not a matter of degree. On the contrary, Bacon legitimates the immense ambition of a dictator who is a state-builder, much like the image of Henry VII conveyed in his *History of the Reign of Henry VII*. Bacon celebrates the Caesars. He celebrates especially Augustus, who ruled the world and obtained an immortality as founder of an enduring world empire.[42] While Locke knows very well of the power of founding patriarchs and monarchs in the history of states, he treats their absolutism as unconstitutional (and only very, very quietly, as perhaps necessary). He is very far from celebrating the Caesars. Jefferson, as is well known, is farther yet.

In short, Bacon's eulogy of ruthless princes is reminiscent of Machiavelli's *Prince*. Like the *Prince*, Bacon takes his bearings as much by the few who would dominate by force and fraud as by the republican peoples who would be protected. Indeed he takes his bearings more by the dominating figures, for a state is "the prince's armor." These doctrines Jefferson hates, and parts of the Baconian "moral sciences" are thus alien to Jeffersonianism. Jefferson could unaffectedly despise "the mean, wicked, and cowardly cunning of the cabinets of the age of Machiavelli."[43] But Bacon was the first and only seventeenth-century philosopher to cite Machiavelli favorably—

indeed, the only one to cite him at all in works published during Machiavelli's lifetime. The references were frequent, and they went to the realistic core of modern political philosophy and modern philosophy in general: "We are much beholden to Machiavel and others, that write what men do, and not what they ought to do."[44] The concentration on real needs may lead to the project to relieve human necessities by inventions political as well as technological. But Baconian political science lacks the rather simple creed of liberty, and of government by consent, that Locke set forth.

Locke's *Second Treatise* seems calculated to stand by itself after the *First* had been more or less forgotten. *The First Treatise* disposed of the political claims of God the Father and of all such allegedly natural or divine authorities. The *Second* would be a modernizing Bible that teaches individuals and peoples how to provide for themselves—by industry, by governing themselves as free peoples, and by overturning the institutions and the customs that keep the majority down. It provides a popular faith that teaches majorities to depend on themselves. It keeps in the background the superiority of the philosopher who plans and provides the new faith.

It would be a grave error to think that Locke's best-known political works, the *Second Treatise* and *Letter concerning Toleration*, are as simple, doctrinaire, and repetitive as they appear. The simplifications are necessary tricks of the enlightener. Like Bacon's science fiction of visions, they are parts of an effort to set forth a new faith, and at every turn, those with eyes to see can see apparently simple doctrines revised, qualified, and developed. Still, the simple creed of rights, representation, and rebellion endeared Locke to Jefferson. It made endearing to him, or at least welcome instruments for him, the later propagandists such as Paine and Priestley who could overlook subtleties and qualifications.

There is cause to think that Jefferson himself understood well enough the difference between simple public doctrines and the whole complicated plan. There is the evidence of his flexible, immense, and varying policies, and there are revealing comments in addition. While Jefferson was reluctant to reveal himself by revealing his judgments of controversial political thinkers—one can almost see him refraining from talking of Rousseau despite remarks by his correspondents—he was once drawn out by Francis Eppes to acknowledge depths beyond depths. In response to Eppes's request for his opinion of Paine and Bolingbroke, Jefferson said that both were "honest men," both "advocates for human liberty." Paine could write freely, however, while Bolingbroke was "restrained by a constitution, and by public opinion." Paine wrote with extreme simplicity and clarity. But Bolingbroke's superiority went beyond his more diffi-cult circumstances. His was "a style of the highest order," and his "conceptions," more penetrating and politic, could reward diverse audiences. "His political tracts are safe reading for the most timid religionist, his philosophical, for those who are not afraid to trust their reason with discussions of right and wrong."[45]

It is necessary here to note Jefferson's attacks upon certain early modern philosophers who had reservations about the revolutionary, democratic, and legalistic simplicities of Locke and his followers. This more cautious and rather undoctrinaire school included Montesquieu and David Hume, and followers such as Sir William Blackstone. Montesquieu's *Spirit of the Laws* is their great work. They turned to remind of the importance of circumstance, habit, and the moderat-ing complications of mixed government, established law, and coun-terbalanced classes. Although the *Spirit of the Laws* was oriented to the basic "security" of peoples and to appropriate liberties, it said little or nothing about natural rights and about consent as the title to government. It distinguished old and simpler democratic repub-lics from the mixed, commercial, and party-oriented British regime that is the best harbor for real security. Montesquieu recommended a senate of the wealthy and select. He celebrated the softening of manners that came with commerce and the harnessing of ambition that came with party conflict. Locke had paid lip service to the Brit-ish mixed regime while advancing doctrines and policies that would democratize, secularize, economize, and constitutionalize it. His *Sec-ond Treatise* had moved almost invisibly toward one house and that rather democratic, although representing somewhat wealth as well as numbers. It had moved more visibly toward a separation of pow-ers and a reduction of monarchical power—with the executive even-tually rather subordinate to the legislative. Locke moved toward majority rule and the party of the rights of man.

Montesquieu recommended a separate president as executive. Locke, paying lip service to a single monarchical executive, had moved almost invisibly, as Bacon had, toward a cabinet of ministers dependent on the legislature. Montesquieu recommended a separate judiciary as a third branch of government, especially to protect the citizens' security from the executive power. Locke had folded the judiciary into the executive magistrates as he subordinated the executive to the legislative. He seemed to fear the independence of courts, perhaps thinking of courts royal and ecclesiastical, and he relied most upon legislatures and majorities for protecting the secu-rity of individuals.

Finally, Montesquieu suggested the possibility of revolution by insinuation. He looked to the mores of commerce and to judicial changes in criminal law and in the private law of contract and inheritance. He thus recurs to the indirection advanced by Bacon. Locke was hardly averse to the influence of new doctrines of economics and private law, but he also and chiefly sought to revolutionize by explicit doctrines of property rights, political rights, and representative government—and by summoning the jealousy and readiness of a middle-class majority produced and enlightened by such doctrines.

Montesquieu's proposals for three branches and two houses had considerable influence on the framers of the actual Constitution of 1787. Also, his very undoctrinaire demeanor rubbed off. Among such framers as Madison, Hamilton, and others, one finds considerable skepticism of universal theories and much attention to the special customs and circumstances suitable for modern republics. Still, all but Hamilton doubted whether Britain, with its unrepresentative House of Lords, could really be considered a model for a republic. But while Montesquiean caution might appeal to the Federalists who dominated the Constitutional Convention and the administrations of George Washington and John Adams, it was anathematized by Jefferson as "Toryism" and "apostasy." The language of heresy, of betrayal of the true faith, marks the power of Jefferson's devotion to the true science of liberty.

Notes

1. "What is Enlightenment?" in Michel Foucault, *The Foucault Reader*, Paul Rabinow, ed. (New York: Pantheon Books, 1984), 42–43.

2. Jefferson to Roger C. Weightman, June 24, 1826, in *The Writings of Thomas Jefferson*, Andrew A. Lipscomb and Albert E. Bergh, eds., 20 vols. (Washington, DC: Thomas Jefferson Memorial Association, 1904–1905), 16:181–182; hereinafter cited as *Jefferson Writings*.

3. Jefferson to Samuel Kercheval, July, 12, 1816, in *Jefferson Writings*, 15:41.

4. This discussion and others to follow rely on Robert Faulkner, "Marshall and Jefferson," in *The Jurisprudence of John Marshall* (Westport, CT: Greenwood Press, 1980), 173–187.

5. Jefferson to Judge John Tyler, June 28, 1804, in *Jefferson Writings*, 11:33.

6. "Nothing can now be believed which is seen in a newspaper. . . . The man who never looks into a newspaper is better informed than he who reads them; inasmuch as he who knows nothing is nearer to truth than he whose mind is filled with falsehoods and errors" (Jefferson to John Norvell, June 11, 1807, in *Jefferson Writings*, 11:224–225).

7. Jefferson to Edward Carrington, January 16, 1787, in *Jefferson Writings*, 6:57–58.

8. Jefferson to Mr. Miles King, September 26, 1814, in *Jefferson Writings*, 14:197ff.

9. Jefferson to John Trumbull, February 15, 1788, in *The Papers of Thomas Jefferson*, Julian P. Boyd, ed., 25 vols. to date, (Princeton, NJ: Princeton University Press, 1950–), 14:561; hereinafter cited as *The Jefferson Papers*.

10. Jefferson to Thomas Law, June 13, 1814, in *Jefferson Writings*, 14:143.

11. "Report on Desalination of Sea Water," November 21, 1791, in *The Jefferson Papers*, 22:319; Jefferson to Dr. Thomas Cooper, August 25, 1814, in *Jefferson Writings*, 14:173.

12. Jefferson to David Rittenhouse, July 19, 1778, and June 12, 1790, in *The Jefferson Papers*, 2:202–203, and 16:485; see also 16:602–617.

13. Richard K. Mathews, *The Radical Politics of Thomas Jefferson: A Revisionist View* (Lawrence: University Press of Kansas, 1984), 28; Charles M. Wiltse, *The Jeffersonian Tradition in American Democracy* (New York: Hill & Wang, 1960), 74.

14. John Locke, *Two Treatises of Government: A Critical Edition with an Introduction and Apparatus Criticus*, 2d ed., Peter Laslett, ed. (Cambridge, England: Cambridge University Press, 1970), II.v.42.

15. The argument of this paragraph especially relies on Faulkner, *The Jurisprudence of John Marshall*, 173–187.

16. Jefferson to Thomas Mann Randolph, May 30, 1790, and to John Norvell, June 11, 1807, in *Jefferson Writings*, 28:30–31 and 11:222–223; see also 10:448.

17. Destutt de Tracy, *A Treatise on Political Economy*, Thomas Jefferson, trans. (Georgetown, Washington, DC: Joseph Milligan, 1817), 113, 138; reprinted in *Psychology of Political Science: With Special Consideration for the Political Acumen of Destutt de Tracy*, John M. Dorsey, ed. (Detroit, MI: Center for Health Education, 1973).

18. Jefferson to Thomas Cooper, July 10, 1812, in *Jefferson Writings*, 13:177.

19. Pierre Jean George Cabanis, *On the Relations between the Physical and Moral Aspects of Man*, George Mora, ed., Margaret Duggan Saidi, trans., 2 vols. (Baltimore: Johns Hopkins University Press, 1981), 1:6–71.

20. Ibid., 1:10.

21. Ibid., 1:17–19.

22. Gordon S. Wood, *The Radicalism of the American Revolution* (New York: Alfred A. Knopf, 1992).

23. Bernard Bailyn, *The Ideological Origins of the American Revolution* (Cambridge: Belknap Press of Harvard University Press, 1967); Bernard Bailyn, "Political Experience and Enlightenment Ideas in Eighteenth-Century America," *American Historical Review* 67, no. 2 (January 1962), 339–351.

24. See Steven M. Dworetz, *The Unvarnished Doctrine: Locke, Liberalism,*

and the American Revolution (Durham, NC: Duke University Press, 1990), 3–38, 97–134; Thomas L. Pangle, *The Spirit of Modern Republicanism: The Moral Vision of the American Founders and the Philosophy of Locke* (Chicago: University of Chicago Press, 1988), 28–39.

25. This sketch of Lockean constitutionalism is defended in Robert Faulkner, "John Locke," in *Encyclopedia of the American Constitution*, Leonard Levy, Kenneth Karst, and Dennis Mahoney, eds., 4 vols. (New York: Macmillan, 1986), 3:1175–1177; Robert Faulkner, "Liberal Plans for the World: Locke, Kant, and World Ecology Theories," in *International Journal on World Peace* 7 (1990): 61–68; and Robert Faulkner, "Constitutional Institutions: Locke's Model" (forthcoming).

26. Jefferson to Ellen W. Coolidge, August 27, 1825, in *Jefferson Writings*, 18:341.

27. Jefferson to William Short, October 31, 1819, in *Jefferson Writings*, 15:221.

28. Jefferson to Isaac H. Tiffany, August 26, 1816, in *Jefferson Writings*, 15:65–66. The Roman republic and its successor states in Italy never have known "one single day of free and rational government." Cicero, Cato, and Brutus "had no ideas of government themselves, but of their degenerate Senate, nor the people of liberty, but of the factious opposition of their tribunes" (Jefferson to John Adams, December 10, 1819, in *Jefferson Writings*, 15:234–235).

29. Jefferson to William Short, August 4, 1820, and to John Adams, July 5, 1814, in *Jefferson Writings*, 15:258 and 14:148–149. See Stuart Gerry Brown, "The Mind of Thomas Jefferson," in *Ethics* 73 (January 1963): 97. The brief interpretations of Baconian thought rely on Robert Faulkner, *Francis Bacon and the Project of Progress* (Lanham, MD: Rowman & Littlefield, 1993), chap. 5.

30. Jefferson to William Short, October 31, 1819, in *Jefferson Writings*, 15:219.

31. Jefferson to anon., 1825, in Edwin T. Martin, *Thomas Jefferson: Scientist* (New York: Henry Schuman, 1952), 36.

32. Jefferson to anon., 1805, in *Thomas Jefferson: Scientist*, 45. Regarding Jefferson's characteristic "utilitarianism" as to science, his favor of "the practical over the theoretical" in chemistry, physics, and all the sciences, see John C. Green, *American Science in the Age of Jefferson* (Ames: Iowa State University Press, 1984), 3–36.

33. Faulkner, *Francis Bacon*, chaps. 9, 10.

34. John Locke, *An Essay concerning Human Understanding*, Alexander Campbell Fraser, ed. (New York: Dover Publications, 1959), IV.xiv–xxi.

35. Locke, *Two Treatises*, I.ix.86, 87.

36. Ibid., I.ix.86.

37. Richard Whately, ed., *Bacon's Essays* (London: Longmans, Green & Co., 1888), nos. 30 and 57, 348–353; and 591–596, respectively.

38. Locke, *Two Treatises*, II.xiii.158.

39. Whately, *Bacon's Essays*, no. 29.

40. Foucault, *The Foucault Reader*, 63–75; Faulkner, *Francis Bacon*, chap. 10.

41. See Bacon's *An Advertisement Touching a Holy War*, discussed in Faulkner, *Francis Bacon*, 224–226.

42. Faulkner, *Francis Bacon*, chap. 6; see also Bacon's "Images" of Julius and Augustus, reprinted as appendices 1 and 3 therein.

43. Jefferson to Colonel William Duane, April 4, 1813, in *Jefferson Writings*, 13:230.

44. Francis Bacon, *Advancement of Learning*, William Aldis Wright, ed. (Oxford, England: Clarendon Press, 1900), II.xxi.9; see also Faulkner, *Francis Bacon*, chap. 3, quotation at 59.

45. Jefferson to Francis Eppes, January 19, 1821, in *Jefferson Writings*, 15:305–306.

3

Jefferson's Machiavellian Moment

Paul A. Rahe

On the face of it, there would seem to be little evidence suggesting that the political science of Thomas Jefferson owed much, if anything, to the speculation of Niccolò Machiavelli. The Virginian appears to have mentioned the Florentine by name but once, and he did so in a manner conveying his disdain for the author of *The Prince*. And yet, as I try to show in this essay, Jefferson's commitment to limited government, his advocacy of a politics of distrust, his eager embrace of a species of populism, his ultimate understanding of the executive power, and the intention guiding the comprehensive legislative program that he devised for Virginia make sense only when understood in terms of the new science of republican politics articulated by Machiavelli in his *Discourses on Livy.*

Jefferson was exceedingly erudite, and he was keenly interested in the education of the young. On more than one occasion, he took care in outlining a course of study for a protégé. But, in doing so, he never saw fit to include on his list of recommended books *The Prince*, the *Discourses on Livy*, *The Florentine Histories*, *The Art of War*, or any of Machiavelli's lesser works.[1] Indeed, in his only book, the *Notes on the State of Virginia*, in his public writings and speeches, and in his letters, he mentions Machiavelli only once—and then only to denounce a wayward colleague in the Continental Congress. Regarding John Francis Mercer, in a letter to James Madison, Jefferson had nothing good to say: *"He is very mischievous. He is under no moral restraint.* If he *avoids* shame he avoids wrong according to *his system. His fondness for Machiavel is genuine and founded on a true harmony of principle.*"[2] Jefferson's allusion to Machiavelli's reliance on appearances suggests that he had both read *The Prince* and assimilated the critique of virtue elaborated in its fifteenth through eighteenth chapters.[3] That he had not adopted as his own the advice proffered therein by the connoisseur of cunning is evident as well.

There was, of course, another Machiavelli who was less easily dismissed—the republican author of the *Discourses on Livy.*[4] And Jefferson was by no means unaware of his existence.[5] In July 1791, at a tumultuous moment in the midst of the French Revolution, the chevalier de Pio wrote to his old friend from Paris, remarking, "Actually, before my eyes, I have none but Locke, Sidney, Milton, J. J. Rousseau, and Th. Payne; that is my entire library; I have burned the rest, except for *Machiavel,* whom all diplomats possess, though they dare not confess it, and whom free men ought to place alongside the *Declaration of Rights.*"[6] Jefferson may never have acknowledged or even recognized what his own republicanism owed to the thinking of this Machiavelli, but that he was as deeply in debt to the Florentine as was the chevalier de Pio we need not doubt. One does not have to cite an author or, for that matter, even peruse his works to absorb something of his doctrine and to come under his sway. Many an artist and many a thinker echoed Jean Jacques Rousseau in the nineteenth century without having studied him in depth or even read him at all, and the same can be said for Martin Heidegger in more recent times. Debts acquired secondhand remain debts whether we are witting or not; and despite his well-earned reputation as a teacher of evil,[7] Machiavelli exercised a species of intellectual hegemony over republican thought in the eighteenth century exceeded by none but John Locke.

The character of that hegemony demands attention. In recent years, it has become common among scholars to speak of Machiavelli and Locke as if they represented rival and opposed traditions in political thought: Machiavelli is often depicted as a "civic humanist" or classical republican, and Locke is treated, in turn, as the paradigmatic liberal.[8] That the two were at odds on some important questions, such as the status of natural right, is clear enough, and this deserves considerable emphasis. But, at a deeper level, in repudiating Aristotle's understanding of the character of politics and its foundations in human nature and in rejecting all his putatively evil works, especially those of his Christian henchmen, the two were in complete accord. Their dispute concerning the natural foundations of justice was a family quarrel as to the implications of a set of presumptions concerning the relationship between reason and passion that they both accepted; and insofar as the Machiavellian strain of republicanism remained a genuine force within the English-speaking world after the Restoration of Charles II, it did so chiefly as an element integrated within, rather than as one excluded from and opposed to, the liberal republican thinking of Algernon Sidney, John Locke, John Wildman, Walter Moyle, John Toland, John Trenchard, Thomas Gordon, Lord Bolingbroke, James Burgh, William Blackstone, and the like.[9]

Politics of Distrust

Politically, Machiavelli can perhaps best be described as a disciple of Heraclitus. The foundation of his teaching concerning politics is his claim that "all the things of men are in motion and cannot remain fixed." By this, he meant to convey something closely akin to what Thomas Hobbes and David Hume had in mind when they asserted that reason is the slave of the passions. As Machiavelli put it by way of explanation, "the human appetites" are "insatiable"; "by nature" human beings "desire everything" while "by fortune they are allowed to secure little"; and since "nature has created men in such a fashion" that they are "able to desire everything" but not "to secure everything," their "desire is always greater than the power of acquisition (la potenza dello acquistare)." As a consequence of accepting this doctrine, the Florentine dismissed as utopian the moral and political teachings advanced by his classical and Christian predecessors; and under its guidance, he rejected the Aristotelian doctrine of the mean, arguing that the pursuit of moderation is a species of folly and contending that in a world in constant flux there simply is not and cannot be "a middle road (via del mezzo)."[10] Instead of succumbing to the snares of moral reason and the moral imagination, he asserted, one must take one's bearings from an appreciation of what he termed, in an elegant turn of phrase, "the effectual truth of the matter." His position, which he slyly attributed to "all who reason concerning civic life (vivere civile)," was that anyone intent on setting up a republic and ordaining its laws must "presuppose that all men are wicked (rei) and that they will make use of the malignity of their spirit whenever they are free and have occasion to do so."[11]

By Jefferson's day, this had become the common wisdom of the age. In the mid-seventeenth century, James Harrington elaborated a revolutionary, new, and thoroughly modern scheme of republican political architecture on the presumption that Machiavelli had been correct in presuming human desire insatiate and that Hobbes was similarly right in concluding that reason is enslaved to the passions. With regard to the Malmesbury philosopher's "treatises of human nature, and of liberty and necessity," he observed, "they are the greatest of new lights, and those which I have follow'd and shall follow." Consequently, he joined Machiavelli and Hobbes in concluding that self-interested rule is the effectual truth of the matter. He restates the former's conclusion that "*it is the duty of a* Legislator *to presume all men to be wicked.*"[12] He quotes with approval the latter's dictum that "*as often as reason is against a man, so often will a man be against reason.*" Moreover, he concedes that, in practice, "*reason* is nothing but *interest,*" and he concludes that "there be divers *interests,* and so divers *reasons.*"[13] And in making these claims, Harrington set the tone for constitutional prudence from his day through the American Revolution.

David Hume is a case in point. It is indicative of the moderate and skeptical pose that he was inclined to take that he should soften and smooth the rough edges of the doctrine that Harrington had adapted from Machiavelli and Hobbes while reasserting its substance. He observed:

> Political writers have established it as a maxim that, in contriving any system of government, and fixing the several checks and controuls of the constitution, every man ought to be supposed a *knave,* and to have no other end, in all his actions, than private interest. By this interest we must govern him, and, by means of it, make him, notwithstanding his insatiable avarice and ambition, co-operate to public good. Without this, say they, we shall in vain boast of the advantages of any constitution, and shall find, in the end, that we have no security for our liberties or possessions, except the good-will of our rulers; that is, we shall have no security at all.[14]

Hume acknowledged that it might appear "somewhat strange, that a maxim should be true in *politics,* which is false in *fact,*" but he contended nonetheless that it is "a just political maxim, *that every man must be supposed a knave.*" He explained this paradox by drawing attention to the fact "that men are generally more honest in their private than in their public capacity." In defense of partisan principles and in pursuit of what they represent to themselves and others as the common good, they are willing to commit misdeeds that they would never even consider if acting simply and solely on their own behalf. It was, strangely enough, man's generous, public-spirited propensity for partisanship that rendered institutional checks of the sort devised by Harrington so essential to good government.

Hume's restatement of the Machiavellian and Hobbesian position was exceedingly popular in America. The young Alexander Hamilton cited the passage with approbation in a pamphlet that he published in 1775 on the eve of the American Revolution.[15] John Adams did the same in a letter written to his cousin Samuel in 1790 when he was vice-president of the United States.[16] Moreover, in his massive, three-volume *A Defence of the Constitutions of Government of the United States of America*, Adams not only expressed his approval of the claim, advanced in Machiavelli's *Discourses on Livy*, that a legislator must presume all men knaves; he demonstrated in detail that the same view was espoused by Thomas Hobbes, James Harrington, Bernard Mandeville, the baron de Montesquieu, Lord Bolingbroke, and Jean Louis de Lolme, as well as by Joseph Priestley and Richard Price.[17] He need not have stopped there. Few, if any, English Whigs and few American patriots were inclined to challenge Montesquieu's claim that "every man who possesses power is driven to abuse it"; few doubted that such a man would "go forward until he discovers the limits."[18] That was their common creed.

James Madison summed up the convictions of the great majority of his English-speaking contemporaries on both sides of the Atlantic in *The Federalist* when he remarked, "If men were angels, no government would be necessary. If angels were to govern men, neither external nor internal controuls on government would be necessary. In framing a government which is to be administered by men over men, the great difficulty lies in this: You must first enable the government to controul the governed; and in the next place, oblige it to control itself."[19] This was a presumption common to Federalists and Anti-Federalists alike: like the earlier successors of James Harrington, they disputed the political architecture appropriate to a modern republic but not the political problem that this architecture was meant to address. Under the guidance of Machiavelli, Harrington, and the Whig writers of the seventeenth and eighteenth centuries, America's Whigs had become practitioners of what we might call "the politics of distrust."

Wolves and Sheep

Among those who accepted Hume's more nuanced reformulation of Machiavelli's argument, Thomas Jefferson was arguably the most eloquent. Although he was convinced that human beings are endowed by nature with an innate moral sense that renders them fit for society, able to manage their own affairs, and capable of cooperative self-government, he nonetheless doubted whether any individual can really be trusted to rule on another's behalf.[20] During his sojourn as an American diplomat in Paris, he had observed firsthand the consequences of a politics of implicit confidence and trust. In Europe, as he put it to his friend and fellow Virginian Edward Carrington, "under pretence of governing they have divided their nations into two classes, wolves and sheep." He feared that the same could only too easily happen in the infant republics in America. "Cherish therefore the spirit of our people, and keep alive their attention," he urged his correspondent.

> Do not be too severe upon their errors, but reclaim them by enlightening them. If once they become inattentive to the public affairs, you and I, and Congress, and Assemblies, judges and governors shall all become wolves. It seems to be the law of our general nature, in spite of individual exceptions; and experience declares that man is the only animal which devours his own kind.[21]

This particular observation owes more to Machiavelli than one might at first suppose. From his premise that the founder of a republic must operate on the presumption that all men are wicked, the Florentine drew a series of conclusions that astonished his contemporaries and would have surprised the ancients at least as much: that classical Rome was as a republic Lacedaemon's superior, that in a republic the people are safer and better guardians of liberty than are the nobles, and that Roman liberty was rooted in a salutary political turbulence. In Machiavelli's judgment, those whom Jefferson feared might turn into wolves and sheep are to be found wherever there is liberty. Those, he wrote, who are inclined to denounce political turmoil and to argue for social and political harmony "have not considered how it is that in every republic there are two diverse humors—that of the people (*popolo*), and that of the great ones (*grandi*)—and that all the laws that made in favor of liberty are born from this disunion." He insisted that "good examples arise from good education, good education from good laws, and good laws from the tumults (*tumulti*) which many so inconsiderately condemn." To those who thought this last claim preposterous, he replied that "every city ought to have modes by which the people can vent their ambition," arguing that "the demands of a free people are seldom pernicious and rarely endanger their liberty: they arise from oppression or from the suspicions that they entertain that they are about to be oppressed; and when these opinions are false, there is a remedy in the public assemblies where a good man can stand up and, in speaking, demonstrate to the people that they are in error." The crucial fact that one has to keep always in mind is that the people "have less of an appetite for usurpation" than the *grandi*; if one ponders the ends that "the nobles" pursue and those pursued by "the ignoble," one will recognize that the former's purposes arise from "a grand desire for domination" and the latter's "solely from a desire not to be dominated"—that the former "desire to acquire" while the latter "fear to lose what they have acquired."[22]

Institutions versus Tumults

Not all of Machiavelli's admirers shared his taste for *tumulti*. The most influential of these dissenters was Thomas Hobbes.[23] The Malmesbury philosopher was perfectly prepared to concede the distinction that the Florentine drew between those "worthy" to be princes and the people,[24] but the natural antagonism between those ambitious to acquire and those fearful of losing what they already possessed was, in his opinion, an argument against republicanism that justified investing arbitrary authority in a single individual.[25] Although James Harrington vociferously declared his admiration for Machiavelli, rejected Hobbes's case for monarchy, and composed his *Oceana* for the purpose of defending the republican cause, he was in many respects much closer to his compatriot than to the Florentine. In most things, apart from the Hobbes's preference for monarchy, Harrington conceded, "I firmly believe that Mr. Hobbs is and will in future ages be accounted the best writer, at this day, in the world." If he "oppos'd the politics of Mr. Hobbs," Harrington readily confessed, it was merely "to shew him what he taught me."[26]

One sentiment that Harrington shared with Hobbes was an emphatic dislike of political turbulence. In dismissing the self-styled "saints" who advocated godly rule in the wake of the Great Rebellion, Harrington borrowed the language of Machiavelli: "*Give us good men and they will make us good Lawes*, is the *Maxime* of a *Demagogue* and (through the alteration which is commonly perceivable in men, when they have power to work their own wills) exceeding *fallible*." In place of this hoary dictum, Harrington embraced the thoroughly modern principles of the Florentine: "*Give us good orders, and they will make us good men*, is the *Maxime* of a *Legislator*, and the most infallible in the *Politickes*." But, in applying Machiavelli's dictum, Harrington made no mention of his argument on behalf of tumults.

Instead, he proposed to eliminate the need for turmoil by devising institutions that would render them nugatory. In his estimation, "the perfection of Government lyeth upon such a libration in the frame of it, that no man or men, in or under it, can have the interest; or having the interest, can have the power to disturb it with sedition." While in Rome, he remarks, he once observed a pageant

> which represented a kitchen, with all the proper utensils in use and action. The cooks were all cats and kitlings, set in such frames, so try'd and so ordered, that the poor creatures could make no motion to get loose, but the same caused one to turn the spit, another to baste the meat, a third to scim the pot and a fourth to make green-sauce. If the frame of your commonwealth be not such, as causeth everyone to perform his certain function as necessarily as this did the cat to make green-sauce, it is not right.[27]

In his *Oceana*, Harrington claimed to have demonstrated that it is possible to construct an *"immortal Commonwealth"* utterly free from every *"internall cause of Commotion."*[28]

Where Machiavelli distinguished between "the *grandi*," driven by the desire for dominion and the lust for more, and "the people," fearful of being dominated and intent on retaining what they have, Harrington spoke of "the natural aristocracy" and "the natural democracy."[29] Harrington was persuaded that initiative in government invariably falls to members of this "natural aristocracy" and that, if allowed to do so, those who have seized or been entrusted with the initiative will inevitably betray the public trust. "A man doth not look upon *reason* as it is *right* or *wrong* in it self," he insisted, "but as it makes for him or against him." Consequently, he added,

> unlesse you can shew such *orders* of a *Government,* as like those of *God* in *nature* shall be able to constrain this or that *creature* to shake off that *inclination* which is more peculiar unto it, and take up that which regards the *common good* or *interest*; all this is to no more end, then to perswade every man in a *popular Government,* not to carve himself of that which he desires most, but to be mannerly at the publick Table, and give the best from himself unto decency and the *common interest.*[30]

Where Machiavelli proposed to rely on the spirit of the people and their capacity to assert themselves through tumults as a constraint on abuse by the *grandi*, Harrington looked to institutions. "There is not a more noble, or usefull question in the Politicks," he wrote, "then that which is started by *Machiavil*, Whether means were to be found whereby the Enmity that was between the Senate and the people of *Rome* might have been removed."[31]

Harrington's strategy for eliminating this enmity was disarmingly simple. Even *"girles,"* he remarked, know how to provide for justice in situations where interests are opposed.

> For example, two of them have a cake yet undivided, which was given between them, that each of them therefore may have that which is due: Divide, sayes one unto the other, and I will choose; or let me divide, and you shall choose: if this be but once agreed upon, it is enough: for the divident, dividing unequally loses, in regard that the other takes the better half; wherefore she divides equally, and so both have right.

In much the same fashion, Harrington contended, "the whole *Mystery* of a *Common-wealth* . . . lyes only in *dividing and choosing*." One need only assign the right of *"debate"* to "the natural aristocracy" while reserving the right to determine the *"result"* to "the natural democracy."[32] In promoting social and political harmony between the *grandi* and the people, where Machiavelli had purportedly failed, Harrington asserted that one might easily succeed by establishing a bicameral legislature and consigning the representatives of the *grandi* to a deliberative assembly and those of the people to a voting assembly called together to approve or disapprove the proposals advanced by this "natural aristocracy." The former were to divide the cake and the latter to choose.

Thomas Jefferson read Harrington and borrowed his language: he, too, spoke of "the natural aristocracy"; and in using that phrase, he referred to those of his compatriots with a potential for accomplishment that would enable them in the wrong circumstances to present themselves as "wolves." But if he honored Harrington for his recognition of the political problem posed by the natural division between those intent on domination and aggrandizement and those eager to escape domination and retain their possessions, he was in no way persuaded by the claim that with well-designed institutions the English republican had managed to eliminate political turmoil. When Jefferson wrote from Paris to Edward Carrington to urge him to "cherish . . . the spirit of our people, and keep alive their attention" and then cautioned him against being "too severe upon their errors," he had in mind what he took to be an overreaction on the part of his compatriots to the uprising in western Massachusetts that came to be known as Shays's Rebellion. In his letter, he described this event quite self-consciously in the language pioneered by Machiavelli as "the tumults in America."[33]

With regard to the question of political turbulence, the republican from Virginia was indistinguishable from his Florentine predecessor. He did not partake of Machiavelli's enthusiasm for the predatory imperialism of republican Rome; and, perhaps for that reason, he evidenced no interest in providing class struggle with the institutional foundations that were said to have made it a spur to that city's conquest of the Mediterranean world. What Jefferson did share with the Florentine was the conviction that every political community "ought to have modes by which the people can vent their ambition"; and he, too, was persuaded that "the demands of a free people are seldom pernicious and rarely endanger their liberty." Like Machiavelli, he was convinced that such demands "arise from oppression or from the suspicions that they entertain that they are about to be oppressed" and that, "when these opinions are false, there is a remedy in the public assemblies where a good man can stand up and, in speaking, demonstrate to the people that they are in error." Thus, after warning Carrington against being "too severe upon" popular mistakes, Jefferson emphasized that he should, instead, seek to "reclaim" the people "by enlightening them." As he put it by way of explanation,

> I am persuaded myself that the good sense of the people will always be found to be the best army. They may be led astray for a moment but will soon correct themselves. The people are the only censors of their governors: and even their errors will tend to keep these to the true principles of their institution. To punish these errors too severely would be to suppress the only safeguard of the public liberty.[34]

In a letter dispatched soon thereafter to Abigail Adams, Jefferson once again spoke in a Machiavellian vein: "The spirit of resistance to government is so valuable on certain occasions," he wrote, "that I wish it to be always kept alive. It will often be exercised when wrong, but better so than not to be exercised at all. I like a little rebellion now and then. It is like a storm in the Atmosphere." To the latter, he remarked that political "turbulence" is an "evil . . . productive of good. It prevents the degeneracy of government, and nourishes a general attention to public affairs. . . . It is a medicine necessary for the sound health of government."[35]

Prerogative

In endorsing Machiavelli's conviction that popular ire is rooted in oppression, in a justified fear of oppression, or in unjustified suspicions that are quite easily dispelled, Thomas Jefferson was by no means peculiar. Few, if any, credited the more extreme claims that Harrington had advanced on behalf of his scheme of political architecture. Indeed, apart, perhaps, from Harrington's close friend and colleague Henry Neville, the English republican was alone among those who contributed to the Whig canon in thinking that constitutional structures would in and of themselves be sufficient to obviate the need for popular vigilance. John Locke is an especially revealing example, for his position on this question was quite similar to Jefferson's, and it owed much more to Machiavelli than to Hobbes or Harrington. From the outset, even before the Restoration, Locke was inclined to ground his politics on the supposition that "our passions . . . dispose of our thoughts and actions." To a friend, he then wrote, "Tis Phansye that rules us all under the title of reason. . . . We are all Centaurs and tis the beast that carrys us."[36] But from that premise, he eventually drew conclusions opposed in one crucial regard to those of his monarchist predecessor and in another to those of that individual's most effective republican critic.

In his *Two Treatises of Government*, Locke presented himself as a proponent of "moderated" monarchy, but he did not hesitate to describe that regime as "the mighty *Leviathan*."[37] His choice of language was by no means fortuitous: for, in contrast with Harrington, he made a point of entrusting the execution of the laws to a single individual. In fact, he insisted on lodging the conduct of war and foreign policy—which he called the "federative power"—in the same individual's hands. He was convinced that the maintenance of domestic tranquillity and a provision for the common defense are inseparable; and though committed in principle to governance "by establish'd *standing Laws*, promulgated and known to the People," he clearly shared Machiavelli's belief that "the things of men" are too much "in motion" to be consistently administered in so orderly and reasonable a way. Moreover, he clearly felt the force of the case that the Florentine had made on behalf of the Roman dictatorship, and he had apparently pondered the argument advanced by Hobbes on behalf of absolute monarchy. In consequence, Locke deemed it appropriate that his monarchical executive be conceded considerable discretion to contravene the precise letter of the law, to suspend it, to act where it is silent, to mitigate the severity of its penalties, and to pardon offenders. He was also quite happy to grant England's king the right to veto acts of Parliament; and while insisting that his ministers be held responsible for all that they did under his direction, he nonetheless asserted the sanctity of the king's person.[38] In the course of Locke's account of executive prerogative, the "wise and godlike" monarch who rules "by established laws of liberty" gradually gives way to something more akin to Machiavelli's Roman dictator who manages to sustain popular support while acting "without or contrary to the Letter of the Law."[39] In Locke's estimation, the public interest requires a remarkable concentration of power and authority in the hands of a single man.

On the face of it, Jefferson would appear to be opposed to Locke on this point. At the time of the Revolution, he was certainly no friend to the executive power. In designing a constitution for Virginia, he was prepared to embrace the notion of a unitary executive, but he saw fit in each of the three drafts that he penned to specify a long list of powers once accorded the king that, in his opinion, should be expressly denied the official he designated as "the administrator."[40] In 1783, when he proposed a new constitution for his state, he specified that "by Executive powers we mean no reference to those powers exercised under our former government by the crown as of it's prerogative"; and once again he expressly listed and denied to Virginia's executive what he termed "the praerogative powers."[41] Moreover, in his *Notes on the State of Virginia*, he denounced in round terms those in the General Assembly of Virginia who had proposed, at a time of great distress in 1776 and again in 1781, conferring temporary emergency powers in the Roman manner on a dictator.

> One who entered into this contest from a pure love of liberty, and a sense of injured rights, who determined to make every sacrifice, and to meet every danger, for the re-establishment of those rights on a firm basis, who did not mean to expend his blood and substance for the wretched purpose of changing this master for that, but to place the powers of governing him in a plurality of hands of his own choice, so that the corrupt will of no one man might in future oppress him, must stand confounded and dismayed when he is told, that a considerable portion of that plurality had meditated the surrender of them into a single hand, and in lieu of a limited monarch, to deliver him over to a despotic one![42]

In making his argument, Jefferson took care to respond to the case advanced by the proponents of the dictatorship, intimating, to begin with, that he understood the linkage between Machiavelli's defense of the Roman institution and Locke's case for prerogative: there is, he insisted, no provision for such an office within the Constitution of Virginia that not only "provides a republican organization," but "proscribes under the name of *prerogative* the exercise of all powers undefined by the laws." To those who reiterated Machiavelli's appeal to "the necessity of the case," Jefferson responded that "necessities which dissolve a government, do not convey its authority to an oligarchy or a monarchy. They throw back, into the hands of the people, the powers they had delegated, and leave them as individuals to shift for themselves." In any event, he added, "the necessity" faced by his fellow Virginians was neither "palpable" nor "irresistible." In answering those who followed Machiavelli in asserting Roman precedent, he contended that "it had proved fatal." Rome was "a republic, rent by the most bitter factions and tumults, where the government was of a heavy-handed unfeeling aristocracy, over a people ferocious, and rendered desperate by poverty and wretchedness." In that polity, there were "tumults which could not be allayed under the most trying circumstances, but by the omnipotent hand of a single despot. Their constitution therefore allowed a temporary tyrant to be erected, under the name of a Dictator; and that temporary tyrant, after a few examples, became perpetual." In Jefferson's estimation, when his fellow Virginians contemplated electing a dictator, they came close to turning their backs on America's nascent experiment in republicanism. As he put it,

> the very thought alone was treason against the people; was treason against mankind in general; as rivetting for ever the chains which bow down their necks, by giving to their oppressors a proof, which they would have trumpeted through the universe, of the imbecility of republican government, in times of pressing danger, to shield them from harm.

To this one might add that, throughout his life, Jefferson was an exceedingly strict constructionist in expounding the Constitution.[43] "I own," he told James Madison quite early on, "I am not a friend to a very energetic government. It is always oppressive."[44] No one spoke with greater force in favor of what Locke called governance "by establish'd *standing Laws*, promulgated and known to the People." And yet Jefferson, as president, was prepared to sanction what, he had no doubt, was a breach of the Constitution; he justified his act in negotiating the Louisiana Purchase and that of Congress in ratifying the treaty and in appropriating the requisite funds in a manner indicating his recognition that Machiavelli, Hobbes, Locke,

Montesquieu, Bolingbroke, Blackstone, and de Lolme were correct in supposing that necessity dictates, even within a republic, the presence of a prince capable of meeting the emergencies forever incident to human affairs. Jefferson, too, believed that the world is in constant motion.[45]

In pondering "whether circumstances do not sometimes occur, which make it a duty in officers of high trust, to assume authorities beyond the law," Jefferson argued that the question was "easy of solution in principle, but sometimes embarrassing in practice." As he put it,

> A strict observance of the written laws is doubtless one of the high duties of a good citizen, but it is not *the highest*. The laws of necessity, of self-preservation, of saving our country when in danger, are of higher obligation. To lose our country by a scrupulous adherence to written law, would be to lose the law itself, with life, liberty, property and all those who are enjoying them with us; thus absurdly sacrificing the end to the means.

In *The Federalist*, Alexander Hamilton had hinted at something of the sort, alluding to the precedent set by Rome's dictatorship, arguing that the distinction between a workable republic and one incapable of providing for domestic tranquillity and the common defense turns largely on the provisions made to ensure the "decision, activity, secrecy, and dispatch" necessary to this end, and contending that the president's extended term of office would enable a public-spirited executive "to expose himself" when necessary, to save "the people from very fatal consequences of their own mistakes," and to procure for himself "lasting monuments of their gratitude" for having had "courage and magnanimity enough to serve them at the peril of their displeasure."

In making this argument, Hamilton was exceedingly cautious: if one were to ignore Hamilton's allusion to the Roman dictatorship, one could easily read the latter passage simply and solely as a defense of the executive veto. Jefferson was much more candid, specifying just what was involved:

> It is incumbent on those . . . who accept of great charges, to risk themselves on great occasions, when the safety of the nation, or some of its very high interests are at stake. An officer is bound to obey orders; yet he would be a bad one who should do it in cases for which they were not intended, and which involved the most important consequences.

That "the line of discrimination between cases" might be "difficult," he was perfectly happy to acknowledge. His point was simply that "the good officer is bound to draw it at his own peril, and to throw himself on the justice of his country and the rectitude of his motives."[46]

Anticipation, Resistance, and Revolution

The willingness of Harrington's Whig successors to embrace the notion of a unitary executive posed a grave difficulty for the proponents of republican liberty: how to prevent an abuse of what Locke called "Prerogative" on the part of an executive graced with dictatorial discretion. It was in part with this problem in mind that Locke asserted the right of popular resistance and made the people's representatives in the legislature and the executive ultimately accountable to the people themselves for their conduct in office. Like Machiavelli, the English philosopher was persuaded that the people are the best, if not the only, safe guardians of their own liberty.[47] Some would, he conceded, attack him for laying "the Foundation of Government in the unsteady Opinion, and uncertain Humour of the People." But such men were in error; and to demonstrate that this was the case, Locke borrowed and adapted the arguments made by Machiavelli against the very same objections. The many may be inclined to resist when "*generally ill treated*," he contended, but they are "not so easily got out of their old Forms, as some are apt to suggest." In fact, if anything, they are too steady in their opinions and too certain in their humors. For the people "are more disposed to suffer, than right themselves by Resistance," and they are "not apt to stir" until "the mischief be grown general, and the ill designs of the Rulers become visible, or their attempts sensible to the greater part." As a consequence, the many tend not to resist oppression until it is already too late for them to be effective; and even when they do, they nearly always fail to initiate the institutional reforms necessary to prevent a recurrence.[48]

To counteract the "slowness" of the people; to lessen, if not expunge, their "aversion" to change; and to encourage them to anticipate oppression to come, Locke introduced a new rhetoric of popular resistance to be deployed by spirited and ambitious *grandi* of the sort that Machiavelli had deemed "worthy to be princes." To arouse the ardor of these natural aristocrats and to elicit from them the requisite jealousy, vigilance, and *virtù*, he mocked the traditional

Christian doctrine of *"Passive Obedience"* and "quiet Submission" to authority, and he rejected the classical commitment to communal solidarity and trust; in their place, he exalted the prudence and foresight, the independence of mind, and the wiliness that had enabled Odysseus to rescue himself from the Cyclops Polyphemus.[49]

Locke harbored no illusions concerning the few men endowed with what he called "a busie head, or turbulent spirit," and he said nothing in their defense. He remained persuaded that reason is dependent on the passions and that "the busie mind of Man" can "carry him to a Brutality below the level of Beasts." He had learned from long and painful experience that the human "imagination is always restless and suggests variety of thoughts, and [that] the will, reason being laid aside, is ready for every extravagant project." "In this State," Locke tells us, "he that goes farthest out of the way, is thought fittest to lead, and is sure of most followers." Consequently, the English philosopher readily acknowledges that "the Pride, Ambition, and Turbulency of private Men have sometimes caused great Disorders in Commonwealths" while "Factions have been fatal to States and Kingdoms." As for those who lay "the foundation for *overturning* the Constitution and Frame of *any Just Government*," he holds them responsible "for all those mischiefs of Blood, Rapine, and Desolation, which the breaking to pieces of Governments bring on a Countrey"; and in his judgment, this makes them "guilty of the greatest Crime" he can imagine "a Man . . . capable of."[50]

But despite, or, perhaps, even to some degree because of, their shortcomings, Locke is eager to enlist these turbulent spirits under the banner of liberty—for he is confident that this natural aristocracy will understand how to make "the ill designs of the Rulers . . . visible" and their "attempts sensible" to the people as a whole. From studying the example that he provides in his *Two Treatises of Government*, they can learn how to unmask the tyranny that lies hidden under "ancient Names, and specious Forms." It was in pursuit of this Machiavellian end that Locke redeployed the natural rights theory devised for other purposes by that enemy of tumults Thomas Hobbes. The rhetoric that Locke employed in his great political tract, in particular his appeal to natural rights as a standard by which to judge the conduct of administration, is an instrument fashioned in such a manner as to enable busy heads to make "visible to the People" the "design" that underlies and accounts for "a long train of Abuses, Prevarications, and Artifices, all tending the same way." When enlightened by the jealous and watchful few, the many "cannot but feel, what they lie under, and see, whither they are going";

and when they both feel and see, "'tis not to be wonder'd, that they should then rouze themselves, and endeavour to put the rule into such hands, which may secure to them the ends for which Government was at first erected."[51]

That his "Doctrine" of anticipation, resistance, and revolution may be "destructive to the Peace of the World" Locke tacitly concedes. But, like Machiavelli, he demands that his readers consider whether the peace so often inculcated from the pulpit can be distinguished from "Violence and Rapine," and he concludes that this peace is "maintain'd only for the benefit of Robbers and Oppressors." Moreover, in posing a rhetorical question, he employs an analogy between man and beast that would soon be appropriated in America by Jefferson. "Who would not think it an admirable Peace betwixt the Mighty and the Mean," he asks, "when the Lamb, without resistance, yielded his Throat to be torn by the imperious Wolf?"[52]

The English philosopher resorts to sarcasm in this context because he clearly discerns an alternative to arbitrary rule. Civil disorder may, he confesses, be "an *Inconvenience . . . that attends all Governments* whatsoever," but that is only because "the Governours have brought it to this pass, to be generally suspected of their people." Such a condition is "the most dangerous state" that rulers "can possibly put themselves in." But "they are the less to be pitied, because it is so easie to be avoided," for it is "impossible for a Governor, if he really means the good of his People, and the preservation of them and their Laws together, not to make them see and feel it."[53]

In restating, elaborating, and adapting Machiavelli's argument that the people are the best guardians of their own liberty, Locke stopped just shy of fully endorsing the case that the Florentine had made in defense of tumults, and he failed at the same time to reiterate the Florentine's closely related contention that, in a free state, liberty depends upon a frequent recurrence to first principles.[54] If there were some, such as Blackstone and Hume, who thought Locke a mite reckless in elaborating a rhetoric of popular resistance, there were others, chiefly among the radical Whigs, who were apparently persuaded that he had erred on the side of caution—and they could cite the pronouncements of the Whig martyr Algernon Sidney in their defense;[55] and among the American colonists, the case that they made in defense of periodic civil disorder fell on especially fertile ground.[56] Like Sidney and his admirers on both sides of the Atlantic, Jefferson repeatedly echoed Machiavelli's conviction that corruption and lethargy can easily deprive a people of the capacity to defend their own liberty.[57]

The Logic of Jefferson's Legislative Program

Some among Jefferson's contemporaries shared Alexander Hamilton's conviction "that there is always a body of firm patriots" that can easily "shake a corrupt administration."[58] Jefferson was not so confident. In writing to yet another correspondent on the subject of Shays's Rebellion, he observed, "God forbid we should ever be 20 years without such a rebellion."[59] He was not especially disturbed by the ignorance of the people; he considered them fully capable of taking instruction. The real danger was that his compatriots would "remain quiet under" their "misconceptions." In this he perceived "a lethargy," which he described as "the forerunner of death to the public liberty." He asked, "What country can preserve it's liberties if their rulers are not warned from time to time that their people preserve the spirit of resistance?" And then he concluded, "Let them take arms. The remedy is to set them right as to facts, pardon and pacify them. What signify a few lives lost in a century or two? The tree of liberty must be refreshed from time to time with the blood of patriots and tyrants. It is its natural manure." It was with the danger of public lethargy in mind that Jefferson fashioned his great program of legislative reform for Virginia.[60]

In 1776, when the General Assembly asked him to revise the laws of the Commonwealth in light of the decision to break with the mother country, Jefferson took his commission as an occasion for disassembling the artificial supports sustaining what little there was in that state reminiscent of England's ancien régime. To lessen the probability that the clergy would exercise through priestly guile a hegemony over the minds of his fellow citizens, he proposed disestablishing the Episcopalian Church. As drafted, Jefferson's bill attacked "the impious presumption of legislators and rulers, civil as well as ecclesiastical, who, being themselves but fallible and uninspired men, have assumed dominion over the faith of others."[61] In this fashion, Jefferson disposed of the clergy's pretensions to tutelage. He then struck a blow at inherited wealth and position. To lessen the likelihood that riches would corrupt and birth dazzle his fellow Virginians, Jefferson "laid the axe to the root of Pseudo-aristocracy" by convincing the assembly to outlaw entails and abolish primogeniture. Deprived of legal props, with their land and their other property being gradually divided by the succession of generations and ultimately dispersed, the great families of Virginia would wither and soon disappear.[62]

After eliminating the privileges reinforcing the power and influence of the clerical and secular *grandi* who stood as rivals to what he termed the "natural aristocracy," Jefferson concerned himself with promoting the advancement of young men of genius who might become genuinely worthy of high office. To encourage the emergence of a class of talented and well-informed individuals suited for public service, and to prepare ordinary Virginians for the task of selecting nature's noblemen from among the pretenders, he proposed "a systematical plan of general education."[63] From 1779 on, he urged the Virginia General Assembly to pass his Bill for the More General Diffusion of Knowledge and thereby establish throughout the Commonwealth a system of publicly supported elementary schools.[64] In a curriculum lasting three years, these schools would instruct all of the state's young residents (male and female alike) not only in reading, writing, and arithmetic, but also in the history of the spirited peoples who had pioneered free institutions—the Greeks, the Romans, the English, and their American successors. These schools were to be under the supervision of a visitor who would choose annually from among the children of parents who lacked the resources to provide for their son's further education "the boy, of best genius in the school" and send him on at state expense to study Greek, Latin, geography, and mathematics at one of the twenty grammar schools to be established within Virginia. After a year or two, "the best genius" was to be selected from among the scholarship students within each class at each of the grammar schools. The others would then be dismissed, and the one boy chosen would continue his studies until he had completed a six-year term. "By this means," Jefferson remarked, "twenty of the best geniusses will be raked from the rubbish annually, and be instructed, at the public expence, so far as the grammar schools go." Upon completion of this extended course of study, ten of the twenty would receive public support to go on to study "all the useful sciences" at the university level. "By that part of our plan which prescribes the selection of the youths of genius from among the classes of the poor," Jefferson observed, "we hope to avail the state of those talents which nature has sown as liberally among the poor as the rich, but which perish without use, if not sought for and cultivated."[65]

The proprietor of Monticello drafted this proposal decades before he first conceived the notion of establishing a university in the Piedmont region of central Virginia.[66] At the time, the only institution of higher education in the state was his own alma mater, the College of William and Mary. Persuaded that this institution, as constituted, failed to meet Virginia's needs in the new era of independence, he urged a thoroughgoing reform of its bylaws and of the curriculum "to aid and improve that seminary, in which those who are to be the future guardians of the rights and liberties of their country may be endowed with science and virtue, to watch and preserve the sacred deposit." To this end, Jefferson set out to change what had been an Anglican establishment into an institution wholly secular—with a thoroughly modern course of study including mathematics as well as political and natural science. To achieve this, he argued for dropping the chairs in theology and oriental languages. After his reform, there would be eight professorships, one to give instruction in moral philosophy, the laws of nature and of nations, and the fine arts; and the others to teach law and police, history, mathematics, anatomy and medicine, natural philosophy and natural history, ancient languages, and modern languages.[67]

Unfortunately, despite considerable and persistent effort on Jefferson's part, his "systematical plan of general education" never passed into law. The General Assembly did make a feeble attempt to encourage the establishment of elementary schools on the local level, and Jefferson was able to effect a partial reform of the College of William and Mary in 1779 when he served as a visitor to that ancient institution.[68] But these meager accomplishments left him unsatisfied.[69] To John Adams, in 1813, he expressed his dismay that his "system" had never been enacted.

> The law for religious freedom . . . having put down the aristocracy of the clergy, and restored to the citizen the freedom of the mind, and those of entails and descents nurturing an equality of condition among them, this on Education would have raised the mass of the people to the high ground of moral respectability necessary to their own safety, and to orderly government; and would have compleated the great object of qualifying them to select the veritable aristoi, for the trusts of government, to the exclusion of the Pseudalists.[70]

Despite its virtues, Jefferson's plan never recommended itself to the general public.

Ultimately, Jefferson had to settle for the establishment at Charlottesville of the University of Virginia on lines similar to those laid out in his plan to transform the College of William and Mary.[71] It is indicative of the Machiavellian roots of his program that he insisted that, had he been given the option, he would have preferred the general education of the many to the higher education of the few. To one close collaborator, he wrote,

> Were it necessary to give up either the Primaries or the University, I would rather abandon the last, because it is safer to have a whole people respectably enlightened, than a few in a high state

of science, and the many in ignorance. This last is the most dangerous state in which a nation can be. The nations and governments of Europe are so many proofs of it.[72]

But Jefferson was denied the opportunity to choose. Though disappointed, he could nonetheless take consolation from the prospect that, at the university he had instituted, the future leaders of Virginia would receive a proper political education and imbibe Machiavelli's politics of distrust as they read Sidney's *Discourses of Government*, Locke's *Second Treatise*, the Declaration of Independence, *The Federalist*, Washington's Farewell Address, and the Virginia Resolutions of 1799 while attending the lectures of an orthodox Whig.[73] As Jefferson put it in a letter to James Madison, "In the selection of our Law Professor, we must be rigorously attentive to his political principles." Before the Revolution, this would have been easy, he explained, for "our lawyers were then all Whigs." Even now, he added, "they suppose themselves, indeed, to be Whigs, because they no longer know what Whigism or republicanism means. It is in our seminary that that vestal flame is to be kept alive."[74]

Popular Education, Ward Republics, and Political Jealousy

The same set of concerns that animated first Machiavelli and then Locke account for Jefferson's frustration at the failure on the part of the framers of the Constitution to include a bill of rights within the document.[75] He harbored few illusions regarding the strength of parchment barriers as a bulwark against the tyrannical rule of a popular majority, but he did think them useful as a rallying point against oppression on the part of a corrupt and distant government. "Above all things," he wrote with this question in mind, "I hope the education of the common people will be attended to; convinced that on their good sense we may rely with the most security for the preservation of a due degree of liberty."[76] Citizens who were fully informed of their rights were much more likely to be able to defend those rights.

Jefferson's commitment to the freedom of the press is explicable in precisely the same terms. In a letter to Edward Carrington, he argued, with regard to tumults, that "the way to prevent these irregular interpositions of the people is to give them full information of their affairs thro' the channel of the public papers, and to contrive that those papers should penetrate the whole mass of the people." He was persuaded that "the basis of our governments" is "the opin-

ion of the people" and that "the very first object should be to keep
that right. . . . Were it left to me to decide whether we should have
a government without newspapers, or newspapers without a government," he wrote, "I should not hesitate a moment to prefer the
latter. But I should mean that every man should receive those papers and be capable of reading them."[77]

Thirty years subsequent to his presentation of "The Revisal of
the Laws, 1776-1786" to the Virginia General Assembly, after observing the manner in which his political enemies in New England had
employed the town meetings to rally the populace of that region
against his embargo, Jefferson added an amendment to his original
proposals. For the purpose of establishing local elementary schools,
he had long supported dividing the counties into "hundreds" or
"wards." Now, he sought the institution of such small districts for
another end as well: they were, he believed, ideally suited for the
establishment of self-government within the localities; and as such,
they could do much to form the political character of the nation's
citizens and to head off political lethargy and corruption. Here again
he had in mind Machiavelli's defense of *tumulti*. The wards were
designed to make the general public attentive to political affairs: they
were to function as "a regularly organized power" enabling the
people "to crush, regularly and peaceably, the usurpations of their
unfaithful agents," free "from the dreadful necessity of doing it in-
surrectionally."[78] "By making every citizen an acting member of the
government, and in the offices nearest and most interesting to him,"
Jefferson attempted to "attach him by his strongest feelings to the
independence of his country, and its republican Constitution."[79] As
he put it,

> Where every man is a sharer in the direction of his ward-republic,
> or of some of the higher ones, and feels that he is a participator in
> the government of affairs, not merely at an election one day in the
> year, but every day; when there shall not be a man in the State
> who will not be a member of some one of its councils, great or
> small, he will let the heart be torn out of his body sooner than his
> power be wrested from him by a Caesar or a Bonaparte. . . . As
> Cato, then, concluded every speech with the words, "*Carthago de-
> lenda est* [Carthage must be destroyed]," so do I every opinion,
> with the injunction, "divide the counties into wards."[80]

It is essential to recognize that Jefferson did not give primacy to
political participation as an end in itself.[81] His desire to foster self-
government in the localities had the same roots as his long-standing
commitment to states rights. Like the Anti-Federalists, he wished to

minimize the responsibilities of those elements of the government set at a great distance from the people and to maximize vigilance on the part of the people by fostering popular control of local affairs. His animating principle is visible in the passage that he inserted in his draft of the Kentucky Resolutions of 1798, arguing that "confidence is everywhere the parent of despotism," that "free government is founded in jealousy, and not in confidence," and that "it is jealousy and not confidence which prescribes limited constitutions, to bind down those whom we are obliged to trust with power."[82]

This Machiavellian predilection for distrust helps explain why Jefferson looked on the Supreme Court of the United States with such suspicion, railing against what he perceived as a propensity for judicial "despotism" and "oligarchy." It was Jefferson's conviction that to concede political supremacy to courts composed of men appointed to office for life would be to make the Constitution "a mere thing of wax in the hands of the judiciary, which they may twist and shape into any form they please."[83] It was his conviction that "to consider the judges as the ultimate arbiters of all constitutional questions was a very dangerous doctrine indeed," for there was and could be "no safe depository of the powers of the society but the people themselves." And he insisted that, "if we think them not enlightened enough to exercise their control with wholesome discretion, remedy is not to take it from them, but to inform their discretion by education."[84]

Precisely the same concern with promoting popular vigilance dictated the desire, which Jefferson shared with the Anti-Federalists and with many a Federalist as well, that the individual citizens of the United States be armed and that they be organized locally under their own officers as a militia. Those who proposed the pertinent provisions in the various state bills of rights, those who enacted the relevant state laws, and those who requested, framed, and ratified what we now know as the Second Amendment to the federal Constitution took as a given William Blackstone's exposition of the parallel passage in the English Bill of Rights. In the United States of America, as in England, the individual's right to bear arms was deemed an "auxiliary right" comparable to freedom of speech and freedom of the press. It was established as a legal or even constitutional right because it was thought essential as a safeguard for the more fundamental, natural rights to life, liberty, and property. To be precise, the right to keep and bear arms was "a public allowance, under due restrictions, of the natural right of resistance and self-preservation, when the sanctions of society and laws are found insufficient to restrain the violence of oppression."[85] Even those who greatly feared political turmoil recognized that measures aimed at suppressing tumults or rendering them impossible or exceedingly difficult might open the way for an elimination of public liberty.[86]

Jefferson never strayed from the position that he outlined in his missive to Edward Carrington. In his last communication, a letter that he drafted to decline an invitation to attend festivities scheduled for the fiftieth anniversary of America's Declaration of Independence, he wrote of that event:

> May it be to the world, what I believe it will be, (to some parts sooner, to others later, but finally to all,) the signal of arousing men to burst the chains under which monkish ignorance and superstition had persuaded them to bind themselves, and to assume the blessings and security of self-government. That form which we have substituted, restores the free right to the unbounded exercise of reason and freedom of opinion. All eyes are opened, or opening, to the rights of man. The general spread of the light of science has already laid open to every view the palpable truth, that the mass of mankind has not been born with saddles on their backs, nor a favored few booted and spurred, ready to ride them legitimately, by the grace of God.[87]

From the outset, Jefferson's goal was to prevent America's *grandi* from becoming wolves who would treat their fellow citizens as if they were sheep. Because he was mindful of the Machiavellian dictum that a legislator must presume all men wicked, he was persuaded that the only way to accomplish this end was to see to it that the American people were never in any fashion sheeplike at all. Such was for Jefferson, as it had been for Machiavelli, Locke, and their admirers, the central core of his understanding of the spirit that one must foster if one is to sustain republican liberty.

Notes

This essay was initially drafted for presentation at a conference on "Thomas Jefferson's Legacy of Liberty," held at the Institute of United States Studies in the University of London on November 22–23, 1993. In revised form, it was presented as part of a panel on "The American Faces of Machiavelli" at the annual meeting of the American Political Science Association held in New York on September 1–4, 1994, and it was published in the *Review of Politics* 57, no. 3 (Summer 1995). It was composed and then reworked while I was a fellow of the National Endowment for the Humanities and the Woodrow Wilson International Center for Scholars in Washington, D.C. I am indebted to these two institutions for their support and to Jean Yarbrough and Anthony Parel, who were free with their criticism. The translations in this essay are my own. In citing passages from sources in English, I have retained the original grammar, spelling, and emphasis. Nicholas Paul and Rosalee Williams helped me check the notes.

1. See, for example, Jefferson to Robert Skipworth, August 3, 1771, to Peter Carr, August 19, 1785, and August 10, 1787, and to Garland Jefferson, June 11, 1790, in *The Papers of Thomas Jefferson*, Julian P. Boyd, ed., 25 vols. to date (Princeton, NJ: Princeton University Press, 1950–), 1:76–81, 8:405–408, 12:14–19, and 16:480–482, respectively; hereinafter cited as *The Jefferson Papers*. See also Jefferson to John Minor, August 30, 1814, in *The Writings of Thomas Jefferson*, Paul Leicester Ford, ed., 10 vols. (New York and London: G. P. Putnam's Sons, 1892–1899), 9:480–485; hereinafter cited as *The Writings of Jefferson*.

2. Jefferson to James Madison, May 7, 1784, in *The Jefferson Papers*, 7:228.

3. On the argument that Machiavelli presents in these chapters, see Clifford Orwin, "Machiavelli's Unchristian Charity,"*American Political Science Review* 72, no. 4 (December 1978; 1217–1228, and Richard H. Cox, "Aristotle and Machiavelli on Liberality," in *The Crisis of Liberal Democracy*, Kenneth L. Deutsch and Walter Soffer, eds. (Albany, NY: State University of New York Press, 1987), 125–147.

4. In this connection, see Gisela Bock, Quentin Skinner, and Maurizio Viroli, eds., *Machiavelli and Republicanism* (Cambridge, England: Cambridge University Press, 1990).

5. He owned Machiavelli's collected works in Italian and in an English translation: see E. Millicent Sowerby, *Catalogue of the Library of Thomas Jefferson* (Washington, DC: Library of Congress, 1983), nos. 169, 1143, 2324, 2351–2353, 4579.

6. Chevalier de Pio to Jefferson, July 22, 1791, in *The Jefferson Papers*, 20:662–663. The original letter is in French.

7. See Victoria Kahn, *Machiavellian Rhetoric: From the Counter–Revolution to Milton* (Princeton, NJ: Princeton University Press, 1994).

8. See J. G. A. Pocock, "Virtue and Commerce in the Eighteenth Century," *Journal of Interdisciplinary History* 3 (1972–1973), 119–134; J. G. A. Pocock, *The Machiavellian Moment: Florentine Political Thought and the Atlantic Republican Tradition* (Princeton, NJ: Princeton University Press, 1975); and J. G. A. Pocock and Richard Ashcraft, eds., *John Locke: Papers Read at a Clark Library Seminar, 10 December 1977* (Los Angeles, CA: William Andrews Clark Memorial Library, University of California, 1980), 3–24.

9. For an extended analysis of the character of Anglo-American republican thought in the early modern period, see Paul A. Rahe, *Republics Ancient and Modern: Classical Republicanism and the American Revolution* (Chapel Hill: University of North Carolina Press, 1992), bk. 2, 231ff.

10. Niccolò Machiavelli, *Discorsi sopra la prima deca di Tito Livio*, 1.6, 37, 2 Proemio, in Niccolò Machiavelli, *Tutte le opere*, Mario Martelli, ed. (Firenze, Italy: Savroni, 1971), 86–87, 119, 145.

11. One should read Machiavelli's, *Discorsi*, 1.3, in *Tutte le opere*, 81–82, in light of *Il principe*, 15, in *Tutte le opere*, 280.

12. James Harrington, *The Prerogative of Popular Government*, 1658, in *Works: The Oceana and Other Works of James Harrington*, John Toland, ed. (London: Booksellers of London and Westminster, 1771), 241, hereinafter cited as *Works of Harrington*; and S. B. Liljegren, ed., *James Harrington's Oceana* (Heidelberg, Germany: G. Winter, 1924), 152, 155.

13. Compare Liljegren, *James Harrington's Oceana*, 22, with Thomas Hobbes, Ep. Ded., *Human Nature*, in *The English Works of Thomas Hobbes of Malmesbury*, Sir William Molesworth, ed. (London: John Bohn, 1839–1845), IV.xiii, and with Thomas Hobbes, *Leviathan*, C. B. Macpherson, ed. (London: Harmondsworth, 1968), 166.

14. This and the following Hume quotes are from David Hume, "Of the Independency of Parliament," in David Hume, *Essays Moral, Political, and Literary*, rev. ed., Eugene F. Miller, ed. (Indianapolis, IN: Liberty Classics, 1985), 42–46, esp. 42–43.

15. "The Farmer Refuted &c," February 23, 1775, in *The Papers of Alexander Hamilton*, Harold C. Syrett, ed., 27 vols. (New York: Columbia University Press, 1961–1979), 1:94–95.

16. John Adams to Samuel Adams, October 18, 1790, in *The Works of John Adams: Second President of the United States*, Charles Francis Adams, ed. (Boston: Little & Brown, 1850–1856), 6:415; hereinafter cited as *The Works of John Adams*.

17. See "A Defence of the Constitutions of Government of the United States of America," in *The Works of John Adams*, 6:408–415, 556–558.

18. Charles de Secondat, baron de La Bréde et de Montesquieu, *De l'esprit des lois*, 2.11.4, in *Oevres complètes de Montesquieu*, Roger Caillois ed. (Paris: Gallimard, 1949–1951), II.395.

19. *The Federalist*, no. 51, in *The Federalist*, Jacob C. Cooke, ed. (Middletown, CT: Wesleyan University Press, 1961), 349.

20. See David N. Mayer, *The Constitutional Thought of Thomas Jefferson* (Charlottesville: University Press of Virginia, 1994), 53–329, esp. 70–74, 83–144, 199–208, 314–329.

21. Jefferson to Edward Carrington, January 16, 1787, in *The Jefferson Papers*, 11:49. Elsewhere, Jefferson employed the same metaphor to similar effect: see Thomas Jefferson, *Notes on the State of Virgina*, William Peden, ed. (Chapel Hill: University of North Carolina Press, 1955), 93, query 11; and Jefferson to James Madison, January 30, 1787, in *The Jefferson Papers*, 11:92–97, at 93.

22. Machiavelli, *Discorsi*, 1.4–5, in *Tutte le opere* 82–84. See in this connection Quentin Skinner, *The Foundation of Modern Political Thought: Volume One—The Renaissance* (Cambridge, England: Cambridge University Press, 1978), 180–186; and Quentin Skinner, *Machiavelli* (New York: Hill

and Wang, 1981), 48–77. For the ancient commitment to political and social harmony, see Rahe, *Republics Ancient and Modern*, bk. 1.

23. Future discussions of Machiavelli's influences on Hobbes will have to begin with Noel B. Reynolds and John L. Hilton, eds., *Three Discourses of Thomas Hobbes* (Chicago: University of Chicago Press, 1995). For a preview, see Noel B. Reynolds and John L. Hilton, "Thomas Hobbes and Authorship of the *Horae Subsecivae*," *History of Political Thought* 14, no. 3 (Spring–Autumn 1993): 361–380.

24. Consider Hobbes, *Leviathan*, 184–185, in light of *Three Discourses of Thomas Hobbes*, 138–139; and for the distinction between "princes" and those "worthy to be such," see Machiavelli, *Tutte le opere*, 75.

25. Hobbes, *Leviathan*, 183–251.

26. Harrington, *The Prerogative of Popular Government*, 241. In this connection, see Paul A. Rahe, "Antiquity Surpassed: The Repudiation of Classical Republicanism," in *Republicanism, Liberty, and Commercial Society, 1649–1776*, David Wootton, ed. (Stanford, CA: Stanford University Press, 1994), 233–269, esp. 251–268.

27. See Liljegren, *James Harrington's Oceana*, 30–32, 56, 185; and Harrington, *The Prerogative of Popular Government: The Art of Lawgiving* (1659), *A System of Politics, Political Aphorisms* (1659), and *A Discourse upon This Saying . . .* (1659), all in *Works of Harrington*, 242–248, 403–404, 468–469, 483, 567–574, esp. 573–574.

28. Liljegren, *James Harrington's Oceana*, 61, 84, 135.

29. See ibid., 23–25, 117–124, esp. 119, 123, 145–146, 174–175; and Harrington, *The Prerogative of Popular Government*, 215, 236–238.

30. Liljegren, *James Harrington's Oceana*, 23.

31. Ibid., 133–139.

32. Ibid., 23–25, 115–117, 142–14, and Harrington, *The Prerogative of Popular Government*, 235–238.

33. Jefferson to Edward Carrington, January 16, 1787, in *The Jefferson Papers*, 11:48–49.

34. Ibid., 49.

35. Jefferson to James Madison, January 30, 1787, and to Abigail Adams, February 22, 1787, in *The Jefferson Papers*, 11:92–93 and 174, respectively.

36. Locke to Tom [Thomas Westrowe?], October 20, 1659, in *The Correspondence of John Locke*, Esmond S. de Beer, ed., 8 vols. (Oxford, England: Clarendon Press, 1976), 1:123.

37. See John Locke, *Two Treatises of Government: A Critical Edition with an Introduction and Apparatus Criticus*, 2d ed., Peter Laslett, ed. (Cambridge, England: Cambridge University Press, 1970), II.xiv.159, with viii.98.

38. See ibid., II.xii.145–148, xiii.151, 154, 156–xiv.168, xviii.205–210, xix.222, with vii.87, ix.131; and consider Machiavelli, *Discorsi*, 1.34, in light of 1.6 and *Il principe*, 18, in *Tutte le opere*, 84–87, 116–117, 283–284.

39. See Locke, *Two Treatises of Government* II.v.42, with xiv.165–166.

40. Thomas Jefferson, "The Virginia Constitution [June 1776,]" in *The Jefferson Papers*, 1:329–365, esp. 341–342, 349–350, 359–360.

41. "Jefferson's Draft of a Constitution for Virginia," 1783, in *The Jefferson Papers*, 6:298–299.

42. For this quote and those following, see Jefferson, *Notes on the State of Virginia*, 126–129, with Machiavelli, *Discorsi*, 1.34, in *Tutte le opere*, 116–117.

43. See Mayer, *The Constitutional Thought of Thomas Jefferson*.

44. Jefferson to James Madison, December 20, 1787, in *The Jefferson Papers*, 12:442.

45. For a thorough examination of the role played by the prince in modern republican speculation, see Harvey C. Mansfield Jr., *The Taming of the Prince: The Ambivalence of Modern Executive Power* (New York: Free Press, 1989).

46. Jefferson to John B. Colvin, September 20, 1810, in *The Writings of Thomas Jefferson*, Andrew A. Lipscomb and Albert E. Bergh, eds., 20 vols. (Washington, DC: Thomas Jefferson Memorial Association, 1904–1905), 12:421–422, hereinafter cited as *Jefferson Writings*; and *The Federalist*, nos. 70–71, in Cooke, *The Federalist*, 471–483.

47. Note Machiavelli, *Discorsi*, 1.4–8, 58, in *Tutte le opere*, 82–90, 140–142; consider Julian H. Franklin, *John Locke and the Theory of Sovereignty: Mixed Monarchy and the Right of Resistance in the Political Thought of the English Revolution* (Cambridge, England: Cambridge University Press, 1978); and see Nathan Tarcov, "Locke's *Second Treatise* and 'The Best Fence against Rebellion,'" *Review of Politics* 43, no. 2 (April 1981), 198–217, esp. 211–217; and Thomas L. Pangle, "Executive Energy and Popular Spirit in Lockean Constitutionalism," *Presidential Studies Quarterly* 17 (1987): 253–265, esp. 259–264.

48. Locke, *Two Treatises of Government*, II.xix.223–224, 230; note also II.xiv.168, and Locke's "Some Considerations of the Consequences of Lowering the Interest and Raising the Value of Money," in *The Works of John Locke*, 9 vols. (London: C. & J. Rivington, 1824), 5:71.

49. Locke, *Two Treatises of Government*, II.xix.223, 228.

50. Ibid., I.vi.58; II.xix.230.

51. Ibid., II.xix.225, 230.

52. Consider *Two Treatises of Government*, II.xix.228, in light of Machiavelli, *Discorsi*, 2.2, 2.3, in *Tutte le opere*, 148–151, 195–197.

53. Locke, *Two Treatises of Government*, II.xviii.209.

54. See Machiavelli, *Discorsi*, 3.1 (with 3 and 49), in *Tutte le opere*, 195–199, 253–254.

55. After reading Neal Wood, "The Value of Asocial Sociability: Contributions of Machiavelli, Sidney, and Montesquieu," in *Machiavelli and the Nature of Political Thought*, Martin Fleischer, ed. (New York: Atheneum, 1972), 282–307, esp. 282–298, consider Blair Worden, "The Commonwealth Kidney of Algernon Sidney," *Journal of British Studies* 24 (1985): 1–40, esp. 13–38; Jonathan Scott, *Algernon Sidney and the En-*

glish Republic, 1623–1677 (Cambridge, England: Cambridge University Press, 1988); Jonathan Scott, *Algernon Sidney and the Restoration Crisis, 1677–1683* (Cambridge, England: Cambridge University Press, 1991); and Alan Craig Houston, *Algernon Sidney and the Republican Heritage in England and America* (Princeton, NJ: Princeton University Press, 1991), in light of Algernon Sidney, *Discourses concerning Government*, Thomas G. West, ed. (Indianapolis, IN: Liberty Classics, 1990), 2.13–14, 24, 26; and see Walter Moyle, "An Essay on the Lacedaemonian Government," 1698, in *The Whole Works of Walter Moyle* (London: J. Knapton, A. Bettesworth [etc.], 1727), 57–58.

56. See Pauline Maier, "Popular Uprisings and Civil Authority in Eighteenth-Century America," *William and Mary Quarterly*, 3d ser., 27 (1970): 3–35, esp. 24–33.

57. Consider Jefferson, *Notes on the State of Virginia*, 120–121, 161, 164–165, in light of Alfredo Bonadeo, *Corruption, Conflict, and Power in the Works of Niccolò Machiavelli* (Berkeley, Los Angeles, and London: University of California Press, 1973); and Riccardo Breschi, "Il concetto di 'Corruzione' nei 'Discorsi sopra la prima deca di tito Livio,'" in *Studi Storici* 29 (1989): 707–735.

58. Alexander Hamilton, speech on June 22, 1787, in *The Records of the Federal Convention of 1787*, Max Farrand, ed., 4 vols. (New Haven, CT: Yale University Press, 1937), 1:381.

59. Jefferson to William Stephens Smith, November 13, 1787, in *The Jefferson Papers*, 12:355–356; subsequent quotes in this paragraph are also from this letter.

60. See Ralph Lerner, *The Thinking Revolutionary: Principle and Practice in the New Republic* (Ithaca, NY: Cornell University Press, 1987), chap. 2, 60–90.

61. Thomas Jefferson, "The Revisal of the Laws, 1776–1786: Bill No. 82: A Bill for Establishing Religious Freedom," in *The Jefferson Papers*, 2:545.

62. Jefferson to John Adams, October 28, 1813, in *The Adams–Jefferson Letters: The Complete Correspondence between Thomas Jefferson and Abigail and John Adams*, Lester J. Cappon, ed., 2 vols. (Chapel Hill: University of North Carolina Press, 1959), 2:387–392. For the laws abolishing entails and primogeniture, see Jefferson's "Bill to Enable Tenants in Fee Tail to Convey Their Lands in Fee Simple," October 14, 1776, and his "The Revisal of the Laws, 1776–1786: Bill No. 20: A Bill Directing the Course of Descents," both in *The Jefferson Papers*, 1:560–562, 2:391–393, respectively.

63. Thomas Jefferson, "Autobiography," in *Jefferson Writings*, 1:70.

64. See Thomas Jefferson, "The Revisal of the Laws, 1776–1786: Bill No. 79: A Bill for the More General Diffusion of Knowledge," in *The Jefferson Papers*, 2:526–535. For a later version, see Jefferson to Joseph C. Cabell, September 9, 1817, with draft of "An Act for Establishing Elementary Schools," in *Jefferson Writings*, 17:417–441.

65. Jefferson, *Notes on the State of Virginia*, 146–148.

66. For the history of Jefferson's efforts on behalf of education, see Merrill D. Peterson, *Thomas Jefferson and the New Nation: A Biography* (New York: Oxford University Press, 1970), 145–152, 961–988.

67. See Thomas Jefferson "The Revisal of the Laws, 1776–1786: Bill No. 80: A Bill for Amending the Constitution of the College of William and Mary, and Substituting More Certain Revenues for Its Support," in *The Jefferson Papers*, 2:535–543.

68. See "Autobiography," in *Jefferson Writings*, 1:70–72.

69. See Jefferson to Dr. Joseph Priestley, January 27, 1800, in *Jefferson Writings*, 10:146–149; and "A Memorandum (Services of Jefferson)," in *The Writings of Thomas Jefferson*, 7:475–477.

70. Jefferson to John Adams, October 28, 1813, in *Adams–Jefferson Letters*, 2:390.

71. For the overall plan as it developed, see "Report of the Commissioners for the University of Virginia (Rockfish Gap Report)," August 4, 1818, in *Early History of the University of Virginia as Contained in the Letters of Thomas Jefferson and Joseph C. Cabell*, Nathaniel F. Cabell, ed. (Richmond, VA: J. W. Randolph, 1856), 432–447; and "An Extract Transcript of the Minutes of the Board of Visitors of the University of Virginia, during the Rectorship of Thomas Jefferson," May 5, 1817, to April 7, 1826, in *Jefferson Writings*, 19:361–499, esp. 407–408, 413–416, 433–452, 454–461. In the mid-1790s, Jefferson toyed with the idea of shifting the Academy of Geneva to Virginia; in 1800, he began talking of establishing a new, thoroughly modern university in the Piedmont. See Jefferson to Francois d'Ivernois, February 6, 1795, and Jefferson, to Dr. Joseph Priestley, January 18 and 27, 1800, in *Jefferson Writings*, 9:297–299, 10:138–143, 10:146–149, respectively; Jefferson to Littleton Waller Tazwell, January 5, 1805, in Thomas Jefferson, *Writings*, Merrill D. Peterson, ed. (New York: Library of America, 1984), 1149–1153, hereinafter cited as Jefferson, *Writings*; and Jefferson to Joseph C. Cabell, September 9, 1817, with draft of "An Act for Establishing Elementary Schools," in *Jefferson Writings*, 17:417–441. In this connection, see Jefferson to Messrs. Hugh L. White and others, May 6, 1810, in Jefferson, *Writings*, 1222–1223. To this project, he turned his attention a few years after he left the presidency. At first, he focused on the establishment of an academy in Albemarle County. See Jefferson to Peter Carr, September 7, 1814, in *Jefferson Writings*, 19:211–221. Perhaps the clearest testimony of the degree to which Jefferson was dedicated to this project is the fact that, though very nearly bankrupt, he nonetheless kept his promise and left his library to the university. See "Thomas Jefferson's Will," in *Jefferson Writings*, 17:465–470, at 469, and vol. 19. See also Peterson, *New Nation*, 961–988, 989–992, 1006–1007.

72. Jefferson to Joseph C. Cabell, January 13, 1823, in *Early History of the University of Virginia*, 266–268.

73. See "An Exact Transcript of the Minutes of the Board of Visitors of the University of Virginia, during the Rectorship of Thomas Jefferson," March 4, 1825, in *Jefferson Writings*, 19:460–461.

74. Jefferson to James Madison, February 17, 1826, in *Jefferson Writings*, 16:156.

75. See Jefferson to James Madison, December 20, 1787, to Alexander Donald, February 7, 1788, to George Washington, November 4, 1788, to Francis Hopkinson, March 13, 1789, and to James Madison, March 18, 1789, in *The Jefferson Papers*, 12:438–443, 12:570–572, 14:328–332, 14:649–651, 659–663, respectively.

76. Jefferson to James Madison, December 20, 1787, in *The Jefferson Papers*, 12:442.

77. Jefferson to Edward Carrington, January 16, 1787, in *The Jefferson Papers*, 11:49.

78. See Jefferson to John Tyler, May 26, 1810, to Samuel Kercheval, July 12, 1816, and September 5, 1816, and to John Taylor, July 16, 1816, in *Jefferson Writings*, 12:391–394, 15:32–44, 15:70–73, 15:44–47, respectively; Jefferson to John Adams, October 28, 1813, in *Adams–Jefferson Letters*, 2:387–392; Jefferson to Joseph C. Cabell, February 2, 1816, in *Jefferson Writings*, 14:417–423; Jefferson to Major John Cartwright, June 5, 1824, in *Jefferson Writings*, 16:42–52. See also Jefferson to Joseph C. Cabell, November 28, 1820, in *Jefferson Writings*, 15:289–294. As this and the previous letter to Cabell cited above make clear, the ward proposal was closely linked with Jefferson's campaign to establish primary schools. The passage quoted in the text is to be found in the second of the two letters to Samuel Kercheval.

79. Jefferson to Samuel Kercheval, July 12, 1816, in *Jefferson Writings*, 15:38.

80. Jefferson to Joseph C. Cabell, February 2, 1816, in *Jefferson Writings*, 14:422–423.

81. See Hannah Arendt, *On Revolution* (New York: Viking Press, 1963), 111–285, esp. 115–137, 234–28; and Hannah Arendt, with Jean Yarbrough, "Republicanism Reconsidered: Some Thoughts on the Foundation and Preservation of the American Republic," *Review of Politics* 41, no. 1 (January 1979): 61–95, esp. 84–92. Arendt's argument has beguiled many a scholar: see Pocock, *The Machiavellian Moment*, 506–552, esp. 550; Richard K. Matthews, *The Radical Politics of Thomas Jefferson: A Revisionist View* (Lawrence: University Press of Kansas, 1984), 77–95, esp. 83–90; and Garrett Ward Sheldon, *The Political Philosophy of Thomas Jefferson* (Baltimore: Johns Hopkins University Press, 1991), 53–111.

82. Draft of the Kentucky Resolutions, [October] 1798, in *The Writings of Thomas Jefferson*, 7:304.

83. Jefferson to Judge Spencer Roane, September 6, 1819, in *Jefferson Writings*, 15:215.

84. Jefferson to William Charles Jarvis, September 28, 1820, in *Jefferson Writings*, 15:276–279.

85. William Blackstone, *Commentaries on the Laws of England*, 4 vols. (Chicago: University of Chicago Press, 1979), 1:119–141, esp. 139.

86. Cf. Robert E. Shalhope, "The Ideological Origins of the Second Amendment," *Journal of American History* 69, no. 5 (December 1982): 599–

614, with Lawrence Delbert Cress, "An Armed Community: The Origins and Meaning of the Right to Bear Arms," *Journal of American History* 71, no. 1 (June 1984): 22–42, and see David T. Hardy, "The Second Amendment and the Historiography of the Bill of Rights," *Journal of Law and Politics* 4 (1987): 1–62; and Joyce Lee Malcolm, *To Keep and Bear Arms: The Origins of an Anglo-American Right* (Cambridge, MA: Harvard University Press, 1994). If I am correct in asserting (Rahe, *Republics Ancient and Modern*, 254–259, 321–334, 347–356, 409–747) that Whigs of all stripes, in America as well as in Britain, were united in accepting Blackstone's dictum that "the public good is in nothing more essentially interested, than in the protection of every individual's private rights" (*Commentaries on the Laws of England*, 1:135), then the current dispute between those who interpret the Second Amendment in terms of individual rights and those who stress communal duties is an artifact of contemporary scholarship grounded on a dichotomy that would have made little, if any, sense to anyone in the eighteenth century. The revolutionary generation disliked standing armies and saw them as a threat to liberty. Even when they conceded the necessity of such an army, they wanted to see the individual citizens armed and organized as a militia in such a way as to help provide for the common defense while safeguarding the right to revolution.

87. Jefferson to Roger C. Weightman, June 24, 1826, in *Jefferson Writings*, 16:181–182.

4

Jefferson and Slavery: A Study in Moral Perplexity

Howard Temperley

Like other exponents of natural rights philosophy, Thomas Jefferson favored arguing from first principles. This was most famously demonstrated in his draft of the Declaration of Independence, but it was a practice he followed throughout his career. Indeed, it is largely on account of it that he is today remembered. To call him a politician many would regard almost as an insult. Rather, he is remembered as a statesman and philosopher, one whose broad vision extended beyond the issues of his own day and who took it upon himself to remind his fellow countrymen of those eternal verities that were their birthright. In a very real sense, it was he who, by spelling out just what those verities were—in particular, his linking the idea of America with the notion of freedom—defined for what that nation stands. That he should be remembered in this way he would have found pleasing. It was an image he did much to cultivate. More than any other president, with the possible exception of Woodrow Wilson, he saw himself as the conscience of his nation.

Needless to say, that is not how his political opponents saw him. The Jefferson whom history honors, and whose likeness appears on Mount Rushmore, bears little resemblance to the unctuous, self-righteous hypocrite of their perception. That posterity should take seriously the statements about freedom and equality that he made his hallmark and went on uttering throughout his career, as if these were qualities he had himself invented and in which he had a personal warranty rather than useful ammunition in a political debate, they would have regarded as one of history's ironies.

Such views can, of course, be attributed to jealousy and to the normal rivalries and vicissitudes of party politics. Nevertheless, it has to be acknowledged that there is a marked asymmetry in Jefferson's case between what he preached and what he practiced. It is, in fact, hard to think of any other president, or even any other major American figure, whose proclaimed ideals and personal lifestyle were more strikingly and embarrassingly at odds. He celebrated the virtues of the American yeoman-farmer, but lived like a European nobleman; he condemned acquisitiveness, yet scoured the world for possessions to display in the mansion he built for himself at Monticello; he praised self-sufficiency, but plunged so deeply into debt that in the end only his reputation saved him from bankruptcy. Most ironic of all, the wealth and leisure that enabled him to engage in politics and allowed him to write his works on liberty were bought with the labor of some 200 slaves.

It was not, of course, Jefferson's choice to be born into a rich planter family. No more than other Americans of his generation is he to be held responsible for the behavior of his ancestors. The problem that faced him, albeit in an exceptionally acute and personal form, was one that faced the entire revolutionary generation. It was not whether or not to have slavery, for slavery already existed and was deeply woven into the fabric of their society, but what to do about it. The choice, in other words, was not between slavery and freedom, but between what existed and something else that could prove a good deal worse, not simply for the slaveholding classes or for whites in general, but conceivably for the slaves themselves.

If Jefferson failed to see a ready solution to this problem, he was no different from most of his contemporaries. Viewed in the abstract, of course, slavery and freedom are polar opposites. This was something of which he, along with others of his generation, was only too well aware. If unalienable rights were indeed unalienable, and self-evident truths were actually self-evident, and had Americans been prepared to act on those principles, they would have set about ending slavery forthwith; and, in fact, that is what many did do, or began to do, in the states north of the Mason-Dixon line. It did not happen in Jefferson's Virginia, which at that time contained rather more than half the slaves in the Union, although some were manumitted by their masters.

So where did Jefferson stand on the issue? Granted that as a Virginian dependent on the support of fellow Virginians, he had to move more cautiously than aspiring politicians from states less dependent on slavery. Does the evidence show that his commitment to natural rights influenced his attitude toward the institution? To some degree it does, although not to such an extent as to alarm his fellow planters.

According to Jefferson's own account, he had made his views known as early as 1769, when, as a newly elected member of the Virginia House of Burgesses, he had supported a bill to allow the private manumission of slaves. This may indeed have been the case, but we have only Jefferson's word for it. The bill, in any case, was rejected.[1] What is known and documented is that among the earliest cases he took up following his admission to the Virginia bar was one on behalf of Samuel Howell, who was suing for freedom. The point at issue was whether the descendant of a free white woman could legitimately be held in bondage. Virginia law provided that mulatto children born to white mothers out of wedlock were to be bound out by the local churchwardens until they attained the age of thirty-one. It was further provided that the same applied to the offspring of mothers thus held in bondage. In this way, a form of temporary servitude could, as in Howell's case, be passed on from generation to generation. Strictly speaking, therefore, it was not a case about slavery at all, but about bounding out. Within a few years Howell would be free anyway. It is not even clear whether, in the eyes of the court, he was considered white or mulatto since he belonged to a third generation of those to whom the law had been applied, and all that is known for certain of his ancestry is that one of his grandparents was white and another either black or mulatto. If he were able to show that less than a quarter of his ancestry was black, as was quite conceivably the case, he would have been entitled to be regarded as white. Nevertheless, the provisions regarding bounding out were plain, and for want of any better recourse, Jefferson chose to appeal to an authority higher than the state of Virginia, arguing that "under the law of nature, men are born free, and everyone comes into the world with a right to his own person, which includes the liberty of moving and using it at his own will." This was no Somerset case, and Jefferson was no Granville Sharp. While pleading on behalf of his client—unsuccessfully as it proved—he was advertising for the return of runaway slaves of his own. Jefferson's willingness to take on such a case and to argue it in the way he did suggests that his views were more liberal than those of many.[2]

Further evidence for this is contained in his 1774 *A Summary View of the Rights of British America*, in which he expresses his righteous

indignation at the British for their participation in the slave trade
and for having imposed slavery on their American colonies. Like
everything else, it was the fault of George III and his ministers. This
was distinctly disingenuous coming, as it did, from a slaveholder.
Nevertheless, it indicates that Jefferson was prepared, at least for
polemical purposes, to represent not only the slave trade but slavery
itself as contrary to American values. Two years later, he attempted
to insert a similar diatribe into the Declaration of Independence but
was overruled by the Continental Congress, which took the view,
very reasonably, that, if the intention were to enlist the sympathy
of the world, to encumber the document with such patently self-
serving claims would weaken rather than strengthen the cause.[3]

Meanwhile, in Jefferson's own Virginia, disquiet was expressed
that appeals to natural rights were getting out of hand. While exult-
ing that the chains holding them in bondage to Britain had been
finally broken, Virginians roundly denounced Lord Dunmore for declaring their slaves free and for welcoming runaways into his lines.
A month before the signing of the Declaration of Independence, the
Virginia Convention, discussing the adoption of a bill of rights, ruled
that its provisions did not extend to slaves. Saying that Americans
were the equals of the English was one thing; claiming that slaves
were the equals of their masters was quite another. Edmund Randolph later recalled it being agreed:

> that with arms in our hands, asserting the general rights of
> man, we ought not to be too nice and too much restricted in the
> delineation of them; but that slaves, not being constituent mem-
> bers of our society, could never pretend to any benefit from such
> a maxim.[4]

Jefferson might, had he wished, have publicly dissented from
this view, but he failed to do so. His own references to men being
created equal and the nature of their unalienable rights were later
taken up by abolitionists, some of whom went so far as to claim that
they implicitly abolished slavery.[5] But there is no evidence to indicate that Jefferson himself attached that meaning to them or that at
the time he saw such unalienable rights as applying to anyone other
than free white Americans.

This is hardly surprising, for in the circumstances of the time, to
have attempted anything more would have been foolhardy. He could
not afford to alienate his fellow planters or anyone else at that
particular juncture. Many years later, at the time of the Missouri
Compromise, John Quincy Adams confided in his diary that a life

devoted to getting rid of slavery would be a life "nobly spent or sacrificed." Yet it was not until fifteen years later, by which time he had ceased to be president, that he voiced his beliefs in public.[6] The issue was simply too explosive. So for Thomas Jefferson, caught up in a struggle for the independence of his country, a prudent silence is hardly an object of wonder.

Yet the two cases are not quite parallel. There is no doubt as to where Adams's sympathies lay. And as his later actions reveal, he was eventually provoked into speaking out. Being a Northerner, of course, it was easier for him. For a Southerner, the situation was more problematic. Misjudge it, say the wrong thing, and political influence would evaporate very quickly. It was an issue that called for careful handling. Yet even when allowance is made for that, Jefferson's attitude remains puzzling. On the one hand, there are the grand generalities, the universal truths; on the other, the equivocations and evasions that his critics saw as indicative of a general shiftiness of character. What did he really think? Was he, as some have assumed, a closet abolitionist? If not in his public pronouncements, then in his private papers there ought to be an answer. Yet among the various and conflicting statements, one looks in vain for any consistency.

It could be argued that this is to underestimate the very real pressures to which, at least in the United States, Jefferson was subjected. It is noteworthy that the most forceful attack on slavery he made was in his *Notes on the State of Virginia*, a private publication written in the early 1780s and published in 1784 while he was serving as American minister to France. It was addressed to a select group of French aristocrats and intellectuals much influenced by Enlightenment thinking. Writing, then, for what he perceived as a sympathetic audience, he was at liberty to unburden himself of his views regarding the unjust and morally corroding influence of slavery, and he proceeded to do so in no uncertain terms. Southerners "nursed, educated and daily exercised in tyranny," he declared, "cannot but be stamped by it with odious peculiarities." Slavery destroyed industry. What kind of society was it that allowed one-half of its population to trample on the rights of another? The slaves would not always remain quiescent. "Indeed I tremble for my country," he went on, "when I reflect that God is just; that his justice cannot sleep forever." What haunted Jefferson's imagination was the fear of a slave uprising, or as he put it, "a revolution of the wheel of fortune, an exchange of situations." Slaves would do to their masters what their masters were already doing to them. Pursuing its present course, America risked a terrible retribution. No abolitionist could have expressed himself more vehemently. Yet he ended rather limply. Things were changing for the better, sentiments were improving. The way was being prepared, he hoped, "under the auspices of heaven, for a total emancipation . . . with the consent of the masters."[7]

So was this what Jefferson really thought? At one level, perhaps, but it is well to remember that he was serving as an American diplomatic representative abroad when he penned these comments, and was eager to enhance the reputation of a country much slighted by European commentators. The image of Virginia that he projected, resembling, as it did, that contained in Crevecoeur's popular *Letters from an American Farmer*, published in France only two years before, was precisely calculated to forestall the criticisms of America's European detractors and enhance the favorable belief in his fellow citizens as comprising a virtuous nation of hardworking small farmers.

Moreover, there was little in his account likely to alarm his fellow planters even though it was hardly the sort of statement he would have composed for their benefit. Many of them disapproved of slavery too, at least in a theoretical way, much as sinners will often be heard disapproving of sin or gamblers of gambling. And for the racists among them, there was much that was reassuring. Blacks were well endowed with musical ability, but in every other respect, so far as could be ascertained, they were intellectually inferior to Europeans. Such matters were difficult to judge, and perhaps science would eventually throw light on them. In the meantime, various achievements held up as examples of native black ability did not much impress him. Most blacks about whom such claims were made showed traces of white ancestry. Was it surprising that from time to time the white inheritance predominated and revealed itself in the display of some unusual talent? This could not be said in the case of Phillis Wheatley, who had been born in Africa, but in his opinion, her poetry was of a very inferior quality. What all these instances went to show was what Samuel Johnson had noted about women's preaching: the marvel was not that it was done well, but that it was done at all. Blacks were a lower order of human being. Physically, they were uglier than Europeans and, besides, they smelled. There were powerful obstacles to emancipation. What would become of the slaves if they were freed? Jefferson could not conceive how blacks could ever be incorporated into white society on equal terms. "It is not against experience," he concluded, "to suppose that different species of the same genus, or varieties of the same species, may possess different qualifications. Will not a lover of natural history, then . . . excuse an effort to keep those in this department of man as distinct as nature has formed them?"[8] The statement is interrogative, but it is plain that Jefferson doubted that all men were created equal or, pending further investigation, equally entitled to life, liberty, and the pursuit of happiness.

And so it went. While in France, momentarily carried away at finding himself in a slave-free, albeit hierarchical, society, he talked of emancipating his slaves and setting them up as share-croppers along with imported German peasants. But once back in America, the notion was soon abandoned, for which he blamed British moneylenders whose demands for repayment were pressing. The trouble was that he had returned to the United States with eighty-six large crates of paintings, statues, furniture, and other treasures he had purchased while he was in Paris. Instead of freeing his slaves, he quietly sold off some fifty of them to placate his creditors, taking care to do so through a third party so as to avoid public attention.[9]

Because of his financial extravagance, Jefferson continued buying and selling slaves throughout his presidency—unlike, it may be noted, George Washington, whose lifestyle was altogether more austere and who had set up a fund to ensure that his slaves were freed and provided for after his and Martha's deaths.[10] In other respects, however, Jefferson appears to have been a kindly master. He knew his slaves by name and was familiar with their characters and foibles. They were his "family" or, as he put it on another occasion, "those who labor for my happiness."[11] He took pride in their achievements, and when those he had trusted were guilty of some lapse, he would often intercede on their behalf to save them from punishment. He managed his affairs, in other words, on much the same principles as an English landowner might manage his estates, which is to say, in the knowledge that efficiency and liberality were not incompatible and that a great deal depended on the energy and cooperativeness of his workforce.

During his lengthy periods of absence, and even when he was in residence, he left the day-to-day running of his plantations to overseers. These were a mixed bunch, and the turnover was high. Among them were several with reputations for cruelty. Jefferson himself did not hesitate to authorize whippings when he considered them deserved, as in the case of habitual runaways, or when he felt that an example should be made to the other slaves. But as often as not, the offenses were of a kind that would merit a punishment in any society, as when one slave struck another with a hammer during a quarrel, severely wounding him. When dealing with slaves whose behavior, as in this case, was seriously disruptive, it was Jefferson's practice, like that of other plantation owners, to rid himself of them by sale. On the other hand, he would go to great lengths to reward those whom he considered had earned his trust. The records show that from time to time he made purchases or agreed to sales in order simply to keep families together.

Surprisingly for one who spent so much time commending the agrarian life, Jefferson's own interests tended toward mechanical pursuits. He took particular pride in the nail-making operation he established at Monticello, which, especially in its early years, he supervised on a daily basis. His operatives were given special food and clothing allowances to encourage a sense of esprit de corps. Later on, he established a textile factory that employed women and children not strong enough to work on the farm. His aim was to ensure that all were employed in tasks suited to their abilities and provided with whatever incentives were necessary to ensure that they worked diligently. Slave artisans and other senior figures in the workforce were given bonuses and gratuities and expected to get on with their tasks virtually unsupervised. Jefferson's boast that American slaves were "better fed . . . , warmer clothed, and labor less than the journeymen or day laborers in England" may well have been true, at least so far as the conditions of work on his own plantations were concerned. Yet his view of his slave dependents was notably different from that of an employer of free workers as when he commented, "I consider the labor of a breeding woman as no object, and that a child raised every 2 years is of more profit than the crop of the best laboring man. In this, as in all other cases, providence has made our interest and our duties coincide perfectly."[12]

The idea that providence smiled on the South's peculiar institution was a product of Jefferson's later years. It is unlikely that the young Jefferson would have expressed himself in quite such terms. Still, the fact remains that Jefferson's slaves fared better than most, not only because of the relative liberality of their master, but also because only a minority were engaged in fieldwork on his four plantations, many of the rest being domestic servants or retainers employed in such ways as his lavish entertaining and gracious lifestyle required.

Among the most privileged of these latter were the members of the Hemings family, inherited from his father-in-law and generally supposed to be Jefferson's late wife's half-brothers and sisters. One of them he had trained in Paris as a chef, and another became a skilled carpenter. Their mother is said to have been the product of a union between a British sea captain and an African woman, and visitors to Monticello were surprised to find among Jefferson's retinue slaves who were to all appearances white. As the duc de La Rochefoucauld-Liancourt noted in 1796, blacks were not the only ones held in hereditary servitude. "I have even seen," he wrote, "and particularly at Mr. Jefferson's, slaves who have neither in their color nor features a single trace of their origin, but they are the sons of slave mothers and consequently slaves." Presumably, he had the Hemings family in mind. Moreover, this was before an appearance of the third generation of Hemingses, many of whom had white fathers and in whose appearance African characteristics were presumably even less detectable. Who their fathers were has been the subject of much speculation, but there is no lack of candidates for this role: overseers, hired artisans, guests of the family, even Thomas Jefferson himself. Being seven-eighths white, the male Hemingses would, if freed, have been entitled to citizenship under U.S. law; but, as Jefferson complacently noted, slave status depended on maternal, not racial, descent. Under Virginia law, he was fully entitled to their services as bondsmen.[13]

Whether Jefferson's slaves were also his kinsfolk, and in some cases even his children, cannot be proven and, unless some means is found of bringing modern genetic testing techniques to bear on the problem, will presumably never be known. On the basis of the available evidence, the truth of one particular story appears unlikely: that after his wife's death Jefferson took Sally Hemings as his mistress and had several children by her. The children in question are more plausibly supposed to have been those of his two young nephews, Peter and Samuel Carr. That was what the servants at Monticello supposed, and they were in a better position than most to know. It is also worth noting that if Jefferson did have a liaison with "Black Sally," as the gutter press of the time claimed, it would have been out of keeping with what is otherwise known about his relations with women. In his journals, he mentions the births and deaths of several of Sally's children, but he does so in the same dry, factual manner he used for recording other routine occurrences around his estate. This was in contrast to his joy and grief at events within his immediate family. But if the children were, indeed, his nephews', his indifference remains curious. It can hardly be accounted for on the grounds of racial antipathy, since those involved were essentially white. This was the case evidently with Sally herself, described by a contemporary as "mighty near white," and presumably more so in the case of her children. Whatever the paternity of the younger Hemingses, it is plain that Jefferson presided over a rather curious household.[14]

What his thoughts on the subject were remain a mystery. His opposition to miscegenation is well documented. It may be that its occurrence within and around his own establishment was a source of personal anguish that he bore with commendable fortitude. If so, it was a pretense that he kept up with remarkable diligence throughout his life. There is no record of his taking relatives or servants to task, of punishments inflicted or individuals banished. This is not to say that such incidents could not have occurred. But on the basis of what is known, it would seem much more probable that he took it all pretty much in his stride. Public disapproval of racial mixing was one thing, intervening in the lives of those who practiced it another, particularly when it was as widespread as was evidently the case in Albemarle County. Besides, in the case of white slaves like the Hemingses, such liaisons hardly amounted to miscegenation. Like slavery itself, miscegenation was something Jefferson's generation had inherited. Race had never been a bar to sexual attraction. And what large household, in Europe or America, he could have reflected, was free of backstairs goings-on? He could even have viewed it all with the amused tolerance with which aristocrats traditionally regard such matters. Whether he himself felt any qualms at having mortgaged his dependents' futures in order to maintain his lavish lifestyle, again, history does not reveal.[15]

So far as the general rights and wrongs of slavery are concerned, he spent his later years trying to avoid the subject. One wonders how often he rued having hitched his wagon to those Enlightenment abstractions. As secretary of state, he was much involved—although without success—in persuading the British to pay compensation for the slaves who made off during the War of Independence, many of whom were later resettled in Sierra Leone. Unlike several of his contemporaries, he did not join an antislavery society. As president, he found it prudent to maintain a masterly silence. He did go so far as to welcome the act providing for America's withdrawal from the slave trade in 1807, but, not wishing to receive black diplomats in Washington, D.C., he adamantly refused to recognize Haiti as an independent republic.[16]

Once retired from the presidency, it would have been easier for Jefferson, as it was for John Quincy Adams, to speak out, but he signally failed to do so. In 1814, he was put to the test by Edward Coles, a fellow Virginian, near neighbor, and former private secretary of James Madison, who wrote asking him to lend his support to a movement for gradual emancipation. Like others of a liberal disposition who wrote to Jefferson, Coles had assumed that he would find in the author of the Declaration of Independence a natural ally. The views of any one of the nation's founders, Coles noted, were bound to carry weight. But, he went on, "it is a duty, as I conceive, that devolves particularly on you, from your known philosophical

and enlarged view of subjects, and from the principles you have professed and practised through a long and useful life."[17] As a declared
champion of the rights of man, Jefferson's views would continue to
resound through the ages.

In reply, Jefferson affected to welcome Coles's initiative. He had
supposed the public had grown apathetic. It was good to know that
there were still those who felt strongly about the issue. Nevertheless, he counseled extreme caution for fear of causing irritation and
arousing opposition. Any other approach would be counterproduc-
tive. Coles would find consolation in the fact that "no good measure
was ever proposed, which, if duly pursued, failed to prevail in the
end." So far as his own participation was concerned, Jefferson begged
off on the grounds that he was too old for such enterprises. In any
case, the time was not ripe. He advised Coles to remain in Virginia,
care for his slaves, and to go on working for the cause, but to do so
behind the scenes so as not to stir up antagonism. Instead, Coles
freed his slaves and migrated with them to Illinois, where he worked
diligently to prevent the reintroduction of slavery, which, given the
number of Southern migrants, was at one time a distinct possibility.
There were, as Coles's actions showed, practical ways in which Virginian planters could express their abhorrence of slavery.

One reason why Jefferson could not follow Coles's example was
the immense burden of debt under which he labored. Another was
his opposition to any plan that did not remove freed slaves from
America. This was not, as some colonizationists have argued, because
whites would not accept them, although that went without saying: it
was because they were quite simply unprepared, and in all probability congenitally unsuited, for life in a free society. Freeing slaves
was like abandoning children. What would become of them? Con-
templation of the possibility conjured up appalling visions of miscegenation, crime, and, ultimately, racial war. "We have the wolf by
the ears," Jefferson declared in 1820, "and we can neither hold him
nor safely let him go. Justice is in one scale, and self-preservation in
the other."[18] The only way of reconciling the two was to get rid
of the problem altogether. Creating a successful biracial society
was an impossibility. The blacks would have to go. Unlike Madison
and Monroe, he did not take the notion of African settlement very
seriously, although he was not unsympathetic. The Far West he saw
as destined for white settlement. However far away blacks were sent,
whites would ultimately catch up with them. Instead, he pinned
his hopes on the Caribbean, especially Haiti; and shortly before his
death, he did come up with a grand design for taking five-year-
old slave children from their parents and training them, in state-run

institutions, for resettlement overseas, the enterprise being paid for in part by the labor of the children themselves.

Here, as on occasion elsewhere, we glimpse the dehumanizing assumptions underlying Jefferson's thinking about blacks. Desperate situations called for desperate remedies, in this case, the seizure and collectivization of five-year-olds. Given that some 60,000 black children were born annually, the cost would be so stupendous it could not conceivably be met by the individual states. The federal government would have to bear the burden, which would exceed the current national debt many times over. More important, the task of locating five-year-olds, compensating their owners, providing for their care and education, overseeing their labor, transporting them overseas, and supervising their resettlement would require an increase in the scope and functions of the central authority far beyond anything envisaged even by Jefferson's Federalist opponents. Gone was any notion of minimal government. The whole American system created by the founding fathers would have to be modified and adapted to meet the overriding necessity of ridding America of its black population. But such sacrifices were justified. The "beatitude" of the plan was that it promised a final solution to America's race problem. Some might object to separating children from parents at such a tender age, but given the alternatives, "to persist in such humanitarian scruples . . . would be straining at a gnat and swallowing a camel."

Needless to say, nothing came of the scheme. It was simply another example of Jefferson's congenital eclecticism. He continued to see himself as the apostle of liberty, but the immediate threat to liberty, in his estimation, was not slavery. It was the urban civilization of banks, industries, and commerce advocated by Alexander Hamilton and his ideological successors. The natural counterweight to this Northern entrepreneurship was the agrarian South. When the question arose of the expansion of slavery into the Louisiana Purchase territories, as it did in the Missouri crisis of 1819-1821, Jefferson strongly supported the Southern belief that the entire trans-Mississippi region should be opened to settlement by slaveholders. This was in striking contrast to his earlier advocacy of keeping them out of the trans-Allegheny region in deference to the superior virtues of America's small farmers. There was no reason, he now sought to show, why slavery would be strengthened by becoming more diffused; indeed, the opposite might well prove to be the case—a judgment that persuaded Lafayette that Jefferson's mental powers were failing. Having started life as an American nationalist and advocate of human rights, he had, by the time of his death, virtually become a spokesman for the Southern interest.[19]

It was Jefferson's fate to believe a number of irreconcilable things, or, more precisely, to subscribe to a variety of incompatible belief systems, for he was not, at least in a philosophical sense, an original thinker. As his *Notes on the State of Virginia* shows, Jefferson was naturally eclectic. He collected information and ideas much as he collected objects, and as a politician he was prepared to make use of what came to hand. In practice, his "immutable moral laws" proved eminently mutable where slavery was concerned. Sometimes he said one thing, sometimes another. When pressed, he would talk reassuringly about the future. Somehow it would all come right in the end. The important thing was to proceed prudently so as not to put people's backs up. Mostly, he simply wished the problem would go away. Occasionally, he dreamed that it had, imagining an America from which both slavery and blacks had been extirpated.

In penning the Declaration of Independence, Jefferson put into words a set of beliefs much cherished by subsequent generations. The meanings attached to them have been various, but preponderant among them has been a commitment to freedom and equality, implying as it does that heredity is of very little importance—that regardless of race, class, or other distinctions of birth, all people are entitled to respect. They come into the world with much the same attributes and possess within themselves a similar potential for development. It is a belief well suited to an immigrant society intent on developing a new continent in that it provides for the discarding of the nonsensical distinctions, hierarchies, and shibboleths of the Old World. Whatever people were before, however different they might be in appearance or ancestry, is of no account as compared with their entitlement to certain basic rights and the privilege of being citizens. Jefferson's words continue to resonate in the appeals of oppressed peoples the world over. Whether, however, they accord with the private beliefs of their author is quite another matter.

On more than one occasion, Jefferson asked to be remembered not for what he said, but for what he did. Judged on this basis, he emerges as a Southern slaveholding gentleman of boundless curiosity whose real passions were not the universal principles for which he is remembered, or even the members of his family, to whom he was admittedly devoted—the white ones particularly—but the lifestyle he created for himself and, above all, Monticello, that eighteenth-century San Simeon he built for himself on his hilltop overlooking Charlottesville and where he received the homage of countless distinguished visitors. To a striking degree, its design and contents mirrored the character of its owner being essentially European in concept, set high on an American hilltop and filled with an amazing variety of objects accumulated over a lifetime in a manner worthy of William Randolph Hearst himself.[20] To maintain all this, he relied on the labor of generations of slaves whose futures he mortgaged to stave off impending bankruptcy. The Jefferson whose likeness appears on Mount Rushmore was, at bottom, an opportunist. The principle to which he was most committed was his own convenience. In his will, he emancipated five slaves—all Hemingses, two of them Sally's children who married white husbands and passed into the white community. Virtually all the rest went under the hammer.[21]

Notes

1. Paul Finkelman, "Jefferson and Slavery: 'Treason against the Hopes of the World,'" in *Jeffersonian Legacies,* Peter S. Onuf, ed. (Charlottesville: University Press of Virginia, 1993), 188–189; hereinafter cited as *Jeffersonian Legacies.*

2. Ibid., 189–190.

3. John Chester Miller, *The Wolf by the Ears: Thomas Jefferson and Slavery* (New York: Free Press, 1977), 6–7; hereinafter cited as *Wolf by the Ears.* This is the most complete account of Jefferson's views on slavery. His confusion of thought, however, is also subjected to detailed examination in Richard Hofstadter's "Thomas Jefferson: The Aristocrat as Democrat," in his *The American Political Tradition and the Men Who Made It* (New York: Alfred A. Knopf, 1984), 18–44; and in Winthrop D. Jordan, *White over Black: American Attitudes toward the Negro, 1550–1812* (Chapel Hill: University of North Carolina Press, 1968), 429–481.

4. Quoted in Henry F. May, *The Enlightenment in America* (New York: Oxford University Press, 1976), 134.

5. William H. Pease and Jane H. Pease, *The Antislavery Argument* (Indianapolis, IN: Bobbs-Merrill, 1965), viii, xxv, 216–218, 281–282.

6. Samuel Flagg Bemis, *John Quincy Adams and the Union* (New York: Alfred A. Knopf, 1956), 327.

7. Thomas Jefferson, *Notes on the State of Virginia*, William Peden, ed. (Chapel Hill: University of North Carolina Press, 1955), 162–163.

8. Ibid., 138.

9. *Wolf by the Ears*, 101–102, 107. Between 1784 and 1794, Jefferson disposed of 161 slaves by gift or sale (Lucia Stanton, "'Those Who Labor for My Happiness': Thomas Jefferson and His Slaves," in *Jeffersonian Legacies*, 148). For details of Jefferson's acquisitiveness and financial profligacy, see Garry Wills, "The Aesthete," in *New York Review of Books* 40, no. 14 (August 12, 1993): 6–9.

10. For the contrast between Jefferson's and Washington's attitudes

toward their slaves, see Wills, "The Aesthete," 9; *Jeffersonian Legacies*, 188; and *Wolf by the Ears*, 107.

11. *Jeffersonian Legacies*, 148–153. Stanton's account is by far the best on Jefferson's personal relations with his slaves.

12. Ibid., 150.

13. Ibid., 152.

14. Ibid., 147–180, quotation at 152.

15. For a general discussion of Jefferson's attitudes and the miscegenation issue, see *Jeffersonian Legacies*, 148–153; and *Wolf by the Ears*, 162–163.

16. *Wolf by the Ears*, 135–141.

17. This quote and the following discussion of the Jefferson-Coles exchange is from David Brion Davis, *The Problem of Slavery in the Age of Revolution: 1770–1823* (Ithaca, NY: Cornell University Press, 1975), 180–184.

18. *Wolf by the Ears*, 241.

19. Ibid., 221–272, quotation at 272.

20. Wills, "The Aesthete," 6. Unlike Hearst, however, Jefferson did not have an income commensurate with his lifestyle. He died owing over $100,000. Virtually everything he had amassed over his lifetime, including the house and the contents, was sold to appease his creditors. Hearst left generous bequests to his dependents, a publishing organization with assets of $160 million, and a charitable trust worth $44 million (W. A. Swanberg, *Citizen Hearst* [New York: Scribner's, 1961], app. 3). Upon Jefferson's death, Monticello was sold to Uriah Lev, and, after passing through various hands, was eventually acquired by the Thomas Jefferson Memorial Foundation. Since Hearst's death, San Simeon has come under the control of the California Parks Service. Similarly situated on the tops of hills, both are popular tourist attractions.

21. *Jeffersonian Legacies*, 147, 169–171.

Part II

Thomas Jefferson, the Common Law, and Constitutionalism

5

Sound Whigs or Honeyed Tories? Jefferson and the Common Law Tradition

James R. Stoner

In February 1826, a few months before his death, Thomas Jefferson wrote what he knew would be his last letter to his longtime friend and political associate James Madison. His concern was chiefly the business of the University of Virginia, especially its chair of law, a position that had become vacant:

> In the selection of our Law Professor, we must be rigorously attentive to his political principles. You will recollect that before the revolution, Coke Littleton was the universal elementary book of law students, and a sounder Whig never wrote, nor of profounder learning in the orthodox doctrines of the British constitution, or in what were called English liberties. You remember also that our lawyers were then all Whigs. But when his black-letter text, and uncouth but cunning learning got out of fashion, and the honeyed Mansfieldism of Blackstone became the students' hornbook, from that moment, that profession (the nursery of our Congress) began to slide into toryism, and nearly all the young brood of lawyers now are of that hue. They suppose themselves, indeed, to be Whigs, because they no longer know what Whigism or republicanism means. It is in our seminary that that vestal flame is to be kept alive; it is thence it is to be spread anew over our own and the sister States. If we are true and vigilant in our trust, within a

dozen or twenty years a majority of our own legislature will be from one school, and many disciples will have carried its doctrines home with them to their several States, and will have leavened thus the whole mass.[1]

It is worth noting that, here, confiding his political hopes to a life-long friend, Jefferson framed them in reference to the common law, and he suggested that the difference between Whig and Tory—which he elsewhere calls "the natural parties into which mankind divide"[2]—corresponded to the difference between the leading oracles of the common law in his day, Sir Edward Coke and Sir William Blackstone.

It takes a moment's pause to realize quite how surprising this is and how incongruous it must seem to latter-day Jeffersonians. Jefferson, after all, is the apostle of reason and natural rights in American political thought, the reformer who celebrated the American republic as something "new under the sun," the philosopher, moreover, who doubted "whether one generation of men has a right to bind another."[3] How could he give credence to a form of law anchored in tradition and precedent, derived from a hierarchical society, its origin hidden in "time immemorial"? The Jeffersonian Republicans, meanwhile, arose in response to a Federalist policy that included the attempt to apply the common law in federal courts as well as acts of legislation defended with reference to common law principles, and in the wake of the Jeffersonian triumph, American conservatism in the early Republic—or at least its Northern branch—came to be associated with the authors of treatises that developed common law in the American context, men such as James Kent of New York and Joseph Story of Massachusetts. What use had the Republic for Jefferson's Saxon constitution or his enthusiasm for the writings of old Coke?

Contemporary historians, when not condemning the echoes of common law in Jefferson as his "darker side,"[4] pass over them as anomalies in the thought of the foremost liberal intellect of his generation. Introducing a recent volume of essays, Joyce Appleby emphasizes the element of novelty in Jefferson's project and overlooks its vestiges of tradition:

Scholarly and philosophical . . . Jefferson boldly levitated himself out of his social milieu and trained his great learning on the real problem of liberty at the end of the eighteenth century: how to make good on the Enlightenment promise that men, born with a capacity for benign self-direction, could work out their own destinies and bring into existence a world that reflected the fulfillment of desire rather than a compromise with despair. Fired by this compelling social ambition, Jefferson put into circulation ideas about a different kind of freedom—one rooted in nature and accessible to reason, its workings explained by abstractions, its validation projected onto the future. Just how radical this departure point was can be judged by considering the English alternative of rights won by extracting concrete concessions from the Crown and implemented through the arcane processes of the common law.[5]

Jefferson biographer Merrill Peterson acknowledges that his subject did not altogether escape from common law arcana, but he explains this in developmental terms:

> Jefferson became an authentic spokesman of this hope of the Enlightenment, this vindication of human nature against the past, which seemed to be the peculiar mission of America. But he reached the position gradually. The progression of his political thought before the Revolution has been described as a movement from history to theory. It was that, and at the same time a movement from the particularism, the local patois, of English law and government to the rationalism and universalism of the natural rights philosophy. In the preliminary stage of the controversy with the mother country, he joined his fellow colonials in the appeal to the English constitution. And even after the ultimate appeal to nature in 1776, the shadow of the English heritage hovered over Jefferson's mind. His political imagination, partly clouded by old historical ideas, had not yet caught up with the principles of reason.[6]

Accurate as these passages are in capturing the spirit of Enlightenment liberalism that pervades his work, both fail to account for why, even in his mature writings, Jefferson repeatedly couples his liberal principles with an appeal to the common law and its ancient constitution. After all, the traditions of common law and liberal political theory begin at odds with each other, and the various attempts at assimilating them typically make one the other's handmaid.[7] Starting with the philosophy of Thomas Hobbes, from his account of law in *Leviathan* to his *Dialogue Between Philosopher and a Student of the Common Laws of England*, liberalism declared war on the common law, rejecting its allowance of tradition as the source of law in favor of the will of the sovereign, discarding its understanding of what Coke had called the "artificial reason" of the judge in favor of analytical rationality, and reformulating its rough and particular liberties in terms of popular consent to government on the one hand and individual freedom from government on the other. A century after Hobbes, Blackstone offered in synthesis a liberalized common law, but this proved inadequate to the liberal mind—Jeremy Bentham plays the Hobbes to his liberalized Coke. A century later and an ocean apart, Oliver Wendell Holmes, Jr., offered a thoroughly historicized common law in which liberal principles replace everything old except the romance. What is unique in this story about Blackstone's younger contemporary, Jefferson, is that his undoubted liberalism led him neither to challenge common law, as Hobbes had, nor to transform it, as Blackstone and afterward Holmes had; rather, he sought a perfect reconciliation between the opposing traditions on apparently equal terms. To understand the character of this reconciliation is to suggest its consequences for American constitutionalism.

The Saxon Constitution, the Rights of Nature, and the Common Law

The basic form of the reconciliation Jefferson proposed appears in the tract he drafted as instructions to the Virginia delegates to the First Continental Congress, printed in pamphlet form as *A Summary View of the Rights of British America*. The thrust of the piece is to present an account of the structure of the British Empire that leaves the colonies entirely free of parliamentary authority: the colonial connection with the British consists entirely in their employment of a common executive, the king of England, while their legislatures are parallel institutions each limited to their territory and its inhabitants. Jefferson anchored this argument in what he called the "right which nature has given to all men, of departing from country in which chance, not choice, has placed them, of going in quest of new habitations, and of there establishing new societies, under such laws and regulations as, to them, shall seem most likely to promote public happiness."[8] He described the colonial emigration as identical to the Saxon emigration to Great Britain from "their native wilds and woods in the North of Europe." Like the Saxons, the American immigrants "thought proper to adopt that system of laws under which they had hitherto lived in the mother country"; unlike them, the Americans thought proper "to continue their union with her [the mother country] by submitting themselves to the same common sovereign," namely, the English king. But both of these decisions were freely made by the choice of the colonists, and thus they could be freely altered. "From the nature of things, every society must at all times possess within itself the sovereign powers of legislation." If Parliament attempts, or the king's governors succeed in, dissolving the colonial assemblies, "the power reverts to the people, who may exercise it to unlimited extent, either assembling together in person, sending deputies, or in any other way they may think proper."[9]

The theory of the sovereignty of the people, anchored in the natural rights of the individual and expressed through a representative legislature in one's own land, was, of course, employed by Jefferson in the Declaration of Independence two years later to justify not only the independence of colonial law from parliamentary interference, but also the rejection of "a prince whose character is thus marked by every act which may define a tyrant." The celebrated introductory paragraphs certainly bear little mark of the common law, although the reference at the outset to the "separate and equal station . . . among the powers of the earth" to which the new United States claims entitlement by "the laws of nature and of nature's God" should serve as a reminder that what follows is not the sketch of an ideology, but an exercise in natural public law. Where the British constitution does appear is in the Bill of Particulars, the list of grievances against the king and Parliament. If the right to rebel against despotism is established by recourse to liberal political theory, despotism is itself defined by violation of the settled practices of the British constitution, at least as interpreted by the Americans in reference to their situation. Indeed, in the *Summary View*, from which Jefferson borrowed freely when composing the Declaration, not only are the principal practices and violations discussed in some detail, but they are placed in the larger context of English history. By referring to "the establishment . . . of the British constitution at the glorious Revolution on its free and antient principles," Jefferson invokes the myth of the ancient Saxon constitution to which he was to appeal throughout his life. As he explains some fifty years later in a letter to the author of a volume on the subject, the "derivation of [the British constitution] from the Anglo-Saxons, seems to be made on legitimate principles," although "It is really wonderful, so many able and learned men should have failed in their attempts to define it with correctness," their failure consisting in exaggerating the sovereignty of Parliament. The crux of the argument of Saxonists was in interpreting the innovations of the Norman kings as usurpations and explaining resistance to the Stuarts as an attempt at restoring the ancient Saxon constitution. Jefferson described it:

> [T]his constitution was violated and set at naught by Norman force, yet force cannot change right. A perpetual claim was kept up by the nation, by their perpetual demand of a restoration of their Saxon laws; which shows they were never relinquished by

the will of the nation. In the pullings and the haulings for
these antient rights, between the nation, and its kings of the races
of the Plantagenets, Tudors, and Stuarts, there was sometimes
gain, and sometimes loss, until the final reconquest of their rights
from the Stuarts.[10]

Although in the same letter Jefferson distances the American Revolution from the English heritage in accents that sound more French
than British—"We had no occasion to search into musty records, to
hunt up royal parchments, or to investigate the laws and institutions
of a semi-barbarous ancestry. We appealed to those of nature and
found them engraved in our hearts"[11]—he elsewhere makes it clear
that English experience was not foreign to the American people.
"Our laws, language, religion, politics and manners," he wrote, "are
so deeply laid in English foundations, that we shall never cease to
consider their history as a part of ours, and to study ours in that as
its origin."[12]

In the *Summary View*, Jefferson's appeal to the Saxons referred not
only to their constitution and the struggle for its recovery, but also
to their law on the possession of land. "Our Saxon ancestors held
their lands, as they did their personal property, in absolute dominion, disencumbered with any superior," and although the Norman
Conquest brought with it feudal duties, these were never universal,
according to Jefferson, but were to be seen as "exceptions out of the
Saxon laws of possession, under which all lands were held in absolute right." The conclusion he drew was that the Saxon laws "still
form the basis or groundwork of the common law, to prevail whereso-
ever the exceptions have not taken place," and that means in Amer-
i- ca, where colonists carried with them the common law but not
necessarily feudal encumbrances. The law of the land was barely
touched upon in the Declaration, but it became central to Jefferson's
work in the Virginia legislature later in 1776 and as part of the Committee of Revisors the following year. As he explains in his "Autobiography," one of the first bills he proposed in the legislature that
revolutionary year involved "declaring tenants in tail to hold their
lands in fee simple," as a means not only of restoring the Saxon order, but of preventing or dismantling the "aristocracy of wealth" that
had grown up under the protection of feudal entail in order to make
way for a republican "aristocracy of virtue and talent."[13] His biographer Dumas Malone sees in the inheritance bill the influence of
Jefferson's earlier study of Coke under George Wythe's direction, as
he sees the mark even of Coke's scholarly style in Jefferson's draft
for the Committee of Revisors' bill proportioning crimes and punishments.[14]

The project of this committee formed an important episode in Jefferson's career of engagement with the common law.[15] Appointed by the Virginia legislature on a motion proposed by Jefferson himself, its membership eventually consisting of Jefferson, Wythe, and Edmund Pendleton—three of the leading members of the state bar, and the last the leader of the opposition to the bill abolishing entail—the Committee of Revisors was assigned the task of collecting and reviewing the laws of Virginia to ensure their consistency with the new republican order. Its report in 1779 of 126 bills, "The Revisal of the Laws, 1776-1786," was not adopted in its entirety, but over the next decade or so, many of its bills were enacted in some form. What is important to note is that the committee agreed at the outset that "The Common Law [is] not to be medled [sic] with, except where Alterations are necessary."[16] This was not a unanimous decision, Jefferson reveals in his "Autobiography," since Pendleton, "contrary to his usual disposition in favor of antient things," preferred to "abolish the whole existing system of laws, and prepare a new and complete Institute."[17] In *Notes on the State of Virginia*, Jefferson explained the "Revisal" by noting that "The common law of England, by which is meant, that part of the English law which was anterior to the date of the oldest statutes extant, is made the basis of the work. It was thought dangerous to attempt to reduce it to a text: it was therefore left to be collected from the usual monuments of it."[18] And in the "Autobiography," he elaborated on the danger and the decision not to start afresh, noting

[T]hat to abrogate our whole system would be a bold measure, and probably far beyond the views of the legislature; that they had been in the practice of revising from time to time the laws of the colony, omitting the expired, the repealed and the obsolete, amending only those retained, and probably meant we should now do the same, only including the British statutes as well as our own; that to compose a new Institute like those of Justinian and Bracton, or that of Blackstone, which was the model proposed by Mr. Pendleton, would be an arduous undertaking, of vast research, of great consideration & judgment; and when reduced to a text, every word of that text, from the imperfection of human language, and it's incompetence to express distinctly every shade of idea, would become subject of questions & chicanery until settled by repeated adjudication; that this would involve us for ages in litigation, and render property uncertain until, like the statutes of old, every word had been tried, and settled by numerous decisions, and by new volumes of reports & commentaries; and that no one of us probably would undertake such a work, which, to be systematical, must be the work of one hand.[19]

Besides his distrust of Blackstone, as already expressly noted, what is striking about this passage is its adoption of a strict interpretation of legislative intent, its concern for the certainty of property, and its cautious attitude toward change—all typical features of the classical mode of the common law mind. What is missing, but what in revolutionary circumstances one should not expect, are Cokean panegyrics on the wisdom of the ancient common law and on its "perfection of reason" through the work of Parliament, bench, and bar.

In his recent essay on Jefferson's involvement with the "Revisal," Ralph Lerner argues that "[a]s a whole . . . the proposed bills testify . . . to a world of high aspiration and intractable circumstance, to a sense of open possibilities and cherished constraints. Wishing to soar, but obliged as sober legislators always to touch Virginian soil," the revisors, or at any rate Jefferson, tempered republican aspirations with a prudence secured by making peace with the common law tradition, although Lerner also notes that the traditional constraints were not entirely foreign to the ends aspired to, since "Jefferson assumed a people already long accustomed to the forms and habits of English law, 'a people fostered & fixed in principles of freedom.'"[20] This nicely captures the tension inherent in Jefferson's synthesis of liberal republicanism and the common law heritage: on the one hand, republican principles demand revision of the law to purge it of monarchical elements, while on the other, attributing principles of liberty to the common law suggests that liberal republicanism is not the complete and adequate source of political good. Jefferson's appeal to the Saxon constitution, although it suggests a primitive republican tradition in England kept alive in common law, did not entirely dissolve the tension, for he did not pretend that the "semi-barbarous" Saxons had the benefit of the modern Enlightenment and thus a knowledge of the rights of man. Blackstone's synthesis of common law and the Enlightenment laid stress on the peculiar adaptability of common law to modern improvements, especially in the hands of an able liberal judge. Why Jefferson chose a different route is the mystery that needs attention.

Common Law and Christianity

The most famous of the bills in the "Revisal" was the statute of religious liberty, passed by the Virginia legislature in 1786 in slightly modified form through the efforts of James Madison, since its author, Jefferson, was then serving the United States as minister to France. Jefferson's self-composed epitaph bears testimony to the centrality of the question of religious liberty in his life's work, as does his characterization of the Declaration of Independence, in the last letter he wrote, as "the signal of arousing men to burst the chains under which monkish ignorance and superstition had persuaded them to bind themselves, and to assume the blessings and security of self-government."[21] The problem with reconciling his insistence on the separation of church and state—formulated most extremely in *Notes on the State of Virginia*, where he argues, "it does me no injury for my neighbor to say there are twenty gods or no god. It neither picks my pocket nor breaks my leg"—with the common law is that the latter, as Jefferson notes only a page before the quotation just given, counted heresy as a capital offense and numbered among its maxims that Christianity is a part of the common law. Jefferson's equivocation in the next query in the *Notes*, where, in the context of a discussion of slavery, he asks whether "the liberties of a nation [can] be thought secure when we have removed their only firm basis, a conviction in the minds of the people that these liberties are of the gift of God," may signal a nod of recognition to the policy of the common law, but if so, it hardly squares with his description of the criminalization of heresy as "religious slavery."[22] How can Jefferson, devoted as he is to the suppression of enforced religious orthodoxy, make his peace with, much less call confidently upon, a common law embedded in the Christianity of the old regime?

Characteristically, Jefferson faced this question early on in his career, in an essay perhaps written in 1774, in the commonplace book he had kept since his student days—an essay Jefferson copied and sent to a correspondent forty years later, reiterated a decade after that in a letter on the Saxon constitution quoted above, and included as an appendix in his posthumously published *Virginia Reports*. "[W]ritten at a time of life when I was bold in the pursuit of knowledge, never fearing to follow truth and reason to whatever results they led, and bearding every authority which stood in their way," wrote Jefferson, the essay is an ingenious attempt to purge the common law of its churchly ties.[23] Working in the law library in Williamsburg, Jefferson uncovered a mistranslation of Law French in Sir Henry Finch's *Law* (1613): where the old Year Book report had Justice Prisot comment, on a case in a common pleas court involving the suit of a bishop, that the common law court gives credence to such laws of the holy church as are in "*ancien scripture*," Finch translates the phrase as "Holy Scripture"; Jefferson was able to show, most cogently, that the original referred not to the Bible, but to the "ancient written laws of the church," in conformity with the well-established doctrine that the common law courts recognize the law

and judgments of courts of separate jurisdiction, including ecclesiastical courts as well as courts of admiralty and the like. His next step
was to suppose that when Chief Justice Hale wrote on a witchcraft
case, *King v. Taylor,* toward the end of the seventeenth century that
"Christianity is parcel of the laws of England,"he must have relied
on Finch's "perverted expression of Prisot," although Hale "quotes
authority." After easily tracing all subsequent repetitions of this
maxim—including Blackstone's—to Hale's case, Jefferson proceeded
to establish the opposite by noting, first, that the common law owes
its origin to Saxons who arrived in England prior to the conversion to Christianity and, then, that the fraudulent prefacing of biblical law to the laws of the Saxon king Alfred had already been discovered. "[T]here is no better instance of the necessity of holding
the judges and writers to a declaration of their authorities than the
present: where we detect them endeavoring to make law where they
found none, and to submit us at one stroke to a whole system, no
particle of which has its foundation in the common law," Jefferson
wrote in an entry in his commonplace book; in the age of John Marshall he called it "judiciary usurpation of legislative powers."[24] The
cause is simple: "In truth, the alliance of Church and State in England has ever made their judges accomplices in the frauds of the
clergy; and even bolder than they are." The correction Jefferson offered shows already his characteristic doctrine of religious and intellectual liberty:

> We might as well say that the Newtonian system of philosophy is
> a part of the common law, as that the Christian religion is. The
> truth is that christianity and Newtonianism being reason and ver-
> ity itself, in the opinion of all but infidels and Cartesians, they are
> protected under the wings of the common law from the dominion
> of other sects, but not erected into dominion over them.[25]

The problem with Jefferson's claim that the fraud of mistranslation lies behind Hale's maxim is, of course, that Hale does not cite
Finch, and Jefferson's complaint that Hale quotes no authority is
hardly warrant for supposing Finch is Hale's source. Just as reasonably, Hale's maxim can be seen not as incorporating the law of Exodus and Acts into the law of England, but as the obverse of the fact
that heresy was a common law crime, a point that Jefferson mentions later in the essay without contradiction. If Hale is the first
to formulate this obverse, that was no doubt because until his
time it was tacitly understood, and at any rate, not publicly con-
tradicted. Jefferson's notion that the separation of common law and

ecclesiastical law protects free inquiry is a topic worth pursuing, and it may help explain how the common law order in America and England was able readily enough to accommodate religious liberty. But as a statement of historical fact, it does not seem warranted: at least as long as heresy remains a crime at common law, that law establishes Christianity among its parcels.

Indeed, what is at issue between Jefferson and Hale, so to speak, is not only a difference of attitude toward Christianity, but a different account of the nature of common law as well. In a letter from Paris to Phillip Mazzei in 1785, in answer to a query concerning the distinction between common law and chancery, Jefferson made the following surprising statement:

> The Common law is a *written law* the text of which is preserved from the beginning of the 13th century downwards, but what preceded that is lost. Its substance however has been retained in the memory of the people and committed to writing from time to time in the decisions of the judges and treatises of the jurists, insomuch that it is still considered as a lex scripta, the letter of which is sufficiently known to guide the decisions of the courts.[26]

The paradox of referring to what is usually considered the unwritten law as though it is written can be explained, if one pays attention to Jefferson's emphasis on legislation. Whether discussing the Saxon constitution or the adoption of the common law in Virginia, Jefferson never attributes to the common law any source besides the people's legislative will. The unwritten law is only natural law, and this goes no further than to establish the natural rights of men and the people's right to legislate their protection. For Hale and the traditional common lawyers including Sir Edward Coke, by contrast, the common law assimilated the customs of the realm, the maxims of the commentators, statutes, precedents, and other authorities, collecting them into a whole through the practical reason of those responsible for judgment in a case at hand. Natural law was as much a part of common law thus understood as was Christianity, but it was similarly in the background, not applicable to everyday cases. And it stood in the background in the sense that natural law stands behind human law in the philosophy of St. Thomas Aquinas, not in the sense that natural law underlies the foundation of the right of sovereignty in the philosophy of Hobbes. Jefferson's synthesis of liberalism and common law, then, requires a reinterpretation of common law as legislation, the particular origins of which are lost in the mists of time, but origins that are in principle discoverable.

His differences with Blackstone, then, involve not a difference of principle, since both trace the authority of law to sovereign legislation, but a difference over who is sovereign, Parliament or the people themselves. And to Jefferson's mind, the answer that one gives to this question is precisely what defines him as a Tory or a Whig.

Conclusion:
Toward Jefferson's Constitutionalism

The working out of the practical meaning of sovereignty of the people characterizes the remainder of Jefferson's political career, and his developing constitutionalism retained a common law flavor throughout. Understanding the perfect consistency Jefferson saw between popular sovereignty and the people's adoption of the common law is the key that unlocks many of its apparent paradoxes. His rejection of a federal common law of crimes[27] follows from his embrace of the common law in the states; and, indeed, his loyalty to the states themselves is not untouched by the fact that they are particular communities bound together by the common law. That Jefferson in the Kentucky Resolutions objected rather to the author than to the substance of the Sedition Act follows as well, and his confidence that interposition as a response to unconstitutional laws would bring about their reformation was not uncharacteristic of the mentality of the traditional common lawyer, for whom the hierarchy of legal command is altogether secondary to the reason in the argument of the case. The same appeal to the priority of law to legal institutions, and thus an unwillingness to tolerate a monopoly of legal interpretation that quenches all legitimate doubt and argument, supported both his doctrine of departmental interpretation of the Constitution and his animus against Marshall's practice of replacing seriatim opinions by the justices with official opinions of the Court.[28] In all of these matters, not to mention the prosecution for treason of Aaron Burr, Jefferson displays something of the spirit of Sir Edward Coke, making some sense of his continued admiration of one whose law he had placed on a new foundation. Whether that spirit can be sensibly maintained when its transcendent moorings have been severed is a question that awaits another day.

In the *Social Contract*, Rousseau develops a theory of the sovereignty of the people and the abstract form of government, but he recognizes that the actual establishment of a republican city requires not a political theorist but a legislator, who will not only develop the details of political institutions, but also design and inspire the mores of his people, which, after all, says Rousseau, form in their hearts "the true constitution of the State."[29] Whether as a result of his reading of Rousseau or of his own parallel course of thought, Jefferson turned to the common law, I think, not for his own republican political theory, but as a source of laws and mores for a free people—and a source requiring not that the American legislator try "changing human nature,"[30] but only that he seize what lay ready at hand in the older Whig tradition. In short, though Jefferson's desire, like Blackstone's, was to reconcile liberalism and the common law, his approach was very different. While Blackstone sought to modernize the common law by teaching it the liberal spirit of accommodation and balance under the guidance of an enlightened class—this is what Jefferson called "toryism," in Blackstone and in the Federalists—Jefferson sought, rather, alongside his scheme of education, to inspirit the forms of liberal republicanism by breathing into them the life of common law liberty, gathered, as Ralph Lerner wrote, from "a people already accustomed to the forms and habits of English law 'a people fostered and fixed in the principles of freedom.'" [31] Again, the question is whether these principles of freedom, embodied in the habits of preliberal England, did not presuppose or carry along with them forms of reason and even of faith ultimately at odds with Jefferson's own.

Notes

1. Jefferson to James Madison, February 17, 1826, in *The Writings of Thomas Jefferson*, Andrew A. Lipscomb and Albert E. Bergh, eds., 20 vols. (Washington, DC: Thomas Jefferson Memorial Association, 1904–1905), 16:156; hereinafter cited as *Jefferson Writings*.

2. "And in fact the terms of whig and tory belong to natural, as well as to civil history" (Jefferson to John Adams, June 27, 1813, in *The Adams–Jefferson Letters: The Complete Correspondence between Thomas Jefferson and Abigail and John Adams*, Lester J. Cappon, ed., 2 vols. [Chapel Hill: University of North Carolina Press, 1959], 2:335; hereinafter cited as *Adams–Jefferson Letters*).

3. Ibid., 2:283–638.

4. The term is from the title of Leonard W. Levy, *Jefferson and Civil Liberties: The Darker Side* (New York: Quadrangle Books, 1973).

5. Joyce Appleby, "Introduction: Jefferson and His Complex Legacy," in *Jeffersonian Legacies*, Peter S. Onuf, ed. (Charlottesville: University Press of Virginia, 1993), 4–5.

6. Merrill D. Peterson, *Thomas Jefferson and the New Nation: A Biography* (New York: Oxford University Press, 1970), 57; hereinafter cited as *New Nation*.

7. See James R. Stoner, *Common Law and Liberal Theory: Coke, Hobbes, and the Origins of American Constitutionalism* (Lawrence: University Press of Kansas, 1992).

8. Thomas Jefferson, "A Summary View of the Rights of British America," in Thomas Jefferson, *Writings*, Merrill D. Peterson, ed. (New York: Library of America, 1984), 105–106, hereinafter cited as *Writings*.

9. Ibid., 118.

10. Jefferson to Major John Cartwright, June 5, 1824, in *Jefferson Writings*, 16:43. For a list of Jefferson's British sources for the Saxon myth, see Peterson, *New Nation*, 58. Interestingly, Blackstone's account is not dissimilar, speaking of a "gradual restoration of that antient constitution, whereof our Saxon forefathers had been unjustly deprived, partly by the policy, and partly by the force, of the Norman" (William Blackstone, *Commentaries on the Laws of England*, 4 vols. [Chicago: University of Chicago Press, 1979], 4:413).

11. Jefferson to Major John Cartwright, June 5, 1824, in *Jefferson Writings*, 16:44.

12. Jefferson to William Duane, August 12, 1810, in *Jefferson Writings*, 12:405. It is characteristic of Jefferson that he gives less credit to England in his letter to an Englishman (Cartwright) than in his letter to the American Duane.

13. Thomas Jefferson, "Autobiography," in *Jefferson Writings*, 1:53–54.

14. Dumas Malone, *Jefferson the Virginian* (London: Eyre & Spottiswoode, 1948), 71–72, 269–270.

15. See the discussion in Ralph Lerner, *The Thinking Revolutionary: Principle and Practice in the New Republic* (Ithaca, NY: Cornell University Press, 1987), chap. 2. For the work of the committee, see Jefferson's "The Revisal of the Laws, 1776–1786," in *The Papers of Thomas Jefferson*, Julian P. Boyd, ed., 25 vols. to date (Princeton, NJ: Princeton University Press, 1950–), 2:303ff.; hereinafter cited as *The Jefferson Papers*.

16. Thomas Jefferson, "The Revisal of the Laws, 1776–1786: Bill No. 1 Plan Agreed upon by the Committee of Revisors at Fredericksburg, January 13, 1777," in *The Jefferson Papers*, 2:325.

17. "Autobiography," in *Jefferson Writings*, 1:62–63.

18. Thomas Jefferson, *Notes on the State of Virginia*, William Peden, ed. (Chapel Hill: University of North Carolina Press, 1955), 137.

19. "Autobiography," in *Jefferson Writings*, 1:63.

20. Lerner, *The Thinking Revolutionary*, 63, 89, quoting Jefferson's draft of the Declaration of Independence.

21. Jefferson to Roger C. Weightman, June 24, 1826, in *Jefferson Writings*, 16:182. See also Harvey C. Mansfield, Jr., "Thomas Jefferson," in *American Political Thought: The Philosophic Dimension of American Statesmanship*, Morton J. Frisch and Richard G. Stevens, eds. (New York: Scribner's, 1971), 28.

22. Jefferson, *Notes on the State of Virginia*, 159, 163.

23. Jefferson to Dr. Thomas Cooper, February 10, 1814, in *Jefferson Writings*, 14:85–97; Jefferson to Major John Cartwright, June 5, 1824, in *Jefferson Writings*, 16:42–52. The reference to its appearance in Jefferson's *Virginia Reports* I owe to the notes accompanying a reprint of the piece in William Addison Blakely, ed., *American State Papers Bearing on Sunday Legislation* (New York: National Religious Liberty Association, 1891), 127.

24. Jefferson to Dr. Thomas Cooper, February 10, 1814, and to Major John Cartwright, June 5, 1824, in *Jefferson Writings*, 14:85–97; 16:42–52.

25. Jefferson to Dr. Thomas Cooper, February 10, 1814, in *Jefferson Writings*, 14:85–97.

26. Jefferson to Phillip Mazzei, November 1785, in *The Jefferson Papers*, 9:67–68.

27. See Jefferson to Edmund Randolph, August 18, 1799, in *Writings*, 1066; also "Observations on the Force and Obligation of the Common Law in the United States . . . ," November 11, 1812, in *Jefferson Writings*, 17:410–417.

28. See Jefferson to Judge Spencer Roane, September 6, 1819, in *Jefferson Writings*, 15:212–216, and Jefferson to Justice William Johnson, October 27, 1822, in *Writings*, 1459–1463.

29. Jean-Jacques Rousseau, *On the Social Contract*, Judith Masters, trans. (New York: St. Martin's Press, 1978), bk. 2, chap. 12, 77.

30. Ibid., bk. 2, chap. 7, 68.

31. Lerner, *The Thinking Revolutionary*, 89.

6

Jefferson's Greatest Vision: The Promise of the Bill of Rights

Robert A. Rutland

Thomas Jefferson, Abraham Lincoln, and George Washington constitute the holy trinity in the experience and secular history of the United States. Even the Roosevelts and the Johnsons, as well as the Tafts and the Coolidges, come and go while these three stay in place. Two and one-half centuries after his birth, Jefferson appears foremost in the hearts of his countrymen and in the conscience of the world—placed perhaps even higher than a Mahatma Gandhi or a Nelson Mandela. As Jefferson's critic Leonard Levy once admitted, Jefferson is "the apostle of liberty," an image wherein "the whole may be larger than the sum of its parts" because "[i]t is the image, more than the reality, that has had the greatest influence."[1]

Americans have become a nation of hero-worshippers, and, while Washington is too formal and Lincoln too saintly, Jefferson is still one of us but also far above us. As Merrill Peterson has noted, Jefferson has become a lightning rod for public opinion in the United States, a phenomenon that reflects "America's troubled search for the image of itself."[2] In a world teeming with bad guys trying to outvote or outshoot the good guys, Jefferson is the consummate good guy.

Jefferson holds this highspot in world opinion because he was a consistent and articulate spokesman for the idea that mankind is capable of and deserving of a life lived in liberty; it is mankind's

119

right to live peaceably in a lawful society without illegal restraints. At least I think this is what we are talking about in Western society when we speak of liberty, although I notice that Gordon Wood has rather confused things by trying to define "liberty" with more precision. In his excellent book *The Radicalism of the American Revolution,* Wood goes to some lengths to spell out what they meant by liberty in 1776 and what is meant today:

> Public or political liberty—or what we now call positive liberty— meant participation in government. And this political liberty in turn provided the means by which the personal liberty and private rights of the individual—what we today call negative liberty—were protected.[3]

Wood goes on to say that in eighteenth-century America, "this classical republican tradition [before the so-called modern distinction between positive and negative liberties] was not yet clearly perceived, and the two forms of liberty were seen as one." To be candid, there are problems when we try to speak of liberty as a "negative" value. Indeed, when James Madison was arguing for a single word on the first U.S. coins in 1790, he insisted on only one word—liberty—and he was not thinking about positives and negatives. He was talking about the universally held perception that "liberty" meant that the government left citizens alone unless they broke the law. In many places in America today, that is still a working definition.

Liberty allows citizens freedom, hence the idea that a bill of rights could curb arbitrary governments: the free are left to their own schemes for the pursuit of happiness. When Lech Walesa and Mikhail Gorbachev are both quoted as expressing their admiration for Jefferson, we know that Jefferson has moved into the world's imagination as America's foremost visionary and apostle of freedom. There is a Jeffersonian shadow cast over the recently enacted Canadian Bill of Rights, and if and when the British respond to pleas for a similar catalog of guaranteed liberties, surely there will be tracings from Jefferson's ideas there too. And no citizen of the world need apologize for these borrowings—Jefferson now belongs to the heritage of the free world. There are no boundary lines blocking the search for liberty.

Even in places where a working bill of rights would be a godsend, such as Haiti or Serbia, people of goodwill pray that Jefferson's philosophy will ultimately reign. In our more comfortable and civilized precincts, we must remind ourselves that the suffering multitudes in Port-au-Prince or Sarajevo are without hope for the future unless Jefferson's implicit call for guaranteed rights for mankind can be some day turned into reality. It is a dream, but that is what we find so appealing in Jefferson. He was a dreamer; and in the long run, we embrace our dreamers more than our pragmatic politicians.

It must be recognized, too, that Jefferson came upon the scene at a magic moment in world history. Without exception, the Americans who were in the thick of the Revolution were convinced that they were onto something of worldwide importance. Consider George Washington's retrospective view, in his final act as commander in chief, when he wrote to the governors of the thirteen states:

> The foundation of our empire was not laid in the gloomy age of Ignorance and Superstition, but at an Epocha when the rights of mankind were better understood and more clearly defined, than at any former period; the researches of the human mind, after social happiness, have been carried to a great extent.[4]

Washington accepted the pressure this achievement had placed on his generation. Jefferson nurtured the same idea throughout his life. Only days before he died, he spoke of the Revolution—some fifty years later—as a model for men everywhere:

> May it be to the world, what I believe it will be, (to some parts sooner, to others later, but finally to all,) the signal of arousing men to burst the chains [of bondage] . . . and to assume the blessings and security of self-government. That form which we have substituted, restores the free right to the unbounded exercise of reason and freedom of opinion. All eyes are opened, or opening, to the rights of man.[5]

The words seem as fresh, and certainly more productive, as those at any current United Nations' meeting.

We are all aware that, in 1776, Jefferson was there, on the ground floor, working with James Madison, George Mason, John Dickinson, and other dedicated patriots with inventive talents and unshakable convictions. When their thoughts turned to creating a model of self-government, they did look to John Locke and Montesquieu for guidance, but depended chiefly on their own experience in colonial government. Proud of their British heritage, they adopted the nomenclature and phrases of the English Revolution, but used them in creating a different kind of mechanism that would establish a representative government unlike anything the world had ever seen. And in the Virginia Convention of 1776, the delegates called for a decla-

ration of rights to precede a "plan of government." Jefferson was in
Philadelphia, busy on his own draft of such a plan; but Mason was
in Williamsburg, his mind unencumbered with Old World jargon.
What should a declaration of rights contain? Nobody knew; but in
the Virginia village where he worked alone, Mason studied Locke
and created some fresh ideas. To give tone to his new country's Revolution, Madison thought, its declaration ought to spell out the details of the much-used watchword: liberty. The rights Mason had
in mind were liberties claimed by the English since 1688, encapsu-
lated in revolutionary documents and given out as every Englishman's birthright by a host of writers from Locke through Thomas
Gordon and John Trenchard in their *Cato's Letters*. In short, Mason
gave an American twist to English-born rights. Thus, with a direct-
ness that has seldom been imitated, Mason set down for Virginians
those rights "which . . . do pertain to them, and their posterity, as
the basis and foundation of government."[6]

Jefferson's own constitutional model for the Convention shows
that his mind and Mason's were working in parallel, but the elder
Virginian had given the overall structure an elevated purpose with
his prefatory catalog of guaranteed rights for a freeman. Where
Jefferson's draft started with an indictment of George III's misrule,
then moved into the construction of a three-branched republic, Mason posited the need for general laws applicable to all citizens of a
free society. The chief variation between Mason's and Jefferson's
approaches was the format: Mason was invoking history and experience to set down rigid rules to curb arbitrary government, while
Jefferson appended his right to "full and free liberty of religious
opinion," the right to bear arms, and freedom of the press in his
section establishing a judiciary. Jefferson's draft went far afield by
also promising a 50-acre grant of land "to every person not owning
nor having ever owned that quantity of lands." In later versions,
Jefferson shifted his catalog of liberties to a section on "Rights
Private and Public," added a prohibition on standing armies, and
tucked in a staggering proposal that "[n]o person hereafter coming
into this country shall be held within the same in slavery under any
pretext whatever."[7] This potential bombshell seems to have been
pretty much ignored, along with most of what Jefferson prepared in
absentia for his distant colleagues.

During the fateful weeks between mid-May and mid-July 1776,
both the Convention and the Congress sorted things out. An eyewit-
ness reported that Mason's plan "swallowed up all the rest" and
became the working draft in Williamsburg; while in Philadelphia,
Jefferson read Mason's first article and liked its ring:

That all men are by nature equally free and independent, and have certain inherent rights, of which, when they enter into a state of society, they cannot, by any compact, deprive or divest their posterity; namely, the enjoyment of life and liberty, with the means of acquiring and possessing property, and pursuing and obtaining happiness and safety.

And so it happened that Jefferson borrowed from Mason, as Mason had borrowed from Locke, and their felicitous words ultimately echoed in Paris, in St. Petersburg, in Saigon, with no end to the reverberations in sight.

But the story does not end there. After independence was declared and Jefferson's place in history soon acknowledged, he was not willing to let the matter rest. In fact, Jefferson was critical of Mason's main constitution and spent a great deal of time during the next decade attempting to replace it with his own handiwork. At the same time, Jefferson was soon aware of the impact of the ideas in Mason's declaration on the other state legislatures forming new governments. Some lawmakers borrowed verbatim from the Virginia Declaration, and others added to the basic categories of protected freedoms; but by 1780, when the state constitution-making phase ended, the prefatory Bill of Rights was a fixture in the American political spectrum.

Some of Mason's friends and colleagues ignored this fact at their peril. Chief among them was James Madison, friend and confidant of both Mason and Jefferson, but a man who was less a dreamer than a doer. After the return of peace in 1783, the American economy lurched forward, but problems domestic and foreign tested the Articles of Confederation as a unifying pact. Unlike Madison, who finally lost patience and became the ramrod for a series of smaller conventions that culminated in the Federal Convention of 1787, Jefferson favored stopgap measures.

The main occurrence that galvanized public men into action in 1787 was Shays's Rebellion. Coming in the midst of cries for reform, the insurrection in Massachusetts was blown out of proportion by those who favored drastic action. Central to their plan was the figure of Washington, for without his endorsement and promised attendance at the national convention, there was little prospect of success. Once Washington was convinced and promised to attend the Federal Convention, a gigantic stage was set. The resulting assembly was, as Jefferson said, a collection of demigods; but he did not like the pall of silence the delegates threw over their deliberations, and he awaited the results with cautious optimism.

In fact, Jefferson first saw the convention's handiwork in Paris, not in a packet sent by Madison, but in a diplomatic pouch forwarded by John Adams from London. Perhaps Madison wanted to wait until he could explain the process and lay out his disappointment; but for whatever reason, Jefferson had several weeks to review the Constitution by the time Madison's version of events was in his hands. In those intervening weeks, Jefferson appears to have realized that the Philadelphia gathering had produced a counterrevolutionary document. When he finally saw a copy of the proposed Constitution in November 1787, Jefferson wrote to Adams in London: "Indeed I think all the good of this new constitution might have been couched in three or four new articles to be added to the good, old, and venerable fabrick, which should have been preserved even as a religious relique."[8]

Perhaps Jefferson was out of touch with what was happening back home, having been ambassador to France since 1784; and perhaps he had already seen Mason's hastily written *Objections* to the proposed Constitution, which began: "There is no Declaration of Rights." Beyond doubt, Jefferson read James Wilson's heated reply to Mason's pamphlet, which ridiculed the need for a bill of rights on the ground that the Constitution was a document of expressed powers and limitations without the need for positive guarantees on human rights.

Of course, Jefferson's impulsive first reaction gave way to more sober thoughts, particularly after Madison sent him a long summary of what had taken place in Philadelphia. Madison told Jefferson of his disappointment over losing his pet scheme of a federal veto over state laws and barely mentioned the last-minute attempt to draft a bill of rights. "Col. Mason left Philada. in an exceeding ill humour indeed. . . . He considers the want of a Bill of Rights as a fatal objection." Madison then surveyed prospects for ratification in the several states and left a dismal view of the national affairs. The Continental Congress was limping along, few states bothered to send delegations, "and it is extremely uncertain when a Congress will again be formed."[9] Madison knew Jefferson too well to predict anything but great uncertainty for 1788.

Jefferson read Madison's lengthy missive and took pen in hand the next day. Promising he would add "a few words" on the proposed Constitution, Jefferson in fact launched a five-page critique. He liked the taxing system and was "captivated" by the compromise of the opposite claims of the great and little states in congressional representation. Jefferson also approved of the presidential veto and the votes in Congress "by persons, instead of . . . by states." Then Jefferson got down to business:

> I will now add what I do not like. First the omission of a bill of rights providing clearly and without the aid of sophisms for freedom of religion, freedom of the press, protection against standing armies, restriction against monopolies, the eternal and unremitting force of the habeas corpus laws, and trials by jury in all matters of fact triable by the laws of the land and not by the law of Nations.

Alluding to Wilson's argument that a bill of rights was unnecessary—because the Constitution dealt only with grants of power and, moreover, the states were not in agreement as to what a bill of rights should encompass—Jefferson was direct. He called Wilson's argument a "gratis dictum, opposed by strong inferences from the body of the instrument."

Jefferson added that it was "a hard conclusion" to say that, because some states guaranteed trial by jury and some did not, the need for the time-honored provision was unjustified. "It would have been much more just and wise to have concluded the other way that as most of the states had judiciously preserved this palladium, those who had wandered should be brought back to it." Reasoning thus, Jefferson said, the convention would "have established general right instead of general wrong."

From his vantage point in Paris, where he was witness to life in a police state that was crumbling, Jefferson was ready to lecture Madison a bit: "Let me add that a bill of rights is what the people are entitled to against every government on earth, general or particular, and what no just government should refuse, or rest on inference."[10]

Now Jefferson was warmed up, and he threw his second verbal grenade at the "abandonment in every instance of the necessity of rotation in office." The abandonment Jefferson alluded to was the provision in the Articles of Confederation limiting congressional terms, and he thought a constitutional door would be opened to reelect a popular president who would, in fact, become "an officer for life."[11]

Still in a lecturing mood, Jefferson told Madison he would not be discouraged if further efforts were needed to mend the ailing confederation. Jefferson knew Madison believed that this was probably a last desperate effort to prove Americans were capable of maintaining a republic. He hinted that the Shays's Rebellion had made too much of an impression in his homeland. But be of good cheer, he came close to saying, for: "After all, it is my principle that the will of the Majority should always prevail. If they approve the proposed Convention in all it's parts, I shall concur in it cheerfully."[12]

Jefferson sounded like a good sport, ready to take things as they came; but, in fact, he was hatching a scheme that he was unwilling to share with his good friend. On the same day Jefferson's pen moved in Paris, Madison was reporting to him from New York of the nearly empty national Treasury. With no cash on hand, the custodians "seem to be in despair of maintaining the shadow of Government much longer."[13] But to free-spending Jefferson, the empty cash box was regarded as a momentary problem. He was far more concerned about a practical way to assure the addition of a bill of rights to the proposed Constitution.

Jefferson's next moves showed that he was more concerned with securing a bill of rights than with speaking to Madison with candor. Early in February, Jefferson wrote John Adams's son-in-law of his pleasure "that the new constitution will undoubtedly be received by a sufficiency of the states to set it a going." Then he entered his caveat:

> Were I in America, I would advocate it warmly till nine should have adopted, and then as warmly take the other side to convince the remaining four that they ought not to come into it till the declaration of rights is annexed to it. By this means we should secure all the good of it, and procure so respectable an opposition as would induce the accepting states to offer a bill of rights. This would be the happiest turn the thing could take.[14]

If Jefferson had dropped his idea after revealing it to a friend in London, his friendship with Madison might not have been strained. But Jefferson was upset, for he explained to Smith:

> I own it astonishes me to find such a change wrought in the opinions of our countrymen since I left them, as that three-fourths of them should be contented to live under a system which leaves to their governors the power of taking from them the trial by jury in civil cases, freedom of religion, freedom of the press, freedom of commerce, the habeas corpus laws, and of yoking them with a standing army. This is a degeneracy in the principles of liberty to which I had given four centuries instead four years.

Of course, Jefferson had to be an optimist. "But I hope it will all come about," he concluded, for his countrymen were "now vibrating between too much and too little government, and the pendulum will rest finally in the middle."[15]

Four days later, Jefferson told Madison of his idea for withholding ratification after a certain trial for the Constitution, but he tossed it out as a wish, not a political plan.[16] It must have thrown

Madison for a loss when he discovered that Jefferson was writing to other Americans, implying that four state conventions should drag their feet "till a declaration of rights be annexed."[17] To send this message to Virginia was to invite its broadcast, as Jefferson surely knew; and in time, his words would be quoted on the floor of the Virginia ratifying convention as a testimonial for the Anti-Federalist position.

How Madison must have winced when he heard the opposition quote from Jefferson and applaud the advice from Paris! From Daniel Carroll, Madison had learned that Jefferson had been quoted at the Maryland ratification as urging his nine-adopt-four-withhold plan. "Col. Forrest show'd this letter," Carroll reported, "without date or name, but said to come under cover. It resembles Mr Jefferson's hand writing."[18]

If Madison was shocked by this disclosure, he kept quiet—but not for long. At the Richmond ratifying convention, their old bête noire, Patrick Henry, let the same cat out of the bag. On June 12, Henry quoted from Jefferson's letter and told delegates, "This illustrious citizen advises you to reject this government till it be amended." Madison was soon on his feet. The mention of Jefferson's name brought Madison up short. "I was much surprised," he said, adding that "I wish his name had never been mentioned." Henry had seized Jefferson's suggestion, pointing out that New Hampshire was probably going to be the ninth ratifying state, and thus it was all the more incumbent on Virginia to withhold its approval of the Constitution. Forewarned, Madison replied by quoting Jefferson's letter of December 20, with its praises of the Constitution. But the incident must have left a small scar.[19]

Unaware of these byplays, Jefferson heard in the late summer of 1788 that nine states had ratified. In half-congratulation, Jefferson wrote Madison that he rejoiced at the news. "It is a good canvas, on which some strokes only want retouching. What these are, I think are sufficiently manifested by the general voice from North to South, which calls for a bill of rights." He repeated his earlier list of what guarantees were needed and expanded his argument. "I hope therefore a bill of rights will be formed to guard the people against the federal government, as they are already guarded against their state governments in most instances."[20]

Jefferson's tactical plan had little effect on the ratification process, but was another indication that judicious concessions were in order. In time, Madison and his pro-Constitution delegates were ready to compromise and ward off the threat of a second national convention. Some urgency was necessary. New Hampshire had already ratified, so the needed nine states had come around, but Virginia and New York were still out, and no real test of the Constitution was possible without them in the Union. Madison offered a list of recommended amendments with an implied promise to offer them to Congress when the new government was under way. The proposition worked, and Virginia narrowly ratified the Constitution in June 1788. New York soon followed, but Jefferson's suggestion was also brought up in the North Carolina Convention, and it helped delay ratification there until 1789. Nothing seemed to work in Rhode Island.

Jefferson reviewed the ratification process as word reached Paris in the fall of 1788, and he professed "infinite pleasure" to Washington on the turn of events. By this time, Jefferson too saw the latent dangers in the call for a second convention. "I am in hopes that the annexation of the bill of rights to the constitution will alone draw over so great a proportion of the minorities, as to leave little danger in the opposition of the residue," he wrote, "and that this annexation may be made by Congress and the assemblies, without calling a convention which might endanger the most valuable parts of the system."[21] The battle was not over, but victory was—in Jefferson's eyes—already half won.

Within a year Jefferson was back in America and helping to form a team committed to making the Constitution work. As secretary of state, he witnessed the labors of Madison in the first Congress, often against bold opposition, to keep the campaign promise alive and finally enacted as a package of amendments sent to the states. Then, in his capacity as secretary of state, he declared the Bill of Rights to have officially become a part of the supreme law of the land on December 10, 1791. Ironically, the Virginia General Assembly had tossed the first-term amendments back and forth until Jefferson's home territory became the last necessary state to vote and ratify the Bill of Rights. Virginians were sometimes a cantankerous lot, as Jefferson well knew, particularly when Patrick Henry was involved in the plotting.

Now the Republic seemed set on its course, but trouble lay ahead when Jefferson and Hamilton began sparring over the direction. When Hamilton became Washington's chief navigator, Jefferson bowed out of the cabinet but not out of political life. Working with Madison, Jefferson in nominal retirement began shaping an opposition to policies deemed aristocratic, pro-English, and unsuited for the agrarian nation Jefferson had envisioned since 1776. In time, the discord would test the limits of political warfare and bring a direct challenge to the First Amendment, with its promise that Congress could pass no law abridging freedom of the press or of speech.

Jefferson's opponents never doubted that their Sedition Act of 1798 would bring upstart Republican editors misery and oblivion. On its face, the act provided punishment for critics of the administration who falsely and maliciously published their creeds with the intention of bringing the president and others into contempt and disrepute. Truth was not the issue: political hay was being made in the afterglow of the quasi war with France. The arch-Federalists, by their miscalculation, gave Jefferson (now vice president) and his friends new ammunition in their search for power.

The problem was compounded by the Federalists' control of the court system and the likelihood that zealous Federalist judges would empanel juries that could punish critics with impunity. Indeed, Madison, Albert Gallatin, and Edward Livingston attacked the Sedition Act for what it was, a partisan effort to squelch the opposition. But a modern critic has insisted that Jefferson "contributed only tired clichés" to the uproar that followed prosecutions and convictions— always of Republican editors or speakers, always in courts where federal judges meted out harsh penalties—coming into the battle late and halfheartedly insofar as freedom of the press was concerned.

To be sure, the Kentucky Resolutions of 1798, which Jefferson wrote (but gave to a friend to mask his authorship), were a lawyer's brief more than a libertarian's outcry. Jefferson based his early argument against the Sedition Act on the ground that Congress had violated the First Amendment prohibition against shackling freedom of religion or expression. Congress had no power to pass such a law, and the legislation itself could not be recognized by "federal tribunals." Since the act was an abridgment of freedom of the press, it was "altogether void, and of no force."[22]

Jefferson had a similar argument for the Alien Act. But it was Jefferson's remedy that has upset his critics. Instead of making a ringing pronouncement on behalf of unlimited freedom of the press, Jefferson lapsed into a lawyer's mood and concluded that the offending laws could be struck down by the states acting in concert. "A nullification of the act is the rightful remedy," the Eighth Resolve advised, "that every State has a natural right . . . to nullify of their own authority all assumptions of power by others."[23] There is a good deal more, including some allusions to bloody revolt, that may have scared a few timid souls. But Jefferson did remind his countrymen that power must be curbed or it will become corrupt:

> Free government is found in jealousy, and not in confidence; it is jealousy and confidence which proscribes limited constitutions, to bind down those whom we are obligated to trust with

power . . . let the honest advocate of confidence read the alien and sedition acts, and say if the Constitution has not been wise in fixing limits to the government it created.[24]

Jefferson spoke too harshly and found few ready to follow his call for state action so that "these acts, nor any others" so egregiously unconstitutional would be nullified. Madison's Virginia Resolves were more temperate, but the entire concept was ridiculed in New England statehouses and pigeonholed elsewhere. Fines were paid, editors were thrown in jail, and Jefferson came to see the obnoxious laws as shaping a plank for the political platform he was building. As the presidential campaigns in those days were even more protracted than they are in our time, we can see Jefferson's eagerness to make the Alien and Sedition Acts into a party issue that went deeper than the contemporary disputes aroused by the XYZ affair and the charges of Federalist partisans.

In what may serve as the first American political platform, Jefferson spelled out a personal philosophy that furnished a guide for his party during the next half century. Writing to Elbridge Gerry, Jefferson said, "I shall make to you a profession of my political faith," and he knew Gerry was going to circulate it in New England as the campaign warmed and political tempers glowed. Along with his professed desire to preserve the Constitution, Jefferson pledged to oppose "the monarchising [of] it's features," to preserve for the states their proper powers, to keep expenses down, to eliminate the national debt, to rely on a militia "solely, till actual invasion," and thus to prevent the formation of a standing army. Jefferson also called for a small defensive naval force, "free commerce with all nations," and no new treaties with European powers. Then came the most interesting part:

> I am for freedom of religion, and against all maneuvres to bring about a legal ascendancy of one sect over another: for freedom of the press, and against all violations of the constitution to silence by force & not by reason the complaints or criticisms, just or unjust, of our citizens against the conduct of their agents.[25]

Coming as this platform did, in the midst of rancorous attacks on the Democratic-Republican societies founded by Jefferson's supporters, Jefferson's statement underscored his commitment to civil liberties stretching back a quarter of a century.

Jefferson became president in 1801 and worked to redeem his campaign pledges. Citizens convicted under the sedition law were pardoned and fines refunded; meanwhile, Jefferson's political opponents tested the limits of free expression in their newspapers. Jefferson did not take the barrage from "the artillery of the press" without complaint, but he generally respected the parchment barriers in the Bill of Rights, although he was not always consistent in his defense of liberty. Of the trinity, Washington and Lincoln were far more consistent than Jefferson in every phase of their public lives. But if he was the most inconsistent, Jefferson was also the most visionary of the three. He dreamed of a world where liberty and the rule of law were paramount, and he thus gained a special niche as a hero of the Western world. We love our dreamers far more than our taskmasters.

The American people have come to their present posture on civil liberties with much travail and thousands of lapses. We still struggle with racial tensions and political demagoguery. Jefferson's vision of liberty is still the goal, however, and it is the most admired aspect of the American character. Jefferson's dream of a world peopled by free men and women endures, and will be a guiding light to generations unborn.

The remaining question is: How can we teach humankind to nurture the Jeffersonian legacy? This is the major challenge of the twenty-first century, and all the high technology in the world will not help us if we forget the priority liberty must occupy in our quest for a better world. Jefferson's vision must take practical shape, or we in the West will have failed to understand our mission.

Notes

1. Leonard W. Levy, *Jefferson and Civil Liberties: The Darker Side* (Cambridge, MA: Belknap Press of Harvard University Press, 1963), xii.

2. Merrill Peterson, *The Jefferson Image in the American Mind* (New York: Oxford University Press, 1960), vii.

3. Gordon S. Wood, *The Radicalism of the American Revolution* (New York: Alfred A. Knopf, 1992), 104.

4. George Washington, "Circular to the States," June 14, 1783, in *George Washington: A Collection*, W. B. Allen, ed. (Indianapolis, IN: Liberty Classics, 1988), 240–241.

5. Jefferson to Roger C. Weightman, June 24, 1826, in *The Writings of Thomas Jefferson*, Andrew A. Lipscomb and Albert E. Bergh, eds., 20 vols. (Washington, DC: Thomas Jefferson Memorial Association, 1904–1905), 16:181–182; hereinafter cited as *Jefferson Writings*.

6. Robert A. Rutland, ed., *The Papers of George Mason: 1725–1792*, 3

vols. (Chapel Hill: University of North Carolina Press, 1970), 1:287; hereinafter cited as *Papers of George Mason*.

7. For Mason's version of the Virginia Bill of Rights, see *Papers of George Mason*, 1:274–291. Jefferson's three drafts of the Virginia Constitution are printed in *The Papers of Thomas Jefferson*, Julian P. Boyd, ed., 25 vols. to date (Princeton, NJ: Princeton University Press, 1950–), 1:337–336; hereinafter cited as *The Jefferson Papers*.

8. Jefferson to John Adams, November 13, 1787, in *The Jefferson Papers*, 12:351.

9. James Madison to Jefferson, October 24, 1787, in *The Jefferson Papers*, 12:280, 284.

10. Jefferson to Madison, December 20, 1787, in *The Jefferson Papers*, 12:439–440.

11. *The Jefferson Papers*, 12:440.

12. Ibid., 12:442.

13. Madison to Jefferson, December 20, 1787, in *The Jefferson Papers*, 12:444.

14. Jefferson to William Stephens Smith, February 2, 1788, in *The Jefferson Papers*, 12:558.

15. Ibid.

16. Jefferson to Madison, February 6, 1788, in *The Jefferson Papers*, 12:569–570.

17. Jefferson to Alexander Donald, February 7, 1788, in *The Jefferson Papers*, 12:571.

18. Daniel Carroll to Madison, May 28, 1788, in *The Papers of James Madison*, William T. Hutchinson, William C. Rachal et al., eds., 21 vols. to date (Chicago: University of Chicago Press, 1962–1977; and Charlottesville: University Press of Virginia, 1977–), 11:64–65; hereinafter cited as *Madison Papers*.

19. Dumas Malone, *Jefferson and His Times*, 6 vols. (Boston: Little, Brown & Co., 1948–81), 2:172–173; Madison's speech, "General Defense of the Constitution," June 12, 1788, in *Madison Papers*, 11:130.

20. Jefferson to Madison, July 31, 1788, in *Madison Papers*, 11:212–213.

21. Jefferson to George Washington, December 4, 1788, in *The Jefferson Papers*, 14:328.

22. "Draft of the Kentucky Resolutions," October 1798, in Thomas Jefferson, *Writings*, Merrill D. Peterson, ed. (New York: Library of America, 1984), 451.

23. Ibid., 453.

24. Ibid., 454.

25. Jefferson to Elbridge Gerry, January 26, 1799, in *Writings*, 1057.

7

Jefferson and the Law

Raoul Berger

The law permeated Jefferson's entire career; the constraints of a memorial address, however, make it necessary to single out a few strands: his legal education, his views of lawyers and judges, and his enduring respect for the law's restraints.

Fortune smiled on Jefferson when it threw him under the tutelage of George Wythe, the foremost lawyer and most learned man of the Virginia bar.[1] Jefferson was not an apprentice in the usual sense; he did not sit in Wythe's office picking up the details of law and law practice. Instead, he traveled at intervals from his home in the distant backwoods to Williamsburg.[2] "The only help a youth wants," he said, "is to be directed what books to read, and in what order to read them."[3] Wythe plunged him into Edward Coke's crabbed comments on Thomas Littleton's *Tenures*,[4] a daunting undertaking at any stage, let alone for a beginner left to his own devices. He spent five years in study,[5] poring over Henry de Bracton and a string of such luminaries, culminating in Matthew Bacon's *Abridgment* (1736).[6] His thoroughness is attested by 556 entries in his commonplace book containing articles analyzing special cases and historical materials.[7] There being no English translation, he read Bracton in the Latin original, with all its archaisms and obsolete terms. He was conversant with the Year Books and translated excerpts from their Law French,[8] a task that was beyond the competence of his American fellows and remains beyond the capacity of almost all American scholars. James Truslow Adams concluded that "from the point of view of legal knowledge he was probably one of the best equipped lawyers of his time."[9]

Although Jefferson had consigned Coke—that "old dull scoundrel"—to the devil in his student days,[10] he came to believe that there was never "one of profounder learning in the orthodox doctrines of the British Constitution or what is called British rights."[11] It was otherwise with William Blackstone. Blackstone's *Commentaries on the Laws of England* had been published about the time that Jefferson entered upon his study of law. To a generation starved for reports of cases and of texts, Blackstone was a welcome repository of the common law. But Jefferson viewed the *Commentaries* with reserve: "A student," he wrote in 1812, "finds there a smattering of everything" and disparagingly compared it with "the deep rich mines of Coke Littleton."[12]

From the rarified sphere of Bracton and Coke, Jefferson plunged into the rough-and-tumble world of law practice. Its nature may be gathered from the fact that Patrick Henry was admitted to the bar after six weeks of desultory reading and, notwithstanding, quickly rose to the top as a jury spellbinder.[13] That gift had been withheld from Jefferson, so not suprisingly, he had a "distaste for the life of an advocate or jury lawyer" and little respect "for the court lawyer's attainments."[14] So he became a consultant to other lawyers and was retained by Wythe, by his great rival Edmund Pendleton, and by Patrick Henry.[15] Consultancy, whereby he supplied analysis and learning to his peers, developed into a lucrative law practice; but he left after eight years.[16] Meanwhile, he had been elected to the Virginia General Assembly. His early experience in practical politics, where he saw the "worst degeneration of legal theory and practice," their disassociation from "the public good," increased his "detestation of lawyers."[17] At the Annapolis Congress, he found 150 lawyers "whose trade," he remarked, "it is to question everything, yield nothing, & talk by the hour," consumed by a "morbid rage of debate."[18] Lawyers generally were in ill repute.

After drafting the Declaration of Independence, he returned to the Virginia assembly where he introduced a number of bills, among them four that were designed to shake the grip of the aristocracy on the government of Virginia. "The governing class," James Truslow Adams observed, "felt that . . . for the preservation of property and society, it was its duty, to govern the whole community,"[19] thus depriving the people of the right to govern themselves. What with his inheritance and that of his wife, Jefferson was one of the greatest landholders in Virginia.[20] But unlike the governing "rich and well-born,"[21] his sympathies were with the commonality.[22] Aware that a change in law could work a change in the social system, Jefferson aimed by his four bills to forestall the growth of a wealthy aristocracy. He summarized their several purposes

> as forming a system by which every fibre would be eradicated of antient or future aristocracy; and a foundation laid for a government truly republican. The repeal of the laws of entail would prevent the accumulation and perpetration of wealth in select families . . . the abolition of primogeniture, and equal partition of inheritances, removed the feudal and unnatural distinctions which made one member of every family rich, and all the rest poor . . . the restoration of rights of conscience relieved the people from taxation for the support of a religion not theirs; for the establishment was truly of the religion of the rich, the dissenting sects being entirely composed of the less wealthy people; and these, by the bill for a general education would be qualified to understand their rights, to maintain them.[23]

Coincident with the four bills, Jefferson moved for revision of the laws of Virginia.[24] Pendleton, the compeer of Wythe, advocated a new system, a code; but Jefferson sagaciously urged that the existing system be revised.[25] A new code, he reasoned, "would involve us in ages of litigation . . . until, like the statutes of old, every word has been tried, and settled by numerous decisions."[26] At every stage, he was so involved in legislation drafting that Julian Boyd remarked, with good reason, that "he was in himself a veritable legislative drafting bureau."[27]

Despite the administrative demands of the high posts Jefferson later held, he retained his lawyerly skills. Thus when Edward Livingston brought suit against him for certain acts while president, presenting complex alluvial issues, Jefferson drafted a brief for his counsel that won high praise from John Adams, himself an accomplished lawyer: "you have brought up to the view of the young generation of lawyers . . . regions of legal information of which they had never dreamed."[28] From the law he learned that "a patient pursuit of facts" is the path to "sure knowledge."[29]

Jefferson had little trust in judges; in this, he was a child of his times.[30] The founding fathers had "a profound fear of judicial independence and discretion."[31] They were influenced by the English Puritans' fears that "the law's meaning could be twisted by means of judicial construction"; they feared "the judges imposition of their personal views."[32] These fears were compounded by a number of factors. Virginia's judges were of indifferent quality; the best lawyers would not desert their lucrative practices for the ill-paid, hard life of a circuit-riding judge.[33] George Nicholas emphasized that a proper administration of justice requires judges who "are superior in legal knowledge to the bar; this cannot be the case until it is an object with the best lawyers to be judges."[34] Then, too, appointees by the governor were chosen for political reasons rather than for their fitness,[35] or they were saddled on the colonists by the Crown, often with little sympathy for, or understanding of, colonial needs. Justice James Wilson explained in 1791 that judges had been derived from a "foreign source . . . [and] were directed to foreign purposes. Need we be surprised that they were objects of aversion and distrust?" He felt constrained to exhort his fellow Americans that it was now time to "chastise our prejudices."[36]

Those prejudices drew on two powerful currents of Jefferson's thinking. First, he wished always to bind all branches "to the fixed letter of the constitution and laws,"[37] thus he criticized Lord Mansfield for rendering uncertain that which his predecessors sought to make certain.[38] For, as Madison stated, all "power is of an encroaching nature, and . . . ought to be effectually restrained from passing the limits assigned to it."[39] So when Chief Justice Marshall validated the establishment of the Bank of the United States by drawing implications from other powers[40]—despite the Federal Convention's rejection of power to charter a bank corporation[41]—Jefferson maintained that "to take a single step beyond the boundaries thus specifically drawn around the powers of Congress . . . is to take possession of a boundless field of power, no longer susceptible of definition."[42] Second, he was deeply committed to the autonomy of the states, which the Constitution reserved to them in all local and internal matters.[43] He believed that a central government was both too large for administration of local matters and that it tended to tyranny.[44] This belief was intensified by the high-handed administration of the Sedition Act by Federalist judges[45] and by the attempt of the Federalists, after being swept from office by the election of 1800, to fasten their grip on the nation by the lame-duck provision for extra judgeships packed with Federalist appointees.[46] This, Gouverneur Morris explained, was necessary because the Federalists were "about to experience a heavy gale of adverse wind; can they be blamed for casting many anchors to windward to hold their ship, through the storm?"[47] Little wonder that Jefferson came to see the Federalist judiciary as "endangering the very life of the Republic."[48]

His objections were not to the judiciary as an institution but, rather, to the inadequacy of judges and to the bias of Federalist judges.[49] In 1810, he wrote, "we have long enough suffered under the base prostitution of law to party passions."[50] He considered that the Federalist majority on the Supreme Court were "bidding defiance to the spirit of the whole nation."[51] Those beliefs led him to say in 1820 that the federal judiciary is "the subtle corps of sappers and miners constantly working underground to undermine the foundations of our confederated fabric,"[52] a charge he repeated again and again.[53] Echoing earlier Puritan misgivings, he came to believe that the judiciary had made of the Constitution "merely a thing of wax" that the Court "may twist and shape into any form they please,"[54] thereby betraying the design that officials would be "bound down from mischief by the chains of the Constitution."[55] He was troubled that the federal courts were "steadily working to undermine the independent rights of the States, and to consolidate all power in the hands" of the federal government.[56] His was a prescient eye, as the course of decision in recent years attests.

Nevertheless, he expressed confidence in the judiciary if "kept strictly to their department,"[57] confining themselves to interpreting, not "making," law, as Francis Bacon long since had counseled.[58] And he favored adding a bill of rights to the Constitution because of "the legal check which it puts in the hands of the judiciary."[59]

Jefferson's Alleged Disrespect for Law

The distinguished American historian Daniel Boorstin asserted that "the contempt for the judiciary which Jefferson expressed freely and repeatedly . . . betray[s] his inability to feel respect for law."[60] It was not disrespect for law but, rather, for judges who twisted the law that Jefferson exhibited. Respect for law was, for him, an abiding article of faith. Although he desired national provision for education, for example, he called for an amendment to make it possible.[61] So, too, his eagerness to establish a great national university yielded to the fact that it was not "enumerated in the Constitution."[62] The bey of Tripoli had been levying tribute on American ships, yet Jefferson ordered the release of a ship seized from the bey because retention was "unauthorized by the Consitution, without the sanction of Congress to go beyond the line of defense."[63] Hamilton, on the other hand, derided Jefferson's scruples against waging war without a declaration of war by Congress.[64] Jefferson expressed similar reservations when urged to take warlike measures against Spain.[65] He refused to endorse Andrew Jackson's candidacy for

President on the ground that "he has had very little respect for laws or constitutions."[66]

The charge that Jefferson had no "respect for law" simply does not square with the facts. Three examples are worth noting. First, the Louisiana Purchase is cited for his disregard for law.[67] Ten years earlier, he had written to Gouverneur Morris that the United States would "contemplate a change of neighbors with extreme uneasiness."[68] Spain's cession of New Orleans and Louisiana to the unappeasable Napoleon threatened to block an indispensable artery of commerce, through which "the produce of three-eights of our territory must pass to market."[69] Congress, writes Arthur Schlesinger Jr., "set up a clamor for Louisiana . . . and passed statutes authorizing the President to receive the purchase."[70] But Jefferson entertained grave doubts concerning the federal authority to annex new territory and proposed an amendment to the Constitution, explaining, "I had rather ask an enlargement of power from the nation . . . than to assume it by a construction which would make our powers boundless."[71] However, an amendment would be time-consuming, and Congress pressed for action before the unpredictable despot could change his mind. Jefferson yielded, but his conduct exemplifies his respect for constitutional limitations.

Second, the centerpiece of Jefferson's alleged "attack on the federal judiciary" is the impeachment of Justice Samuel Chase,[72] which, it has been charged, "had no real substance."[73] Most historians regard Chase as an "American Jeffreys,"[74] a bitter critic from the bench of republicanism,[75] who had become "the hated symbol of partisanship."[76] According to the consensus of scholarly opinion, the Alien and Sedition Acts and their implementation ignited a "reign of terror."[77] The Federalist judiciary, Dumas Malone concluded, "amounted to an arm of that party," and "its object was the silencing of the opposition press."[78] Chase, a superheated Federalist, had agitated for passage of the Sedition Act and became its fanatical enforcer.[79] A glance at one trial must suffice.

James Callender, an unsavory character, was charged with violation of the Sedition Act by contemptuous utterances about President John Adams.[80] Luther Martin, Chase's counsel in the impeachment trial, testified that he had underscored passages in Callender's book and had given it to Chase.[81] A respected lawyer, John Mason, testified that Chase told him he "would certainly punish Callender."[82] To James Triplett he remarked, "it is a pity that you have not hanged the rascal."[83] Chase admitted that the "atrocious" libel "excited" his "indignation"; he feared lest an "atrocious offender" would escape punishment.[84] Plainly, Chase had prejudged the case and demonstrated his bias against Callender.[85] Throughout the trial, Chase exhibited partiality to the prosecution. Albert Beveridge, John Marshall's biographer, noted the "sarcastic contempt" with which Chase treated defense counsel and that his frequent interruptions were "extremely well calculated to abash and disconcert counsel."[86] In a recent study of the trial, Chief Justice William Rehnquist observes that there is an "obligation upon the judge to refrain from ridiculing or making light of the lawyers."[87] Chase acknowledged that "'vexatious interruptions of counsel', and manifestation of 'indecent solicitude' . . . for the conviction of a most notorious offender" are "no doubt improper and unbecoming in . . . a judge," but, he urged, they were not defined as a crime.[88] Impeachment, however, is not confined to indictable crimes.

The Constitution provides that "judgment in cases of impeachment shall not extend further than removal from office . . . but the party convicted shall nevertheless be liable and subject to Indictment . . . and Punishment."[89] Thus the sanction for impeachment is removal; criminal prosecution is left to a separate proceeding. To view removal from office as a crime is to court double jeopardy, forbidden by the Fifth Amendment. Impeachment, said Blackstone, requires maladministration in office.[90] By the Judiciary Act of 1789, a justice is to be sworn to "impartially discharge" his duties;[91] Chase's partiality violated his oath. Then, too, the Supreme Court declared that "a fair trial in a fair tribunal is a basic requirement of due process."[92] Chase's incontrovertible bias deprived Callender of due process, a gross subversion of his office. English judges, wrote Justice Joseph Story, had been impeached "for acting grossly contrary to the duties of their office."[93]

Chase was acquitted for reasons unrelated to his guilt. The chief prosecutor was the erratic John Randolph, who was utterly unpracticed in trying cases. His two and one-half hour speech, wrote John Quincy Adams, had "as little relation to the subject matter as possible."[94] His searing criticism in the congressional debates of his fellow Republicans had led them to "hate" him.[95] "To a very large extent Chase's acquittal," Richard Ellis concludes, "was a direct result of Randolph's opposition to a number of important Republican measures . . . the final vote was probably more against Randolph than for Chase."[96] Although that deep-dyed Federalist Timothy Pickering complained of the "virulence of the party prosecuting," it was the Federalists themselves who exhibited unquenchable partisanship. The "Federalist Senators, sitting as judges, *had caucused . . . before the trial began*" and had determined "to vote as a body, before hearing a word of evidence, for the acquittal" of Chase.[97] The acquittal represented a failure of justice.[98]

Finally, as an example of his disrespect for the law, it has been asserted that Jefferson's sacking of the "midnight judges" was blatantly unconstitutional.[99] After being overwhelmingly swept from office in 1800, the lame-duck, Federalist-dominated Congress created sixteen judgeships by the Judiciary Act of 1801, and at "the last hour Adams appointed sixteen Federalists to the new circuit judgeships."[100] Merrill Peterson portrays the scene:

> On March 3 the Senate was in session late into the night confirming the last batch of nominations, and Adams spent his final hours in the executive chair hurriedly signing nocturnal commissions. The indecency of the proceeding capped two crowded months of Federalist office-packing. What was this for unless to stack the cards against the new regime?[101]

"Most historians," a critic of Jefferson acknowledges, regard the Judiciary Act of 1801 "as a blatant attempt to entrench the Federalists on the bench . . . thus to secure the one branch of the national government not yet lost to the Federalists."[102] Gouverneur Morris admitted as much.[103]

Understandably, Jefferson refused to be hog-tied and moved to repeal the 1801 act; he was met by the argument that repeal was barred by the constitutional provision for judicial life tenure.[104] But the Federalists could hardly maintain that argument because they themselves had provided by section 24 of the 1801 act that "the district courts of Kentucky and Tennessee shall be and hereby are abolished."[105] Moreover, Article 1, section 8(9) of the Constitution gives Congress power to establish inferior courts. With the power to establish goes the power to abolish, as the Federalists recognized by section 24. Judicial tenure was not designed to compel maintenance of a court no longer needed simply to provide a sinecure for an incumbent left with no duties to perform. In 1803, Chief Justice Rehnquist observes, "the Supreme Court—consisting of Federalist appointees—upheld the constitutionality of the repealer."[106]

Wide ranging as were Jefferson's talents—someone said he was "a prodigy of talents"—what emerges for me is the transcendent goodness of the man. Abigail Adams, wife of his great rival John Adams, described him as one of the "choice ones of the earth."[107] "You can never be an hour in this man's company," said John Quincy Adams, "without something of the marvellous."[108] Across 250 years, strained through cold print, that sense of the marvelous perdures.

Notes

1. James Truslow Adams, *The Living Jefferson* (New York: Scribner's, 1936), 32; Stanley Elkins and Eric McKitrick, *The Age of Federalism* (New York: Oxford University Press, 1993), 203.

2. Merrill D. Peterson, *Thomas Jefferson and the New Nation: A Biography* (New York: Oxford University Press, 1970), 16; hereinafter cited as *New Nation*.

3. Ibid., 17.

4. Ibid., 16.

5. Ibid., 13.

6. Jefferson to Dr. Thomas Cooper, January 16, 1814, in *The Writings of Thomas Jefferson*, Andrew A. Lipscomb and Albert E. Bergh, eds., 20 vols. (Washington, DC: Thomas Jefferson Memorial Association, 1904–1905), 14:54–63; hereinafter cited as *Jefferson Writings*. Jefferson was familiar with Ranulph de Glanvill and praised Matthew Bacon.

7. Gilbert Chinard, *Thomas Jefferson: The Apostle of Americanism*, 2d ed., rev. (Boston: Little, Brown & Co., 1948), 28.

8. Jefferson to John Adams, January 24, 1814, and to Thomas Cooper, February 10, 1814, in *Jefferson Writings*, 14:71–79, 85–97.

9. Adams, *The Living Jefferson*, 39.

10. Albert J. Nock, *Jefferson* (Washington, DC: Harcourt, Brace, 1926), 19.

11. Edward S. Corwin, *The Doctrine of Judicial Review: Its Legal and Historical Basis and Other Essays* (Princeton, NJ: Princeton University Press, 1914), 31.

12. Julian S. Waterman, "Thomas Jefferson and Blackstone's *Commentaries*," *Illinois Law Review* 27 (1933): 629, 634. The English did not regard Blackstone as an oracle; his *Commentaries* were viewed as "a popular exposition of the laws of England," a "handbook of the law for laymen," rather than "a legal treatise." He "has been much criticized for his superficiality and lack of historical sense," having "only the vaguest possible grasp of the elementary conceptions of law" (*The New Encyclopedia Britannica*, 15th ed., 32 vols. [Chicago: Encyclopedia Britannica, Inc., 1987], 2:264). When "Blackstone compiled his lectures," said Lord Ellenborough in 1812, "he was comparatively an ignorant man" (Waterman, "Jefferson and Blackstone's *Commentaries*," 629n7).

Presumably, Jefferson was influenced by his view that "Blackstone and Hume have made Tories" of young Americans. With Hume, he underscored, Blackstone had "done more towards the suppression of the liberties of man, than all the millions of men in arms of Bonaparte." Of Blackstone's "abettor," Lord Mansfield, John Quincy Adams wrote, "Is not Lord Mansfield most responsible of all men of that age, for the war of the American Revolution?" Jefferson expressed fears "of the 'sly poison' of Mansfield's legal innovations" (Waterman, "Jefferson and Blackstone's *Commentaries*," 635, 643, 645, 642n9).

13. Nock, *Jefferson*, 37–38. John Marshall likewise obtained the whole of his formal legal training in six weeks (Albert J. Beveridge, *The Life of John Marshall*, 4 vols. [Boston: Houghton Mifflin, 1916], 1:154).

14. Nock, *Jefferson*, 37.

15. Saul K. Padover, *Jefferson* (London: Jonathan Cape, 1942), 24.

16. Ibid., 25.

17. Nock, *Jefferson*, 39. Lawyers were in ill repute; for the reasons, see Richard E. Ellis, *The Jeffersonian Crisis: Courts and Politics in the Young Republic* (New York: Oxford University Press, 1971), 112; hereinafter cited as *Jeffersonian Crisis*: "Most evangelical ministers had little use for lawyers whom they considered to be an avaricious and depraved lot" (255); and John Quincy Adams complained that "the most innocent and irreproachable life cannot guard a lawyer against the hatred of his fellow citizens"(114).

18. Padover, *Jefferson*, 117–118. Later, Jefferson referred to "a dry technical lawyer [who] would not believe two and two made four, unless you could prove it by an adjudged case," and he urged that lawyers should have "more general science and more common sense" (ibid., 322).

19. Adams, *The Living Jefferson*, 76. In Virginia, "power was riveted solidly to wealth, breeding, and status" (*New Nation*, 37).

20. Padover, *Jefferson*, 31.

21. Hamilton divided the community into "the rich and well-born . . . [and] the other the mass of the people," the latter being "a great beast . . . needing a strong hand to keep them in order" (Nock, *Jefferson*, 183).

22. Jefferson wrote, "man is the only animal which devours his own kind, for I can apply no milder term to the governments of Europe, and to the general prey of the rich on the poor." In France, he wrote, monarchy and aristocracy render "existence a curse for 24 out of 25 parts of the inhabitants" (Adams, *The Living Jefferson*, 189). This motif occurs again and again (Nock, *Jefferson*, 84, 88).

23. Adams, *The Living Jefferson*, 114–115.

24. Padover, *Jefferson*, 72; Mason and Lee dropped out of the committee (73).

25. *New Nation*, 111.

26. Ibid.

27. Ibid., 112: "He drafted and reported bills on every conceivable subject" (156).

28. Nock, *Jefferson*, 45.

29. *New Nation*, 145.

30. Ibid., 117, 79. See also Adams, *The Living Jefferson*, 191.

31. Gordon S. Wood, *The Creation of the American Republic, 1776–1787* (New York: W. W. Norton, 1969), 298.

32. H. Jefferson Powell, "The Original Understanding of Original Intent," *Harvard Law Review* 98, no. 5 (March 1985: 892, 891).

33. *Jeffersonian Crisis*, 116–117.

34. Ibid., 129.

35. Ibid., 6.

36. Robert Green McCloskey, ed., *The Works of James Wilson*, 2 vols. (Cambridge, MA: Belknap Press of Harvard University Press, 1967), 1:292, 293.

37. *New Nation*, 155.

38. Jefferson to Phillip Mazzei, November 1795, in *The Works of Thomas Jefferson*, Paul Leicester Ford, ed., 10 vols. (New York: G. P. Putnam's Sons, 1892–1899), 4:115.

39. *The Federalist*, no. 48, in Jacob C. Cooke, ed., *The Federalist* (Middletown, CT: Wesleyan University Press, 1961), 332.

40. *M'Culloch* v. *Maryland*, 17 US 316 (1819).

41. Max Farrand, ed., *Records of the Federal Convention of 1787*, rev. ed., 4 vols. (New Haven, CT: Yale University Press, 1937), 2:615–616.

42. *New Nation*, 434.

43. *The Federalist*, no. 39, in Cooke, *The Federalist*, 250. For additional citations, see Raoul Berger, *Federalism: The Founders' Design* (Norman: University of Oklahoma Press, 1987), 53–54. "The true theory of our constitution," Jefferson wrote in 1800, is "that the states are independent as to everything within themselves, & united as to everything respecting foreign nations" (Padover, *Jefferson*, 386).

44. Padover, *Jefferson*, 386.

45. See the text accompanying notes 75–78 below.

46. *Jeffersonian Crisis*, 14.

47. William H. Rehnquist, *Grand Inquests: The Historic Impeachments of Justice Samuel Chase and President Andrew Johnson* (New York: Morrow, 1992), 50.

48. Chinard, *Apostle of Americanism*, 387; see also Nock, *Jefferson*, 269; cf. Padover, *Jefferson*, 387.

49. Padover, *Jefferson*, 385.

50. Jefferson to John Tyler, May 26, 1810, in *Jefferson Writings*, 12:391.

51. Jefferson to Ceasar A. Rodney, September 25, 1810, in *Jefferson Writings*, 12:425.

52. Jefferson to Thomas Ritchie, December 25, 1820, in *Jefferson Writings*, 15:297.

53. Jefferson to Charles Hammond, August 18, 1820, to Monsieur A. Coray, October 31, 1823, and to Edward Livingston, March 25, 1825, in *Jefferson Writings*, 15:330–333, 15:480–490 and 16:112–115, respectively.

54. Leonard Levy, ed., *The Supreme Court Under Earl Warren* (New York: Quadrangle Books, 1972), 9, 10.

55. Jonathan Elliot, *Debates in the Several States Conventions on the Adoption of the Constitution*, 2d ed., 4 vols. (Washington, DC: J. Elliot, 1836), 4:520, 543.

56. Thomas Jefferson, "Autobiography," in *Jefferson Writings*, 1:121–122.

57. Jefferson to James Madison, March 15, 1789, in *The Writings of Jefferson*, 5:81.

58. Richard Whately, ed., *Bacon's Essays with Annotations* (London: Longmans, Green & Co., 1888), 582.

59. Helen E. Veit et al., eds., *Creating the Bill of Rights: The Documentary Record From the First Federal Congress* (Baltimore, MD: Johns Hopkins University Press, 1991), 218.

60. Quoted in Stephen B. Presser, "The Original Misunderstanding: The English, the Americans, and the Dialectic of Federalist Constitutional Jurisprudence," *Northwestern University Law Review* 84 (1989): 144; Presser concurs, 147.

61. *Jeffersonian Crisis*, 281.

62. Claude G. Bowers, *Jefferson in Power: The Death Struggle of the Federalists* (Boston: Houghton Mifflin, 1936), 348–349. Jefferson requested an amendment that would permit Congress to legislate in matters of internal improvements (Herbert Sloan, "The Earth Belongs in Usufruct to the Living," in *Jeffersonian Legacies*, Peter S. Onuf, ed. [Charlottesville: University Press of Virginia, 1993], 281, 302).

63. Bowers, *Jefferson in Power*, 84–85.

64. Ibid., 90.

65. Ibid., 314.

66. Padover, *Jefferson*, 374–375fn4.

67. Presser, "The Original Misunderstanding," 147.

68. Chinard, *Apostle of Americanism*, 278. "There is on the globe one single spot," he later wrote, "the possessor of which is our natural and habitual enemy. It is New Orleans, through which the produce of three-eights of our territory must pass to market" (Jefferson to the U.S. Minister to France, April 18, 1802, in Thomas Jefferson, *Writings*, Merrill D. Peterson, ed. [New York: Library of America, 1984], 1105, hereinafter cited as *Writings*; see also Adams, *The Living Jefferson*, 318).

69. Jefferson to the U.S. Minister to France, April 18, 1802, in *Writings*, 1105.

70. Arthur M. Schlesinger Jr., *The Imperial Presidency* (Boston: Houghton Mifflin, 1973), 23. Compare Presser's statement that Jefferson "lacked official authorization" for the purchase (Presser, "The Original Misunderstanding," 147).

71. Jefferson to Wilson Carey Nicholas, September 7, 1803, in *Writings*, 1140–1141.

72. Bowers, *Jefferson in Power*, 268–293.

73. Stephen B. Presser, "Et tu Raoul? Or the Original Understanding Misunderstood," *Brigham Young University Law Review* 4 (1991): 1489.

74. Ibid., 1478.

75. In a charge to a Baltimore grand jury, Chase declared that the Maryland extension of suffrage would "certainly and rapidly destroy all protection to property and all security to personal liberty, and our republican Constitution will sink into mobocracy" (Padover, *Jefferson*, 326). He condemned the modern doctrine of Jefferson: "that all men in a state of society are entitled to enjoy equal liberty and equal rights [has] brought this mighty mischief upon us" (Bowers, *Jefferson in Power*, 274).

76. Stephen B. Presser, *The Original Misunderstanding: The English, the*

American, and the Dialectic of Federalist Jurisprudence (Durham, NC: Carolina Academic Press, 1991), 27; hereinafter cited as *Original Misunderstanding*.

77. Ibid., 118.

78. Dumas Malone, *Jefferson and His Times*, 6 vols. (Boston: Little, Brown & Co., 1970), 4:458, 466.

79. In his State Trials, Francis Wharton stated that the Sedition Act was pressed by Judge Chase with "inquisitorial energy, and executed with intolerant vigor" (*State Trials of the United States* [New York: B. Franklin, 1970], 45).

80. Chase explained that Callender's offense was "to assert that Adams, as a professed aristocrat, was an enemy to republican government" (*Original Misunderstanding*, 135). Compare Chase's own remarks to the Baltimore grand jury in Padover, *Jefferson*, 326.

81. *Annals of Congress*, 2d ed. (Washington, DC: Gales & Seaton, 1850; print bearing running head "History of Congress"), 14:245–246.

82. Ibid., 216–217.

83. Ibid., 217–218.

84. Ibid., 135–136.

85. Blackstone stated that "tyrannical partiality of judges" is a "crime of deep malignity" (William Blackstone, *Commentaries on the Laws of England*, 4 vols. [Chicago: University of Chicago Press, 1979], 4:140). Hamilton put it simply: "who would be willing to stake his life and his estate upon the verdict of a jury, acting under the auspices of Judges who had predetermined his guilt?" (*The Federalist*, no. 65, in Cooke, *The Federalist*, 443).

86. Beveridge, *The Life of John Marshall*, 3:190. Such comments are prejudicial because the jury tends to identify the defendant with his or her counsel.

87. Rehnquist, *Grand Inquests*, 84.

88. *Original Misunderstanding*, 157.

89. US Constitution, Article 1, section 3(7). For more extended discussion, see Raoul Berger, *Impeachment: The Constitutional Problems* (Cambridge, MA: Harvard University Press, 1973), 53–102. Hamilton stated, "after having been sentenced to a perpetual ostracism from the esteem and confidence, and honors and emoluments of his country; he will still be liable to prosecution and punishment in the ordinary course of law" (*The Federalist*, no. 65, in Cooke, *The Federalist*, 442).

90. Blackstone, *Commentaries*, 4:121.

91. Judiciary Act of 1789, chap. 20, sec. 8, 1 stat. 76 (1789).

92. *In Re Murchison*, 349 US 133, 136 (1954). Judicial impartiality, Thomas Hobbes observed, is "a law of nature" (*Leviathan* [New York: E. P. Dutton, 1933], 80).

93. Joseph Story, *Commentaries on the Constitution of the United States*, 5th ed., 2 vols. (Boston: Little, Brown, 1905), 1:584.

94. *Jeffersonian Crisis*, 101. For a colorful account of the trial, see Bowers, *Jefferson in Power*, 273–279.

95. *Jeffersonian Crisis*, 85.

96. Ibid., 104.

97. Bowers, *Jefferson in Power*, 280, 278.

98. Berger, *Impeachment*, 224–251.

99. Presser, "The Original Misunderstanding," 157. The Federalist arguments and Republican replies are quoted in some detail in Bowers, *Jefferson in Power*, 117–123.

100. "Judiciary Act of 1801," in *Encyclopedia of the American Constitution*, Leonard Levy, Kenneth Karst, and Dennis Maloney, eds., 4 vols. (New York: Macmillan, 1986), 3:1077. Richard Ellis concluded that "the Judiciary Act of 1801 was a purely partisan measure. Passed by a lame duck legislature, and signed by a defeated President, all the judges appointed under it were Federalists" (*Jeffersonian Crisis*, 15).

101. *New Nation*, 668.

102. *Original Misunderstanding*, 5.

103. Rehnquist, *Grand Inquests*, 50.

104. For an account of the debate, see Bowers, *Jefferson in Power*, 115–134.

105. Bowers, *Jefferson in Power*, 121.

106. Rehnquist, *Grand Inquests*, 52.

107. *New Nation*, 302.

108. Ibid., 727.

Part III

Thomas Jefferson and the Pursuit of Equality in American History

8

Jefferson as Nationalist

Colin Bonwick

I

As is well known, Thomas Jefferson wished to be remembered for three things. The first two were documents of which he was the principal author: the Declaration of Independence and the Virginia Statute for Religious Freedom; the third was his role as father of the University of Virginia. This choice tells a lot about his own order of priorities; it tells us, for example, of his commitment to freedom of the human intellect. It also goes far to explain his role as a father figure of American democracy, but it obscures other of his contributions to the development of the American republic that were at least as important, if not more so. The list made no mention of his being secretary of state, vice president, and president, for instance, nor of his leadership of a highly successful political party. These services, however, are familiar to historians. One of the least obvious elements of Jefferson's career was his nationalism. This sense of nation lay at the heart of his being and ran throughout his private as well as public life, but it is frequently masked by his well-known insistence that authority should be exercised at the lowest practicable level in order to make it responsive to the will of the community and protective of the liberties of the citizen. Thus Jefferson is generally regarded as an advocate of states rights rather than national authority. Such judgments are doubly misleading, for on the one hand they misconstrue Jefferson, and on the other they misunderstand the substantive nature of the United States as it moved from the eighteenth century to the beginning of the nineteenth century. For the first quarter century after independence was a critical period that extended far beyond the decade of the 1780s to which John Fiske attached the title. Jefferson's part in ensuring a smooth transition was literally vital.

One of the oddities of American historiography since the mid-twentieth century has been that so much attention has been paid to social characteristics in the microworld of small New England communities, yet so little to the macrocommunity of the United States as a whole. We know an enormous amount about the structure and behavior patterns of small communities and the reasons for their cohesion, but very little about the reasons for the cohesion of the national Union. It is assumed to have emerged full-fledged out of the Revolutionary War. Shortly afterward, it was reshaped at the Philadelphia Convention, and thereafter continued confidently onward until challenged by disaffected Southerners during the following century. The bloodshed of the Civil War was horrifying, but the outcome was never seriously in doubt. These assumptions deserve question and require careful investigation, though some lie outside the province of this chapter.

Perhaps the greatest impediment to our understanding of the revolutionary and early national periods—and thus Jefferson's contribution to American development—is the modern map of the United States. That vast swath of territory has acquired such an imperative logic that it is all too easy to forget the existence of several other possible lines of development. The United States was formed from only thirteen of about twenty colonies. Florida, Bermuda, Nova Scotia, and, above all, Quebec declined for various reasons to join the rebellion. Nor was there any natural unity among the thirteen colonies.[1] Each was politically and legally distinct from its neighbors, and each possessed its own social and commercial characteristics and thus had divergent interests.

The outbreak of war undoubtedly stimulated unity, since, as Benjamin Franklin famously remarked, "if we don't hang together we shall all hang separately," but it did not guarantee permanent union. The thirteen original states managed to declare independence together, but there was so much diversity among them that they refused to accept a proposal that a single model constitution should be drafted for uniform implementation in every state.[2] And who could doubt that Virginia and probably several other states could have survived as separate nations? Congress achieved much but depended heavily on the states throughout the war for men, material, and finance, and of necessity, the Articles of Confederation explicitly acknowledged state sovereignty. As Rowland Berthoff and John M. Murrin have argued, "the Revolution created a national government, but not a national community."[3]

There were also nodes of attraction elsewhere in North America. In the 1780s, some people feared that as settlement moved south-westward from the Appalachian Mountains, many settlers would be attracted to allegiance to Spain, and the argument over the Gardo-qui Treaty was conducted along sharply sectional lines. Later, in the nineteenth century, the settlement of many areas—from the region divided between New England and the remaining British colonies on the Atlantic seaboard across to western New York and southwest Ontario, the Red River of the north and the Oregon country in the Far West—swept on with little concern for the political boundary with British North America.

The conclusion is inescapable: provided there was a broad simi-larity (which there was) between one political regime and another, the Eurosettlers of North America were largely indifferent to the political color of the areas they chose to inhabit. The development of the American Union after independence was an optional choice, not an imperative. Whatever the formal legal position may have been, the Union in the 1780s was substantively one of states rather than individual citizens. Congress lacked the capacity to coerce either the states or large organized bodies of determined or distant citizens. Thus the debate over the nature of the Union, which was central to the revolutionary era, continued long after the war had been brought to a triumphant conclusion. Construction of a long-term viable union would be a challenging task, especially if the United States was to become, in Julian P. Boyd's happy if optimistic phrase, an "empire of liberty."[4] Certainly, it could not survive, let alone flourish, if its government attempted to replicate the prescriptiveness, incipient centralism, and authoritarianism inherent in the old British Empire.

II

As a nationalist, Jefferson made three major contributions to the development of a nation that remained frail and susceptible to disintegration long after the formal achievement of independence. First—and most familiar—he set an ideological agenda for the future. His other two contributions, both of which have been underestimated to a lesser or greater degree, were interlocked. These contributions to the federal Union were made during its critical first quarter century. Thus his second and partially familiar concern was for an expansive union in terms of western development and foreign relations, both of which required an activist national government. But his third and least familiar contribution was his understanding of the need to maintain the existing union of states if the nation was to consolidate and expand. This task was fundamental and required qualities of sensitive and subtle federal government very different from those needed for the successful conduct of foreign affairs and western expansion. It was especially important since the states were the basic building blocks of political cohesion— everything else depended on keeping this balance sweet.

Of the three, Jefferson's ideological agenda is most familiar and needs less attention. Jefferson was not a systematic and professional philosopher, but a *philosophe* and a working politician who was obliged to practice his art in a frequently changing world. His ideas were not worked out in a rigorously consistent system, but were sometimes subtlely modified to meet the imperatives of varying circumstances. Perhaps it is for this reason that they became so attractive to many—and detested by others. To introduce a metaphor suited to his musical interests, as a violinist he took a number of familiar tunes and developed and transformed them in a manner that enabled future generations to compose fresh variations. His approach to political problems rested on an essentially optimistic view of human nature and conduct. As he wrote John Adams late in life, "My temperament is sanguine. I steer my bark with Hope in the head, leaving Fear astern. My hopes indeed sometimes fail; but not oftener than the forebodings of the gloomy."[5] This buoyancy was coupled with a conviction that man was by nature a social being; he had no truck with the hermit and believed that men could only benefit from immersion in a social environment. Jefferson also believed that man possessed the capacity for reason, a belief exemplified by the hymn to the spirit of human inquiry incorporated in his preamble to the Virginia Statute for Religious Freedom. Moreover, and not entirely consistent, Jefferson was an adherent of the Scottish commonsense philosophy that insisted that men possessed an innate capacity for moral judgments. But his actions were also driven by that quality possessed by every successful operator: instinct. Taken together, they made Jefferson a pragmatic politician, but not a cynical calculator or a Metternich.

Jefferson's principles were not the only available to revolutionary America. His friend John Adams's honest if pessimistic constitutionalism and his opponent Alexander Hamilton's political economy, for example, had much to commend them, especially to those with a less confident opinion of human nature than Jefferson shared. But his principles were undoubtedly more attractive. When articulated through his major public documents such as the Declaration of Independence and his First Inaugural Address, his views of humanity had important consequences for national political culture. Like the Puritans, he believed that individuals were morally responsible for their own actions; but whereas the Puritans believed they were responsible for their sinful guilt in a predestinarian world, Jefferson was convinced that they possessed the capacity for their own development and enjoyed the ability to advance themselves. In particular, the Declaration provided a national set of values that was sufficiently broad as to be as attractive to New Englanders as to Southerners and could be extended to incorporate those groups such as African Americans and all women who were currently excluded from the political universe. Above all, they could incorporate all white men, not only the elite; and, indeed, Jefferson trusted the people far more than he did their rulers. As he wrote Samuel Kercheval, "I am not among those who fear the people. They, and not the rich, are our dependence for continued freedom."[6]

Since individuals could command themselves, it followed that the United States was, in important respects, a self-creating nation with control over its own character and destiny; hence, Jefferson's imperative that citizens should be emancipated from the shackles of the past, from dependence on others, and, above all, from restrictions on the freedom of intellectual speculation. These values had particular worth in such an ethnically and culturally diverse society as the United States, since they were secular rather than confessional in nature and could not only adapt to the diversity of Protestant sects, but also accommodate other Christians and non-Christians. And each generation was entitled to control its own life, hence his belief that regular revolutions were necessary.[7] But if Jefferson constructed an attractive national ideology, there was also irony. For in the context of his own lifetime, much of it could be implemented only by the states. Thus his attack on primogeniture and entail, his extension of the white male suffrage, his demolition of religious discrimination, and his educational proposals, to take only most prominent instances, applied only to Virginia; other states were required to work out their own salvation. This was, of course, wholly consistent with Jefferson's views on the location of political authority, but it had great significance for the national Union.

III

The proposition that Jefferson was a covert nationalist may seem perverse since he undoubtedly advocated strict constitutional construction and states rights. He strongly approved a written constitution, but considered it insufficient to separate the three branches of government, important though he thought that division was if the liberty of the citizen was to be adequately protected. It was also essential to maintain a second division. This latter division concerned the federal relationship in which government powers were divided between the central and local governments. Writing from Paris shortly after independence, he told his close friend and associate James Madison that "To make us one nation as to foreign concerns, and keep us distinct in Domestic ones, gives the outline of the proper division of powers between the general and particular governments," a point he repeated many times.[8] Within this balance, he insisted that Congress possessed only enumerated powers and could use only essential means to implement them. As he urged where arguing against the constitutionality of the Bank of the United States in 1791, the Constitution "was intended to lace them up straitly within the enumerated powers, and those without which, as means, these powers could not be carried into effect."[9] Later, he affirmed the principle of states rights and a theory of the Union as a compact among the several states in his draft of the Kentucky Resolutions of 1798: the states did not owe unlimited submission to the general government; rather, they had "delegated to that government certain definite powers, reserving, each State to itself, the residuary mass of right to their own self-government; and that whensoever the general government assumes undelegated powers, its acts are unauthoritative, void, and of no force."[10] He repeated his states rights doctrine in limited form in his First Inaugural Address in 1801, when he argued that government should be limited in extent and that state governments should be supported in all their rights, "as the most competent administrations for our domestic concerns and the surest bulwarks against antirepublican tendencies."[11] But should these apparently clear propositions be taken at full face value?

There are, of course, some familiar instances of Jefferson taking a strongly nationalist stance. He appreciated the need for vigorous national government in appropriate circumstances, but believed that different sectors of national activity required drastically different approaches; in particular, he recognized that external affairs demanded activist government even if domestic affairs demanded deference to the individual states. Put differently, as Robert W. Tucker and David C. Hendrickson have argued, his "vision of domestic society was contingent on the fulfillment of expansive goals."[12] These external affairs can be coarsely defined as incorporating western expansion as well as the more obvious matters of foreign relations. Here, Jefferson's nationalism emerges very clearly. On his return to Congress after the Revolutionary War, he was responsible for drafting a land ordinance in 1784 that established principles of surveying western lands, dividing them into communities when sufficient people had settled there, and admitting them into the Union by democratic methods and on equal terms with the original thirteen states. Jefferson's ordinance was overtaken by events, but it had provided a solution to the colonial problem that Great Britain had so manifestly failed to devise, and its essential principles survived. Moreover, Jefferson's confidence that republicanism was compatible with extensive territory (provided it was based on compact and equality) survived long after he had left office; indeed, the two were mutually dependent, for, as he put it, "My hope of its duration is built much on the enlargement of the resources of life going hand in hand with the enlargement of territory, and the belief that men are disposed to live honestly, if the means of doing so are open to them."[13]

These expansive goals also required an activist foreign policy in the customary sense of that term. Tucker and Hendrickson argue that Jefferson's conduct was very similar to those of European old regimes: for "what he regarded as the necessities of the state and nation overrode the principles that appeared to jeopardize these necessities, including principles that had otherwise commanded his undeviating allegiance."[14] This sort of behavior has laid Jefferson open to accusations of hypocrisy, trimming, and the abandonment of principles in the interest of convenience. Jefferson was aware of the gravity of the accusations of inconsistency and realpolitik and justified himself by reflecting late in life that "It is a melancholy law of human societies to be compelled sometimes to choose a great evil in order to ward off a greater."[15] His successful campaign against the Barbary pirates is interpreted as a remarkable example of vigorous action, as is the purchase of Louisiana from Napoleon. But the constitutional basis for the Louisiana Purchase was widely challenged at the time and has continued to be questioned by later scholars. Lastly, of course, there are the five Embargo Acts (1807–1809) restricting American trade. Here, he extended the doctrine of implied powers to such a point that Leonard Levy, one of Jefferson's severest critics in matters of civil liberties, heatedly declares that it remains the most repressive and unconstitutional legislation ever enacted by Congress in time of peace. No peacetime president ever sought or received, such a vast concentration of power as did Jefferson and at the expense of provisions in the Bill of Rights which he himself once advocated as necessary checks against tyranny.[16]

IV

Jefferson's nationalism was more subtle than the above examples suggest. His actions in domestic affairs, as much as in foreign policy, were undoubtedly shaped by deep-seated principles, but they were also tempered by the need to take account of circumstances as he found them, and one major element of those circumstances was the continuing importance of the states. Right at the beginning, the Declaration of Independence implied a level of unity that did not exist at the time. For if some Americans were deeply pessimistic about the prospects for the Union in the 1780s, historians have been very unwise to take the notion of unity for granted. Thus Julian P. Boyd correctly argues that "the cardinal principle of Jefferson's life was his uncompromising devotion to the Union because of its identity with human rights."[17] Beyond that, however, he assumes that the Union was already secure before the end of the eighteenth century; thus he declares that "the monumental achievements of American constitutionalism—the Declaration of Independence, the Articles of Confederation, the Northwest Ordinance, the federal Constitution— were the written expressions of a people already unified in ideals, as Jefferson clearly perceived."[18] But if Boyd's ideological proposition is correct, his implication that the Union was also secure was, at best, unexamined, and, at worst, mistaken.

There was a further problem. If Thomas Burke's suggestion that each state should go its own way after the attainment of independence should be dismissed as too extreme, then a division into three or perhaps four separate confederacies had much to commend it. North American geography emphasized sectional unities such as New England, the Chesapeake Bay region, and the lower South, not a single seaboard union. The Appalachians similarly separated the Atlantic states from the interior before the completion of the Erie Canal in 1825, but in many respects, lateral bonds from east to west and separated by the Ohio River made more sense than a North-South union—a proposition demonstrated by the pattern of migration in which Southerners opened the old southwest well before the New England diaspora opened the Northwest. Continuing development toward the American Union that actually emerged was an optional choice, not a geographical, economic, cultural, or political imperative.

Jefferson instinctively understood this. Whatever the legal position may have been—and this remained open to vigorous debate—the Union of the 1780s was one of states, not of individual citizens forming a single nation. Throughout Jefferson's long life and for many years thereafter, the states remained far more important as units of social organization and political and public activity than they are at present. Each was politically and legally distinct from its neighbors, and each possessed its own social and commercial characteristics and thus had divergent, as well as convergent, interests. Long after 1789, they retained enormous powers in comparison with those of the federal government, including property law, family law, public morality, public health, education, penal law, and commercial law. It was no coincidence that two of the three achievements of which Jefferson was most proud, the Statute for Religious Freedom and the University of Virginia, were both the work of a state legislature, not the federal government. As the political scientist Theodore Lowi has argued, the national government did relatively little during the nineteenth century, especially in comparison with the states. Rather, as he points out, it kept close to the functions expressly delegated to it in Article 1, section 8 of the Constitution.[19] The practice of government naturally inclined to the division of authority Jefferson articulated, and an essential duty of government was to discourage centrifugal tendencies among the states and promote their convergent interests. It followed that the federal relationship between states and central government was far more important than it became in the twentieth century—and national union was therefore far less secure.

The new Union created by the Constitution of 1787 demanded the construction of an additional layer of government and thus the transfer of some authority from local communities to the center. Section 8 of Article 1, which set out certain powers of the federal government; sections 9 and 10 of the same article, which imposed restrictions on Congress and the states, respectively; and especially Article 4 began the test of defining the new system, but left many questions as to the balance between federal and state authority unresolved. Was central authority to be strong or weak? Alexander Hamilton, who is frequently described as a realist, especially in contrast to Jefferson, had no doubts. Yet his proposed solution to the problem of union was absurd. His remedy at Philadelphia was creation of a national sovereignty and reduction of the states to no more than municipal corporations.[20] His financial program as secretary of the Treasury and his insistence that the federal government had been granted implied as well as specified powers undoubtedly strengthened the Union in the long run, but his preference for commercial interests did much to divide the embryonic nation. It took time, but by the middle of the 1790s, a new structure was in place. The states had founded themselves on the basis of popular sovereignty, and a national Union had been constructed through the medium of the federal Constitution of 1787, the work of George Washington as president and Alexander Hamilton as secretary of the Treasury and the unexpected and unwelcome emergence of the first party system. Yet this was not enough. As Jefferson himself insisted, the earth belongs to the living.[21] But if successive generations can build on their predecessors' achievements, they can also make a mess of things.

At first sight, Jefferson appears to have performed a modest, even a negative, part in this process. Yet superficial appearances are sometimes misleading. In reality, he played a vital role in articulating the linkage between the revolutionary era and the advancement of the United States into the nineteenth century, but he did more than provide an ideological agenda. His understanding derived in good measure from the particular cast of his mind. He also possessed a good deal of political experience, ranging from his days in the Virginia legislature and as its governor to national service in Congress and as American minister in Paris. These qualities made his years as a national politician between 1790, when he became secretary of state, and 1809, when he left the presidency, the most important of his life.

Perhaps the first and crucial thing that Jefferson understood was that the United States was an artificial human construct. In a very literal sense, the United States had created itself. To use Benedict Anderson's terminology, a nation is an imagined community whose communion lives in the minds of members who cannot be expected to know one another. It is also, in Anderson's terms, limited by finite boundaries and is sovereign "because the concept was born in an age in which Enlightenment and Revolution were destroying the legitimacy of the divinely-ordained hierarchical dynastic realm."[22] In the American case, it was sovereign because it had repudiated the prescriptive authority of parliamentary sovereignty. Jefferson himself had, of course, played a central role in its birth. But he realized instinctively that if the blood of patriots and tyrants was the natural manure of liberty, the health and prosperity of the nation also required care and nourishment. He also understood the somewhat ambivalent relationship between the nation and its political system, and it is striking that he uses the terms "union" and "general government" far more frequently than he does the term "nation"—a word that does not, for example, appear in the Declaration of Independence.

Jefferson was in Paris while the Constitution was being drafted and ratified, but he had been alarmed by what he regarded as the want of energy in the old confederation, and he therefore appreciated the value of the new system.[23] His correspondence from France contains surprisingly few immediate comments on it. His only major criticism concerned the possibility of unlimited reelection of the president, instead of the rotation in office that he preferred, and what he considered to be its insufficient protection for individuals; here, he joined those who wished to attach a bill of rights. Perhaps surprisingly, he applauded the ingenious device that permitted representation by population in the House of Representatives and by states in the Senate, but he did not remark on the restrictions imposed on the states.[24]

He also realized that the Constitution offered an invitation to national development, but not a promise of success, and appreciated the distinction between the document itself and the institutions established under its authority. For political structures and institutions are live and active. They are the creation of people's goals and rivalries and the product of their compromises. They consist of human beings, but paradoxically, they are not autonomous; they cannot be relied upon to be predictable. To adapt Jefferson's phrase, institutions belong to the living, yet the decisions and policies of one generation in practice often create firm, binding precedents for its successors. Jefferson, of course, argued that they should be regularly adjusted to changing conditions and needs. Particular driving forces created the Constitution—economic interests, ideology, defense, and immediately perceived needs—but could not keep it alive, hence the need for understanding and subtlety. Too much weight imposed on a frail structure would collapse it. Hamilton's nostrums would have done that; fortunately, he was sidetracked. But, conversely, if too little attention was given to its development, the Union would evaporate like a bubble of soap.

Even so, Jefferson's meaning is sometimes unclear. Shortly before his death, he described the Constitution as "a compact of independent nations," but this was the statement of an old man and surely gives too strong an impression.[25] His sense of the division between state and central authority was often ambivalent. As he told President Washington in 1793,

> I consider the people who constitute a society or nation as the
> source of all authority in that nation, as free to transact their com-
> mon concerns by any agents they think proper, to change their
> agents individually . . . when ever they please; that all the acts
> done by those agents under the authority of the nation, are the
> acts of the nation.[26]

Furthermore, "sooner or later public opinion, an instrument merely
moral in the beginning, will find occasion physically to inflict it's
sentences on the unjust."[27]

But how could power be channeled within the nation, and the responsibility of government to its citizens be preserved? As he argued
to Daniel Tompkins, governor of New York, in February 1809, "By
all, I trust, the union of these [states] will ever be considered as the
Palladium of their safety, their prosperity and glory, and all attempts
to sever it will be frowned on with reprobation and abhorrence."[28] It
is here that Jefferson's nationalism emerges at its strongest. His sense
of its structure had three components: the people, the federal government, and the states.

V

Naturally, the people were the first pillar on which the new regime was to rest. This proposition could be derived on theoretical
grounds from Jefferson's general philosophy, but it had a pragmatic
justification as well. The best vindication of it came during his second administration. It was the influence of the people that contributed so greatly to the defeat of the Burr conspiracy; in other
countries, only an army could have defeated it, but the event "has
proved that government to be the strongest of which every man feels
himself a part."[29] Indeed, Jefferson constantly insisted that it was the
duty of the president "to unite in himself the confidence of the whole
people. This alone, in any case where the energy of the nation is
required, can produce a union of the whole."[30] And as John Quincy
Adams recognized, "The power of the [Jefferson] administration rests
upon the support of a much stronger majority of the people throughout the Union than the former administration ever possessed."[31]

Above all, of course, he used the instrument of political party as
an agent of national union by weeding out from government offices
those whom he believed were politically unreliable, a practice that,
it has been argued, he extended to army commissions as well as to
civil appointments and to favoritism toward banks known to be run

by Republicans. All this was in addition to his proven methods of persuading and influencing Congress. There can be no doubt that Jefferson was a highly effective party leader, even though he constantly denied that he was a party man. But implicitly, and perhaps disingenuously, he equated republicanism as a principle with republicanism as a party.

The second element was, of course, the states, of which little more needs to be said. Jefferson's sympathy for them was different from the fierce localism, agrarianism, and individualism of men like John Randolph of Roanoke and John Taylor of Caroline. Just as Hamilton had brought the states on the side of the federal government by encouraging them to invest in the Bank of the United States, so Jefferson worked through the states as a means of strengthening his government. Thus he applauded Governor Edward Tiffin for Ohio's part in suppressing the Burr conspiracy.[32] Later, when foreign affairs deteriorated from 1807 onward, Jefferson allowed state governors such as William H. Cabell of Virginia and Daniel Tompkins of New York to organize defense. But symbolically, although the troops used were state militia, they were already nominally controlled by federal regulations.

The third leg essential to the Union was the federal government. Jefferson did not want a weak central government, and his pruning of the federal government on entering office should not be misconstrued. Rather, he wanted one that was strong as well as simple in character and frugal in cost.[33] Yet the weakness of the national government was palpable. It was called upon to administer the common affairs of a territorially vast country with a small and scattered population, even though it had few civil servants and only a few hundred soldiers.

From 1787 onward, Jefferson clearly understood that the Union was a national one rather than a confederation. He recognized that the new Constitution had produced a consolidated government and applauded the creation of a federal government "which could walk upon it's own legs, without leaning for support on the state legislatures."[34] He opposed Madison's nostrum of a congressional veto on state legislation—but he supported the principle that appeals could be made from state courts to the federal court on matters controlled by national law—even at the risk of encroaching on the jurisdiction of state courts.[35]

Here, indeed, was a basis for nationalist development. In a country as extensive and expansive as the United States, a Hamiltonian unitary government was impractical, and an articulated system had important advantages. The distinction Jefferson made was that the citizens had formed themselves into one nation as to outsiders but several states as to themselves. A division of functions followed: the united nation was responsible for external and mutual relations and the preservation of republican institutions, but individual states were responsible for "the care of our persons, our property, our reputation, and religious freedom."[36]

So far, so good; but when it comes to a consideration of the relationship between the states and the federal government, Jefferson's meaning is sometimes unclear. In January 1802, he declared that "State rights & State sovereignties, as recognized by the Constitution, are an integral & essential part of our great political fabric. They are bound up by a common ligament with those of the National government, and form with it one system, of which the Constitution is the law and the life."[37] It would be possible to interpret this as implying that the Union was a union of states, with all that that might imply. More likely, though, he was using the term "state sovereignty" loosely and thus ambiguously, in the same way that his inaugural affirmation that "We are all republicans, we are all federalists" also causes a lot of problems of interpretation. It is also notable that Chief Justice John Marshall used the terms in a very similar way in his judgment in *M'Culloch* v. *Maryland*. Perhaps, though, the clincher is what Jefferson also said to the Rhode Island Assembly in 1801: "It is a momentous truth, and happily of *universal* impression on the public mind, that our safety rests on the preservation of our Union."[38] This was especially so since he believed that "the true barriers of our liberty in this country are our State governments"; moreover, there was a terrible example if power was concentrated in one place. In France, the republican government was lost *"without a struggle"* because the government was centralized and "no provincial organizations existed to which the people might rally under authority of the laws," and this made possible Napoleon's coup d'état.[39]

The point about Jefferson's constitutionalism is that he saw the federal government and the states as part of an integrated system. And, of course, he was correct in arguing that the states retained most domestic authority. He presumably would have agreed with Richard Neustadt's judgment that the Philadelphia Convention did not create a government of separated powers, but a government of separated institutions sharing power—only he would have extended it beyond the federal government to include the states.[40] To quote James Madison, it was neither wholly national or wholly federal; and to cite Alexis de Tocqueville, it was no longer a federal government but an incomplete national government.[41] Jefferson's theoretical position was thus fully compatible with the actuality of a strong national system that permitted extensive powers to the states. And "the genius of states' rights within the framework of a more energetic national union was to secure sectional interests without directly acknowledging their legitimacy and durability," as Cathy Matson and Peter Onuf have argued.[42]

This division was essential, bearing in mind the weakness of the national government. Jefferson respected the states. Throughout the final stages of his career, he was not only afraid of the unconstitutional extension of federal authority such as the Alien and Sedition Acts, he was also afraid that the Union would disintegrate. During the Alien and Sedition Acts crisis, he rejected John Taylor's argument that it was time to reconsider secession. Similarly, he was continually afraid that the New England states might attempt to secede. But, he insisted, in 1798, times were not natural and they should be ridden out. This fear of secession ran throughout his presidency and came to a climax during the Embargo Crisis when he told several friends that he was convinced that the New England states were about to hold a convention that might propose separation. And the experience of his presidency suggests that if New England had made a serious attempt to secede, the federal government lacked the capacity to suppress it. After all, President Lincoln had very great difficulty in suppressing the Southern rebellion in the 1860s in spite of the massive growth of the country's industrial strength.

Jefferson believed that if one state seceded, others would follow. Soon the Union would disintegrate into a number of smaller confederacies. He had no objection to this taking place in new territories—indeed, he seems to have expected it—but this did not apply to the original Union that achieved independence from Great Britain. It was the nest from which all America was to be peopled. It had to be carefully protected, especially since he estimated in 1806 that about 100,000 people had emigrated from the Atlantic states to the western country the previous year and that emigration was taking about half the country's natural increase each year.[43] He was much more vigorous, even ruthless, in dealing with external affairs. He was insistent that New Orleans and the Mississippi navigation should be obtained, as well as Florida for its strategic dominance of the Caribbean. This concern also helps to explain his bitter hostility toward Aaron Burr and his determination to punish him for his adventurism in the Southwest; there was, Jefferson realized, a real possibility that as adventurist settlements were established, they might be drawn away from a United States the center of political gravity of which was still east of the Appalachian Mountains. In this respect, and in relation to American maritime rights during the Napoleonic Wars, Jefferson clearly placed reasons of state above other considerations. Ironically, his Embargo Act of 1807, which attempted to deploy American commercial strength as a coercive weapon, would achieve success only if the local interests of American shipping—especially in New England—could be subordinated to national interest. The situation was very similar to that in which the colonies had found themselves in the 1760s when Britain attempted to centralize control of the empire in the common interest of defense. But Jefferson also discovered the validity of his earlier insistence on popular sovereignty. He claimed to rely on popular support to defeat Burr's scheming, but it was popular sentiment that threatened once again the possibility of New England secession and defeated the embargo. The lesson was one that he already knew. The development of the Union depended not on the construction of a powerful coercive government, but on a respect for local rights and local interests. His political aims were essentially those of Alexander Hamilton, but his methods were more subtle, more national in their attractiveness, and, above all, more successful.

Shared common values and a strong desire to remain a single nation were literally vital, and certainly more important than geographic and economic ties, but any assumption that they were sufficient is mistaken. As Jefferson himself anticipated, it was entirely feasible for separate but ideologically similar countries to emerge and grow to maturity in North America: the success with which the rump of the first British Empire was transforming itself into the transcontinental Dominion of Canada was proof of that. He appreciated the legitimacy of both national and state interests. He realized that the Union and the liberty of its citizens could survive only in a reticulated system where every government stood on its own feet but depended on, and was interlocked into, the others. The greatest risk was of disintegration. Jefferson's achievement was to cement the federal Union, and in this crucial respect, he was as much a nationalist as Alexander Hamilton. Their grand political objective was the same, but their strategies were radically different. Hamilton failed. Jefferson succeeded.

Notes

1. See John M. Murrin, "The Great Inversion, of Court versus Country: A Comparison of the Revolution Settlements in England (1688–1721) and America (1776–1816)," in *Three British Revolutions: 1641, 1688,*

1776, J. G. A. Pocock, ed. (Princeton, NJ: Princeton University Press, 1980), 386–387.

2. Willi Paul Adams, *The First American Constitutions: Republican Ideology and the Making of the State Constitutions in the Revolutionary Era*, Rita Kimber and Robert Kimber, trans. (Chapel Hill: University of North Carolina Press, 1980), 55–56.

3. Rowland Berthoff and John M. Murrin, "Feudalism, Communalism, and the Yeoman Freeholder: The American Revolution Considered as a Social Accident," in *Essays on the American Revolution*, Stephen G. Kurtz and James H. Hutson, eds. (Chapel Hill: University of North Carolina Press, 1973), 288.

4. Julian P. Boyd, "Thomas Jefferson's 'Empire of Liberty,'" *The Virginia Quarterly Review* no. 4, no. 24 (Autumn 1948): 538–554.

5. Jefferson to John Adams, April 8, 1816, in *The Adams–Jefferson Letters: The Complete Correspondence between Thomas Jefferson and Abigail and John Adams*, Lester J. Cappon, ed., 2 vols. (Chapel Hill: University of North Carolina Press, 1959), 2:467.

6. Jefferson to Samuel Kercheval, July 12, 1816, in *The Writings of Thomas Jefferson*, Andrew A. Lipscomb and Albert E. Bergh, eds., 20 vols. (Washington, DC: The Thomas Jefferson Memorial Association, 1904–1905); 15:39, hereinafter cited as *Jefferson Writings*.

7. Jefferson to James Madison, January 30, 1787, in *The Papers of Thomas Jefferson*, Julian P. Boyd, ed., 25 vols. to date (Princeton, NJ: Princeton University Press, 1950–), 11:92–97; hereinafter cited as *The Jefferson Papers*.

8. Jefferson to James Madison, December 16, 1786, in *The Jefferson Papers*, 10:603.

9. Henry Steele Commager, ed., *Documents of American History*, 9th ed., 2 vols. (Englewood Cliffs, NJ: Prentice-Hall, 1973), 1:160.

10. Noble E. Cunningham Jr., *In Pursuit of Reason: The Life of Thomas Jefferson* (Baton Rouge: Louisiana State University Press, 1987), 217.

11. Commager, *Documents*, 1:189.

12. Robert W. Tucker and David C. Hendrickson, *Empire of Liberty: The Statecraft of Thomas Jefferson* (Oxford, England: Oxford University Press, 1990), 234.

13. Jefferson to Monsieur Barre de Marbois, June 14, 1817, in *Jefferson Writings*, 15:131.

14. Tucker and Hendrickson, *Empire of Liberty*, 234.

15. Jefferson to William Short, Esq., November 28, 1814, in *Jefferson Writings*, 14:213.

16. Leonard W. Levy, *Jefferson and Civil Liberties: The Darker Side* (Cambridge, MA: Harvard University Press, 1963), 139.

17. Julian P. Boyd, "Thomas Jefferson's 'Empire of Liberty,'" in *Thomas Jefferson: A Profile*, Merrill D. Peterson, ed. (New York: Hill & Wang, 1967), 186.

18. Ibid., 184.

19. Theodore J. Lowi, *The Personal President* (Ithaca, NY: Cornell University Press, 1985), 24–26.

20. Max Farrand, ed., *The Records of the Federal Convention of 1787*, rev. ed., 4 vols. (New Haven, CT: Yale University Press, 1937), 1:282–293.

21. Jefferson to James Madison, September 6, 1789, in *The Jefferson Papers*, 15:392.

22. Benedict Anderson, *Imagined Communities: Reflections on the Origin and Spread of Nationalism*, rev. ed. (London: Verso, 1991), 7.

23. Jefferson to Archibald Stuart, January 25, 1786, in *The Jefferson Papers*, 9:217–219.

24. Jefferson to James Madison, December 20, 1787, in *The Jefferson Papers*, 12:438–442.

25. Jefferson to Edward Everett, April 8, 1826, in *Jefferson Writings*, 16:162.

26. Jefferson to George Washington, April 28, 1793, and Jefferson's "Opinion on the Treaties with France" in *The Jefferson Papers*, 25:604–607.

27. Jefferson to James Madison, April 23, 1804, in *The Works of Thomas Jefferson*, Paul Leicester Ford, ed., 10 vols. (New York: G. P. Putnam's Sons, 1892–1899), 8:300; hereinafter cited as *Works of Jefferson*.

28. Jefferson to Daniel Tompkins, February 24, 1809, in Jefferson Coolidge Collection (Boston: Massachusetts Historical Society), reel 12.

29. Jefferson to Edward Tiffin, February 2, 1807, in *Jefferson Writings*, 11:147.

30. Jefferson to Garland Jefferson, January 25, 1810, in *Jefferson Writings*, 12:353.

31. Robert M. Johnstone Jr., *Jefferson and the Presidency: Leadership in the Young Republic* (Ithaca, NY: Cornell University Press, 1978), 311.

32. Jefferson to Edward Tiffin, February 2, 1807, in *Jefferson Writings*, 11:146–147.

33. Jefferson to Comte de Volney, April 20, 1802, in Jefferson Coolidge Collection, reel 9.

34. Jefferson to Richard Price, January 8, 1789, in *The Jefferson Papers*, 14:420.

35. Jefferson to James Madison, June 20, 1787, in *The Jefferson Papers*, 11:480–484.

36. Jefferson to the General Assembly of Rhode Island and Providence Plantations, May 26, 1801, in *Jefferson Writings*, 10:262–263.

37. Jefferson to the Georgia Legislature, January 15, 1802, in the Jefferson Papers (Charlottesville: University of Virginia), reel 5.

38. Jefferson to the General Assembly of Rhode Island and Providence Plantations, May 26, 1801, in *Jefferson Writings*, 10:262–263.

39. Jefferson to DeStutt de Tracy, January 26, 1811, in *Jefferson Writings*, 13:19–20.

40. Richard Neustadt, *Presidential Power: The Politics of Leadership from FDR to Carter* (New York: John Wiley & Sons, 1960), 26.

41. Anthony King, ed., *The New American Political System*, 2d ed. (Washington, DC: AEI Press, 1990), 231, 244–245.

42. Cathy D. Matson and Peter S. Onuf, *A Union of Interests: Political and Economic Thought in Revolutionary America* (Lawrence: University Press of Kansas, 1990), 123.

43. Jefferson to Archibald Stuart, January 25, 1786, in *The Jefferson Papers*, 9:217–219 and Jefferson to Comte de Volney, February 11, 1806, in *The Works of Jefferson*, 8:419–421.

9

A Respectful Revisionism:
Lincoln and the Jeffersonian Legacy
in the Civil War Era

Peter J. Parish

The American civic religion has its own secular trinity: George Washington, the father; Abraham Lincoln, the son; and Thomas Jefferson, the guiding spirit. Their monuments in Washington, D.C., are temples of that civic religion. The atmosphere that is so assiduously cultivated at Jefferson's home at Monticello can inspire similar feelings of reverence, almost of veneration, as any modern visitor can testify.

For Americans of Lincoln's generation, too, Thomas Jefferson was clearly a figure to command respect, even reverence. But he also belonged to a very recent past. He had been dead only twenty years when Lincoln was elected to the House of Representatives, and only thirty-five years when Lincoln entered the White House. For Americans of 1860, his death was almost as close as the assassination of John F. Kennedy is for Americans today. For all that, he was already a legend, a massively powerful symbolic figure. He had become a national oracle whose words and deeds were constantly invoked, in support of all manner of causes. Like others who have achieved the same kind of oracular status, from Jesus Christ to Karl Marx, Jefferson had a certain protean quality. He and his words could and did provide a source of support for almost any conceivable point of view on such fundamental questions as liberty, republicanism, democracy, equality, states rights, and, of course, slavery. If he had acquired the status of a demigod, he was also a very serviceable and adaptable one.[1]

It was the richness and diversity of the Jeffersonian legacy that enabled Lincoln, onetime Whig and then Republican, to resolve one particular problem. As well as being one of the great founding fathers of the American republic, Jefferson was also the founding father and patron saint of the opposing party, the Democratic Party (the choice of the name "Republican" for the new party born in the mid-1850s struck the right note and staked a claim for a share in the Jeffersonian legacy). Like other leaders of the new party in the 1850s and 1860s, Lincoln realized that Jefferson could be neither ignored nor condemned. Lincoln was always careful to accord him proper respect. Jefferson, he said in 1854, "was, is, and perhaps will continue to be, the most distinguished politician of our history." As presidential candidate in 1860, Lincoln dismissed as a base forgery a newspaper quotation from a speech he had allegedly made in 1844, in which Jefferson's character was denounced as repulsive. In a reply probably planted by Lincoln himself in a friendly newspaper, it was asserted that he had always held up Jefferson as "one of the ablest statesmen of his own or any other age" and had frequently referred to him as "one of the greatest apostles of freedom and free labor."[2]

Having established himself as a respectful admirer of Jefferson, Lincoln could go about the business of claiming his support for his own purposes and causes. He was even able to find Jefferson texts in support of such unlikely causes as the protective tariff and internal improvements. In the wake of the Supreme Court's *Dred Scott* v. *Sanford* decision in 1857, Lincoln gleefully cited Jefferson in support of the proposition that it was dangerous to put too much power into the hands of the judges.[3] On these issues, and on the great issues of liberty and equality, slavery and its further extension, Lincoln revised, adapted, extended, perhaps distorted, and certainly transformed Jefferson's meaning and purpose in order to serve his own ends, the needs of his party, and his conception of American democracy and nationhood. Like many others before and since, he made selective use of Jefferson's words and actions, reinterpreted or redefined his position, and extended their meaning and application in directions that might well have made them unrecognizable to Jefferson himself (just as Karl Marx would wish to distance himself from many modern Marxists, Thomas Jefferson would no doubt wish to disown some latter-day Jeffersonians).

The classic, and most frequently cited, example of Lincoln's appropriation of the Jeffersonian legacy occurred in April 1859, in his response to an invitation to a Jefferson birthday dinner in Boston. The letter displays Lincoln's art and his artfulness in full measure. Initially, he commented ironically on the way in which the Democratic Party and its opponents had swapped roles as champions of personal rights:

> The democracy of to-day hold the *liberty* of one man to be absolutely nothing, when in conflict with another man's right of *property* [i.e., property in slaves]. Republicans, on the contrary, are for both the *man* and the *dollar*; but in cases of conflict, the man *before* the dollar.

Then comes the opposite, and inevitable, story:

> I remember once being much amused at seeing two partially intoxicated men engage in a fight with their great-coats on, which fight, after a long, and rather harmless contest, ended in each having fought himself *out* of his own coat, and *into* that of the other. If the two leading parties of this day are really identical with the two in the days of Jefferson and Adams, they have performed about the same feat as the two drunken men.

Now the challenge was to save the principles of Jefferson from total overthrow.

> The principles of Jefferson are the definitions and axioms of free society. And yet they are denied, and evaded, with no small show of success. One dashingly calls them "glittering generalities"; another bluntly calls them "self-evident lies"; and still others insidiously argue that they apply only to "superior races."

Such views were the vanguard of returning despotism, and "we must repulse them, or they will subjugate us." Lincoln goes on:

> This is a world of compensations; and he who would *be* no slave, must consent to *have* no slave. . . . All honor to Jefferson—to the man, who, in the concrete pressure of a struggle for national independence by a single people, had the coolness, forecast, and capacity to introduce into a merely revolutionary document, an abstract truth, applicable to all men and all times, and so to embalm it there, that to-day, and in all coming days, it shall be a rebuke and a stumbling-block to the very harbingers of reappearing tyranny and oppression.[4]

Thus Lincoln was able both to voice his admiration for Thomas Jefferson and what he stood for and to adapt his principles to serve his own purposes. This recurrent theme of "respectful revisionism" in Lincoln's relationship with Jefferson may be explored and illustrated in relation to four separate but interrelated topics: Jefferson as author of the Declaration of Independence; Jefferson and free soil— that is to say, the limitation or prevention of the further spread of slavery; Jefferson and the debate over slavery itself—that is to say, both the proslavery and antislavery arguments; and, in conclusion, Jefferson's fundamental beliefs on questions of liberty, equality, democracy, and power.

The Declaration of Independence

Lincoln's respect for Jefferson stemmed above all else from his reverence for the Declaration of Independence. In February 1861, on his way to Washington, D.C., for his inauguration, he declared that he had "never had a feeling politically that did not spring from the sentiments embodied in the Declaration of Independence" (it may not be irrelevant to note that he was speaking in Independence Hall, Philadelphia, at the time).[5] The key phrases of the second paragraph of the Declaration, on the "self-evident truth" that "all men are created equal," on "unalienable rights" including "life, liberty and the pursuit of happiness," on governments deriving their just powers from the consent of the governed—these were at the very heart of Lincoln's political thinking, and he invoked them constantly.

Like Daniel Webster and other champions of the Union before him, Lincoln set great store by the argument that the Union pre-dated the Constitution, and that the Declaration of Independence was its founding document.[6] In that sense, the states were the creation of the Union, rather than vice versa. In his *Lincoln at Gettysburg*, Garry Wills places great emphasis upon the argument that Lincoln saw the Declaration as the fundamental statement of the ideals and principles of the American republic and that the Constitution of 1787 was simply one attempt at the practical application of those ideals. At any given moment, such endeavors would, of necessity, involve compromise with existing realities.[7]

This is not a new argument; it has been aired by earlier Lincoln scholars, and it is more solidly supported by the words of Lincoln himself than some of Wills's more speculative conclusions. In a speech on the *Dred Scott* decision of 1857, Lincoln argued that the authors of the Declaration were not asserting "the obvious untruth" that all men were then actually enjoying equality, nor that they were about to have it conferred upon them, nor that they were equal in all respects. The Declaration intended "simply to declare the *right*, so that the *enforcement* of it might follow as fast as circumstances should permit." It set up "a standard maxim for free society . . . constantly looked to, constantly labored for, and even though never perfectly attained, constantly approximated." Lincoln had always thought, he said, that "the Declaration contemplated the progressive improvement in the condition of all men everywhere."[8] He seemed to regard the concession in the Constitution to slavery and slave owners as a recognition of the immediate realities of the newly independent United States in the 1780s.

In 1858, one of the issues of heated debate between Lincoln and Stephen A. Douglas (and more generally between Northern Republicans and Southern defenders of slavery) was whether or not the bold declaration of 1776 that "all men are created equal" applied to blacks. Douglas insisted that it clearly did not. Not only Thomas Jefferson but many other signatories of the Declaration were slave owners and continued to be so. It would not have entered the heads of the men of 1776, he believed, that their Declaration would embrace blacks. In the Galesburg debate with Lincoln, Douglas declared frankly that "in my opinion, this government was made by our fathers on the white basis. It was made by white men for the benefit of white men and their posterity forever."

Lincoln's response took various forms, at different times and in different places. He claimed that, from 1776 until about three years before his debate with Douglas, no one, to his knowledge, had affirmed that blacks were excluded from the Declaration (he did not acknowledge that the explanation may well have been that this was taken for granted). It was only in the mid-1850s that the exigencies of the Democratic Party, and its desperate need to placate the South, had led to the assertion that blacks were excluded. As for Jefferson himself, Lincoln conceded that he had retained his slaves, but he had also agonized over the danger slavery had posed for the Republic. On this very subject, Jefferson, he noted, had "trembled for his country when he remembered that God was just." He suggested that a little trembling of the same kind from Douglas would be welcome.[9]

At the same time, Lincoln was careful to limit the implications of any commitment to inclusion of blacks within the Declaration that "all men are created equal." In his debates with Douglas, as elsewhere, he was always aware of the need to appease the feelings and prejudices of his own electorate—and he was frank at times in declaring his own views about the superiority of the white race. He believed that the physical difference between the two races "will probably forever forbid their living together on the footing of perfect equality." The Declaration of Independence, he thought, did not mean that all men were created equal in all respects. But, he went on,

> there is no reason in the world why the Negro is not entitled to all the rights enumerated in the Declaration of Independence—the right of life, liberty and the pursuit of happiness. I hold that he is as much entitled to these as the white man. I agree with Judge Douglas that he is not my equal in many respects, certainly not in color—perhaps not in intellectual or moral endowments; but in the right to eat the bread without leave of anybody else which his own hand earns, *he is my equal and the equal of Judge Douglas, and the equal of every other living man.*[10]

Here, in these remarkable final words, Lincoln is surely adding new social and economic dimensions to the words of the Declaration. He is stretching Jefferson's meaning to its limit, and perhaps beyond; this is not so much revision as redefinition.

In debating these issues with Douglas, Lincoln earned high marks for ingenuity in argument and for gaining the more elevated moral ground. However, if the prize were to have gone to whichever protagonist had the better of the historical argument, and whichever showed more respect for the historical evidence, Douglas might well have won it on the ground that he was less guilty of distortion, or creative rewriting, of Jefferson's record.[11]

Against the background of Northern disputes on this issue, it is worth glancing at the Southern attitude toward Jefferson as the author of the statement that all men are created equal. Merrill Peterson has depicted Southern embarrassment on this point. It was explained away as sentimental rhetoric, or as having no possible application to blacks, or it was blamed on sinister French influences upon Jefferson or upon his irreligion. In the immediate antebellum period, some of the more extreme proslavery ideologues, notably George Fitzhugh, were ready to dismiss Jefferson as a wild theorist, and a dangerous revolutionary who had earned the title of godfather of abolitionism. Fitzhugh even dismissed the Declaration of Independence as a collection of "bombastic absurdities" and a powder cask of abstractions. Its authors were "silly, thoughtless, half-informed, speculative charlatans."[12]

In his Farewell Address to the Senate in January 1861, the future president of the Confederacy, Jefferson Davis, explained the decision of his state of Mississippi to secede in the following terms:

She has heard proclaimed the theory that all men are created free and equal, and this made the basis of an attack upon her social institutions; and the sacred Declaration of Independence has been invoked to maintain the position of the equality of the races. That Declaration of Independence is to be construed by the circumstances and purposes for which it was made. The communities were declaring their independence; the people of those communities were asserting that no man was born—to use the language of Mr. Jefferson—booted and spurred to ride over the rest of mankind; that men were created equal—meaning the men of the political community, that there was no divine right to rule; that no man inherited the right to govern; that there were no classes by which power and place descended to families, but that all stations were equally within the grasp of each member of the body-politic. These were the great principles they announced; these were the purposes for which they made their declaration; these were the ends to which their enunciation was directed. They have no reference to the slave.[13]

Not for the first or the last time, Jeffersonian arguments on one side of the question were deployed to counter Jeffersonian arguments advanced on the other. What is striking about the statement of Jefferson Davis is the confidence and specificity with which he pronounced upon the meaning of the Declaration of Independence and the strict limits of its application. In their 1858 debates, both Lincoln and Douglas discussed the Declaration in more general, and often more speculative, terms. What distinguished Lincoln from both Douglas and Davis was his readiness to expand upon the few brief key phrases of the Preamble to the Declaration and to extend their meaning to meet the condition of mid-nineteenth-century America. Five years later, he would continue that process, with much greater dramatic effect, in a few brief phrases of his own, in the Gettysburg Address.

The Northwest Ordinance of 1787
and the Restriction of Slavery

The question of the further extension of slavery was, of course, the headline political issue of the antebellum period. The desire to restrict or prevent any such extension inspired the Wilmot Proviso in 1846, fueled the outcry against the Kansas-Nebraska Act in 1854, and became the central plank in the platform of the Republican Party. Naturally, those who championed the policy of free soil searched for the most respectable authorities, and the most compelling precedents, to support their case. They went back to the Northwest Ordinance of 1787, passed by Congress under the Articles of Confederation, at the very time when a convention in Philadelphia was drafting a new constitution. In its plan for the future of the Northwest Territory—the vast area between the Ohio River and the Great Lakes—the ordinance contained a clause excluding slavery from the whole region.[14]

In 1830, in his debate with Robert Hayne, Daniel Webster advanced the claims of his fellow New Englander, Nathan Dane, to be the chief author of that provision.[15] During the 1830s and 1840s, there was a lively political and historical debate over the authorship of the ordinance of 1787. One school of thought claimed that Jefferson was its true father, but his paternity in this case is at least as difficult to prove as in the matter of Sally Hemings's mulatto offspring. The great obstacle to awarding him the credit for the ordinance is that he was on the other side of the Atlantic at the time. But only the fainthearted were deterred by this objection. The case for Jefferson rested upon the fundamental principles of the document rather than direct authorship. First, he had done much to inspire Virginia's cession of its claims to the western lands. Second, and more important, he had drafted the earlier ordinance of 1784 that provided for the exclusion of slavery from all the territories of the United States (not just the Northwest Territory)—but this was not to take effect until 1800. The ordinance of 1784 remained a dead letter, but, so the argument runs, it inspired the more limited exclusion of slavery in the Ordinance of 1787. The modern historian of the ordinance, Peter Onuf, argues that Jefferson established the basic principle that the Northwest Territory was to be an area for the expansion of freedom. The final wording of the 1787 ordinance was simply the best available deal on slavery at the time.[16]

The historical debate over the direct or indirect authorship of the ordinance of 1787 spilled into the turbulent politics of slavery extension. Merrill Peterson claims that the Wilmot Proviso of 1846 was widely referred to as the Jefferson Proviso, though exactly how widely may be a matter for debate. Certainly, Thomas Hart Benton so described it, but Benton was never renowned for understatement. The Northwest Ordinance was to Jefferson, he exulted, what the *Republic* was to Plato and *Utopia* was to Thomas More. Salmon P. Chase also linked the Wilmot Proviso to Jefferson (it is worthy of note that both Benton and Chase were Democrats).[17]

Among later participants in the debate over the provenance of the ordinance of 1787 was Abraham Lincoln. His language was more measured than that of Benton, but his grasp of the actual history was little more secure. In various speeches in 1854, he attacked the Kansas-Nebraska Act for overturning decades of federal policy that had restricted slavery in the territories and excluded it from large parts of them. These attacks involved brief and somewhat erratic excursions into American history—and they generally began with the ordinance of 1787. In Lincoln's eyes, the first hero of the story was none other than Thomas Jefferson who, although a citizen of the slave state of Virginia and a slaveholder himself, had initiated the policy of slavery exclusion from the Northwest Territory. Jefferson's precise paternal or authorial relationship with the ordinance of 1787 posed no great problem to a master politician and wordsmith like Abraham Lincoln. In a speech of September 26, 1854, he said: "Under the auspices of Jefferson, an Ordinance was enacted in 1787 prohibiting slavery forever in that territory."[18] ("Under the auspices of" was the perfect phrase to cover a multitude of sins or to evade awkward historical questions.)

In his Peoria speech a few weeks later, Lincoln went out of his way to make the point that the policy of prohibiting slavery in new territory originated with the author of the Declaration of Independence. A speech delivered five years later, in 1859, suggests that Lincoln (and Douglas, whom he was seeking to rebut) had been brushing up on their history during the intervening years. Now Lincoln made his first direct reference to the earlier ordinance of 1784, which was clearly Jefferson's handiwork, and he devoted a passage in his speech to an elaborate attempt to relate that abortive measure to the ordinance passed three years later.[19]

Harry Jaffa insists that, for Lincoln, exclusion of slavery from the territories was a matter of both legality and morality. He saw laws such as the ordinance of 1787, which restricted slavery in the territories, as an expression of the moral sense of the people. Jaffa continues:

> The moral sense which condemned slavery naturally demanded a law preventing its extension, and the demand for the law was simultaneously a demand for the preservation of that moral sense. Lincoln was certain, not that the Northwest Ordinance as such had excluded slavery from the territory north of the Ohio, but that the moral condemnation of slavery which demanded and was embodied in the ordinance had kept it out.[20]

Jefferson was an extremely convenient witness in support of this argument. As a slaveholder deeply concerned about the problems posed by slavery for the future of the Republic, he had proposed its exclusion from all the territories in the ordinance of 1784 and had thus influenced, however indirectly, the more limited exclusion embodied in the ordinance of 1787.

While Lincoln was pressing Jefferson into service in support of the cause of free soil, Stephen A. Douglas and his supporters were insisting that the policy of popular sovereignty—of letting the people of the territory decide for themselves the question of slavery or no slavery—sprang from pure Jeffersonian sources. Its emphasis on local self-rule and noninterference by the federal government, it was claimed, was fully in accord with the core principles of Jeffersonian democracy. Meanwhile, the third party in the triangular debate over slavery in the territories—the slaveholding South—was only too willing to point to the apparent absurdity of citing the large-scale slave owner Thomas Jefferson in support of an antislavery policy. Once again, Jefferson was, or could be made to be, all things to all men.[21] No one was more adept than Abraham Lincoln at playing this particular game, but it was a much more difficult challenge when the issue was not the exclusion of slavery from the territories, but the existence of slavery itself.

Jefferson: Proslavery or Antislavery?

When the focus is shifted from the further extension of slavery to the institution of slavery as it existed in the Southern states, Jefferson had rather less to offer as a guide to Lincoln's thinking. However, Jefferson's thoughts on the subject exercised some indirect influence at least, as the earlier discussion of the Declaration of Independence, the Northwest Ordinance, and the question of slavery in the territories has already indicated. Reflecting the position of the Republican Party in the 1850s, the prepresidential Lincoln was antislavery but not abolitionist. In other words, he opposed any further extension of slavery and he was unambiguous in condemning slavery as morally repugnant, but he respected the convention that slavery in the states where it already existed was beyond the reach of the federal government. As president in the 1860s, engaged in a life-and-death struggle to save the Union, Lincoln's thoughts and actions on slavery were shaped by the immediate exigencies of war (and wartime politics), rather than by the more distant and deeply divided Jeffersonian legacy.

Basically, the choice for would-be interpreters of Jefferson on slavery was (and is) between his deeds and his words. Defenders of slavery could simply point to the fact that, whatever he may have said or written on the subject, Jefferson remained a substantial slave owner throughout his life; indeed, he steadily increased his slave-holding and sought to recover slaves who ran away. On the other hand, antislavery spokesmen, including Lincoln himself, could point to Jefferson's declared intention to free his slaves, his laments over the evil of slavery, his attempt to restrict its spread, and his fears for the damage it would inflict upon the long-term health of the American republic.[22]

Whatever the ideals that found their highest expression in the Declaration of Independence, Jefferson was also a practical man and a subtle and resourceful politician, living in a particular place at a particular time. A favorable interpretation of his record would say that he looked to patience, persuasion, and perseverance over a long period to bring slavery to an end. Such an approach has attracted harsh criticism from both Jefferson's contemporaries and from historians in our own time. John Quincy Adams, never notable for the charity of his judgments, deplored Jefferson's unwillingness to take any risks in order to bring slavery to an end; but then, he added, "Mr. Jefferson had not the spirit of martyrdom."[23] In his book *The Road to Disunion*, William Freehling portrays Jefferson as an "apologizing procrastinator" on the subject of slavery.[24]

It would be hard to better Peterson's description of the tension between the commands of conscience and the limitations imposed by history, as the unfortunate Jefferson was posthumously pushed and pulled in both directions by the serried ranks of proslavery and antislavery forces:

> Jefferson was the crucial figure in American history both for slavery and for abolition. Partisans on both sides sought justification in him, while they also indicted him for their distresses. Jefferson, the Virginia planter, who had written the Kentucky Resolutions, and established the Republican party under Southern leadership, had also penned the Declaration of Independence, raised up the democratic spirit, and opposed slavery all his life. Behind the facade of Jeffersonian politics, the abolitionists discovered the Slave Power. And the republican slavocracy discovered that Jefferson's visionary ideas had produced a democratic giant. The *real* Jefferson, if he ever existed, was lost from sight as the fragments of his mind were parceled out among bitter antagonists and as legacies of discord were laid to him.[25]

When that discord culminated in the Civil War, the clash of arms drowned out the voice of Thomas Jefferson. As Lincoln pursued his complicated and circuitous route toward emancipation, there were no further invocations of the name of the sage of Monticello. It is true that, in the Gettysburg Address, Lincoln portrayed the war as a test of the viability of a nation based on the principles of the Declaration of Independence. But, in its 272 words, the address makes no specific reference to slaves or slavery, or to whether African Americans were to share fully in the equality to which that new nation had been dedicated.[26] In his Second Inaugural Address in March 1865, Lincoln interpreted the war as a divine punishment for the sin of slavery, but he made no reference to the question of equality or equal rights.

On the other hand, he had pressed hard for the Thirteenth Amendment to the Constitution, which abolished slavery once and for all, and which, in the eyes of some modern constitutional historians, contained within it the seeds of all the subsequent attempts to legislate equal rights during Reconstruction. But the tragic death of Lincoln in the moment of victory has denied to subsequent generations any certain knowledge of where the Great Emancipator's intellectual development, moral vision, and political acumen might have led him during the years of postwar Reconstruction. On the question of the long-term relationship of black Americans to the proposition that all men are created equal, Jeffersonian ambivalence gave way to Lincolnian ambivalence. For the good of their own reputations, in relation to this issue at least, Jefferson probably lived rather too long, while Lincoln did not live long enough.[27]

Jefferson, Lincoln, and the Meaning of Liberty and Equality

Lincoln had a long history of respect and admiration for Jeffersonian principles of liberty and equality. However, during the 1850s, and much more during the Civil War, he carried his own conception, and implementation, of those principles into areas untrodden, or indeed unimagined, by Thomas Jefferson. In the face of economic growth and social change, and then of civil war, this was hardly surprising. Gabor Boritt quotes W. H. Auden on this point: "The words of a dead man / Are modified in the guts of the living."[28] If the Jeffersonian legacy was to retain any value and purpose for later generations, it could not be frozen in time, or treated as something akin to a museum exhibit. If it was to live, it had to evolve.

The interesting and important question to ask is how, and in what direction, did Lincoln adapt or amend, transform or transcend, Jeffersonian ideas on liberty and equality? In his recent book, Garry Wills claims that, in the Gettysburg Address, Lincoln converted the

Declaration of Independence into a founding constitutional document and then proceeded to give it new meaning by making a national commitment to equality its central principle. "By accepting the Gettysburg Address," Wills says, "[and] its concept of a single people dedicated to a proposition [that all men are created equal], we have been changed. Because of it, we live in a different America."[29] These are dramatic words, but their meaning is not fully worked out by Wills whose rhetoric is not always matched or supported by sustained analysis.

It is to be noted, however, that Jefferson's "self-evident truth" that all men are created equal has become Lincoln's "proposition"—and a proposition is something that needs to be demonstrated and confirmed in action. In his sensitive discussion of the Gettysburg Address, Phillip Paludan suggests that Lincoln was seeking to integrate three basic American ideas of democracy, equality, and government. Before the Civil War, democracy and equality had often been on opposite sides of the political debate; for example, in the clash between Douglas's belief in a "popular sovereignty" that permitted a form of government under which blacks were denied equality and Lincoln's claim that the statement in the Declaration of Independence that all men are created equal embraced blacks as well as whites. In the reconciliation of the ideals of democracy and equality, and in the demonstration and implementation of the principle that all men are created equal, government had a crucial role. According to Paludan, "an older idea of liberty from government was being transformed into a vision of liberty because of government."[30]

Paludan's interpretation builds upon the work of other historians. In their constitutional history of the Civil War, Harold Hyman and William Weicek offer a similar assessment of the direction in which Lincoln's thinking on liberty and equality was carried by the pressures of the war for the Union and wartime emancipation. In 1865, they say, Lincoln had moved "beyond Jefferson's position that liberty existed so that individuals might, on their own, seek and protect their rights, to one that perceived liberty as equality, as obligations under society actively to support individuals in their efforts to enjoy rights."[31] The Thirteenth Amendment was a major breakthrough in that direction, and it paved the way for the Fourteenth and Fifteenth Amendments to carry the process further.

James McPherson has advanced a similar explanation of the transformation in the relationship between liberty and power as a result of the Civil War and Reconstruction, and he sees Lincoln as a major agent of that change. McPherson borrows from Isaiah Berlin the distinction between negative and positive liberty; negative liberty is essentially freedom *from*, while positive liberty is essentially freedom *to* (some critics object to this distinction between two kinds of liberty, but, if they are used as descriptive terms, without necessarily conveying a value judgment, they can promote and clarify understanding of the subject).

In McPherson's view, the American tradition (and certainly the Jeffersonian tradition) before the Civil War was essentially one of negative liberty. The great threat to liberty came from government and its coercive power; the Constitution, and notably the Bill of Rights, enshrined the concept of negative liberty. They specified in great detail what government could not do. In contrast, the Thirteenth, Fourteenth, and Fifteenth amendments established the power of government to preserve and protect the rights and liberties of citizens. They enshrined the principle of positive liberty. Instead of being the great threat to liberty, the federal government became its guarantor. Through his words at Gettysburg, his actions in promulgating the Emancipation Proclamation, and his pressing for the Thirteenth Amendment, Lincoln was a leading actor, perhaps the leading actor, in that transformation scene.[32]

There is at least one other way in which the Jeffersonian view of liberty and equality was extended, and perhaps transformed, in the age of Lincoln. The concept of liberty in the mind of Jefferson, as with most of the founding fathers, was closely linked to the rights of property. A key element in liberty was independence, and property gave one independence. Those who did not own property, and therefore had to work for others, could not be truly independent. By Lincoln's day, there was a much more substantial number of non-property owners in American society. Partly for this reason, it was understandable that Lincoln should often speak of liberty and equality in terms of opportunity and equality of opportunity. As Gabor Boritt has reminded us over and over again, Lincoln attached enormous importance to "the right to rise"—"the principle that clears the path for all—gives hope to all—and, by consequence, enterprize and industry to all." Boritt narrows the argument by his insistence that the mainspring of Lincoln's thought was economic and that "the central idea of America was economic." But, surely, "the right to rise," as Lincoln saw it, involved much more than economic improvement and material advancement; it embraced a whole set of social, cultural, and ideological values, most of them closely bound up with the Republican concept of "free labor."[33]

The Jeffersonian definition of rights would not have included the right to rise, as Lincoln understood it; Jefferson's concept of equal rights scarcely extended to equality of opportunity. Two quotations from Lincoln may illustrate just how, in paying his respects to Jefferson, he was extending the meaning of rights and liberties. In that same speech at Independence Hall in Philadelphia where he acknowledged his profound debt to the Declaration of Independence, Lincoln affirmed that the liberty enshrined in the Declaration "gave promise that in due time the weights should be lifted from the shoulders of *all* men, and that *all* should have an equal chance. This," said Lincoln, "is the sentiment embodied in that Declaration of Independence." But is it? In any event, just over four months later, in his first message to Congress, President Lincoln put the same idea into more eloquent words:

> This is essentially a People's contest. On the side of the Union, it is a struggle for maintaining in the world, that form, and substance of government, whose leading object is, to elevate the condition of men—to lift artificial weights from all shoulders—to clear the paths of laudable pursuit for all—to afford all an unfettered start, and a fair chance, in the race of life.[34]

Perhaps the conclusion to be drawn is that the Jeffersonian concept and structure of rights and liberties, in their original form, were only viable in an era and a polity of minimal government, decentralization, states rights, and local self-rule. As such, they were inevitably overtaken by the evolution of a more complex, interdependent, modern society—and then by a crisis of civil war. Certainly, during the war, in the Northern backlash against the kind of states rights doctrine that shattered the Union, Jefferson came in for severe criticism. Andrew Dixon White, who, before the war, had been eagerly planning a biography of Jefferson, dropped the project, and later castigated the theory of states rights:

> Perhaps no doctrine ever cost any other country so dear as Jefferson's pet theory of State rights cost the United States: Nearly a million of lives lost on battlefields, in prisons, and in hospitals; nearly ten thousand millions of dollars poured into the gulfs of hatred.[35]

But Jeffersonian ideas and ideals were not, in fact, done to death by the Civil War. For that, some of the credit belongs to Abraham Lincoln, as Peterson has observed. Lincoln's devotion to the Declaration of Independence, and his insistence upon a strong democratic basis for the new nation that emerged from the war, meant that, even if he transformed much of the Jeffersonian legacy, he also preserved much of it. Credit belongs, too, to Jefferson himself, and for that very ability to be so many things to so many different people, which has often inspired criticism or skepticism. In Peterson's words:

> Jefferson . . . was protean, capable of infinite reinterpretation within the shared faith of the American people. The same Jefferson who was implicated in the Union's tragedy survived as the symbol of its irreversible ideals and its democratic processes.[36]

In his own presidential Inaugural Address in 1801, Jefferson wrote:

> I know, indeed, that some honest men fear that a republican government can not be strong, that this Government is not strong enough; . . . I believe this, on the contrary, the strongest government on earth. I believe it the only one where every man, at the call of the law, would fly to the standard of the law, and would meet invasions of the public order, as his own personal concern. Sometimes it is said that man can not be trusted with the government of himself. Can he, then, be trusted with the government of others? Or have we found angels in the forms of kings to govern him? Let history answer this question.[37]

Sixty years later, history was forced to provide an answer. The Southern secessionists, under the Jeffersonian banner of states rights, challenged that republican government, threatened the public order that it protected, and tested its true strength. A mass of citizens did indeed fly to the standard of the law. With their support, that government, which Jefferson had proclaimed as the strongest on earth, proved strong enough to meet the challenge, though at a cost beyond Jefferson's blackest nightmares. As he always had done, Lincoln continued to respect the Jeffersonian legacy, but, in the process of securing its survival, he redefined large parts of it. In Lincoln's hands, it was respectful revisionism that won the day.

Notes

1. By far the fullest and most authoritative study of the Jeffersonian legacy, and the fluctuations in Jefferson's reputation, is Merrill D. Peterson, *The Jefferson Image in the American Mind* (New York: Oxford University Press, 1960); hereinafter cited as *Jefferson Image*. I wish to acknowledge my debt to Professor Peterson's work, on which I have relied heavily throughout this essay.

2. Lincoln, speech at Peoria, Illinois, October 16, 1854, and letter to Anson G. Chester, September 5, 1860, in *The Collected Works of Abraham*

Lincoln, Roy P. Basler, ed., 8 vols. (New Brunswick, NJ: Rutgers University Press, 1953), 2:249, 4:111–112, respectively; hereinafter cited as *Collected Works*.

3. Campaign circular from Whig Committee, March 4, 1843; Lincoln speech in U.S. House of Representatives on Internal Improvements, June 20, 1848; speech at Springfield, Illinois, July 17, 1858; and Fragment: Notes for Speech, August 21, 1858, in *Collected Works*, 1:310, 485, 487; 2:516–517, 552, respectively.

4. Lincoln to Henry L. Pierce and others, April 6, 1859, in *Collected Works*, 3:374–376. The phrase "glittering generalities" is probably a reference to Rufus Choate's letter to the Maine Whig State Central Committee, August 9, 1856, which, in an attack on the new Republican Party, spoke of "the glittering and sounding generalities of natural right which make up the Declaration of Independence." See *The Works of Rufus Choate, with a Memoir of His Life*, Samuel G. Brown, ed., 2 vols. (Boston: Little, Brown, 1862), 1:215; hereinafter cited as *Works of Choate*.

5. Lincoln, speech in Independence Hall, Philadelphia, February 22, 1861, in *Collected Works*, 4:240.

6. See, for example, Charles M. Wiltse and Alan R. Berolzheimer, eds., *The Papers of Daniel Webster: Speeches and Formal Writings, 1800–1833*, 2 vols. (Hanover, NH: University Press of New England, 1986), 1:330, 339–340, 577–578; hereinafter cited as *Papers of Daniel Webster*.

7. Garry Wills, *Lincoln at Gettysburg: The Words That Remade America* (New York: Simon & Schuster, 1992), 85–89, 101–103, 129–132, 145–147.

8. Lincoln, speech at Springfield, Illinois, June 26, 1857, in *Collected Works*, 2:406–407.

9. Fifth debate, Lincoln with Stephen A. Douglas at Galesburg, Illinois, October 7, 1858, in *Collected Works*, 3:216, 220.

10. First debate, Lincoln with Stephen A. Douglas at Ottawa, Illinois, August 21, 1858, in *Collected Works*, 3:16.

11. For a thoughtful assessment of the historical arguments of Lincoln and Douglas in relation to the Declaration of Independence, see Harry V. Jaffa, *Crisis of the House Divided: An Interpretation of the Lincoln-Douglas Debates* (New York: Doubleday, 1959), chap. 14, esp. 317–329. A reappraisal of the debates has been facilitated by the recent publication of a new text, which relies on actual transcripts, rather than the revised and "polished" versions produced by partisans of the two speakers; see Harold Holzer, ed., *The Lincoln-Douglas Debates: The First Complete Unexpurgated Text* (New York: HarperCollins, 1993).

12. *Jefferson Image*, 164–170.

13. Linda L. Crist and Mary S. Dix, eds., *The Papers of Jefferson Davis*, 7 vols. (Baton Rouge: Louisiana State University Press, 1992) 7:21.

14. The best study of the ordinance is Peter S. Onuf, *Statehood and Union: A History of the Northwest Ordinance* (Bloomington: Indiana University Press, 1987); hereinafter cited as *Statehood and Union*.

15. *Papers of Daniel Webster*, 1:293–294, 297–298; Maurice G. Baxter, *One*

and Inseparable: Daniel Webster and the Union (Cambridge, MA: Belknap Press of Harvard University Press, 1984), 184–185.

16. *Statehood and Union*, 141–145.

17. *Jefferson Image*, 189–192.

18. Lincoln, speech at Bloomington, Illinois, September 26, 1854, in *Collected Works*, 2:235. See also Lincoln, speech at Springfield, Illinois, October 4, 1854, in *Collected Works*, 2:240–241.

19. Lincoln, speech at Peoria, Illinois, October 16, 1854, in *Collected Works*, 2:249–250; Lincoln, speech at Columbus, Ohio, September 16, 1859, in *Collected Works*, 3:414–415.

20. Jaffa, *Crisis of the House Divided*, 296.

21. *Jefferson Image*, 195–197, 209–214.

22. Ibid., 187–189. For a fuller discussion of Jefferson and slavery, see John C. Miller, *The Wolf by the Ears: Thomas Jefferson and Slavery* (New York: Free Press, 1977). For a vigorous brief discussion, sharply critical of Jefferson, see William W. Freehling, *The Road to Disunion: Secessionists at Bay, 1776–1854* (Oxford, England: Oxford University Press, 1990), 121–131.

23. *Jefferson Image*, 174.

24. Freehling, *Road to Disunion*, 142.

25. *Jefferson Image*, 188.

26. Wills, *Lincoln at Gettysburg*, 90, draws attention to these omissions.

27. Lincoln to John D. Defrees, February 8, 1864, note 1; Reply to Committee Notifying Lincoln of His Renomination, June 9, 1864; Annual Message to Congress, December 6, 1864; Resolution Submitting the Thirteenth Amendment to the States, February 1, 1865; and Second Inaugural Address, March 4, 1865, in *Collected Works*, 7:172–173, 380–382; 8:149, 253–255, 332–333, respectively. Two thoughtful discussions of Lincoln's ideas and attitudes on race are: George M. Fredrickson, *The Arrogance of Race: Historical Perspectives on Slavery, Racism, and Social Inequality* (Middletown, CT: Wesleyan University Press, 1988), chap. 3; and Don E. Fehrenbacher, *Lincoln in Text and Context: Collected Essays* (Stanford, CA: Stanford University Press, 1987), chap. 8.

28. Gabor S. Boritt, *Lincoln and the Economics of the American Dream* (Memphis, TN: Memphis State University Press, 1978), 158.

29. Wills, *Lincoln at Gettysburg*, 145–147.

30. Phillip Paludan, *The Presidency of Abraham Lincoln* (Lawrence: University Press of Kansas, 1994), 230.

31. Harold M. Hyman and William C. Weicek, *Equal Justice Under Law: Constitutional Development, 1835–1875* (New York: Harper & Row, 1982), 276–278.

32. James M. McPherson, *Abraham Lincoln and the Second American Revolution* (Oxford, England: Oxford University Press, 1991), 61–64, 136–138, and, more generally, chaps. 3 and 7.

33. Boritt, *Lincoln and Economics*, esp. 157–162. For a concise and convenient summary of Boritt's thesis, see his "The Right to Rise," in *The*

Public and Private Lincoln: Contemporary Perspectives, Cullom Davis, ed. (Carbondale: Southern Illinois University Press, 1979), 57–70. The classic study of the Republican free labor ideology is Eric Foner, *Free Soil, Free Labor, Free Men: The Ideology of the Republican Party before the Civil War* (Oxford, England: Oxford University Press, 1970).

34. Lincoln, speech in Independence Hall, Philadelphia, February 22, 1861, and Message to Congress in Special Session, July 4, 1861, in *Collected Works*, 4:240, 438.

35. *Jefferson Image*, 216.

36. Ibid., 226.

37. James D. Richardson, *A Compilation of the Messages and Papers of the Presidents, 1789–1897*, 10 vols. (Washington, DC: Government Printing Office, 1896), 1:322.

10

Jeffersonianism in the Progressive Era

Jeffrey Leigh Sedgwick

There is a profound irony in imagining that Thomas Jefferson could have left a legacy to the Progressive Era. In the popular mind, Jefferson will forever be associated with rural life, agriculture, limited government, and his beloved state of Virginia. None of these associations is particularly representative of the Progressive Era. The end of the nineteenth century and the beginning of the twentieth were marked by a decisive turning away from rural and agrarian life in the United States; urban and industrial development aided by a national government increasingly dominant over the states took center stage.

The presidential election of 1896 signified a rejection of agrarianism as reflected in William Jennings Bryan's famous "Cross of Gold" speech on acceptance of the Democratic Party's nomination for president. The victorious Republican Party adopted the full lunch bucket and belching smokestack as partisan symbols. The late-nineteenth-century emergence of a new American state signaled the rejection of traditional limited government. A professional civil service, a reformed and reorganized military, and an energized (and energizing) executive branch headed by a powerful president firmly ensconced in his bully pulpit characterized this new way of government. In short, there is much to suggest there is very little Jeffersonian legacy to the Progressive Era.

We should not be too hasty in this judgment, however, for there is much evidence that Thomas Jefferson *did* leave an important and substantial legacy to the Progressive Era. Herbert Croly characterized his, and Theodore Roosevelt's, "New Nationalism" as an attempt to adapt Hamiltonian means to Jeffersonian ends.[1] Woodrow Wilson consciously posed his "New Freedom" as an attempt to protect Jeffersonian values from the encroachment of industrialism and corporate capitalism.[2] That the principal intellectual architects of progressivism in both the Republican and Democratic Parties cited Jefferson is suggestive but hardly conclusive. To understand fully Jefferson's legacy to the Progressive Era, we must first explore the fundamentals of both Jeffersonianism and progressivism.

Jefferson's Liberal Republicanism

The inherent complexity of Thomas Jefferson's political philosophy, also the variety of roles he played during his lifetime, makes understanding his thought extraordinarily difficult. It is a challenging task to sort what is said for partisan or polemical purpose from what the author thinks to be true; this is especially so in a short essay. It seems, however, that Jefferson's political legacy can best be understood in light of his attitudes toward science, toward history, and toward liberty.

In his essay in this volume, Robert Faulkner illuminates the close connection between the Enlightenment and the "new science of politics," which sought, as its end, the liberation of humanity from both civil and ecclesiastical moralities. Faulkner sees Jefferson as an enthusiastic student of the new science of politics, a partisan and propagandist of both liberty and science. Consider in this regard Jefferson's own sense of his legacy: the Declaration of Independence; the Virginia Statute for Religious Freedom; and the University of Virginia. Jefferson had a strong faith in modern science (taught in properly formed public academies) to better man's estate and to lead to a progressive improvement in human nature (befitting people for selfrule in matters both secular and sacred).

This attitude toward science and the improvement of human nature set the Virginian Jefferson radically at odds with John Adams of Puritan Massachusetts. Adams was profoundly skeptical that human nature either had improved or could improve much at all; Jefferson took a decidedly different tack. Looking back on the partisan quarrels of their earlier years, Jefferson wrote to Adams that:

> One of the questions you know on which our parties took dif
> ferent sides, was on the improvability of the human mind, in

science, in ethics, in government etc. Those who advocated reformation of institutions, pari passu, with the progress of science, maintained that no definite limits could be assigned to that progress. The enemies of reform, on the other hand, denied improvement, and advocated steady adherence to the principles, practices and institutions of our fathers, which they represented as the consummation of wisdom, and akmé of excellence, beyond which the human mind could never advance.[3]

This disagreement over the efficacy of science (or anything else, for that matter) to alter human nature underlies the very real and heated disagreements between American Anglophiles (the Adams-led Federalists) and Francophiles (Jefferson's Democratic Republicans) in the 1790s.

One other aspect of Jefferson's faith in science is notable as well. As Faulkner notes, Jefferson considered Francis Bacon, John Locke, and Isaac Newton to be the three most outstanding philosophers in human history. Significantly, both Bacon and Locke (proponents of the experimental method and materialist psychology) rank higher than Newton in Jefferson's estimate. This may well prefigure the Progressive Era, where the paradigmatic scientist will have changed from Isaac Newton, the physical scientist with his central image of a solar system held in a dynamic equilibrium of countervailing forces, to Charles Darwin, a biological scientist with his central image of evolutionary and progressive development.

Jefferson's treatment of history similarly points to his emphasis on progress and change. He does not consider history a seamless narrative of a people's or nation's development from which one cannot easily escape. Rather, Jefferson treats it as a collection of particular case studies from which one may, as an astute observer, induce universal rules of human behavior.[4]

In his essay in this volume, Howard Temperley correctly calls attention to Jefferson's odd penchant for collecting things—odd because of both his precarious personal finances and the eclecticism of his tastes. I think Temperley misses, however, the instructive point, for Jefferson treated acquisitions as he treated natural history: an aggregation of discrete and apparently unrelated items from which he was free to derive universal principles. I note only in passing that universals are by their nature *general*; consequently, they who dare to universalize will, no doubt, find themselves charged with purveying "glittering generalities" at odds with the particularities of their own lives.

Compare Jefferson's treatment of history, both natural and civil, to that of Edmund Burke's, for example. For Burke, the narrative history of a people contained natural wisdom, born of experience, from which they could not and ought not try to escape. A community was defined by the very particularity of its experience over time in a defined geographic place. In contrast, consider Jefferson's plantation home, his community: a Palladian mansion set atop a hill in Piedmont, Virginia, crammed with European artwork, Indian artifacts, skeletons and bones collected on the Lewis and Clark expedition, scientific instruments and inventions of all sorts. It was an extraordinary and eccentric place, given unity and coherence only by the tastes and interests of its owner.

The idiosyncrasy of Jefferson's tastes and interests, reflected in his acquisitions, undermines the argument that Jefferson was a civic humanist or classical republican. Paul Rahe points out in his essay herein that classical or traditional republicanism promoted martial qualities among the citizenry, praised devotion to the community and a willingness to sacrifice oneself for the common good, and opposed change since change was identified with decay rather than with progress.

On all these counts, Jefferson was no classical or traditional republican. Among his generation, both George Washington and Alexander Hamilton better embody martial virtue. Jefferson's obvious willingness to spend himself into debt to build, furnish, and maintain his elaborate personal mansions (his primary home, Monticello, and his "hunting lodge," Poplar Forest) gives little evidence of a willingness to sacrifice personal interest to the transcendent good of the community. Most important, Jefferson's enthusiasm for progress and change shows that he was no advocate of classical republicanism.

The persistent image of Jefferson as a classical or traditional republican owes much to a fundamental misunderstanding of eighteenth-century agriculture. Jefferson held a special regard for the agrarian way of life. In an oft-quoted passage from his *Notes on the State of Virginia*, Jefferson said that:

> Those who labour in the earth are the chosen people of God, if ever he had a chosen people, whose breasts he has made his peculiar deposit for substantial and genuine virtue. It is the focus in which he keeps alive that sacred fire, which otherwise might escape from the face of the earth. Corruption of morals in the mass of cultivators is a phaenomenon of which no age nor nation has furnished an example. It is the mark set on those, who not looking up to heaven, to their own soil and industry, as does the husbandman, for their subsistence, depend for it on the casualties and

caprice of customers. Dependance begets subservience and venal-
ity, suffocates the germ of virtue, and prepares fit tools for the
designs of ambition. This, the natural progress and consequence
of the arts, has sometimes perhaps been retarded by accidental
circumstances: but, generally speaking, the proportion which the
aggregate of the other classes of citizens bears in any state to that
of its husbandmen, is the proportion of its unsound to its healthy
parts, and is a good-enough barometer whereby to measure its
degree of corruption.[5]

From this, one might well conclude that Jefferson advocated a non-
commercial, nonpecuniary, self-sufficient agrarian economy popu-
lated with virtuous yeomen-farmers. Many scholars, including
Richard Hofstadter, arrived at just such an understanding.[6]

Jefferson's alleged agrarianism was an important element in Hofstadter's interpretation of American history. Hofstadter juxtaposed
the admittedly mythical vision of the sturdy yeoman-farmer to the
emerging commercial realities of American economic life to explain
the stresses and strains that resulted in periodic reform impulses,
including the Progressive Movement. Later scholars have used Jefferson's agrarianism differently, juxtaposing the stability, social cohesion, and neighborly concern of farming communities with the
innovation, social differentiation, and alienation of urban, industrial
life. In this latter view, Jefferson becomes a conservative, fighting
against the forces of modernity to protect classical ideas of civic virtue.[7]

The reality of eighteenth-century agriculture, however, was different. Due to rapid population growth, food shortages occurred in
the West Indies, the Iberian peninsula, and even in the British Isles.
American farmers responded rapidly:

From the middle colonies came wheat, flour, biscuits; from New
England salted fish and meat. Throughout the South lands of marginal efficiency for tobacco production were planted in wheat and
corn. Whole new urban networks took form in response to the
demand for New World foodstuffs. The backcountry of the Caro-
linas and the interior valleys of Pennsylvania, Maryland, and Virginia were drawn into the Atlantic trade world almost as quickly
as the colonists pushed westward. The trade in grains was particularly promising, for only rice came under navigation act
restrictions. Nor were colonial food growers pushed by foreign
competition like the British West Indian sugar growers. Indeed,
as European population began its steady climb, North American
farmers stood to become the principal beneficiaries of the vital

revolution. Well might Thomas Paine exult in 1776 that America would always have a commerce to enrich herself "while eating is the custom of Europe."[8]

In short, agriculture in the United States in the second half of the eighteenth century was largely *commercial* agriculture, linking American farmers to European markets and encouraging innovations that would increase productivity and raise farm incomes.

Jefferson played an important part in the improvement of American commercial agriculture. He invented a threshing machine, improved the moldboard plow, successfully introduced new breeds of sheep, and advocated soil conservation through crop rotation. As Joyce Appleby has said:

> Agriculture did not figure in his plans as a venerable form of production giving shelter to a traditional way of life; rather, he was responsive to every possible change in cultivation, processing, and marketing that would enhance its profitability. It was exactly the promise of progressive agricultural development that fueled his hopes that ordinary men might escape the tyranny of their social superiors both as employers and magistrates.[9]

Viewed in this light, the dispute between Jefferson and Hamilton was less a contest between traditional (agrarian) and modern (commercial) societies than a dispute over two alternate modes of commercial development (agricultural versus manufacturing).

In short, Jefferson was a *liberal* republican whose liberalism betokened a commitment to human liberty. Other writers in this volume have nicely pointed to the multiple dimensions of Jefferson's devotion to liberty. On the one hand, his commitment to liberty reflects a type of Machiavellian moment, an encouragement of civic prickliness, rather than civic friendship, with the anticipated result of political conflict conducive to change and progress. It was this aspect of Jefferson's liberal republicanism that led to his critique of friendship, patronage, and social cohesion as public virtues.

Consider, in this context, President Jefferson's refusal to replace Federalist appointees in the national administration with Republican friends and supporters. He observed, "no man who has conducted himself according to his duties would have anything to fear from me, as those who have done ill would have nothing to hope, be their political principles what they might." For Jefferson, his standard was clear: "Malconduct is a just ground of removal: mere difference of political opinion is not." Jefferson's liberal commitment was clearly reflected in his defense of this practice: "The right of opinion shall suffer no invasion from me. Those who have acted well have nothing to fear, however they may have differed from me in opinion."[10]

Similarly, Jefferson's reading of the common law tradition, guided by Edward Coke's *Institutes*, in no way inhibited his enthusiasm for change or search for universal truths. Rather than seeing the common law as a particular history of a given people in a concrete place, Jefferson understood the common law tradition as a universal teaching about the true source of political sovereignty. Further, he concluded from his study of the common law that long experience with individual liberty resulted in the responsible exercise of that liberty. According to James Stoner's essay herein, Jefferson's commitment to the common law was designed to emphasize the maturation and development of Whig or liberal values among his fellow citizens. These values, such as individualism and freedom of thought, produce a civic "offishness" or desire to withdraw all or in part from the public space.

Withdrawal from the public space might take many forms. It might be as simple as the propensity to say no to the existing order, to disagree, to go over to the opposition. Consider in this light Jefferson's willingness to create an opposition political party when he could no longer agree with the policies of the Federalist majority. Or it might take the form of a flight to the frontier, there to begin anew on the fringes of civilization where one is free to create a new world free from the bonds of tradition and expectation.

Viewed from this perspective, Jefferson's little world atop a hill in Charlottesville takes on decisive significance; as Henry Adams so perceptively noted, "He built for himself at Monticello a chateau above contact with man." There he was free to create as he willed precisely because he was so detached from the particularities of traditional Virginia society. It is this connection of liberty and progress to abstraction or universalization that is Jefferson's profoundest legacy to the Progressive Era.

Progress, Universality, and the Progressive Era

By the third quarter of the nineteenth century, many Americans had come to feel that there was something desperately wrong with their society and their government. The rise of industrialism and corporate capitalism, while providing economic plenty, threatened to destroy both economic and political freedoms. The response to this challenge, however, was oddly ambiguous.

On the one hand, there was a strong Populist element shown most clearly in the agrarian and small town imagery of Woodrow Wilson that hearkened back to Jeffersonian democracy:

> In all that I may have to do in public affairs in the United States, I am going to think of towns such as I have seen in Indiana, towns of the old American pattern, that own and operate their own industries, hopefully and happily. My thought is going to be bent upon the multiplication of towns of that kind and the prevention of the concentration of industry in this country in such a fashion and upon such a scale that towns that own themselves will be impossible. . . . [I]f America discourages the locality, the community, the self-contained town, she will kill the nation. A nation is as rich as her free communities; she is not as rich as her capital city or her metropolis.[11]

On the other hand, there was an equally strong Progressive impulse that stressed newness, a sense that everything had irretrievably changed:

> [The] singular fact is that nothing is done in this country as it was done twenty years ago. . . . The old political formulas do not fit the present problems; they read now like documents taken out of a forgotten age. The older cries sound as if they belonged to a past age which men have almost forgotten.[12]

These two excerpts from Wilson's speeches during the 1912 presidential campaign reflect the ambiguity of the response to industrialization and corporate capitalism.

The ambiguity lay not in Wilson's thinking alone. Indeed, the Progressive Movement eventually split in the election of 1912. Followers of Theodore Roosevelt (and Herbert Croly) accepted the growth of monopoly and trusts as natural and sought merely to regulate them through a strong, activist, "Hamiltonian" state. The followers of Woodrow Wilson (and his mentor, Louis D. Brandeis) rejected both monopoly and political concentration as unnatural, inefficient, and harmful to American individualism.[13] What united these two wings of the Progressive Movement and gave the movement its distinctive character was its moral, or "high-minded," tone and reformist posture. Characteristically, morality was to be understood in contrast to self-interest, especially as far as morality was general and abstract, while self-interest was private and particularistic. And, as the name so clearly suggested, Progressives sought change or progress in addressing the nation's problems.

For Wilson and many other Progressives of similar mind, the nation at the turn of the century faced social issues that were essentially moral and spiritual. Dynamic moral leadership was necessary to facilitate open and public debate on these great issues; the nation needed to breathe "the bracing air of thorough, exhaustive, and open discussions."[14]

The principal impediment to the needed debate was the Congress. Of Congress, Wilson observed:

> There is no one in Congress to speak for the nation. Congress is a conglomeration of inharmonious elements; a collection of men representing each his neighborhood, each his local interest; an alarmingly large proportion of its legislation is "special"; all of it is at best only a limping compromise between the conflicting interests of the innumerable localities represented.[15]

This penetrating criticism artfully juxtaposes "the nation" with a "conglomeration of inharmonious elements." Representatives and Senators cannot be leaders because they are wedded to parochial interests. Even in its collective capacity, Congress can speak only for "the innumerable localities represented" and in the voice of a "limping compromise."

Wilson's desire for dynamic moral leadership led inevitably to a study of the American presidency and the nature of presidential leadership. He asserted that presidential power comes from a president's "contact with and amenability to public opinion."[16] The president is in a unique position to exercise leadership once he receives the public's mandate:

> For he is also the political leader of the nation, or has it in his choice to be. The nation as a whole has chosen him, and is conscious that it has no other political spokesman. His is the only national voice in affairs. Let him once win the admiration and confidence of the country, and no other single force can withstand him, no combination of forces will easily overpower him. His position takes the imagination of the country. He is the representative of no constituency, but of the whole people. When he speaks in his true character, he speaks for no special interest. If he rightly interpret the national thought and boldly insist upon it, he is irresistible.[17]

One might well consider the implications of such presidential power for the balance of powers between the executive and legislative branches.

Wilson's understanding of the comparative legitimacy of the president and Congress rests upon an assumption that a national will exists independent of the brokering and compromising of interest-based political parties. He also assumes this national will can be summoned by a presidential candidate during his election campaign. This almost-Rousseauian conception of the national will, as articulated by the president, takes precedence over the collective voice of Congress, which is little more than the product of bartering in smoke-filled back rooms or closed committee chambers.

This progressive assumption of a homogeneous national will can also be seen at work in the reform of the civil service. During the nineteenth century, three different approaches to staffing the executive branch of government were tried. During the founding era, the character of the public service was congruent with the Federalist understanding of the nature and role of executive leadership. Both presidential selection and appointment to the public service were based largely on merit and insulated from partisanship.

This was a period of "government by gentlemen." Leonard White has correctly noted that the definition of "fitness" during this period has implications for the way in which the parts of the new nation were bound together in the new national government:

> Fitness did not mean to him [Washington] technical competence (except in legal and a very few scientific appointments), nor can it be said that in Washington's time technical competence was recognized generally as a prerequisite for selection. A review of the President's letters and other material leads to the conclusion that, apart from personal integrity, standing in the community was one of the principal ingredients of fitness. . . . In his dignified defense of the nomination of Benjamin Fishbourn, who had been rejected by the Senate (the first such case), Washington made much of the fact that Fishbourn had been repeatedly elected or appointed to offices in his own state and community. In adopting the rule of good standing in the public eye the President was deliberately seeking to consolidate the position and prestige of the new government among the people in all parts of the country.[18]

This definition of merit, which included a strong element of local standing, served to embed in the national government (particularly, in the executive branch) a voice for the localities that comprised the nation.

Many scholars date the opening of the Progressive Era to 1883 and the passage of the Pendleton Act, creating a politically neutral civil service. The Jacksonian era had subordinated both the administration and the presidency to logrolling and compromising politics in the form of patronage-based political parties. One important consequence of this was that politics and administration were, in practice, made coextensive. The public interest was conceived as little more than the aggregation of private interests. The Progressive Movement rejected this conception of the public interest in favor of a unitary conception conceptually distinct from an aggregation of private interests. Therefore, to pursue the public interest, the Progressives sought to insulate both the president and the administration from political bargaining.

The creation of a politically neutral public service changed the way in which local interests and issues were reconciled with national policy. Whereas both "government by gentlemen" and the spoils system had integrated localism into the executive branch (although in different ways), the Progressives' strategy of civil service reform significantly altered the degree to which localism was voiced in the executive branch.

The political neutrality of the national public service created space for the evolution of professionalism in the public service. Professionalism, though, profoundly affected the way in which the parts of the nation were integrated into the whole. As Samuel Beer has noted:

> [T]here is . . . an inherent tendency for professional knowledge to promote governmental centralization. The knowledge of the professional as of the scientist is theoretical and general. It can be applied to similar problems wherever and whenever they arise. What the professional brings to government is not just knowledge of how to cope with a particular problem at a certain time and place, but rather a preparation to deal with all such problems anywhere, anytime. His professional equipment directs him to work through and enlist the initiative of the widest possible jurisdiction.[19]

Progressive reform of the public service eased the growth of public-sector professionalism, replacing the debate between the parts of the nation and the whole with a fragmentation among different functions. Each function was professionalized; each, as a result, tended toward homogenization and centralization.

The Progressives' understanding of the presidency and the public service can most clearly be seen in Franklin Roosevelt's New Deal. Under the combined impact of the Great Depression and the Second World War, the national government came to understand itself not simply as the provider of routine services, but also as the initiator of progress and change. This activist role for administrators was defended from charges of political irresponsibility by subordinating administration to a popularly elected president, assumed to hold a public mandate by virtue of electoral success. The clearest statement of this defense of administration is found, of course, in the 1937 *Report of the President's Committee on Administrative Management* by the Brownlow Committee.

The main theme of this report was the centralization of power and responsibility in the president. Executive power was said to include administrative power that, in turn, included both execution of established policies and initiative in designing new policies. The Brownlow Committee's report thus reflected Wilson's understanding of good government secured through an efficient and nonpartisan bureaucracy subordinated to a popularly elected executive held responsible at the polls for his faithfulness to public opinion.

In this formulation, there was an assumption that a viable national community had evolved in the United States that could speak for itself directly through the election of a president. No longer was it thought that a conception of the public interest must be built from the clash of different local and state interests subject to the restrictions of the national Constitution. Rather, the executive branch was charged with efficiently carrying out the public's will as articulated in presidential elections.

> Modern liberalism promised community—but now *without* the state, local and private institutions that the Anti-Federalists had considered the very source of community. Liberals were, in fact, hostile to local institutions, as such institutions were notoriously backward and provincial. As Arthur Schlesinger Jr. put it recently, "local government historically has been the . . . last refuge of reaction." It was no longer necessary to pay the price of provincialism for community, however; liberalism's "great community" would be drawn together by a powerful, progressive national government, and especially by a powerful, progressive President, using his office as a "bully pulpit" to preach selfless devotion to the common national good.[20]

This is community derived not by debate among parts different in kind, but by abstraction from difference. It is the triumph of the universal over the particular.

This rejection of particularity is reflected in the Progressive understanding of liberty or freedom. Consider, for example, Woodrow Wilson's argument in *The New Freedom*. He begins by suggesting that modern commerce and industrialism submerge the individual:

> You know what happens when you are the servant of a corpora-
> tion. You have in no instance access to the men who are really
> determining the policy of the corporation. If the corporation is
> doing the things that it ought not to do, you really have no voice
> in the matter and must obey the orders, and you have oftentimes
> with deep mortification to co-operate in the doing of things which
> you know are against the public interest. Your individuality is
> swallowed up in the individuality and purpose of a great organi-
> zation.[21]

The assumption of sinister intent by the industrialist was shared by
other thinkers as well. For example, Croly consistently used phrases
such as "unscrupulous devotion," "unscrupulous will," and the "unscrupulous businessman" in discussing the development of the business specialist.[22]

However, the Progressive Movement was not interested in res-
cuing either freedom or the individual as defined by eighteenth-
century thinkers. In a revealing image, Wilson observed that after
Progressive reforms, men could "live as a single community, cooperative as in a perfected, co-ordinated beehive" flexible enough to
be alterable according to the "necessities of their lives."[23]

This organic image of community, which follows a criticism of the
Constitution as thoroughly Newtonian in character and thus ill suited to an age where "living political constitutions must be Darwin-
ian in structure and in practice," suggests that individuality and
self-interest are to be submerged in an organic national community
where each plays his or her proper part. If all the parts of the community are correctly coordinated, then each can be said to be free:

> Liberty for the several parts would consist in the best possible
> assembling and adjustment of them all, would it not? If you want
> the great piston of the engine to run with absolute freedom, give
> it absolutely perfect alignment and adjustment with the other parts
> of the machine, so that it is free, not because it is let alone or
> isolated, but because it has been associated most skilfully and care-
> fully with the other parts of the great structure.[24]

Wilson's desire to overcome the particularity of self-interest through
inclusion in an organic community is virtually indistinguishable in
its end, if not in its process, from Theodore Roosevelt's New Nationalism, in which large trusts would be regulated in the public interest
by powerful, independent regulatory commissions.

The Progressives believed that community could be had only by
abstracting from the differences among human beings. The particu-

larity of self-interest must be overcome in the name of fellowship and the national ideal. Vigorous moral leadership grounded in the effective use of public rhetoric by the president was the vehicle for accomplishing this task.

Jeffersonianism and Progressivism

Speaking on Jefferson Day, April 16, 1906, to a group of party faithful in New York, Woodrow Wilson insisted that

> Jefferson's objects have not fallen out of date. They are our own objects, if we be faithful to any ideals whatever; and the question we ask ourselves is not, How would Jefferson have pursued them in his day? but How shall we pursue them in ours? It is the spirit, not the tenets of the man by which he rules us from his urn.[25]

Wilson's apt turn of phrase captured the odd embrace of Jeffersonianism and progressivism.

The rise of industrial capitalism in the United States at the end of the nineteenth century appeared to challenge Jeffersonianism in all its particulars: agrarianism was receding, the notions of private property and economic freedom had been captured and transformed by the corporation, limited government appeared less to protect individual freedom than to expose it to destruction at the hands of the trusts. Yet Jeffersonianism captured the aspirations of the Progressive reformers.

Despite this challenge, Jefferson became an American hero *only* in the twentieth century. It was in this century that his face was enshrined on Mount Rushmore, his home at Monticello was reopened to the public under the ownership of the nonprofit Thomas Jefferson Memorial Foundation, and the Jefferson Memorial in Washington, D.C., took its place next to the Lincoln Memorial and the Washington Monument. What explains the celebration of Jefferson at exactly the time his philosophy and image seems most irrelevant?

The answer lies in the abstract and universal quality of Jefferson's thought. Jefferson could triumph in the twentieth century only to the extent his primary political aims of human liberty and progress could be divorced from his chosen means of limited government. The Progressive Movement's commitment to an energetic executive and a nonpartisan civil service bore fruit in the New Deal, but the result was not limited government.

The New Deal paid homage to Jefferson in a unique way. According to Peterson,

The New Deal lacked a consistent philosophy, but it possessed a sense of tradition, a faith in democratic ideals, a set of symbols and conventions, which served some of the purposes of a philosophy. Addressing the Jefferson Day dinner at St. Paul, Minnesota during his pre-convention campaign in 1932, Franklin D. Roosevelt called for the renewal of the old social contract on the new terms of American life. The "long and splendid" day of Jeffersonian individualism was over, Roosevelt announced. Americans who shared Jefferson's faith in the ability of free men to work out their own destiny might safely undertake to plan and direct their social and economic life. . . . To make the national government "a refuge and a help," in the present circumstances, was not to negate but to affirm the tradition.[26]

Jefferson lived in essence, divorced from means. He became an ethereal figure, a philosopher but not a statesman, a spokesman but not a political leader.

Having retreated to Monticello after his disastrous second term as president, Jefferson remained there in collective memory. Far above contact with man, his "glittering generalities" emboldened the reformers of the Progressive Era. His quest for universal truths suited his philosophy for adoption by Progressive reformers who sought to rise above the particularism of individual self-interest and local claims.

Notes

1. Herbert Croly, *The Promise of American Life*, Arthur M. Schlesinger Jr., ed. (Cambridge, MA: Belknap Press of Harvard University Press, 1965).

2. Woodrow Wilson, *The New Freedom* (Englewood Cliffs, NJ: Prentice-Hall, 1961).

3. Jefferson to John Adams, June 15, 1813, in *The Adams-Jefferson Letters: The Complete Correspondence between Thomas Jefferson and Abigail and John Adams*, Lester J. Cappon, ed., 2 vols. (Chapel Hill: University of North Carolina Press, 1987), 332.

4. Joyce Appleby has noted that Americans of the revolutionary period "operated within an empiricist scientific tradition in which universal laws operated inexorably. It may be clear to us that their models of social behavior were theoretical and their general principles *a priori*, but this was not their self-image. They brought to human history the ahistoricity of a natural scientist. Not having a sense that a historical event cannot be understood independent of when it happened, they collected historical instances as a naturalist collects fossils—as empirical data to be worked into general laws" (*Liberalism and Republicanism in the Historical Imagination* [Cambridge, MA: Harvard University Press, 1992], 191).

5. Thomas Jefferson, *Notes on the State of Virginia*, William Peden, ed. (Chapel Hill: University of North Carolina Press, 1955), 164–165.

6. Richard Hofstadter, *The Age of Reform from Bryan to F.D.R.* (New York: Alfred A. Knopf, 1956).

7. See, for example, J. G. A. Pocock, *The Machiavellian Moment: Florentine Political Thought and the Atlantic Republican Tradition* (Princeton, NJ: Princeton University Press, 1975), 529–533; Lance Banning, *The Jeffersonian Persuasion: Evolution of a Party Ideology* (Ithaca, NY: Cornell University Press, 1978), 269; and Drew R. McCoy, *The Elusive Republic: Political Economy in Jeffersonian America* (Chapel Hill: University of North Carolina Press, 1980), 10.

8. Joyce Appleby, "Modernization Theory and Anglo-American Social Theories," in *Liberalism and Republicanism*, 112.

9. Joyce Appleby, "The 'Agrarian Myth' in the Early Republic," in *Liberalism and Republicanism*, 269.

10. Leonard D. White, *The Jeffersonians: A Study in Administrative History, 1801–1829* (New York: Macmillan, 1951), 350–351.

11. Wilson, *The New Freedom*, 166–167.

12. Ibid., 19.

13. Two useful discussions of this split in the Progressive ranks are William E. Leuchtenburg's introduction to Wilson's *The New Freedom*, and Arthur S. Link, *Woodrow Wilson and the Progressive Era, 1910–1917* (New York: Harper & Row, 1954), chap. 1.

14. "Cabinet Government in the United States," *International Review* 7 (August 1879): 21.

15. Ibid., 30.

16. James W. Ceaser, *Presidential Selection: Theory and Development* (Princeton, NJ: Princeton University Press, 1979), 184.

17. Richard Hirschfield, ed., *The Power of the Presidency: Concepts and Controversy* (New York: Atherton Press, 1968), 92.

18. Leonard D. White, *The Federalists: A Study in Administrative History, 1789–1801* (New York: Macmillan, 1959), 259.

19. Samuel Beer, "Political Overload and Federalism," in *Polity* 10, no. 1 (Fall 1977): 10.

20. William A. Schambra, "The Roots of the American Public Philosophy," *The Public Interest* 67 (Spring 1982): 44.

21. Wilson, *The New Freedom*, 20.

22. Croly, *The Promise of American Life*, 106, 108, and 109, respectively.

23. Wilson, *The New Freedom*, 44.

24. Ibid., 163. It is striking that having just criticized the founders for their mechanical, rather than organic, understanding of government and the nation, Wilson himself returns to a mechanical image to discuss individuality.

25. Merrill D. Peterson, *The Jefferson Image in the American Mind* (New York: Oxford University Press, 1960), 330.

26. Ibid., 355.

11

Jeffersonianism and the New Deal

Morton J. Frisch

"A wise and frugal government which shall restrain men from injuring one another, shall leave them otherwise free to regulate their own pursuits of industry and improvement, and shall not take from the mouth of labor the bread it has earned. This is the sum of good government."

Thomas Jefferson, First Inaugural Address, March 4, 1801

Jeffersonianism, as Jeffrey Leigh Sedgwick explains elsewhere in this volume, was a way of thinking on Thomas Jefferson's part that celebrated agrarian or rural life over the cities; that embraced states rights against the pretensions of a big national government; and that had grave doubts that the commercial world of factories was good for the human spirit.

In order to examine the relation between Jeffersonianism and the New Deal, one would have to consider the relation between the transformed Jeffersonianism of the early twentieth century and that later twentieth-century movement in the Great Depression associated with Franklin D. Roosevelt. But even the transformed Jeffersonian liberalism of Louis D. Brandeis and Woodrow Wilson during the Progressive Era represented a considerable departure from traditional Jeffersonian liberalism. Although they looked to the resuscitation of Jeffersonian democracy against the special interests perverting republican government in America, the Progressives believed that the exigencies of modern industrial society, especially the concentration of economic power in the form of huge corporations, required a different understanding of freedom than that held by Jefferson. One only has to read the legal memoranda of Brandeis and the political speeches of Wilson to see the extent to which their brand of progressivism had already accommodated itself to urban industrial capitalism; but their thought falls far short of the orientation of New Deal liberalism, not to mention the New Nationalism of Herbert Croly and Theodore Roosevelt. It is sometimes suggested that the New Deal represents a synthesis of Jeffersonianism and Hamiltonianism, but this is made questionable by the fact that the Jeffersonian tradition of liberal democracy had already become radically altered in response to the new conditions of industrial capitalism.

Moreover, the great reforms of the New Deal—economic regulation and economic redistribution—cannot usually be described as the employment of Hamiltonian means for Jeffersonian ends, for the ends of the regime themselves had become substantially enlarged by the Roosevelt revolution. The most one could say is that, rhetorically speaking, there was a Jeffersonian undercurrent in Franklin Roosevelt's and Henry Wallace's concern for the plight of the common man; but as far as its philosophy of government was concerned, the New Deal was decidedly Hamiltonian in essence. The liberal tradition in American politics has been largely associated with Jeffersonian principles, but it would be difficult to imagine brain trusters like Rexford G. Tugwell, Adolph A. Berle Jr., and Raymond Moley as Jeffersonians. I would suggest that there was something more to New Deal liberalism than the New Freedom, or the New Nationalism for that matter, namely, economic redistribution. The Social Security Act, the keystone of the New Deal's welfare legislation, was no more New Nationalism than it was Jeffersonianism.

I do not exactly want to assert that the crisis of American democracy in the twentieth century has been at heart a crisis in the Jeffersonian philosophy, as the Jeffersonian biographer Merrill Peterson maintains, for Jeffersonianism was already well on the wane by that time; but it would be probably correct to say, as he does, that "the New Deal killed the Jeffersonian philosophy as a recognizable and usable tradition in American government and politics," or another way of expressing the same thought, that the New Deal could not possibly be Jeffersonian.[1]

Roosevelt's New Deal constituted a profound modification of the traditional American democracy, a modification arrived at through a decisive break with the liberalism of the early twentieth century. We can see most clearly what that break effected by the New Deal means when examining the establishment of the welfare state. Owing to the economic exigencies created by the depression, it became necessary to reassess the earlier liberalism with a view to whether its understanding of the relationship between the government and the economy was adequate. The central errors of Brandeisian-Wilsonian progressivism were its unrestricted individualism, its policy of encouraging smallness and discouraging economic concentration (that is, its antitrust approach of breaking down and destroying concentrated economic power), and its narrow and inflexible view of the functions of government. The Brandeisian-Wilsonian creed was avowedly Jeffersonian in character.

Brandeis was a vigorous advocate of decentralization in political and economic affairs, believing that the self-governing unity needed to be small, cohesive, and have its citizens close to the instruments of government. He outlined the division between Rooseveltian and Wilsonian progressivism in the presidential campaign of 1912. He wrote that our position

> insists that competition can be and should be maintained in every branch of private industry; that competition can and should be restored in those branches of industry in which it has been suppressed by the trusts; and that, if at any future time monopoly should appear to be desirable in any branch of industry, the monopoly should be owned by the people.

The opposing position

> insists that private monopoly may be desirable in some branches of industry, or at all events, is inevitable; and that, existing trusts should not be dismembered or forcibly dislodged from those branches of industry in which they have already acquired a monopoly but should be made good by regulation.

The Roosevelt party "does not fear commercial power, however great, if only methods for regulation are provided," whereas "we believe that no methods of regulation ever have been or can be devised to remove the menace inherent in . . . overweening commercial power."[2]

Brandeis's aggressive antitrust approach that was intended to foster a competitive economy rested on his profound antistatism. Wilson created the slogan "New Freedom" to distinguish between the New Nationalism and his call for the restoration of "free enterprise." His New Freedom doctrine, taken largely from Brandeis, was essentially an attempt to restore, as far as possible, competitive conditions through antitrust action. Through antitrust legislation, it could stop combination and merger.

In his campaign speeches of 1912, Wilson called for reform that would free business from the plague of monopoly and special privilege and, that would restore competition in the economy, but he also cautioned against the political danger of centralized government control, for as he had earlier remarked: "The history of liberty is the history of the limitation of governmental power, not the increase of it." He had a distinct distrust of centralized political power. He believed that politics must be purified. The government had been corrupted by its association with privileged monopolies. The debate between Wilson's New Freedom and Theodore Roosevelt's New Nationalism, the two idioms of progressive thought, might well be regarded as one of the crucial debates in American history, at least insofar as it set the tone for FDR's later reinterpretation of the liberal tradition in America, a tradition that has been commonly associated with its Jeffersonian origins.

The earlier progressive liberals and the New Dealers shared the view that the concentration of economic power constitutes a threat to liberal democracy, but the earlier Progressives had similar fears about the concentration of governmental power. Accordingly, they sought to decentralize concentrations of economic power, while the New Dealers were more inclined, with some exceptions, to use regulatory legislation to control such concentrations. The New Dealers, in contradistinction to Wilson and Brandeis, viewed a cooperation, not a conflict, between governmental power and private economic power, but with the government as the controlling element. Roosevelt gave liberalism a new dimension when he insisted that

> all reasonable people must recognize that government was not instituted to serve as a cold public instrument to be called into use after irreparable damage had been done. If we limit government to functions of punishing the criminal after the crimes have been committed, of gathering up the wreckage of society after the devastation of an economic collapse, or of fighting a war that reason might have prevented, then government fails to satisfy those urgent human purposes, which . . . gave it its beginning and provide its present justification.[3]

Brandeis's criticism of the New Deal during the 1930s as a member of the Supreme Court rested on decentralization in political and economic affairs. After the National Industrial Recovery Act was declared unconstitutional in the case of *Schecter Poultry Co. v. United*

States in 1935,[4] he told one of the president's closest advisers, Tom Corcoran: "This is the end of this business of centralization, and I want you to go back and tell the President that we're not going to centralize everything. It's come to an end. As for your young men, you call them together and tell them to get out of Washington—tell them to go back to the states. This is where they must do their work."[5] Brandeis wanted a political system that would be as free as possible from centralized direction and, hence, would not sap the vitality of the local communities. Bigness, as he saw it, was a curse. The argument for federalism is that it prevents centralization, thus mitigating some of the evil effects of bigness.

The earlier liberalism with its individualistic bias could be characterized as follows. The more fundamental issue of economic reconstruction is almost entirely subordinated to the restoration of the old competitive system, that is, improving private competition or freedom of competition, which would require only a minimum of government interference. That liberalism called for the destruction of monopolies and trusts, not their regulation. There was an ill-defined recognition that some regulation was needed, which showed up in the first Wilson administration with the creation of the Federal Trade Commission in 1914, whereas in the New Deal, there was a principle clearly stated that government must undertake the responsibility for the maintenance and health of the economy as a whole to the point of rearranging that economy, if necessary, and redistributing its benefits. Woodrow Wilson, incidentally, disliked the paternalism of the welfare state almost as much as he objected to the invidiousness of the trusts.

To understand the welfare state in its essential character means to understand it in its relation to the Lockean-Jeffersonian tradition, and that means moving backward to the pristine liberalism of the American founding. The Declaration of Independence defines the function of government in terms of a certain understanding of the relation between happiness and the conditions of happiness. According to that understanding, life, liberty, and the pursuit of happiness constitute the conditions of happiness, and it is the function of government to guarantee those conditions, but not happiness itself. FDR, on the other hand, believed the function of government to be that of achieving the greatest happiness for the greatest number. He seemed to consider happiness as well-being, and he defined his own understanding of the change in terms of the movement from political to economic rights. It is this fundamental change in emphasis that gives the New Deal its distinctive character as a political movement, for from then on, government furnished not only the conditions of

happiness, but also, to a considerable extent, the enjoyment or possession of material happiness, which might properly be called well-
being. Well-being or welfare is a kind of in-between concept, in
between the conditions of happiness and happiness itself. The welfare state is a society in which material happiness or well-being is
no longer merely privately pursued, but now becomes a matter of
governmental concern.

The particular cause of the transition from traditional liberalism
to the welfare state is the introduction of that new principle of governmental pursuit of well being, but there is a sense in which that
principle forms a part of the Hamiltonian viewpoint. The notion that
the well-being or welfare of the greater number is to be provided
for by government is implicit in the Constitution's Preamble,
which states that one of the great ends of government is to "promote the general welfare." It could reasonably be argued that the
New Deal was in a real sense only attempting to carry out that purpose announced in the Preamble, that is, that the New Deal's intention of furthering the general welfare by governmental provision for
material well-being could be construed as something stated in the
Preamble—deflected perhaps by Roosevelt's turn of mind. That statement of purpose, moreover, is not limited to the Preamble, but is
mentioned in the main body of the Constitution, in the clause grant-
ing the taxing power.

Fundamental to the welfare-state position was the contention that
"government has the final responsibility for the well-being of its citizenship," that is, for securing the material happiness or well-being
of its citizens, while the earlier liberalism, setting society apart from
government, continued to believe in government only as being necessary under certain conditions. But although the virtues of individualism continued to mean for FDR what they had meant for the
earlier tradition of progressive liberalism, he knew that individualism was not enough. It was apparent to him that individual interests
do not always operate in the public interest, and that unrestrained
individualism has a natural tendency to turn individuals away from
the public interest.

As a result of the climactic experience of the Great Depression,
and the manner in which that depression was understood, the earlier liberalism underwent a radical reassessment in the 1930s. The
contribution that the New Deal made to the American political tradition consisted in correcting the earlier liberalism to the extent that
it amended its narrow understanding of the functions of government
(or of the relationship between the government and the economy),
and only in this light can we see how un-Jeffersonian the New Deal

was. The essential failure of Jeffersonian liberalism as it projected itself through the nineteenth century and into the twentieth consisted in a one-sided and oversimplified concentration on individualism and all that this implies for politics and government. Roosevelt, not a consummate Jeffersonian, transcended some of the limitations of liberalism and even enlarged its horizons by explaining that a liberal democratic society requires for its preservation the promotion of equality of opportunity through government provision for well-being or welfare.

In the liberal movements early in the twentieth century, governmental regulation found a limited place. Theodore Roosevelt and Woodrow Wilson presided over the country during the introduction of some regulatory measures, but those regulations were not based on explicit reflections on the relation between politics and the economy. The government regulation of that period did not reexamine the doctrines of nineteenth-century liberalism, according to which the happiness of the individual, understood in terms of economic well-being, was thought to be beyond the reach of government. The subordination of the economy to the government that the New Deal sought to accomplish through regulation integrates economic well-being into the purposes of government.

FDR rejected the notion that an economic system such as the American republic would regulate itself automatically by the uncontrolled competition of private enterprise, and therefore government had to impose regulations and controls on the economy as a whole. But this was accomplished only with very great difficulty, as it involved a struggle against an established pattern of earlier liberal beliefs and attitudes. FDR said that "heretofore, Government had merely been called upon to produce the conditions within which people could live happily, labor peacefully, and rest secure. Now it was called upon to [raise the standard of living for everyone, to bring luxury within the reach of the humblest, . . . and to release everyone from the drudgery of the heaviest manual toil.]"[6] He continued: "It is a relatively new thing in American life to consider what the relationship of government is to its starving people and its unemployed citizens, and to take steps to fulfill its governmental duties to them. A generation ago people had scarcely given thought to the terms social security, minimum wages, or maximum hours."[7]

To indicate the departure from the Jeffersonian tradition of individualistic democracy that Roosevelt's thinking represented, we must realize that he would never have said, as Jefferson did, that the powers of the national government were restricted by the Constitution to those enumerated plus those absolutely necessary to carry those that were enumerated into effect.[8] In his Address to the Young Democratic Clubs in 1935, FDR knows how the consequences of extreme individualism can be corrected without undermining that individualism altogether:

> The crucial suffering of the recent depression taught us unforgettable lessons. We have been compelled by stark necessity to unlearn the too comfortable superstition that the American soil was mystically blessed with every kind of immunity to grave economic maladjustments, and that the American spirit of individualism—all alone and unhelped by the cooperative efforts of Government—could withstand and repel every form of economic disarrangement or crisis. . . . [But] let me emphasize that serious as have been the errors of unrestrained individualism, I do not believe in abandoning the system of individual enterprise. The freedom and opportunity that have characterized American development in the past can be maintained if we recognize the fact that the individual system of our day calls for the collaboration of all of us to provide, at the least, security for all of us. Those words freedom and opportunity do not mean a license to climb upwards by pushing other people down.[9]

But once Roosevelt takes the consequences of individualism into account, he ceases to advocate that mode of thought. As he stated in his Commonwealth Address in 1932:

> Where Jefferson feared the encroachment of political power on the lives of individuals, Wilson knew that the new power was financial. He saw, in the highly centralized economic system, the despot of the twentieth century, on whom great masses of individuals relied for their safety and their livelihood, and whose irresponsibility and greed (if they were not controlled) would reduce them to starvation and penury.[10]

But even Wilson's program of broadening the role of the national government remained in its essentials devoted to the decentralization of governmental power, something that FDR omitted.

Roosevelt was deeply concerned about the danger to our freedoms caused by economic inequality, and as a result of that concern, there evolved in his mind an understanding of the problem of freedom that went beyond the Jeffersonian understanding. The problem of freedom, as he indicated, is necessarily concerned with economic as well as political considerations. It is generally recognized that political freedom rests on restraint and that the broadening of that freedom may necessitate increased restraints on the particular freedoms of some individuals. The restraints derive their justification from the kind of action they curtail, or in the kind of society in which such restraints (and freedoms, for that matter) are exercised. In this sense, it is no longer a matter of increasing and decreasing restraints, but of organizing them to secure conditions understood as necessary for the common good.

Roosevelt wrote to David Sarnoff in 1940 that "in order to maintain our American system of private initiative and private enterprise, it must function as a system that will do the greatest good for the greatest number. It is only by keeping our economy socially conscious that we can keep it free."[11] Roosevelt's view of the common good amounts to a preference for the greatest good of the greatest number; and he regarded that objective as the best political scheme, the proper end or purpose of government. The greatest good of the greatest number may very well appear to be the good of everyone, but it is actually the good of the large majority, perhaps even the good of the common people as distinguished from the good of the wealthy. The greatest good of the greatest number may even require severe limitations on the freedom of the wealthy to some extent. The problem of freedom, therefore, becomes one of finding that point of coincidence between freedom and restraint on which the greatest good of the greatest number, or the common good, rests.[12] Roosevelt's New Deal did not wish to place property at the mercy of the propertyless or freedom at the mercy of the propertied. The New Deal attempted to find the right mean, not by avoiding restraints on the processes of the economy on the one hand and the freedom of the individual on the other, but by integrating restraints and freedoms into a regime that could provide for the greatest good of the greatest number. The public philosophy of the New Deal asserts that political freedom must be maintained not as freedom from government, but as freedom through government.

Merrill Peterson suggests that "the New Deal's attack on the economic royalists was in the spirit of Jefferson's attack on the corrupt monarchists," but this cannot be considered a very satisfactory analogy.[13] It would be more accurate to say that "a moderate welfare state does not quarrel with inequalities per se, but with entrenched economic disparities per se, but which threaten to crush those of ability and effort. (This is what FDR meant by economic royalism.)" As Clifford Orwin has argued,

> the moderate welfare state like the notion of equal opportunity itself . . . does not deny—indeed, it presupposes—that public policy should promote equal chances to achieve unequal things, and

to reap the fruits thereof. . . . It neither questions the reality of distinctions of merit, nor doubts that those are *ipso facto* distinctions of worth.[14]

But we may hasten to add that the moderate welfare state has become transformed into an enormously active government the primary goal of which seems to be to provide goods and services to a greatly expanded body of citizens, rather than the equality of opportunity contemplated by FDR.

There is, moreover, a downside to welfarism. FDR did not seem to realize that, in constantly seeking to strengthen economic equality, the human propensity could, in fact, become submerged in the interest of a better-regulated economic life, with its emphasis on health, welfare, and freedom from want. FDR may not have foreseen it, but the human passion for welfarism could result in what Alexis de Tocqueville referred to as a soft despotism that

> makes the exercise of free choice less useful and rarer, restricts the activity of free will within a narrower compass, and little by little robs each citizen of the proper use of his faculties. . . . It does not break a man's will, but it softens, bends and guides it; it is not at all tyrannical, but it hinders, restrains, enervates, stifles, and stultifies so much that in the end each nation is not more than a flock of timid and hard working animals with the government as its shepherd.[15]

FDR did not perceive that the claims of the welfare principle, pushed steadily toward its utmost extreme, could be fatal to the development of the human faculties, and we can assume that Woodrow Wilson had something like this in mind in his own reflections.

Notes

1. Merrill D. Peterson, *The Jefferson Image in the American Mind* (New York: Oxford University Press, 1960), 330, 332.

2. Memo, "Suggestions for Letter of Governor Wilson on Trusts," Louis D. Brandeis to Woodrow Wilson, September 30, 1912, in *Letters of Louis D. Brandeis,* Melvin I. Urofsky and David W. Levy, eds., vol. 2 (Albany, NY: State University of New York Press, 1972), 688.

3. Franklin D. Roosevelt, *The Public Papers and Addresses of Franklin D. Roosevelt,* S. I. Rosenman, ed., 13 vols. (New York: Random House, 1938; New York: Macmillan, 1941; New York: Harper, 1950), 4:422; hereinafter cited as *Roosevelt Papers.*

4. *Schechter Poultry Co.* v *United States*, 295 US 495 (1935). In *Schechter*, the Supreme Court found the National Industrial Recovery Act, which authorized the president to adopt fair codes of competition for virtually all aspects of the American economy, unconstitutional. The Court held that Congress could not delegate such sweeping powers to an executive body.

5. Arthur M. Schlesinger Jr., *The Age of Roosevelt: The Politics of Upheaval* (Boston: Houghton Mifflin, 1988), 280.

6. *Roosevelt Papers*, 1:747.

7. Ibid., 2:442.

8. See, for example, Jefferson's remarks on the constitutionality of a U.S. bank in Peterson, *Jefferson Image*, 76-78

9. *Roosevelt Papers*, 4:338-339, 341.

10. Ibid., 1:749.

11. Ibid., 9:596.

12. Ibid., 2:186; 3:288; and 9:596.

13. Peterson, *Jefferson Image*, 357.

14. Clifford Orwin, "Welfare and the New Dignity," *The Public Interest* 71 (Spring 1983): 89.

15. Alexis de Tocqueville, *Democracy in America*, J. P. Mayer, ed., George Lawrence, trans., 2 vols. (London: Fontana Press, 1994), II.iv.6.692.

Part IV

Thomas Jefferson and the Pursuit of
Equality in American Politics

12

Jefferson and the Pursuit of Equality

J. R. Pole

If it is true, as Joyce Appleby has remarked, that Thomas Jefferson is the only American president to have given his name to a philosophy, it is no less true that Americans have taken widely differing views of that philosophy.[1] Some have agreed that he believed in literal and universal equality of individual rights, but have differed violently about the merits of that belief; others have held that that was not what he meant at all. A man of Jefferson's length of life, intellectual curiosity, and variety of interests is surely at least entitled to the usual Emersonian quota of inconsistency. Jefferson himself has contributed to the difficulty by his habit of adopting strongly felt moral and political positions without fully or rigorously thinking out the implications. We employ the word "philosophy" itself in a comparatively relaxed fashion in this connection, meaning not so much a self-consistent system of thought as an outlook on life, a composition of imperfectly reconciled sentiments and opinions, and sometimes impulses. Many of them, of course, reflected the thought of his time and have survived to create deep resonances in the subsequent history of American thought. Posterity has strained to catch the note. "What would Mr. Jefferson have said?" is a question still sometimes asked in Virginia.

Jefferson's name and authority are invoked in the context of equality more than in any other cause. In the Declaration of Independence, the "self-evident" truth that all men are created equal precedes the

219

enumerated rights both literally and logically. It is true that the right
to life, to liberty, and to the pursuit of happiness are then specified.
But if the doctrine underlying that affirmation is to be understood, it
is first to be understood that the rights all people share to these
things are *equal* rights. No one person can logically lay claim to a
superior share. Other important equalities—the equality of the sovereign states, the equality claimed by Americans as a people with
other peoples, notably the British—are not inconsistent with this doctrine and in no way impair its efficacy; it is in that sense, with the
proclamation of this doctrine by the Continental Congress, that
the United States was born as an equal among nations and a nation
of equals.

Whatever the sources and complexities of Jefferson's own thought
on these matters—and they have been the subject of numerous studies—the central principle of his Declaration was adopted because it
was acceptable to the Congress and, by inference, to at least that
section of the American people that took sides with the Congress in
what became the American cause. If it had not been acceptable, it
could not have been made the centerpiece of the American rallying
cry. We are not here concerning ourselves with merely personal opinion; it is Jefferson's rendering of a public principle. This principle
was a product of Enlightenment thinking, and the rights claimed
were natural rights. The deeper context to be comprehended is that
of the Enlightenment view of nature. One of Jefferson's achievements,
due in no small part to what John Adams described as his "peculiar
felicity" of style, was to transmit these ideas to later generations, and
not only in America.

The ideal of nature as the universal touchstone of value was
in no sense original to the Enlightenment. "Non-equality given to
equals, dissimilar positions given to similar persons—these are contrary to nature and nothing contrary to nature is fine,"—a statement
bearing on the themes of both equality and nature, appears in Aristotle's *Politics*, while the *Nicomachean Ethics* also discusses nature
as the source of good.[2] In Renaissance evaluations of artistic merit,
likeness to nature was a defining criterion. Since both Judaism and
Christianity regarded nature as emanations of God's will, these doctrines made up a coherent whole, available to Americans of varying
faiths and convictions, while leaving some scope for disagreements
as to what might in fact be natural in any given situation.

The Enlightenment not only had many sources, but also many
manifestations, varying in different national contexts.[3] But Jefferson,
as a product and exemplifier of the Enlightenment, recognized that
a particular thrust in the direction of what appeared to be *verifiably*

natural had occurred with Francis Bacon—a contemporary, as it happened, of the first English colonists. As Robert Faulkner argues elsewhere in this volume, the natural philosophers who followed him in the seventeenth century demonstrated that nature's truths could be reduced to scientific laws. The greatest of these was Isaac Newton. And it was significant that the adjective "universal" was so often attached to Newton's most cosmic discovery, the law of gravitation. These advances in the scientific understanding of the cosmos did not in themselves dictate the laws of right and wrong. They did, however, give altogether new force to the concept of nature as the source of values. If the laws of nature were universal, how could the values associated with nature differ with differences of circumstance? The harmony that prevailed in the order of the universe was a potent exemplar of the universality of moral principles on earth. What went against nature in previous ages had appeared morally wrong in principle; what went against nature was now *demonstrably* wrong. The God who had given the one set of laws had given the other. But here, the human mind, gifted with the power of reason, held an indispensable key to comprehension. Reason was God's gift to man for the understanding of nature; it was, in fact, the one respect in which humans could be thought to resemble God. Reason was itself inherent in human nature; and as the values of nature were universal, varying not from one age or region to another, so the faculty of reason was universal among men. (The question of women was, for the time being, undecided.)

It was by virtue of the natural equality of men that John Locke was able to establish his claim for the contractual origin of the state. And it is wholly in keeping with these principles that Jefferson should have remarked to Alexander Hamilton that Bacon, Newton, and Locke were "my trinity of the three greatest men the world had ever produced."[4] Of the three, Locke was the most influential intellectual source of the intense individualism that also characterized Jefferson's political thought. "Can any reason be assigned," Jefferson had demanded in his *Summary View of the Rights of British America*, written for the Virginia delegation to the Continental Congress in 1774, "why 160,000 electors in the island of Great Britain should give law to four million in the states of America, every individual of whom is equal to every individual of them in virtue, in understanding, and in bodily strength?"[5] There is no contradiction between these views that appear again and again in early American state papers, and not least in the declarations of rights enacted by early state governments. What is indeed more paradoxical is the prevalence of individualistic views of the origins of political society amid the manifest facts of community life that could be observed in the families, villages, towns, churches, markets, and courts in which Americans did most of their transactions. There were some aspects of life, particularly in religious observances and regulations, in which individual preferences were subordinated to those of a collective; but none of this detracted from the underlying principle of equality of rights, which Americans translated into public doctrine when they subscribed to the Declaration of Independence.

Jefferson followed the current teaching of Scottish moral philosophers in ascribing to all men a share of common, innate moral sense. These were human qualities shared by virtue of being human, along with essential biological needs. None of this prevented Jefferson from recognizing that human beings differed from one another in significant ways and extents. Montesquieu, who influenced Jefferson's generation more than any other thinker of continental Europe, had perceived cultural differences arising from different environments. While in the *Persian Letters* he employed a mock-foreign standpoint to probe the peculiarities of the French state and its customs, he advanced a more fully environmental view of law and culture in his much more widely read book, *The Spirit of the Laws*, which had been translated in the early 1750s. Universal human nature thus did not necessarily everywhere yield similar human behavior or institutions. For Jefferson (who thought Montesquieu had misled more than one generation of readers), greater intellectual difficulties, which he never resolved, arose from the problem of accounting for differences within the same environment, which were obvious among the different peoples of America, or, to take the matter on a larger scale, within the same framework of original creation.

The only point we need to take from these considerations is that none of these differences among people living in differing climates and environments could detract from the universality of a philosophy that ascribed identical rights to all men, everywhere and at all times. What followed from this in the political sphere was that society owed to all individuals—we shall come in a moment to certain exceptions—an equal assurance of the right to pursue happiness. And this must seem to imply that every individual had an equal right to make his own decisions for himself.

American society was in many respects mobile. Particularly since about the mid-1740s, fortunes had been made, and lost. The goods of fortune did not come as a gift; the word "pursuit" was not a mere flourish of rhetoric. Moreover, the colonies had not been founded in equality, either material or philosophical, and it was a natural condition of this situation that equality itself was an object that often had to be pursued.[6] It is consistent with Jefferson's individualism to think that he regarded the pursuit of happiness as a process of self-improvement. (There are other ways of thinking about individualism.) He could have found an explicit formulation of this theme in Adam Smith's first book, *The Theory of Moral Sentiments*, which, whether or not it was read at the College of William and Mary when Jefferson was a student there, was likely to have been transmitted along with other teachings of the Scottish school by Jefferson's tutor, Professor William Small. Smith took note of the emulation that ran "through all the different ranks of men" and asked what purpose it served other than "that great purpose of human life which we call bettering our condition?"[7] Jefferson would in any case have observed it around him. Some twenty-five years later, he was so highly impressed by the thought of his French contemporary Destutt de Tracy that he corrected a translation of his *Treatise of Political Economy*, which appeared (without attribution) in 1817. Jefferson's main interest was in refuting Montesquieu's views on human nature and government. He found in de Tracy a highly sympathetic account of men's personal aspirations for self-fulfilment and a justification of self-interest moderated by harmonizing powers, which he also found in human nature.[8] This subsequent evidence does not prove anything about Jefferson's thinking in or around 1776, but the sentiment is wholly compatible with his demonstrable views on individualism and equality of rights, and it is at least consistent with the belief that he had these aims in mind when he drafted the Declaration of Independence.

None of this dictated a specific form of government. But for any republican government, it must mean freeing people from artificial barriers and impediments. In Jefferson's Virginia, it meant the abolition of such artifices as primogeniture (in cases of intestacy) and the entailment of estates. These aims he was able to accomplish in his capacity as a member of the legislature, particularly as a member of a committee to revise the laws, and they constitute a familiar part of the record of the times. Where voting rights and political equality were concerned, the suffrage was based on a 50-acre freehold; and for Jefferson, equality at the political level meant the policy of offering a 50-acre freehold farm to every willing taker—the assumption being that the takers would be white males. Jefferson had not liberated himself from the conventional view that the right to vote should be qualified by the possession of some traditional indication of a stake in society: equality was not the attribute of the unpropertied individual. Rather, he wanted to work the other way round, by conferring the property qualification on the individual. But this was too much for his fellow legislators, who were content to leave things where they stood.

A republic required republican citizens, and the citizens must be capable of making competent judgments about public affairs. Jefferson's interest in education reflected as much concern for the public interest as for the welfare of individuals; but in a republican government, the two principles were mutually supporting. As a member of the legislature in the late 1770s, Jefferson worked out a plan for a three-tier system of public education at public expense, which, if acted on, would certainly have improved the opportunities available to whites of the male sex. By a system of selective examinations, he explained, "twenty of the best geniuses will be raked from the rubbish annually, and be instructed, at the public expense, so far as grammar schools go."[9] This was not quite the sort of language with which modern politicians flatter the electorate, and Jefferson, in trying to lighten the prospective burden of taxation, hinted that most of those who took advantage of it would in fact come from the propertied classes. But, in any case, the legislature proved unwilling to impose the tax burden on its constituents. It was only much later in life that Jefferson was able to fulfill his ambition to raise a university in his native state. In order to make state funding of the university possible, he had to relinquish the funding of elementary education to local initiative.

There was no aspect of the pursuit of equality to which Jefferson was more passionately attached than that of religion. Much more anticlerical than most of his American contemporaries—in this he was more akin to the French Enlightenment—he regarded religious intolerance and the enforced imposition of religious conformity as both absurd and blasphemous. He had drafted a statute on religious freedom, which (he later remarked) brought on "the severest contests I have known." But as ambassador in Paris, he was obliged to leave the parliamentary business to James Madison, who was more than equal to the occasion. From their point of view, it was not good enough that all religious sects should be equally entitled to support under the law; Jefferson and Madison wanted to keep the state's hands out of religion altogether. This position implied a fundamental respect for the moral integrity of the individual, who should be equally free to join any sect or no sect at all. The Virginia Statute for Religious Freedom (1785) was one of Jefferson's proudest achievements, which he caused to be introduced into the next edition of the *Encyclopedia* and to be recorded on his tombstone.[10] The Virginia statute set a precedent for the principles of the First Amendment's provisions on religion, also engineered by Madison. The English Bill of

Rights of 1689 had declared England to be a Protestant country and placed restrictions on Catholics; in America, by contrast, the state became a neutral among religions and was formally excluded from entering into religious matters.

If Americans of European descent were perceived as individuals, the same cannot be said of either Native Americans or Africans. The universalism of Jefferson's principles stopped short of these peoples, and in a sense, though on somewhat different grounds, it stopped short of women of any race or people. On the differences between Native Americans and whites he was reluctant to commit himself and tended to attribute the major differences to different stages of civilization, observing that it had taken Europe sixteen centuries after the introduction of the alphabet to produce a Newton.[11] His attitudes were ambivalent. On the one hand, he appeared to consign Native Americans to the fate of removal or even extermination as a weaker civilization. Yet, on the other, he studied them, showed considerable respect for their various cultures, and composed a dictionary of Indian languages (the manuscript of which was lost in a storm on Chesapeake Bay). His interest in them, as Merrill Peterson has remarked, was essentially anthropological. But he did not exclude the possibility that they could be civilized (by European standards) and even incorporated into the white community.[12]

There was no racial repugnance in this attitude, which was essentially cultural. But Jefferson always seems to have found it more difficult to regard African Americans as individuals, notwithstanding the presence of slaves in his household entourage. He was not quite as inactive about slavery as some of his critics claim; he wrote a strongly worded denunciation of the enslavement and importation of Africans in his first draft of the Declaration of Independence (though its force was somewhat obscured by the circuitous reasoning that cast the blame on George III), but this proved more than his Southern colleagues were willing to accept. He made sporadic, but never very persistent, moves against slavery in Virginia and was responsible for the clause forbidding slavery in the Northwest Territory, which featured in the proposed ordinance of 1784. The ban was eventually incorporated in the Northwest Ordinance of 1787. Jefferson successfully introduced into the Virginia legislature a bill to prohibit slave importation—a measure passed before independence, but vetoed by the Crown. But Jefferson's celebrated denunciation of slavery in his *Notes on the State of Virginia* speaks as strongly of his fears for the effects on the masters as on the slaves.[13] He doubted whether Africans were equal to whites in natural abilities, and he even raised the question of a separate origin—a grave speculation for one who believed in a single act of creation. His repugnance made it impossible for him to contemplate incorporating them into white society, and any plan of emancipation was associated with the removal of the freed slaves. It is often observed that in his will he freed only five of his own slaves.[14]

Though Jefferson never ceased to believe that emancipation would come, he never overcame these obstacles, nor did he take advantage of his later years to address himself to them politically. In his later years, when appealed to for help in the cause, he was wearily content to hand the problem on to a future generation. Yet he seems to have been willing to reconsider his views on the question of blacks' abilities, expressing, later in life, some degree of hope that his doubts would be refuted. "But," he added, "whatever their degree of talent it is no measure of their rights."[15] The differences between Africans and Europeans seemed to Jefferson more insuperable than in the case of the American Indian. This difference he regarded as basically cultural, and therefore bridgeable. The differences between Europeans and Africans, however, were *natural*, and therefore, for Jefferson, culturally unbridgeable. This perception caused doubts that gave him lifelong anguish, but he never resolved them. For were not the rights to which they were entitled in Jefferson's book also *natural* rights?

It was not customary to consider the position of women as being in the same category with slaves (this aperçu was developed after Jefferson's time by early female abolitionists). Such an idea would not have occurred to Jefferson. Toward women of his own class and circle, he was capable of affectionate respect for their abilities and tastes, while remaining fundamentally paternalistic (an exception must be made for the English painter Maria Cosway, with whom he fell in love in Paris). But his respect for the intelligence of women who were his social equals did not for one moment imply the fitness of admitting women to the political sphere. When, in 1807, his secretary of the treasury, Albert Gallatin, suggested appointing suitably qualified women to public office in view of the dismal shortage of suitable men, Jefferson replied, "The appointment of a woman to public office is an innovation for which the public is not prepared, nor am I."[16]

The concept of legal distinction based on natural differences was to have a long life. In 1872, the Supreme Court denied a woman's claim to vote with a reference to differences that lay "in the nature of things."[17] The same phrase significantly reappeared in the Supreme Court's validation of racial segregation in *Plessy* v. *Ferguson* in 1896.[18]

All these views were legacies of a philosophy that based human arrangements in what was perceived as the order of nature. Reflection on the history of racial, ethnic, or gender relationships, as well as that of claims to political authority, suggests that the order of nature is very much what men and women make of it at any one time and place. Such views are not, however, legacies that can be equated with Jefferson's or the Enlightenment's universalism. Jefferson saw no problem with regard to gender, which was hardly a political issue in his active lifetime. With regard to race, although he felt the dilemma acutely, it left him helpless. Jefferson was a product of his time and a member of a master class. But he was also an individualist. There was nothing inevitable about his position; such contemporaries as Benjamin Rush, Samuel Stanhope Smith, Alexander Hamilton, and John Jay, to say nothing of contemporary Virginian planters who took the occasion of the Revolution to free their slaves, held more optimistic views of African potential and were willing to espouse them in public.

For all Jefferson's doubts and hesitation, nothing could extinguish the flame lit by his universalist rhetoric. The antislavery movement, which was already growing in strength before the end of Jefferson's life, seized the torch. In 1860, when the Republican Party convention showed signs of wavering, the elderly abolitionist Joshua Giddings made a fiery speech that persuaded—or shamed—the delegates into endorsing the Declaration of Independence. Thus, while Stephen A. Douglas and his followers were struggling to save the Union by pursuing a course of *regional* pluralism that necessitated acceptance of a doctrine of moral pluralism, the Republicans—despite some anxious internal opposition—held in principle that, as Abraham Lincoln himself had recently said, a house divided against itself could not stand. In his Gettysburg Address, Lincoln described the principle that "all men are created equal" as a "proposition." A proposition, according to Euclid, whom Lincoln had once studied, meant a truth that remained to be demonstrated. Lincoln did not live to complete the demonstration. Jefferson might have doubted whether a *self-evident* truth required such a demonstration. But he would hardly have denied the truth of the proposition.

Universalism is, by definition, available to all. When an organized women's movement began to forge its own claims on African society toward the middle of the nineteenth century, its leaders also availed themselves of the language of the Declaration of Independence. The Declaration of Sentiments adopted by the women of the Seneca Falls Convention in 1848 began by holding it "self-evident that all men and women are created equal," and went on with a parody of the grievances listed in 1776.[19] Jefferson might have been surprised, even alarmed, by this, but he could hardly have complained.

Today, we are invited by many spokespersons for ethnic, religious, or linguistic groups to regard the right of political equality as an entitlement, not to individuals in their individual capacities, but only to individuals identified as members of those groups. This view, which now exerts considerable influence on the design of electoral districts, has certain claims to recognition in American constitutional history. The judgment and opinion of the Supreme Court in validating the doctrine of "separate but equal" in *Plessy* v. *Ferguson* had recognized racial groups as having a basis in constitutional law. Many legally enforceable residential and economic arrangements had long been based on such distinctions before they began to crumble in the aftermath of the Second World War. The claim that race or ethnicity constitutes a legitimate basis for political recognition—that it yields a political *entitlement*—is consistent with these earlier, and discredited, doctrines.

For these policies, this essay finds no support either in the philosophy of Jefferson or—if the matter is taken further—in the Constitution where the ethical and legal foundations of political rights were grounded in the equality of individuals.[20] Perhaps it is just as well that Thomas Jefferson is not available to answer the question, "What would Mr. Jefferson have said?"

Notes

1. In Peter S. Onuf, ed., *Jeffersonian Legacies* (Charlottesville: University Press of Virginia, 1993), 1ff.

2. Aristotle, *Politics*, T. A. Sinclair, trans., rev. Trevor J. Saunders (London: Harmondsworth, 1983), VII.iii.6; and *Nicomachean Ethics*, J. A. K. Thomson, trans., rev. Hugh Tredennick (London: Harmondsworth, 1983). Ernest Barker's earlier translation of the *Politics* has: "nothing contrary to nature is right" (Oxford, England: Oxford University Press, 1948).

3. See, in general, Roy Porter and Mikulus Teich, eds., *The Enlightenment in National Context* (Cambridge, England: Cambridge University Press, 1981); and, in particular, J. R. Pole's essay in this collection, "Enlightenment and the Politics of American Nature," 192–214.

4. Bernard Mayo, ed., *Jefferson Himself: The Personal Narrative of a Many-Sided American* (Charlottesville: University Press of Virginia, 1970), 163. (Hamilton replied by ascribing the accolade to Julius Caesar.)

5. Thomas Jefferson, "A Summary View of the Rights of British America," in *The Papers of Thomas Jefferson*, Julian P. Boyd et al., eds., 25 vols.

to date (Princeton, NJ: Princeton University Press, 1950–), 1:126. For a fuller exposition of the individualist theme, see J. R. Pole, "The Individualist Foundations of American Constitutionalism," in *To Form a More Perfect Union: The Critical Ideas of the Constitution,* Herman Belz, Ronald Hoffman, and Peter J. Albert, eds. (Charlottesville: University Press of Virginia, 1992), 73–106.

6. For an exploration of these problems at greater length, see J. R. Pole, *The Pursuit of Equality in American History,* 2d ed. (Berkeley: University of California Press, 1993), esp. in this connection chap. 1, "The Idea of Equality in a Hostile World."

7. Adam Smith, *The Theory of Moral Sentiments,* D. D. Raphael and A. L. Macfie, eds. (Oxford, England: Clarendon Press, 1976), 50.

8. Joyce Appleby, "What Is Still American in Jefferson's Political Philosophy?" in *Liberalism and Republicanism in the Historical Imagination* (Cambridge, MA: Harvard University Press, 1992), 304–309.

9. Merrill D. Peterson, *Thomas Jefferson and the New Nation: A Biography* (New York: Oxford University Press, 1970), 148; hereinafter cited as *New Nation.*

10. See Merrill D. Peterson and Robert C. Vaughan, eds., *The Virginia Statute for Religious Freedom: Its Evolution and Consequences in American History* (Cambridge, England: Cambridge University Press, 1988); and Pole, *Pursuit of Equality,* 89–97.

11. Mayo, *Jefferson Himself,* 39.

12. *New Nation,* 258–259.

13. Thomas Jefferson, *Notes on the State of Virginia,* William Peden, ed. (Chapel Hill: University of North Carolina Press, 1955), 162–163.

14. Ibid., 138–143; on page 143 he discusses the possibility that blacks might be a distinct race.

15. Mayo, *Jefferson Himself,* 292.

16. Charles A. Miller, *Jefferson and Nature: An Interpretation* (Baltimore, MD: Johns Hopkins University Press, 1988), 78.

17. *Bradwell* v. *Illinois,* 83 US 130 (1873), 445–446. See, in general, Pole, *Pursuit of Equality,* chap. 12.

18. *Plessy* v. *Ferguson,* 163 US 537 (1896), 544.

19. Elizabeth Cady Stanton, *History of Woman Suffrage,* E. C. Stanton, S. B. Anthony, and M. J. Gage, eds., 6 vols. (New York: Fowler & Wells, 1881), 1:69–71.

20. For an extension of this theme with regard to the Constitution, see Pole, "The Individualist Foundations," 73–106.

13

Civil Rights and Civil Religion: The Jeffersonian Legacy

Richard King

The 1930s marked the crucial watershed in Thomas Jefferson's relevance for mainstream American political culture. Because the New Deal squared the ideological circle by combining Hamiltonian means and Jeffersonian ends, "there was," according to Merrill D. Peterson, "no 'return to Jefferson.'"[1] In the wake of this sea change in political consciousness, post–Second World War historiography embraced the notion of consensus and the "givenness" (Daniel Boorstin's term) of American political institutions and values. Neo-orthodox theologian Reinhold Niebuhr and ex-southern agrarian turned tragic moderate Robert Penn Warren, noted Peterson, attacked Jefferson's "optimistic rationalism," a view that survives in Gordon Wood's recent characterization of Jefferson as a "pure American innocent."[2] The quasi-theological mood, the evocation of the "tragic," the darkness at noon of those years were a far cry from the clear, bracing prospect offered by the architect of Monticello. "Bogart liberals" and "NATO" intellectuals (C. Wright Mills's characterization) viewed anything smacking of political rationalism or utopianism with deep suspicion. Where Jefferson's Declaration of Independence once was, there Madison's *Federalist Paper*, number 10, would be. Political realism and the end of ideology were the order of the day.

But if Jefferson's influence had waned seriously as the 1960s swung into view, the Civil Rights Era, far from making a resurrection of his reputation, saw its virtual extinction among activists and political intellectuals. In a decade when even Abraham Lincoln, the Great Emancipator himself, was scored for his racism and temporizing on slavery, Jefferson was never a likely candidate for heroic status in the eyes of Civil Rights, New Left, or, needless to say, Black Power militants.

This is not to say that Jefferson has disappeared from view; only that he is no longer pressed into active ideological service in contemporary political debates. Along with John Locke, John Stuart Mill, and Benjamin Constant, Jefferson is routinely mentioned as one of the founders of modern liberalism, though more as an example of the intellectual in politics than as a political philosopher of any great achievement. The American right has never felt comfortable with Mr. Jefferson. But the fact that in 1990 George Will, hardly a man of the left, viewed Jefferson as "the Person of the Millennium . . . what a free person looks like—confident, serene, rational, disciplined, temperate, curious" suggests perhaps a certain rapprochement.[3] Still, most conservatives detect in Jefferson too much of the Enlightenment skeptic, the supporter of the French Revolution, and the cosmopolitan humanist to fit their taste for spiritual certainties and authorized traditions.

Contemporary academic historians are generally detached about the sage of Monticello. But even Jefferson's champions among American historians can get trapped in the ambiguities of his life and reputation. Joyce Appleby recently claimed that "Freeing the human spirit was Jefferson's lifetime crusade," the kind of judgment once confidently offered in reference to Jefferson. Yet no sooner had Appleby delivered her judgment at a symposium on Jefferson in the fall of 1992 at Charlottesville, Virginia, than she had to modify it— in effect, negate it—with the telling admission that Jefferson's appeal to nature entailed the exclusion of blacks, women, and Native Americans from the realm of equality.[4] An African American historian such as Vincent Harding, a onetime adviser to the Student Nonviolent Coordinating Committee (SNCC) and associate of Martin Luther King Jr., hardly gave a nod to Jefferson in *There Is A River: The Black Struggle for Freedom in America*.[5] One might well conclude from Harding's silence that Jefferson was so marginal to an assessment of the black freedom struggle that attacking him was hardly worth the effort. Or perhaps it was that, as Mary Berry and John Blassingame bitingly observe in their *Long Memory: The Black Experience in America*: "Nat Turner, the slave, had a better understanding of the Declaration than his fellow Virginian patriot Jefferson."[6]

Thus the contemporary view of Jefferson, as a man and as a political figure, is one of ambivalence and, occasionally, rejection. Gordon Wood has suggested that Jefferson was a kind of eighteenth-century man without qualities who "scarcely seems to exist as a real historical person."[7] Robert Dawidoff's recent witty, sharp-edged meditation on the tension between individual distinction and equality in American political thinking names Jefferson the "first American limousine liberal"; that is, his "principles . . . did not interfere significantly with his own life."[8] Such a judgment echoes Richard Hofstadter's mordant observation in *The American Political Tradition*—that though Jefferson was attracted to "advanced and liberated ideas," he was "not in the habit of breaking lances trying to fulfill them."[9] Yet Dawidoff also notes that Jefferson was the "quintessential and founding American class-traitor—who in America is the liberal not the radical."[10] Clearly, it is difficult to warm up to Jefferson: he is not folksy enough for populism, not traditional enough for the conservatives, not radical enough for radicals. By now, it is not so much that he is all things to all people; rather, it is that he sometimes seems to mean little or nothing to anyone.

Jefferson's Reputation in the Civil Rights Era

From one point of view, the Civil Rights Movement itself and those academics whose work was substantially shaped by it had quite convincing reasons for rejecting Jefferson. In three large areas— states rights, slavery, and race—Jefferson's thinking was simply out of line with the liberal views of the contemporary left.

On the issue of states rights, a deep irony emerges. The one set of pronouncements that most marked Jefferson as radical in his time— the Kentucky Resolutions of 1798 against the Alien and Sedition Acts—became the constitutional keystone of Southern states rights doctrine, both in the antebellum resistance to the attack on slavery and in the era of resistance to desegregation that followed the Supreme Court's landmark decision in *Brown v. Board of Education*.[11] Peterson describes Jefferson as the "Father of Democracy and the Father of States Rights."[12] Yet in the original context, Jefferson would have seen no contradiction between the two. As Ed Ayers and Scott French suggest, Jefferson "invoked states rights to protect freedom of expression not to defend slavery or racial subjugation."[13]

Indeed, there is potentially another ironic turn to the doctrines of nullification and, ultimately, of secession. With the emergence of Black Power and black separatist ideologies in the late 1960s, the

defense of group rights, rather than individual rights, could arguably have been cited by African American groups wishing to strike
a blow for cultural and political autonomy. But on this issue, mainstream civil rights thinking was adamant: states rights in whatever
form had served historically as an ideological smoke screen for segregation and indirectly as a hindrance to federal intervention in the
legal, political, and economic-social affairs of the states. Thus, in
matters having to do with racial justice and government intervention to promote equality, states rights was all but dead.

But it was on the twinned issues of slavery and race that Jefferson was most vulnerable, a weakness that the historiography of the
1960s and 1970s analyzed in excruciating detail. Henry May was not
quite accurate when he asserted that "until very recently historians
almost ignored" Jefferson's record on race and slavery.[14] Historians
in the 1950s and 1960s had, in fact, noted the inconsistencies in Jefferson's thinking on these matters. Not only Peterson in *The Jefferson
Image*, but also John Hope Franklin, in *From Slavery to Freedom*; Benjamin Quarles in *The Negro in the American Revolution*; Lerone Bennett, in *Before the Mayflower*; and Staughton Lynd, in *The Intellectual
Origins of the American Radicalism*, all writing just before things
heated up, set forth Jefferson's racial views without trying to white-
wash them, but also without making his moral or personal reputation hinge on them entirely.[15]

For instance, New Left historian Lynd's use of Jefferson displayed
a wide gap between the fact of noting Jefferson's dubious positions
and registering their full impact. For Lynd, Jefferson's views on slavery and on states rights remained somehow tangential rather than
central to his life and thought. Along with Tom Paine and other dissenting radicals, Jefferson was still a valuable source of radical ideas
and impulses. But it took the increasingly radical self-consciousness
of the movement and the burgeoning awareness of the centrality of
racism in American history as the 1960s gave way to the 1970s to
make Jefferson's views appear in all their damaging starkness.

The case against Jefferson, however expressed, was pretty convincing. Though Jefferson spoke eloquently, if formulaically, against
slavery privately—and occasionally, publicly—throughout his lifetime, he took no concrete action as president on the issue, except to
urge congressional action to enforce the ban on the slave trade; nor
in his private capacity as planter and slave owner did he do much
to weaken, much less abolish, the peculiar institution. As David
Brion Davis has emphasized, it was not just pervasive racism that
clouded his vision; it was also the quite conscious fear of economic misfortune that held Jefferson back from adopting a more rad-

ical stance against slavery.[16] And when he did speculate on the fate of ex-slaves, his deliberations suggested colonization as a solution.

Moreover, in the sectional crisis of 1819-1820, notes Gordon Wood, Jefferson contended that "Only each state has the 'exclusive right' to regulate slavery." But, according to Davis, "when the chips were down, as in the Missouri crisis," Jefferson "threw his weight behind slavery's expansion."[17] If South Carolina and John C. Calhoun hijacked the doctrine of nullification, it was Jefferson who left the doors unlocked and the motor running. Overall, then, Jefferson showed more profile than courage on the issue of slavery. To quote Garrett Ward Sheldon: "In Jefferson's hierarchy of values, the emancipation of slaves occupied a lower position than either his personal lifestyle or the ideal republic."[18]

The consensus now seems to be not, as August Meier and Elliott Rudwick once wrote, that Jefferson was among the "most advanced thinkers on the subject" of race and slavery.[19] Rather, it is to place him somewhere in the moderate center. Nor, it should be said, was Jefferson greatly agonized about the issue. But his views on race and slavery have come under such scrutiny precisely because he tried to think through these issues and commit his views to public scrutiny. Indeed, David Walker's *Appeal* of 1829 salvaged the racial views Jefferson presented in *Notes on the State of Virginia*. But the definitive analysis of Jefferson's views on race was Winthrop Jordon's monumental *White over Black*. The importance of Jordan's work lay not only in its rigorous analysis of Jefferson's racial thought, but also in its suggestion that Jefferson's racism was more than conventional or perfunctory. Instead, Jordan claimed that Jefferson had a deep psychosexual investment in sexualizing racial difference and then rejecting blacks, especially black women, as inferior. Though Jordan acknowledged that racist stereotypes easily "acquired autonomous energy and a viability independent of emotional underpinnings," he convincingly argued that "the depth of emotional intensity underlying his [Jefferson's] thinking about the Negro seems sufficiently evident."[20]

Edmund Morgan's *American Slavery, American Freedom* shifted the focus from Jefferson's personal psychology by suggesting that for most eighteenth-century white Virginians, there was no necessary contradiction—and thus little emotional or moral ambivalence on their part—between republican freedom for whites and chattel slavery for those of African descent, since a notion of differential humanity, according to which blacks were human but in crucial respects inferior, was widely accepted at the time. In the mid-1970s, John Diggins also suggested that neither Jefferson's psychological makeup nor shared atavistic, racial cultural bias entirely explained the persistence of slavery and racism in the age of Enlightenment. Indeed, noted Diggins, there was a crucial contradiction at the heart of the Enlightenment sensibility between appeals to nature as the foundation of equality and the appeal to experimental evidence as the basis of truth. Empirical evidence pointed to black inferiority, thus contradicting the metaphysical assumption of natural equality. Put another way, equality did not seem to be natural. By appealing to empirical evidence to confirm or refute the doctrine of black inferiority, as he did in *Notes on the State of Virginia*, Jefferson all but ensured its confirmation.[21]

Again, the case against Jefferson seems irrefutable. As Davis put it in the mid-1970s, the "Jefferson image . . . has taken on a villainous hue."[22] Thus, if Jefferson was to be elevated "whiggishly" in terms of his use to the present, particularly in the struggle for civil rights and racial equality, he had to be rejected out of hand. Nor is it obvious why Jefferson should not have been so judged, however much one might have sympathized with his dilemmas and admired his intellect, however strongly the attempt should have been made to avoid self-righteous, unnuanced pronouncements.

However, what most distinguishes studies of Jefferson since the late 1960s is the way Jefferson fails to appear in very favorable light, even when judged in his own, *not* our, context. Writing in 1963, one of Jefferson's most astringent critics, Leonard Levy, noted that while Jefferson cannot "be held responsible for having been born a white man in eighteenth century Virginia," he deserved much harsher judgment on matters concerning the Fourth Amendment and civil liberties, since the "ban on general search warrants and the guarantee of freedom against unreasonable searches and seizures were well understood" at the time.[23]

Something like Levy's judgment could be implied by the positions expressed by Morgan and Diggins above: trapped by racial assumptions of his time, Jefferson could not escape the framework of assumptions that enclosed him. But the works of Jordan, Davis, and Wood suggest otherwise. Any number of other white Virginia planters—and not just marginal visionaries or African Americans such as Benjamin Banneker, who obviously wanted to believe in racial equality—thought and acted differently than Jefferson. As Paul Finkelman has concluded:

> the test of Jefferson's position on slavery is not whether he was better than the worst of his generation, but whether he was the leader of the best; . . . whether he was able to transcend his eco-

nomic interests and his sectional background to implement the ideals he articulated. Jefferson fails the test.[24]

On the matter of Jefferson's racial views, Finkelman is just as damning: "Jefferson's negrophobia was profound."[25] With all this in mind, it is not difficult to understand why during, as well as in the wake of, the Civil Rights Movement, neither Jefferson's actions nor words on race and slavery were of actual or symbolic aid in the struggle for racial equality.

Enlarging the "Text of Civil Instruction"

Having said all this, there are ways other than dead ends to get from Jefferson to the Civil Rights Movement. If we take up the general idea of what Robert Bellah has called "civil religion"—that is, the shared, if loose, national consensus on the central values and institutions, texts and rituals, holidays and martyrs characterizing the political tradition—then it is clear that the mainstream of the Civil Rights Movement made ample use of the rhetoric of the American civil religion in its efforts to destroy Jim Crow. Interestingly, in his First Inaugural Address in 1801, Jefferson himself appealed to such a common ground, or consensus, by first differentiating "differences in principle" from "differences of opinions" and then going on famously to assert: "we are all republicans—we are all federalists." He also spoke of the "principles" (and enumerated them) that "should be the creed of our political faith—the text of civil instruction—the touchstone by which we try the services of those we trust."[26]

It was the genius of the Civil Rights Movement, at least that part represented by Martin Luther King Jr. from the mid-1950s to the late 1960s, to realize that the movement had to draw upon, and appeal to, the "text of civil instruction" embodied in the sacred documents of the political tradition—the Declaration of Independence and the Constitution—if it were to be successful. Ironically, then, just as analysts of Jefferson were exposing his inconsistency and contradiction, King shifted the focus, as it were, from the contradictions in Jefferson the man to the document of which he was the principal author, the Declaration.

It is important to draw out the implications of this shift from the man to the text since it implies a particular kind of textual address. First, what is important is not so much who wrote a text, but what it says or can be construed to say. Moreover, it is not only the original intentions informing the text or the contextual limitation on the document that is important, but how the text may be interpreted at a later time. Indeed, the best way to understand the main ideas articulated in, for instance, the Civil Rights Movement, claim several recent scholars, is not through hard-line intellectual history of the Skinnerian (or Straussian) sort or a close analytical unpacking of concepts. More profitable, in this view, is an essentially rhetorical analysis of how concepts change in meaning and implication over time. Ideas such as rights and equality, freedom and justice are best understood, suggest Celeste Condit and John Lacaites in *Crafting Equality*, as "ideographs" to be deployed rather than concepts with fixed meanings, determined by original intentions.[27] What is crucial, in other words, is the "use value," not the "truth value," of an idea.

What, then, are the implications of this approach for Jefferson's Declaration of Independence and its relation to the Civil Rights Movement? First, in this view, Jefferson functions less as a specific individual than as an "author function," a term indicating the locus of appearance of the Declaration. Second, the Declaration becomes more than a fixed verbal phenomenon; it can also be seen as a form of action, a performative utterance, as it were, that develops in meaning over time rather than remaining fixed.[28] Indeed, Abraham Lincoln's importance in the story of the Declaration, as Garry Wills has noted, is to have recognized what Martin Luther King might have called the "promissory" nature of the Declaration's equality of rights assertion:

> They [the Declaration's signers] meant simply to declare the right, so that enforcement of it might follow as fast as circumstances should permit. . . . The assertion that "all men are created equal" . . . was placed in the Declaration not for that ["separation from Great Britain"] but for future use.[29]

That is, as Wills asserts in his *Lincoln at Gettysburg*, the Declaration was not only a "founding document," but also a "transcendent ideal to be approximated."[30] Or, put slightly differently, by virtue of its articulation in a public document, equality of rights demanded recognition and realization. But the relevant issue, Lincoln to the contrary, is not what the signers, including Jefferson, thought they were doing, but how the Declaration has been used to sanction and implement the idea of equality. Finally, in light of this way of thinking, it is plausible to claim that the presence of Jefferson and the Declaration in the discourse of the Civil Rights Movement was of considerable impact, whatever the "truth" of Jefferson's own life and private thoughts on race, slavery, and states rights may have been.

To tell this story of how Jefferson's Declaration became a main ingredient in the movement's political culture, particularly in the movement's grand public moments, several broad generalizations must be made. First, as almost everyone agrees, American political and legal culture has been historically dominated by "rights talk" and Jefferson's writings, especially the *Summary View* of 1774 and the Declaration of 1776, played a major role in authorizing this rights discourse. Yet not until the mid-1820s did the Declaration come into its own as a source for arguments for and against slavery, with the South understanding the "hard core meaning of Natural Rights [as] a collective right" and the antislavery forces understanding it in terms of the individual rights of the slaves. In 1833, notes Daniel Rodgers, the American Anti-Slavery Society proclaimed, "we plant ourselves upon the Declaration of our Independence";[31] and it was later part of the Liberty Party platform and appropriated through rewriting by the women at the Seneca Falls Convention.

More important, the Declaration was already cited by black petitioners against slavery during the 1770s and 1780s. Between 1828 and 1838, one-third of the documents of black abolitionist discourse referred to the Declaration and others used words and phrases from it.[32] The important point here is that Jefferson's Declaration was "rewritten," both expanded in range to include blacks and women and made more specific, by seeing rights and equality as grounded in society rather than posited prior to it. The distinction between civil, political, and social rights was articulated and developed prior to, as well as after, the Civil War. Thus Jefferson's "influence" in the history of black America is indeed significant, if we focus on the influence of "his" Declaration.

Yet it is just as important to emphasize that the Declaration has been actively and creatively "misread," rather than merely passively received. For the Declaration was the creation of those who came after its original composition and publication, particularly those involved in the antislavery cause. Lincoln, it seems plausible to say, could not have incorporated the commitment to equality into the political culture or civil religion without the efforts of black and white abolitionists prior to, and contemporaneous with, his own political career. This whole process is particularly difficult to bring into explicit focus, since, unlike in the literary tradition where originality is considered a prime virtue, in the American legal-political tradition subservience and faithfulness to the founding texts (and their informing intentions) are emphasized. Yet modifications, including major revisions, are continually being worked on supposedly fixed texts and permanent meanings.[33]

If these claims about the rewriting of the Declaration are roughly the case, then it is correct to insist that it is wrong to "claim that America's public values are 'white' and that black Americans have played no role in the intellectual work of constructing our national heritage" or to assume that "key value terms possess a fixed meaning."[34] What Harding has called the "Great Tradition" of black struggle and what might be called a kind of radical liberalism with expanding rights claims at its core derive from, but have in turn modified, the mainstream legal and political culture. Indeed, the way in which the Great Tradition has always been a step or so ahead of the dominant understanding of what equality meant and what rights entailed can be detected in a statement of Martin Luther King:

> Negroes have proceeded from a premise that equality means what it says. . . . But most whites in America in 1967, including many persons of goodwill, proceed from a premise that equality is a loose expression for improvement. White America is not even psychologically organized to close the gap.[35]

To see how the Civil Rights Movement—a term encompassing the National Association for the Advancement of Colored People's legal and constitutional battle, first, for enforcement of "separate but equal" and, then, against segregation and also such activist organizations as the SNCC, and the Southern Christian Leadership Conference, and the Congress of Racial Equality—revitalized the power of rights talk, another important development should be kept in mind. With the passage of the Reconstruction amendments, assertions of equality (for blacks and women) were grounded explicitly in the Fourteenth Amendment. But concomitantly, the rhetoric of rights and equality based on a direct appeal to the Declaration declined after the Civil War. Indeed, when not rejected altogether, natural rights and natural law ideas became the resort of conservatives, trying to justify property rights and protect business and corporate prerogatives against state restrictions and interventions. Thus, much of the social and economic reform from the Progressive Era to the New Deal was justified not by appeal to rights, but to the will of the people as expressed in representative bodies against elitist courts and judges. Sociological jurisprudence and legal realism, the creations of legal and political progressives, were deeply suspicious of talk about natural rights and natural law as an outmoded, metaphysical hangover from less enlightened times. If elites were needed, then legal and social science elites were preferable to the conservative judges who dominated the legal system.[36]

Yet the fight against segregation was carried on within the court system, rather than in the legislature, and was eventually, of course, articulated in terms of the "Equal Protection" clause of the Fourteenth Amendment. Fascinating in this context is the rebuke Thurgood Marshall received from Felix Frankfurter in 1952 in the first round of argument for what was to become *Brown* v. *Board of Education*. Said Frankfurter: "Then you have to face the fact that this is not a question to be decided by an abstract starting point of natural law, that you cannot have segregation. If we start with that, of course, we will end with that."[37] Frankfurter's caution to Marshall suggested, of course, that the argument against segregation (and earlier slavery) edged perilously close to a kind of natural rights or natural law doctrine, rather than being grounded in popular legislation and constitutional precedent. Far from dead, rights talk was revived in the postwar world, as witnessed in the *Presidential Commission Report on Civil Rights* of 1947 ("To Secure These Rights") and the formulation and dissemination of the *United Nations Declaration of Human Rights*.

The final chapter of this version of the equal rights story concerns the movement itself. At the beginning in Montgomery in 1955, and at the end in Memphis in 1968, King alluded to a kind of metarights theory, perhaps a way of reviving a notion of civil rights grounded in an idea of natural right or natural rights: "the great glory of American democracy is the right to protest for right."[38] To be sure, "right," a term of moral discourse, is not the same as a "right" that is a legal concept. But King was here groping for the thought—on the analogy of the Constitution as a grounding for positive law—that there was an order to things in light of which implementation of civil and political rights was itself morally right. With this, he firmly planted himself in the Great Tradition.

Indeed, King used the Declaration, as well as the Constitution, to give foundational backing to his philosophy of nonviolent direct action. No better examples exist of this use of the texts of civil instruction than two crucial documents of 1963: "Letter from Birmingham Jail" and the "I Have a Dream" speech delivered in August of that year. Keith Miller has traced the origins of King's Lincoln Memorial speech back to a postemancipation tradition of black preaching and public oratory from which King borrowed quite liberally. In this tradition, Lincoln was the presiding moral presence, while the Declaration and religious texts such as the Golden Rule, the Ten Commandments, and the Sermon on the Mount were the repository of the values underlying the African American version of the civil religion. It is also important to note that in this tradition, Lincoln, not Jefferson, personified the national commitment to equal rights.

In the "I Have a Dream" speech, King placed Jefferson's "We hold these truths . . ." at the center of the American "creed." King, of course, did not call attention to the fact that "interposition and nullification," the words that luridly dripped from the lips of the governor of Alabama, George Wallace, were also Jeffersonian concepts. Very importantly, the "I Have a Dream" address, like all of King's speeches, mixed discourse and genres—the central documents of the civil religion with the black Protestant sermon or jeremiad. It should also be noted that the much more militant speech of SNCC chairman John Lewis at the Lincoln Memorial that day also alluded to "the unfinished work of the revolution of 1776." Overall, in Miller's words, "'I Have a Dream' is a brilliant speech because it is brilliantly conventional."[39]

Though not a public address, "Letter from Birmingham Jail" also drew upon mixed political and religious rhetorics to great effect, in part because it was aimed explicitly at white clergy and was published with a predominantly white liberal readership in mind. At once a jeremiad and a quasi-Pauline epistle, a tract in political theory and an explanation of political strategy, the "Letter" touches all the bases. In it, the Jeffersonian connection is alluded to three times: in a reference to "Constitutional and God-given rights," to the time "before the pen of Jefferson etched the majestic words of the Declaration of Independence," and to the Constitution and Declaration as "great wells of Democracy."[40] The point is clear: the mainstream of the Civil Rights Movement, the strategy and vision of which were articulated by Martin Luther King Jr., owed much of its public rhetoric to political ideas and rhetoric threading back through the history of black protest and the rights tradition to Jefferson's Declaration of Independence.

Beyond the Civil Religion

King's brief discussion of just and unjust laws and the obligation—not option—to disobey the latter in his "Letter" raised the civil disobedience issue as a valid form of political action for civil rights activists and not just for founding fathers in the far-distant past. By so doing, it implicitly suggested the way the movement sought to act on the often perfunctorily cited patriotic and religious rhetoric of the civil religion, including the tradition of rights talk. Or at least it tried to give the civil religion a dissenting, oppositional dimension.

That having been said, in its assault upon segregation, the Civil Rights Movement drew upon traditions of political thought and action other than the rights tradition. In fact, Jefferson was not only one of the founding fathers of the American liberal tradition of rights, but he stood squarely in the republican tradition of emphasis upon citizen virtue and participation in public affairs. The constitutional tocsin of "equal protection," along with a definite bias toward negative freedom, stands at the heart of American liberal thought. Though sometimes linked with the right to dispose of one's own property, the ideas of negative freedom or rights, for American liberalism generally, derive from the Jeffersonian belief in liberty of conscience and from a firm bias against state support of what John Rawls calls a "comprehensive idea of the good."[41] Still, radical liberalism's commitment to civil disobedience challenges most mainstream notions of what constitutes normal politics—the pursuit of self-interest through the medium of political parties. Though pursuit of self-interest was certainly a component of the Civil Rights Movement's goals, the ethos of the movement suggested something more was at stake.

Indeed, that something more might be likened to civic virtue. Here, the student wing of the movement, represented most clearly by the SNCC, pursued a kind of republican emphasis upon participatory politics and community organization. If civic humanism splits between an emphasis upon a virtuous elite to direct political life and an emphasis upon democratic participation by the citizen body, then the SNCC version of politics was definitely—and defiantly—of the latter sort. (It should be added that the SNCC was deeply suspicious of King's emphasis upon single leaders and mass movements.) What is fascinating here is that there are dimensions of Jefferson's political vision—his idea of a local, ward-based politics—that were compatible in spirit with civil rights and New Left politics of the 1960s. But the SNCC was never able to institutionalize its idea of decentralized, grassroots political organization and thus create, in Hannah Arendt's terms, the "lasting institutions" to preserve the commitment to political freedom (in her sense) that the movement was so clearly instrumental in rekindling. For that matter, as Arendt pointed out in *On Revolution*, neither was Jefferson.[42]

Certainly, the mainstream of the Civil Rights Movement aimed at more than a value-neutral political order; or, at least, the talk of the "beloved community," to be realized through nonviolent direct action, a position that called for a specific form of moral self-understanding, would suggest as much. Again, this was not far removed from the idea that citizen action should be in the service of some set of communal values, rather than merely pursuing self-interest. Finally, that participants in the movement were willing to risk their lives suggests a commitment to some collective good beyond the calculation of self-interest. In developing new and/or reviving old notions of what was involved in political action, the Civil Rights Movement gave expression to an impulse that has emerged periodically throughout American political history.

It is fair to say, however, that two other dimensions of the movement's culture were neither shaped by nor reminiscent of Jeffersonian traditions. Beyond the radical liberal and the civic republican forms of politics, the movement also displayed a form of specifically post–French revolutionary politics, in which collective political action becomes a means of effecting individual and group transformation. Politics involves more than winning independence from external control or even the creation of lasting institutions to preserve a space of freedom. Most centrally, it is about achieving a new sense of individual and collective self.

Though King edged toward a kind of "redemptive" politics, he never embraced its more extreme forms. From the mid-1950s onward, one central theme of King's political rhetoric was the need for black self-respect, for a sense of "somebodyness" to replace the fear, apathy, and lingering sense of inferiority endemic in much of the black population. In the rhetoric of freedom, this was a radical form of positive freedom, which eventually defined authenticity and identity in terms of an elusive quality called "blackness." Underlying a black aesthetic grounded on black consciousness was the assumption that there was some black "general will," some shared black interest, in terms of which all political-aesthetic choices and attitudes could be judged. The ultimate expression of this therapeutic form of identity politics (though downplaying the specifically racial dimension) was found in the writings of Martinique-born, Algerian revolutionary Frantz Fanon, who wrote eloquently—and frighteningly—of the creation of a new form of humanity that would emerge out of the violent struggles against the colonizer. In the wake of the Civil Rights Movement proper, groups such as the Black Panthers brought a specifically Fanonist understanding of political action to the American urban scene.[43]

Finally, and perhaps most important, was the collective, religiously derived self-consciousness that characterized the southern movement. If any form of political expression was foreign to the letter or spirit of Jeffersonian politics, it was this model of the politics of collective liberation from the bondage of slavery, both actual (in the Civil War) and metaphorical (on the analogy of the children of

Israel's deliverance from Pharaoh), and of segregation.[44] Where Jefferson was the quintessential product of the Enlightenment, the Civil Rights Movement was thoroughly grounded in southern black Protestantism's biblical faith. In that tradition, there was an understanding of history founded not on secular progress in rationality and rights, but on religious understanding of history as under God's guidance and judgment. In this vision of history, black Americans were, like the Puritans and the children of Israel, chosen to redeem the nation. Made coherent not by a political idea such as freedom or equality, but by the story of freedom and deliverance recorded in Exodus, this religious aspect of southern black political culture was the glue that held the Civil Rights Movement together. Though the central image of the Exodus story was one of physical departure, not legal secession, "Afro-Americans," writes Charles Henry, "have been unique in their use of the chosen people metaphor to affirm their inclusion in the larger society rather than their separateness."[45] Finally, in the story of collective deliverance, equality was grounded in the fatherhood of God, not in any doctrine of natural or inalienable rights.

Conclusion

Like much of American politics, the Civil Rights movement drew upon both secular and sacred, political and religious understandings of history and politics. Specifically, some of its key ideas and ideals such as freedom and equality reflected the dual sources of the political culture. Yet African American political culture is also distinctive in the particular spin it gives to this political tradition. Though some recent analysts of the Civil Rights Movement such as Keith Miller and Charles Henry have stressed, too emphatically perhaps, its African American roots at the expense of its grounding in the essentially secular discourse of modern Western and American political thought, there is no doubt that black politics has seen, as Henry puts it, the "inclusion of a wider variety of political expression and demand, by its emphasis on identity and self-respect . . . , by its dependence on rhetoric and charisma, and by its rootedness in black church tradition that blends sacred and secular vision."[46]

It is not clear whether it matters what *the* main goal of the movement was, whether it was, broadly speaking, equality or freedom. At least rhetorically, a case can be made for the priority of freedom, however defined: from the slogan "Freedom Now!" to "Freedom Summer," the prize on which everyone had their eyes was freedom. But what did freedom mean, and was it compatible with equality? Just as with the relationship between power and freedom, equality and freedom can be posed as opposites; yet other formulations allow them to become all but synonymous or mutually dependent. For instance, participatory freedom implies citizen equality, though the latter condition can exist with little or no access to the public realm. Substantive equality is thought to be inimical to freedom of choice. Yet to exercise one's freedom, one needs certain substantive provisions that may imply an equalizing requirement. And so the argument can go.

The dynamism of the movement derived primarily from non-Jeffersonian sources in which freedom, rather than equality, was central. Jefferson's Declaration was certainly crucial among the political texts that the Civil Rights Movement invoked and upon which it drew. But it was the movement itself that brought the various political and religious traditions to a focus and thereby created its own tradition, forging new meanings, or at least applications, for old concepts and stories. That remains its great importance in, and interest for, recent American history.

Notes

1. Merrill D. Peterson, *The Jefferson Image in the American Mind* (New York: Oxford University Press, 1960), 448.

2. Peterson, *Jefferson Image*, 452; Gordon S. Wood, "The Trials and Tribulations of Thomas Jefferson," in *Jeffersonian Legacies*, Peter S. Onuf, ed. (Charlottesville: University Press of Virginia, 1993), 413, hereinafter cited as *Jeffersonian Legacies*.

3. *Jeffersonian Legacies*, 446.

4. Joyce Appleby, "Introduction: Jefferson and His Complex Legacy," in *Jeffersonian Legacies*, 3, 10.

5. Vincent Harding, *There Is a River: The Black Struggle for Freedom in America* (New York: Harcourt Brace Jovanovich, 1981).

6. Mary Frances Berry and John W. Blassingame, *Long Memory: The Black Experience in America* (Oxford, England: Oxford University Press, 1982), 56.

7. *Jeffersonian Legacies*, 395.

8. Robert Dawidoff, "The Jeffersonian Option," *Political Theory* 21, No. 3 (August 1993): 438.

9. Richard Hofstadter, "Thomas Jefferson: The Aristocrat as Democrat," in *The American Political Tradition*, reprint ed. (Norwich, England: Fletcher & Son, 1971), 25.

10. Dawidoff, *Political Theory*, 439.

11. *Brown* v. *Board of Education*, 347 US 483 (1954).

12. Peterson, *Jefferson Image*, 37.

13. Scott A. French and Edward L. Ayers, "The Strange Career of Thomas Jefferson: Race and Slavery in American Memory, 1943–93," in *Jeffersonian Legacies*, 421.

14. Henry F. May, *The Enlightenment in America* (New York: Oxford University Press, 1976), 300.

15. John Hope Franklin and Alfred A. Moss Jr., *From Slavery to Freedom: A History of African Americans* (New York: McGraw Hill, 1994); Benjamin Quarles, *The Negro in the American Revolution* (Chapel Hill: University of North Carolina Press, 1961); Lerone Bennett, *Before the Mayflower: A History of the Negro in America, 1619–1964*, rev. ed. (Baltimore, MD: Penguin Books, 1966); and Staughton Lynd, *The Intellectual Origins of American Radicalism* (London: Faber & Faber, 1969).

16. David Brion Davis, *The Problem of Slavery in the Age of Revolution, 1770–1823* (Ithaca, NY: Cornell University Press, 1975), 166–167.

17. *Jeffersonian Legacies*, 411; Davis, *The Problem of Slavery*, 184.

18. Garrett Ward Sheldon, *The Political Philosophy of Thomas Jefferson* (Baltimore, MD: Johns Hopkins University Press, 1991), 139.

19. August Meier and Elliott Rudwick, *From Plantation to Ghetto* (London: Constable & Co., 1965), 48.

20. Winthrop D. Jordan, *White over Black: American Attitudes toward the Negro, 1550–1812* (Chapel Hill: University of North Carolina Press, 1968), 471, 460.

21. Edmund S. Morgan, *American Slavery, American Freedom: The Ordeal of Colonial Virginia* (New York: W. W. Norton, 1975); and John P. Diggins, "Slavery, Race, and Equality: Jefferson and the Pathos of the Enlightenment," *American Quarterly* 28, no. 2 (Summer 1976): 206–228.

22. Davis, *The Problem of Slavery*, 166. See French and Ayers, "The Strange Career of Thomas Jefferson," for a short discussion of Jordan, Morgan, and Davis on Jefferson.

23. Leonard W. Levy, *Jefferson and Civil Liberties: The Darker Side* (New York: Quadrangle Books, 1963), ix.

24. Paul Finkelman, "Jefferson and Slavery: 'Treason against the Hopes of the World,'" in *Jeffersonian Legacies*, 181.

25. Ibid., 185.

26. Thomas Jefferson, "First Inaugural Address (1801)," in *The Portable Jefferson*, Merrill D. Peterson, ed. (New York: Penguin [Viking Portable], 1975), 292, 294.

27. Celeste Michele Condit and John Louis Lacaites, *Crafting Equality: America's Anglo-African Word* (Chicago: University of Chicago Press, 1993). The authors define an ideograph as a "culturally biased, abstract word or phrase drawn from ordinary language, which serves as a constitutional value for a historically situated collectivity" (xii). It "identifies the range of acceptable public beliefs and behaviors within any publicly constituted community" (xiii). Though this rhetorical approach can be very fruitful,

concepts such as "equality" cannot have just any meaning. That is, concepts also have histories as well as contexts, and thus their meaning(s) can transcend specific historical contexts. In sum, the rhetorical approach needs supplementing by an intellectual-historical approach.

28. In Hannah Arendt, *On Revolution* (New York: Viking Press, 1963), 127; the author notes this performative dimension of the Declaration, though she does not use the term "performative," which derives from speech act theory. For a more extensive analysis of this issue, involving both Jefferson and Arendt, see Barbara Honig, "Declarations of Independence: Arendt and Derrida on the Problem of Founding a Republic," *American Political Science Review* 85, no. 1 (March 1991): 97–113. For the idea of "author function," drawn from Foucault and applied in reference to Martin Luther King's writings, see Richard H. King, *Civil Rights and the Idea of Freedom* (Oxford, England: Oxford University Press, 1992), 108–114.

29. Garry Wills, *Inventing America: Jefferson's Declaration of Independence* (New York: Doubleday, 1978), xviii.

30. Garry Wills, *Lincoln at Gettysburg: The Words That Remade America* (New York: Simon & Schuster, 1992), 131–132.

31. Daniel T. Rodgers, *Contested Truths: Keywords in American Politics since Independence* (New York: Basic Books, 1987), 71, 76.

32. Condit and Lacaites, *Crafting Equality*, 85–86, 288.

33. I am adverting here to Harold Bloom's ideas of the "anxiety of influence" and "misreading" as they might be applied in areas other than the post-Enlightenment literary tradition.

34. Condit and Lacaites, *Crafting Equality*, 2.

35. Harding, *There Is a River*; Charles P. Henry, *Culture and African American Politics* (Bloomington: Indiana University Press, 1990), 1–2.

36. For a thorough discussion of the legal thought of the interwar years, see Edward A. Purcell Jr., *The Crisis of Democratic Theory: Scientific Naturalism and the Problem of Value* (Lexington: University Press of Kentucky, 1973).

37. Leon Friedman, ed., *Argument* (New York: Chelsea House, 1969), 44.

38. King, *Idea of Freedom*, 103.

39. Keith Miller, "Touchstones, Authorities, and Marian Anderson: The Making of 'I Have a Dream,'" unpublished paper, 23.

40. Martin Luther King Jr., *Why We Can't Wait* (New York: Harper & Row, 1964), 81, 97, 99.

41. John Rawls, *Political Liberalism* (New York: Columbia University Press, 1993), 173–211.

42. Arendt, *On Revolution*, 234–242.

43. See King, *Idea of Freedom*, chap. 7, for an extended discussion and analysis of the politics of self-respect and Fanon's therapeutics of violence.

44. J. C. D. Clark, *The Language of Liberty, 1660–1832: Political Discourse and Social Dynamics in the Anglo-American World* (Cambridge, England: Cambridge University Press, 1994), makes clear that the idea of the "chosen people" as prefigured by the "children of Israel" was a trope deeply embedded in Anglo-American political consciousness and not confined to the New England Puritans. Thus, to say that it was foreign to Jefferson's political vision is not to say that it was foreign to American political culture generally.

45. Henry, *Culture and African American Politics*, 61.

46. Ibid., 107.

14

Women and Equality:
Promise or Deception?

Elizabeth Fox-Genovese

Surely one of the great curiosities of the late twentieth century must be that our political culture congratulates itself for having rejected all intellectual and moral justifications of inequality, except—with growing bad faith—inequality of wealth. Yet, proverbially, the repressed return. Claims of illegitimate inequality haunt us at every turn, and inequality of wealth seems to do nothing but grow. Toward the end of *The Pursuit of Equality in American History*, J. R. Pole wryly notes, "Equality had proved to be an infinitely more complex subject than it had seemed to most of its exponents and devotees of earlier generations."[1] Our own times have more than confirmed his observation, especially with respect to the equality of women.

I

When Mary Wollstonecraft, a contemporary of Thomas Jefferson, entered the rights of woman on the revolutionary agenda of the late eighteenth century, she portentously cloaked women's status in the emerging political language of individualism, if only by assimilating it to the explosive and unambiguously political language of the rights of man.[2] That she did not actually demand political representation for women does not mitigate the implications of her appeal, but it did augur some understandable confusion. As Pole states, Wollstonecraft's primary concern remained to claim for women an intellectual and moral independence equal to that of men. She never claimed that women and men were, in other respects, identical, but simply that manners and morals, rather than nature, should be credited with women's indisputable proclivity for fashion and frivolity. Women, she believed, should be treated as serious, accountable beings, who were fully capable of intelligent reflection upon themselves and society.

In retrospect, we may recognize that Wollstonecraft was drawing upon a venerable Christian tradition of holding each soul accountable for its own relation with God. That tendency within Christianity always coexisted with tolerance, indeed enthusiasm, for a myriad of inequalities between women and men, variously justified by Scripture and nature, but Christianity could never forsake its fundamental tenet that, like every human being, women were responsible for their sins and rewarded for their virtues—that women must cultivate personal relations with God. Throughout the medieval and early modern periods, specific women, notably Christine de Pisan, had drawn upon this tradition to defend women's intrinsic capacity for excellence.[3] At an accelerating rate during the seventeenth and eighteenth centuries, a few women and even fewer men had begun to expand the tradition to include women's intellectual capacities, and perhaps even intellectual equality to men, on the grounds that, as one put it, "in mind there is no sex at all." So when Wollstonecraft wrote, the problem of women's spiritual and intellectual equality with men was not entirely new.

Wollstonecraft innovated by adopting the language of politics and, more significantly, of radical politics to call attention to her message. The full significance of her strategy may best be understood if we recognize that the results of the French Revolution, from which she borrowed, included the overthrow of the ascriptive inequalities of legal estates and the virtual identification of man and citizen with its implied claim that human beings are inherently political beings. The possible implications for women of Wollstonecraft's formulation were thus twofold: first, that women, in all their social and personal diversity, could be subsumed under the essential category of woman; and second, that women, as naturally endowed with rights, might also be seen as political beings. And although Wollstonecraft did not herself press the political implications of her claims, her successors would not take long to do so. Her evocation of the universal woman, however, had more immediate significance, if only by counterpoising women as a group to men as a group and demanding equality between them.

Wollstonecraft wrote during the dusk of a world in which differences of power and prestige among women might well be as significant, if not more so, than those between women and men within social groups and the dawn of a world in which all women, regardless of social position and resources, were equally excluded from public positions. The imaginative division of the world between public and private—male and female—spheres, which was emerging in Wollstonecraft's Britain and triumphed in Western societies after her death, provided the context within which subsequent advocates of women's rights read her words. And their experience of systematic legal exclusion or disadvantage on account of their sex in turn led most of them to shape their discussions of women's rights as a claim for women's equality with men. Some, to be sure, turned to the ideology of separate spheres to celebrate women's difference from men, but even they, sooner or later, were normally drawn to demand equal political rights for women, if only to permit them to defend their distinct morality in the public sphere. Both groups of women activists, moreover, accepted virtually without question the assumption inherent in Wollstonecraft's use of the singular "woman," namely, that women, by virtue of their sex, shared similar interests.

In retrospect, we may see that Wollstonecraft's most important legacy was simultaneously to erase possible inequalities among women from the discussion and implicitly to tie the defense of women's rights to the defense of the equality of women and men. Above all, Wollstonecraft, much in the manner of her male peers, successfully generalized her own experience to cover the experience of all women. A century after Wollstonecraft's death, when the political defense of the rights of woman had become an active struggle, the tensions between their justification on the grounds of "equality" and on the grounds of "difference" had surfaced in forms that Wollstonecraft might never have imagined. Both tendencies in what was finally being called "feminism" could nonetheless be traced to her assumptions about woman as a universal category.

When, during the mid-1970s, I began to teach *A Vindication of the Rights of Woman*, I was astounded by how contemporary the students found it and how easily they assimilated it to their own experience. It was as if, during these two centuries, nothing had changed. Their sense of the immediacy of Wollstonecraft's voice apparently derived from their conviction that she, like them, wanted the freedom to combine womanhood and professional accomplishment and that, like them, she wanted to respect herself and enjoy the respect of others. They especially responded to her conviction that women were reared to think and behave like girls rather than independent individuals. They instinctively understood her claim that women's dependence derived from things they did to themselves as well as things that were done to them. And they embraced her plea, "Let woman share the rights and she will emulate the virtues of man; for she must grow more perfect when emancipated, or justify the authority that chains such a weak being to her duty."[4]

In retrospect, it seems clearer to me than it did at the time that Wollstonecraft's immediacy in large part derived from her uncanny ability to convey the psychological nuances of one woman's response to her situation—to personalize women's disadvantages in a way that invited students' personal identification. But that immediacy also derived from the pervasive radicalism of her politics. For although she refrained from detailing specific reforms, she did insidiously suggest that, at some time in the future, "all will *be* right."[5] And by all being right, she clearly meant that women like herself, notably women intellectuals, would be equal to the men of their group. Her reluctance to make specific proposals inevitably suggested that "equality" was an abstraction, even as her sensitive evocation of women's feelings about their own inequality suggested that the essence of equality lay less in political institutions than in women's feelings about themselves.

II

The struggle for the passage of the Equal Rights Amendment (ERA) during the 1970s and the early 1980s placed the issue of women's equality squarely on the national agenda, even as it exposed persisting doubts among Americans as to whether absolute equality between women and men was possible or even desirable. The failure of the amendment gave victory to the skeptics, but simultaneously fueled a piecemeal struggle that would, within a decade, effectively transform the meaning of equality in ways that few were willing to acknowledge candidly.[6] The ERA itself was simple enough, claiming only that "Equality of rights under the law shall not be denied or abridged by the United States or by any State on account of sex" and providing that Congress should have the power to enforce the provisions of the article.

The ERA, which had originally been proposed in 1923 by Alice Paul and the Woman's Party, effectively claimed to extend and guarantee the fundamental promise of American citizenship to women, namely, the uncontested enjoyment of the full rights of a citizen. Its insistence upon the Congress as the ultimate guarantor of those rights was especially significant, in that it seemed to bind women as equal players into the political life of the country. The promise of the ERA lay in its extending to woman the rights that the American political tradition had long granted man. As Raoul Berger argued, if the equality of women as a group was not acknowledged as a matter of natural law, their interest would continue to require repeated judicial intervention.[7] Even before the amendment's defeat, however, it was becoming clear that the most radical feminists were unlikely to settle for this abstract equality of opportunity. In the end, what feminists above all retained from the struggle to pass the ERA was the conviction that women's goals should be expressed and defended as "rights." They thus borrowed prestige and legitimacy from the language of politics even as they increasingly turned to the Supreme Court—the least democratic of our institutions—to secure the validation of their goals.

The turn to the courts to secure women's equality had begun before the defeat of the ERA, notably with the campaign to establish and defend abortion rights. *Roe v. Wade* had not itself been explicitly drafted in the language of equality, but had defended the availability of abortion under the rubric of the right to privacy.[8] In the wake of the defeat of the ERA and mounting conservative challenges to *Roe*, feminists were increasingly drawn to describe abortion as a fundamental right, analogous to those enunciated in the Declaration of Independence.[9] During the same years, affirmative action, which had originated to guarantee equality of opportunity, was increasingly defended as a means of securing equality of outcome.

For feminists, the most sobering affirmative action battle was probably *Equal Employment Opportunity Commission v. Sears, Roebuck & Co.*, for that case exposed the abiding tension between difference and equality in women's situation and divided feminist scholars and activists in an acrimonious debate.[10] The case served as a disillusioning reminder that the evocation of sexual difference was a two-edged sword that could easily be turned against women. Few, however, drew from their unpleasant brush with the dangers of difference an unambiguous commitment to equality of opportunity. At the extreme, postmodern feminists, notably Joan Scott, unilaterally repudiated the artificial dichotomy between difference and equality as invidious and illegitimate, because that dichotomy "denies the way in which difference has long figured in notions of equality and it suggests that sameness is the only ground on which equality can be claimed."[11]

But even feminists who did not initially follow Scott into the thickets of postmodernist theory began to look for ways to promote equality without repudiating all vestiges of sexual difference.

Notwithstanding a strong current in feminist theory that actively celebrated women's difference from—and, frequently, superiority over—men, few feminists who paid any attention to women's situation in society and the economy were willing to repudiate the notion of equality entirely, and many embraced it enthusiastically. As in the time of Alice Paul, those most likely to defend equality were primarily concerned with the situation of elite professional women whose lives most closely resembled those of the men of their class and for whom "joint-parenting" and the availability of high-quality child care effectively negated the irreducible physiological differences between women and men. Even these feminists demonstrably benefited from programs to enforce affirmative action and punish sexual harassment, but they nonetheless tended to believe that undue emphasis on the differences between women and men would hinder, rather than advance, their professional prospects.

Feminist reluctance to emphasize the significance of sexual difference derived from fear of the ways in which the "protection" of women's difference could result in their exclusion from desirable opportunities such as military combat, hazardous industrial work, or even, as in the *Sears* case, commission sales. Similarly, many feminists opposed provisions for maternal leave on the grounds that it reinforced the notion that women were naturally responsible for children, thereby reinforcing the identification between women and reproduction. As the battle over *Roe* persisted into the early 1990s, many of the arguments for the availability of abortion increasingly emphasized women's right to be freed from their reproductive capacities. But these and related concerns about the ways in which difference might penalize women did not necessarily lead most feminists into an unambiguous defense of equality.

Most feminists persisted in a vague feeling, much like Wollstonecraft's, that women labored under the legacy of their historical subordination, which adversely affected—even precluded—their ability to compete on an entirely equal footing with men. Most, also like Wollstonecraft, were loathe to argue that nature had disadvantaged women relative to men, for that admission would effectively undercut the hope for equality in the future. But they were willing, if not eager, to endorse a variety of measures that would compensate for men's long-standing oppression of women in public and private relations. In this spirit, some feminists supported affirmative action initiatives that strongly resembled quota systems; others supported comparable worth; while still others, primarily on college campuses, supported a variety of speech and behavior codes.

By the early 1990s, some feminists were becoming nervous about a growing tendency among some women to promote so-called victim feminism. In popular books, first Katie Roiphe and then Naomi Wolf opened broadsides against women who were claiming ever more official protection for their purported sexual vulnerability, notably with respect to acquaintance rape. Roiphe, especially, offers a merciless picture of young victim feminists who were terrified of the sexual adventures with which they regularly flirted and who would turn morning-after regrets about consensual sex into formal charges of abuse.[12] In different ways, Roiphe and Wolf both suggest that it is high time for feminists to grow up and take responsibility for their lives, rather than turning to increasingly paternalistic institutions to protect them.

Even feminists who are most hostile to any emphasis on the significance of sexual difference have, nonetheless, refrained from attacking all manifestations of affirmative action out of hand; and very few, even of those who are most enthusiastic about sexual equality, have insisted that women should simply be left to fend for themselves in the world that men have created. Virtually all feminists, in other words, remain attuned to one or another way in which women and men are not equal, and virtually all of them are happy to see persisting inequalities redressed—if need be, by the police, the Congress, or, especially, the courts. So, even as differences about the most salient forms of inequality and about appropriate remedies persist, feminists continue to harbor an uneasy feeling that equality remains an elusive goal.

III

Feminists' sense that equality keeps slipping through women's fingers betrays, among other things, a pervasive disagreement about the meaning of equality. Many feminists, eschewing the view of both left-wing radicals and right-wing traditionalists, scornfully dismiss equality in the sense of equality of opportunity as a bad joke, and some even see a malicious male conspiracy. The postmodernists' attack on the bad faith embedded in the implicit understanding of equality as "sameness" resonates among growing numbers of frustrated feminists who must constantly grapple with the knowledge that women are neither identical to men nor, as Western culture had traditionally held, their opposites. Notwithstanding the cogency of their critique, it, no less than the view it attacks, rests upon its own dubious assumptions.

At the core of much feminist theory, notably its postmodern variants, lies an unexamined assumption about the relation between politics and personal psychology or, to put it differently, politics and the subjective self. This assumption dangerously conflates what Charles Fried, in another context, has called "an effect of the principle" with "the principle itself."[13] Fried is protesting the limitations that many campuses have imposed on the First Amendment right of liberty of speech in the name of protecting the sensibilities of those unrestricted free speech might disparage and who might accordingly tend to be silenced by it, thereby losing their freedom of speech. As Fried insists, the argument is specious, and the policies enacted in its name are decisively altering the quality of intellectual exchange on many campuses. The ideological origin of the conflation of content with result is hardly a secret, although somehow we are compelled not to notice. But who does not know that this very conflation was the bedrock of Stalinism, which bluntly proclaimed that a reactionary result proved reactionary intent? That doctrine was, we might recall, the foundation for the charge that since the victims of the great purge trials had advocated policies objectively favorable to fascism, they were thereby proven to be fascists. Yet some feminists, notably Catharine MacKinnon, apparently oblivious of the ghastly history of her preferred doctrine, defend restrictions of male speech as necessary to women's freedom to speak, and any number of "multiculturalists" have done the same.[14]

The defense of freedom of speech, like other principles of liberty and democracy, depends upon an assumption about equality, namely, that the rules of free speech operate in an arena in which those who observe and benefit from the rules meet in some sense as equals. The defense of free speech is compatible with the assumption that those who benefit from it will also observe some minimal standards of manners or civility and respect other relevant laws. Free speech, in other words, has not normally been taken to legitimate the willful shredding of the arena in which it operates. Understood in this way, the principle of free speech adheres to a community rather than to individuals per se. Obviously, individuals exercise the right of free speech, but they do so because of their membership in a polity that has embraced free speech as a principle. Free speech and other liberties derive from community consensus and agreement, not from natural law; they are political, not natural, rights. Inequality among individuals should not affect their freedom of speech since they are indeed equal in their right to exercise it.

It has become a commonplace that uniform, abstract principles do not favor all individuals equally. Laurence Tribe, for example, has insisted that the right of free speech does not operate neutrally with respect to unions and corporations and must be understood as allocational rather than distributional.[15] Thus he argues that the tendency to see First Amendment rights as applying to society as a whole inevitably obscures the inequalities that prevent all people from benefiting equally from those rights. The received wisdom that to those that have shall be given obtains in countless situations of formal equality. But it does not logically follow that because formal equality may easily benefit the powerful more than the weak, especially when the unequally distributed power is economic or social, equality must ipso facto be repudiated as a principle. The hard truth remains that the principle of equality does not normally produce equality of effect. Nor is it clear that society would be freer or materially better off if it did.

As a political principle, equality has traditionally abstracted from the countless palpable inequalities that differentiate individuals. Were we to start with the attributes of individuals, we should be forced to acknowledge that the principle of equality is no principle at all, but a deceptive myth. No two individuals are, or ever will be, equal. But this fundamental truth has hardly escaped the attention of many political theorists who have defended the principle of equality as a cornerstone of modern democratic polities. It accordingly seems probable that most political theorists have accepted the principle of political equality as a worthy fiction, even as they have acknowledged that it is unlikely to alter substantial inequalities of temperament, character, talent, and material advantages. Nor does their provisional acceptance of the principle mean that they have not probingly criticized its failure to promote substantive equality in practice. Indeed, in our own time, political theorists have paid increasing attention to what equality means or does not mean.

One thing remains clear. In our time, at the level of general perception, equality means, above all, personal equality among individuals. It has become unacceptable to define anyone with reference to difference lest such reference be, in some way, disparaging or demeaning. Thus, in a fit of macabre humor, my husband has taken to referring to our dog and cats as "species-challenged persons." I fear that campus speech codes confirm that these are no laughing matters. But it is difficult not to suspect that even the fanatical attention to the signs of personal worth—self-esteem as it is known—themselves mask a deeper concern.

Presumably, we would not be witnessing such obsessive concern with personal status were status itself not up for grabs. Having discredited all rationales for difference in status, we have condemned ourselves to a society ordered by the vagaries of the market. At issue in most of the discussions of equality is economics, but since few are willing to talk openly about money, we talk about everything else. Difference figures prominently in these discussions, but primarily as a rationale for compensating for the presumed liabilities it imposes upon individuals. In our highly technical, global economy, adequate incomes increasingly depend upon jobs that require intellectual certification, normally one or more university degrees, and, in the United States, that carry benefits as well. Under these conditions, successful completion of a university degree amounts to a meal ticket. Broad recognition of this necessity has resulted in growing pressure on universities—again, especially in the United States, where so many universities are expensive—to grant students degrees almost independent of the quality of the work they perform.

Unfortunately, universities apparently find it more convenient, not to mention less expensive, simply to grant inadequately prepared students degrees than to make the effort to prepare them to earn them. This procedure invites angry denunciations of traditional standards, and even entire subjects, as sexist or racist or whatever. And if the university concurs that, for example, chemistry or seventeenth-century English literature are inherently hostile to women, whose self-esteem and comfort they do not foster and whose personal identification they do not invite, the university thereby frees itself of the obligation to educate women in those subjects without jeopardizing its sense of its own mission. All the university need do is transform its mission from the obligation to offer a demanding education into the responsibility to ensure the comfort of very different kinds of students. But the comfort of celebrating one's difference really means the equality of receiving the degree with its promise of employment. Thus the principle of education ends by being subordinated to the effect of the degree. And thus does the unspoken concern with economic equality shape our discussion of such principles as freedom of speech.

The ambiguities that reach fever pitch on university campuses in some measure pervade affirmative action programs beyond the university as well. As Stephen Carter has argued in *Reflections of an Affirmative Action Baby*, the issues defy easy solution.[16] In many instances, affirmative action programs have genuinely opened opportunities to individuals who would have been barred from them through prejudice, not through lack of talent. But as is widely recognized, affirmative action programs may easily slide into abuses that result in the dilution of requirements for members of specific groups, or even in the wholesale repudiation of requirements. These practices receive theoretical justification from postmodernists who argue that standards are inherently suspect because they inescapably embody the interests and experience of those who have designed them. Since, they argue, we all view the world through the prism of our own experience, the pretense that we may abstract rational or universal standards from that partial and self-interested experience cannot be sustained.

One would think that this postmodern argument must lead to a critique of equality, if not to a justification of inequality, but apparently, such candor would be asking too much. For at the core of the postmodern agenda lies a fierce commitment to impose equality of condition more or less by fiat. And this determination leaves no doubt that, in our time, equality has decisively shifted from equality of opportunity to equality of result, just as the defense of equality has moved from the elimination of barriers to their imposition.

IV

As the pursuit of equality is increasingly taken to dictate the neutralization of the differences among individuals, the list of salient differences has increasingly grown. But even as the legally suspect differences multiply, differences of race and sex retain special significance. The arguments about race command extensive discussion; but, with all due respect to race, it is plausible to argue that the differences that derive from sex are of primary theoretical and practical significance in any consideration of equality. Common sense would suggest that men and women are not and never will be equal in the strict sense of identical, if only because of their respective bodies. But common sense would no less forcefully suggest that there is a rapidly shrinking number of things that men do that women cannot also do, frequently as well, sometimes better. In an expanding sphere of life, the salient inequalities between any given man and any given woman may have little or nothing to do with sex but, rather, with native intelligence, organizational skills, concentration, determination, ambition, whatever.

This being the case, it would seem reasonable to allow individual women to compete directly with individual men for jobs, scholarships, raises, promotions, and all the rest. Many feminists, however, argue that men, notably in the case of such public arenas as work and politics, continue to enjoy an unfair advantage over women that must be redressed. Although we are far from perfect agreement about the nature of the advantage, the most common views include men's continuing numerical preponderance in most public arenas, men's propensity to take sexual advantage of women, men's comparative freedom from domestic responsibilities, or simply the residual attitudes of many supervisors toward women. Each of these presumed male advantages has given rise to policies and regulations that will, it is hoped, level the playing field to ensure greater equality between women and men. And whether one approves or disapproves of the various measures, it is difficult not to concur that their imposition has resulted in a reduction of individual liberty.

Feminists do not invariably concur, for, normally, they believe that some reduction in men's liberty must occur if the liberty of women is to increase. Thus, they might argue, there has not so much been a reduction in liberty as a redistribution. They are wrong, both theoretically and practically, for attempts to regulate people's behavior and expression, however nobly intended, are manifestations of a social engineering that does limit public liberty. But many feminists do not much worry about reductions in liberty that are intended to protect victims against their alleged oppressors. In criticizing this victim feminism, Naomi Wolf enthusiastically argues that it is high time for women to claim their rightful place as accountable adults and to relinquish a victim identity that only demeans them. I largely agree with her. But whatever one's position on women's ability to compete directly with men, the more serious issue remains the danger that the policies to protect women poses to the nature of the polity.

As a rule, feminists are reluctant to attribute women's disadvantage in the worlds of work and politics exclusively, or even primarily, to their sexuality, preferring to focus upon the long history of women's systematic subordination. In other situations, however, women's sexual difference moves to center stage. In recent years, for example, women's sexual vulnerability has been taken to justify speech and behavior codes that will protect women from its consequences—that is, will equalize results. Take the case of acquaintance rape, which has recently attracted so much attention in the United States and the United Kingdom. Notwithstanding pro forma acknowledgments that women can rape and batter men, it has proved virtually impossible to discuss acquaintance rape as if women and men were sexual equals. The very essence of acquaintance rape consists in the assumption that a man has, through physical advantage, forced a woman to have sex against her will. Buried in this assumption lies the primary assumptions that men are sexual predators, women sexual victims, and each will always behave according to his or her nature. In different ways, both Naomi Wolf and Katie Roiphe vehemently insist that these assumptions dangerously perpetuate the sexual ideology that relegated women to the stewardship of men on the grounds that without male protection they would inevitably fall victim to sexual abuse.

Wolf and Roiphe, in effect, are arguing for sexual equality between women and men, at least in the sense of taking responsibility for one's own sexuality. Neither underestimates the gravity of rape as a crime, but both deplore victim feminists' tendency to view all sexual relations between women and men as a form of rape.[17] Surely, they protest, that is not what we have been fighting for. Sex is fun for women, and on the occasions in which a woman has had too much to drink, fallen into bed with a man, and awakened the next morning with a hangover and a gnawing sense of regret, she should take responsibility for her own actions and write the evening off to experience. To assuage one's personal regrets by accusing the man of rape demeans the woman and trivializes the crime of rape, including acquaintance rape.[18]

Wolf and Roiphe applaud the emergence of a world in which women have earned the right to sexual freedom, which they take to mean that women have finally achieved at least a measure of sexual equality with men. Their argument does not mean that women and men are sexually identical, nor does it deny the possibility that men may impose sex upon women by force. It simply assigns to women individual responsibility for their own sexuality. Writing out of the marrow of a class and professional world in which women compete directly and often successfully with men, they are warning other accomplished women of the cultural elite that if this micromanagement nonsense does not cease, women will end up being protected out of their most rewarding opportunities and may well lose the freedom to compete with other women as well. They belong, in other words, to the small but growing number of women who are prepared to fend for themselves rather than risk having others tell them what they may and may not do. And Wolf, who candidly admits to enjoying the amount of money she makes, openly celebrates capitalism as the royal road to individual success.

Wolf's frankly hedonistic position perhaps reveals more than she intends. For the combination of her opposition to victim feminism—she prefers power feminism—and her celebration of capitalism implicitly confirms that the point of various regulations, even those on sexual behavior, is ultimately to promote equality of outcome. And although Wolf delights in using her money to help others, she no less clearly delights in the control that allows her to decide whom to help. Thus, while she calls herself a humanitarian leftist, it seems unlikely that she wishes to promote leveling among individuals. She is committed to an equality of opportunity that is entirely compatible, indeed depends upon, the principle of liberty.

Those whom she calls victim feminists favor curtailment of liberty in principle precisely to ensure leveling between women and men. Regulations and codes such as those that now prevail at Brown University, Antioch College, and elsewhere impose strict standards on the behavior of male students, thus limiting their liberty presumably to increase the liberty of their female peers. Roiphe mercilessly mocks such codes, as she does marches to "take back the night" and young women's public confessions of their experiences of rape. In her view, rape is now being invoked to describe the give-and-take of relations between young women and men in an age of sexual freedom. Roiphe delights in sexual adventure, much as Wolf delights in her ability to earn money. My conversations with young women suggest that many have not adjusted as effortlessly as she to the world of sexual liberation. But many of those who do not want to play the game have absorbed enough to want to go to the party. They cannot take a lighthearted view of acquaintance rape, for the possibility haunts them. For, unsure of their own desires and resilience, they have difficulty in saying yes. And the more difficult they find it to say yes, the more difficult they find it to say no. No, they do not, at least with respect to sex, want to be treated as young men's equals, if that means playing by young men's rules. They also do not want to miss out on all of the fun.

Roiphe falls wide of the mark in insisting that all young women should welcome sexual adventure. Manifestly, many do not. Indeed, many, if my sources are reporting accurately (and I have no reason to believe that they are not), still want "relationships" much more than they want sex, and they only want sex if it is softened by a relationship—if the young man wants to talk meaningfully to them over breakfast. And some young women still remain virgins by choice, without manifesting any signs of neurosis. I am more than prepared to believe that young women's dreams of relationships are at least as worthy of respect as the dreams of the young women who delight in sexual adventure. But I remain astonished, perhaps thereby betraying my own generation, that they think that the way to realize those dreams is to go, scantily clad, to a party at which they drink more than usual, return to a young man's room, pet heavily, and then exercise their right to just say no. No matter how they have behaved, they emphatically have the right to say no; and no matter how they have behaved, the young man who fails to respect it is no gentleman. But a rapist?

Obviously, everything depends upon how one defines "rapist," and I should be the last to begrudge young women maximum protection. But I remain uncomfortable with the scenario. There was a time when fathers, brothers, dress codes, and curfews used to provide that protection, but women have righteously rejected all of the above as illegitimate—dare one say, patriarchal—restrictions on their independence and equality. In those bad old days, protection was privately provided by families and institutions that acknowledged their in loco parentis responsibilities while trying not to infringe upon the principle of liberty. Today, a significant number of feminists, rejecting such private infringements upon women's liberty, want to restrict the principle of liberty instead. But it is hard to believe that we gain by tying women's right to equality to their right to behave as if they wanted sexual adventure when they do not. Would it not be better to encourage them to exercise prudence in their choice of where they go and how they dress, thereby taking responsibility for themselves? No one has the right to force them to do so, but doing so would spare them traumatic encounters. And, possibly, it would even enhance their self esteem.

The sexual inequality between women and men cuts to the heart of our discussions of equality in the abstract, but does not exhaust them. For it is conceivable that should women determine to protect what we recognize as our own vulnerabilities, including the ways in which most of us differ from men—that is, to assume responsibility for our own sexuality—we could, by our own initiative, do what fathers and brothers have traditionally done for us, namely, remove ourselves from situations that expose those vulnerabilities. Those who fancy sexual adventure could pursue it, prepared to take occasional knocks. Those who do not could look for relationships in more propitious circumstances.

V

Sexuality increasingly figures at the center of the feminist imagination, but, if truth be told, it is not the most difficult issue. Feminists, after all, are the first to insist that rape is not about sex but about power. Difficulties persist in drawing hard-and-fast lines between rape as a crime and men's tendency to abuse their physical advantage, but the police and the courts are making steady progress in this regard; and if rape convictions still fall woefully short, they are increasing.[19] Thus even as we acknowledge that men and women are not sexually equal in the sense of sexually identical, we may imagine a world in which they share equal access to a principle of sexual freedom and take personal responsibility for its effects in their own lives.

Women's reproductive capacities are another matter entirely. Tellingly, neither Wolf nor Roiphe dwells upon children. Yet the ability to bear children and the disproportionate responsibility for rearing them decisively jeopardize women's equality with men. Many feminists nonetheless reject the notion that women's reproductive capacities should receive special protection, precisely on the grounds that the continuing association with children seems to condemn women to inequality.[20] The logic of this argument obviously points to freeing women from children, although few admit as much in so many words, much less discuss how the freedom should be effected in practice. We may nonetheless assume that an unarticulated desire to free women from children accounts for some of the passion of feminist rhetoric about women's right to choose to have an abortion. Feminist defenses of abortion are regularly cast in the language of equality—for women to be equal, they must have the right to sever their traditional association with reproduction. And in *Planned Parenthood of Pennsylvania v. Casey,* the Supreme Court effectively concurred.[21]

In *Casey,* the Supreme Court sustained pro-choice advocates' insistence upon abortion as a necessary guarantee of women's equality, but moved the emphasis from sexual equality to the equality of participation in the economy. The Court thus effectively argued that women must not be hindered from providing for their own economic support. *Casey* implicitly retreated from the logic of affirmative action and equalization of economic effects by defending the principle of equality of access to economic freedom. This position logically throws support for the children women choose to have back upon women themselves, with no guarantee of assistance from society, or even from the children's fathers.[22] Thus the many pro-choice activists who bitterly denounced the decision seem to have missed its significance, which was, unambiguously, to confirm a woman's right to choose to have an abortion.

In the light of *Casey,* the right to choose to have an abortion may be understood as an effort to remove women's reproductive capacities from discussions of women's equality with men and thus to strengthen the commitment to the principle of equality independent of its possible effects. Notwithstanding some feminist objections, it is reasonable to argue that with respect to women as individuals, the benefits of defending equality in principle, understood to mean equality of opportunity, outweigh the dangers of attempting to engineer equality of results—to argue that the best, and most just, way to defend equality is to defend it as an abstract principle that we do not expect to produce equality of results. Equality thus reduces, or is elevated, to equality of political and economic rights—the equal right to political and economic participation.

Since the time of Mary Wollstonecraft, and at an accelerating rate in our own time, many, including feminists, have insisted that equality of political rights easily reduces to a sterile formality in societies in which economic and social resources are unequally divided. But the attempts of feminists and others to rectify social and economic inequalities through curtailing liberty in principle present no less serious dangers. The arguments that the rights of entire groups of "victims" require the curtailment of liberty in principle are especially dangerous because the members of those groups are not socially and economically equal, or even comparable. As a result, a curtailment of liberty in principle may, in the end, benefit only a minority of the group, leaving the majority as—or more—socially and economically impoverished than ever. If, in other words, liberty in principle is to promote the effect of greater economic equality, then we must discuss the issue in economic terms without regard to sex, race, or ethnicity.

Should such a discussion occur, it would be reasonable to argue that greater economic equality benefits society as a whole and hence justifies curtailment of the liberty that society enjoys, although counterarguments are also strong. In contrast, it is less easy to argue that society as a whole benefits by favoring some groups of its members over others simply to rectify inequalities in presumed personal attributes and resources. No more than in the past will acceptance of the principle of equal opportunity guarantee equality among the various members of society, although in a democracy like our own, it may well be the best guarantee of maximum liberty for society and its members. Since the French Revolution first invoked the rights of man and the citizen, it has been clear that absolute liberty and absolute equality would never be compatible. The goal of democracies, in their various ways, has been to strike the best possible balance between liberty and equality.

With respect to women as individuals, the balance between liberty and equality remains fragile and an abiding source of controversy. The case of children exposes it as a farce, for neither liberty nor equality obviously benefits children for whom adult rights are, to borrow the words of Elizabeth Wolgast, "wrong rights."[23] Yet the protection of children's vulnerability, like provision for their health and education, should be a preeminent concern of society as a whole. Reproduction stands alone in any consideration of justice, for without reproduction, a society wills itself to destruction. Society must, in one way or another, protect its own reproduction, which means exempting that reproduction from the principles that govern relations among consenting adults. The struggle to ensure women's equality as consenting adults has, however unintentionally, opened the question of who participates in reproduction and, accordingly, benefits from its privileged status.

Historically, social reproduction has been taken to include the biological participants in it: mother, father, child. Recent decades have effectively—many would say, disastrously—released men from that association, thereby undoing in one stroke the work of centuries. The logic of feminism might seem to portend the release of women from it as well. If that logic triumphs, children will be left to depend upon the whims of individuals or to fend for themselves, unless we decide to treat them all as wards of society. If women are released from their traditional association with reproduction, they will thereby remove the main obstacle to their equality with men—and with it, the only compelling justification for abridging society's liberty to compensate for their inequality.

Notes

1. J. R. Pole, *The Pursuit of Equality in American History*, rev. and exp. ed. (Berkeley: University of California Press, 1993), 454.

2. Mary Wollstonecraft, *A Vindication of the Rights of Women*, 2d ed., Carol H. Poston, ed. (New York: W. W. Norton, 1988; 1st ed., 1792).

3. Christine de Pisan, *The Book of the City of Ladies*, Earl Jeffrey Richards, trans., foreword by Marina Warner (New York: Persea Books, 1982). See also Elizabeth Fox-Genovese, "Culture and Consciousness in the Intellectual History of European Women," *Signs: Journal of Women in Culture and Society* 12, no. 3 (Spring 1987): 529–547.

4. Wollstonecraft, *Vindication of Rights*, 194.

5. On Wollstonecraft's political radicalism, see Elissa S. Guralnick, "Radical Politics in Mary Wollstonecraft's *A Vindication of the Rights of Woman*," *Studies in Burke and His Time* 18 (1977): 155–166; reprinted in Wollstonecraft, *Vindication of Rights*, 308–317.

6. On the ERA, see Jane J. Mansbridge, *Why We Lost the ERA* (Chicago: University of Chicago Press, 1986), and Donald G. Mathews and Jane Sherron De Hart, *Sex, Gender, and the Politics of ERA* (New York: Oxford University Press, 1990).

7. Raoul Berger, *Government by Judiciary: The Transformation of the Fourteenth Amendment* (Cambridge, MA: Harvard University Press, 1977), 259–262, 280. See also Elizabeth Fox-Genovese, "Women's Rights, Affirmative Action, and the Myth of Individualism," *George Washington Law Review* 54, nos. 2 and 3 (January and March 1986): 338–374.

8. *Roe* v. *Wade*, 410 US 113 (1973). For the origins of the right to privacy, see *Griswold* v. *Connecticut*, 381 US 479 (1965).

9. See Elizabeth Fox-Genovese, "Feminism and the Rhetoric of Individual Rights, Part 1," *Common Knowledge* 1, no. 1 (Spring 1992): 43–53, and "Feminism and the Rhetoric of Individual Rights, Part 2," *Common Knowledge* 1, no. 2 (Fall 1992): 63–93; Mary Ann Glendon, *Abortion and Divorce in Western Law: American Failures, European Challenges* (Cambridge, MA: Harvard University Press, 1987), and Glendon's *Rights Talk: The Impoverishment of Political Discourse* (New York: Free Press, 1991).

10. *Equal Employment Opportunity Commission* v. *Sears, Roebuck & Co.,* 628 F.Supp. 1264 (N.D. Ill. 1986). See also the discussion in Elizabeth Fox-Genovese, *Feminism without Illusion: A Critique of Individualism* (Chapel Hill: University of North Carolina Press, 1991), esp. 70–75, 142.

11. Joan Wallach Scott, "Deconstructing Equality-versus-Difference: Or, the Uses of Poststructuralist Theory for Feminism," *Feminist Studies* 14, no. 1 (Spring 1988): 46.

12. Katie Roiphe, *The Morning After: Sex, Fear, and Feminism* (Boston: Little, Brown & Co., 1993); Naomi Wolf, *Fire with Fire: The New Female Power and How It Will Change the 21st Century* (London: Chatto & Windus, 1993).

13. Charles Fried, "The New First Amendment Jurisprudence: A Threat to Liberty," in *The Bill of Rights in the Modern State*, Geoffrey R. Stone, Richard A. Epstein, and Cass R. Sunstein, eds. (Chicago: University of Chicago Press, 1992), 226.

14. Catharine A. MacKinnon, *Feminism Unmodified: Discourses on Life and Law* (Cambridge, MA: Harvard University Press, 1987), 163–165, 168–171.

15. Laurence H. Tribe, *Constitutional Choices* (Cambridge, MA: Harvard University Press, 1985).

16. Stephen L. Carter, *Reflections of an Affirmative Action Baby* (New York: Basic Books, 1992).

17. On the generalization of rape, see Emilie Buchwald, Pamela Fletcher, and Martha Roth, eds., *Transforming a Rape Culture* (Minneapolis, MN: Milkweed Editions, 1993).

18. For a discussion of acquaintance rape, see Linda A. Fairstein, *Sexual Violence: Our War against Rape* (New York: William Morrow & Co., 1993).

19. Fairstein, *Sexual Violence*.

20. Nicky Hart, "Procreation: The Substance of Female Oppression in Modern Society, Part One: The True Proletariat," *Contention* 1, no. 1 (Fall 1991): 89–108; my response, "Part Two: Feminism and the Spirit of

Capitalism," *Contention* 1, no. 3 (Spring 1992): 217–225; and Nicky Hart's response to me, *Contention* 1, no. 3 (Spring 1992): 227–236.

21. *Planned Parenthood of Pennsylvania v. Casey*, 112 S.Ct. 2791 (1992).

22. Tellingly, although the decision required minors to consult a parent, guardian, or judge, it did not require adult women to consult their husbands.

23. Elizabeth H. Wolgast, *The Grammar of Justice* (Ithaca, NY: Cornell University Press, 1987), chap. 2.

15

The Moral Sense, Character Formation, and Virtue

Jean M. Yarbrough

Jefferson's belief in the moral sense goes to the heart of his understanding of what the character of free men and women should be. For while character may be influenced by politics and rights, it is essentially about morality and virtue. Thus, for Jefferson, it involves reflection upon those innate moral sentiments that, when cultivated and strengthened by steady practice and example, define the moral core of the individual. The main assumptions of the moral sense doctrine as Jefferson understood it were fourfold. First, the capacity for virtue is natural to all human beings everywhere. The moral sense is the perfect expression of Jefferson's faith that human beings are naturally endowed with a capacity to perceive right and wrong, which, if reinforced by habitual exercise from childhood and fortified by modest instruction in the "little rules of prudence,"[1] will enable citizens to govern themselves and to reach a level of moral perfection in their social relations hitherto reserved only for the few.

In maintaining that morality is part of our natural endowment, Jefferson did not mean to suggest that it was the whole of our constitution, or even its most powerful component. Nor did he mean to deny the influence of history and culture upon the morals of a particular society. In different circumstances, people might draw different conclusions about the moral sentiments all human beings feel.

271

And everywhere, these original moral impulses could either be improved by education and the right institutions or be corrupted by their opposites. Still, no matter how savage, ignorant, or misguided a society might be, it was never completely bereft of moral feelings. Human beings everywhere are born with the capacity to perceive certain moral sentiments. All people desire justice, admire gratitude, and approve of benevolence and generosity (at least within their own tribe or society), even if they disagree about what these things mean or how they can be combined or reconciled.[2] It is the human capacity for moral judgment, located in a distinct faculty of perception, that elevates humankind above all other creatures and endows it with moral dignity.

Second, because morality arises out of certain sense impressions that the moral sense perceives and approves, virtue requires no uncommon degree of reason to give it effect. Although Jefferson does not go so far as to deny reason any role at all in the operation of the moral sense, he is drawn for political reasons to those moral philosophers who would severely restrict its province. If moral knowledge depended exclusively upon right reason (as the ancient philosophers had insisted), very few individuals would be capable of independent moral judgment. "For one man of science, there are thousands who are not. What would have become of them?"[3] Yet in grounding morality upon sentiment rather than reason, Jefferson insists upon the primacy of the social over the selfish passions. The duties we owe to others can never be discovered by consulting our own interests or self-love:

> self love . . . is no part of morality. Indeed, it is exactly its counterpart. It is the sole antagonist of virtue, leading us constantly by our propensities to self gratification in violation of our moral duties to others. Accordingly, it is against this enemy that are erected the batteries of moralists and religionists as the only obstacle to the practice of morality.[4]

Morality is neither a matter of reason intuiting certain principles of right action, nor a function of the selfish desire to avoid pain and enjoy pleasure. It arises out of certain moral sentiments that are inherent in our nature as social beings.

Third, although Jefferson's analogy to the senses gives the impression that virtue is as automatic as seeing or hearing, it clearly is not. That nearly all human beings can perceive certain impulses from which arise their moral obligations does not mean that these feelings guarantee right action. The moral sentiments require continual exercise and encouragement to develop into the established habits and dispositions that form our character. On the other hand, Jefferson does seem genuinely to believe that the exercise of virtue is on the whole both easy and pleasant and that, if we but follow our hearts, all will be well. It was part of nature's benevolent plan to lay "the foundation of happiness"[5] in virtue and reward its exercise with feelings of pleasure. Missing from much of his discussion is any suggestion that virtue is sometimes painful, or that vicious things can also give us pleasure.[6] Jefferson assumes that under the right circumstances, that is, in a republican society, moral education can get most people to take pleasure from what is good.

Fourth, and finally, that we seek the approval of others and, in turn, pass judgment upon their actions testifies to the essentially social character of the moral sense. Accordingly, the virtues that emerge as the most praiseworthy are those that preserve and perfect us as social creatures: justice ranks higher than the "frigid speculations" of philosophy,[7] and benevolence ranks highest of all. All this Jefferson learned from the Scots, and it found powerful affirmation in Jefferson's unorthodox reading of the New Testament. It was this marriage of moral sense philosophy and Christian ethics (shorn of its miraculous and nonrational elements) that Jefferson held up as the model of virtue for republican America.

Empiricism, Egoism, and the Foundations of Morality

Jefferson was attracted to the Scottish moral sense philosophers because they attempted to resolve one of the great problems posed by modern empiricism. If, as Locke had argued, all knowledge arises out of sense impressions or in the mind's reflection upon these sensations, from where does morality come?[8] Is morality derived from the selfish desire to avoid what is painful, or is there some other ground for virtue that is natural to human beings? In seeking a different foundation for moral action, but one that was compatible with Lockean empiricism, the earliest of the Scottish philosophers posited the existence of a distinct moral faculty capable of perceiving genuine moral sensations arising out of the social, as opposed to the selfish, passions.[9]

Francis Hutcheson was the first of the Scottish school to locate the seat of morality in the moral sense. Hutcheson divided moral virtue into three branches: the duties we owe to ourselves, the duties we owe to others, and the duties we owe to God. The affections or desires that give rise to these different branches of virtues are, respectively, self-love, goodwill or benevolence, and piety. Although Hutcheson acknowledged a role for self-love in perfecting the individual, this part of his moral philosophy received little attention. What attracted notice, then as now, was Hutcheson's argument that all the social virtues, or duties we owe to others, are ultimately traceable to benevolence or goodwill. It is this generous affection that moves us to seek the happiness of others independent of any selfish motives. For Hutcheson, we are so constituted by nature that the moral sense tends to "approve every kind affection either in ourselves or others and all publicly useful actions which we imagine flow from such affection, without our having a view to our private happiness in our approbation of these actions."[10]

Reacting against the "utopian" assumption that, regarding the duties we owe to others, benevolence is the sole "principle of action" that the moral sense approves, Lord Kames (Henry Home), sought a more realistic foundation for this faculty. Kames did not deny, indeed he agreed with Hutcheson, that "benevolence and generosity are more beautiful and more attractive of love and esteem"[11] and that "nothing ennobles human nature more than this principle or spring of action,"[12] but he doubted that benevolence could account for all the social virtues and, in particular, for "justice, and every thing which may be strictly called Duty."[13] Although benevolence is natural to humankind, it is limited in its scope to family and friends. Through imagination and abstract reasoning, it may be extended beyond our immediate circle to religion or country, but it cannot be stretched to include an equal universal duty to all. Such extensive benevolence may belong to some people as individuals, but "there is no such general fondness of man to man by nature."[14] The moral sense may approve these generous sentiments, but it does not oblige us to act on them.[15]

If, however, the social virtues cannot all be traced back to the social affection of benevolence, neither are they thrown back upon "absolute selfishness." Following Hutcheson, Kames insists that human beings are endowed with both selfish and social passions; therefore, "to contend that we ought only to regard ourselves and be influenced only by the selfish passions is against nature."[16] Instead, Kames seeks to ground morality on those sentiments or "springs of action" that give rise to a sense of duty or obligation. As social beings who need the company of others, we naturally feel bound to honor compacts and agreements. This duty arises out of the moral sentiment of fidelity, which Kames considers a social affection. At the same time, since many of the compacts we respect preserve the sanctity of private property, this duty is not simply social. The "feeling for private property" is rooted in the natural desire for self-preservation as well as self-love. Together, these social and selfish impulses give rise to the virtue of justice. Justice, according to Kames, is "that moral virtue which guards property and gives authority to covenants."[17] The desire for justice is one of the strongest desires of human beings everywhere; it is solidly rooted in human nature. And because it is necessary for the preservation of society, justice is the one virtue that government may legitimately compel.[18]

One other aspect of Kames's theory deserves mention. Because Kames insists that the moral sense is natural to human beings at all times and in all places, he must try to account for the cruelty and brutality that primitive peoples visit upon one another. If the moral sense has always been present, why does it not restrain such behavior? Kames must satisfy those critics who argue that morality is not natural to human beings, but is acquired only with civilization and education.

Kames replies that the moral sense has always existed, but that conditions do not always initially permit its full development. Rude and illiterate people have not yet developed the capacity for complex ideas and abstract propositions; consequently, they tend to be governed by their immediate selfish passions. Under these circumstances, he concedes, it is *as if* the moral sense did not exist, since it is still too weak to influence behavior. But gradually, as people develop the capacity to form more complex ideas and to think abstractly, they are able to act upon more general principles, the seeds of which are always there. Thus, as humankind becomes more civilized, the selfish passions are brought into submission and the social affections gain ascendancy. The important point is that reason and education do not create these affections, they merely help to refine and improve them. Nurture completes, it does not replace, nature's intention; reason remains the handmaiden of feeling.

Yet the central question that Hutcheson and Kames could not convincingly answer was, Did such a faculty of moral perception actually exist? If there were such a sense, where was its organ of perception? We see with the eyes, taste with the tongue, and so on, so what is the analogous organ that perceives moral sensations? If such an organ existed, it would not function in the same way as do the sense organs. While we exercise the five senses automatically from birth without training or instruction (we do not need to be taught to see), virtue requires a long period of regular exercise and instruction before it develops.[19] These difficulties led David Hume and Adam Smith to reflect upon the following question: if what the moral sense does is approve the moral sentiments, might we not focus directly upon those sentiments and locate approval in some other known faculty of the mind, such as reason or, better still, the imagination? Acting upon this insight, Hume and Smith shifted the focus of their inquiries. While retaining the phrase "moral sense," both of them tended to analyze moral knowledge in terms of the operation of the most basic human passions directly on the mind. In so doing, they moved the discussion away from the moral sense as a distinct faculty of sense perception akin to hearing, seeing, and so forth, to an examination of those sentiments that prompt us to virtuous action.

For both Hume and Smith, the sentiment that moves us to moral approbation and action is sympathy. By sympathy, they do not mean pity or compassion, but the more neutral propensity of human beings as social creatures to enter imaginatively into the feelings and actions of others and to approve of those actions if they meet with our sense of what is "useful and agreeable," in the case of Hume, or with propriety and merit, in the case of Smith. For both philosophers, the foundation of morality is the innate human capacity to identify with the joys and sorrows of others. It is the faculty of imagination, acting by itself or in conjunction with reason, that makes moral judgment possible.

There was, however, one important difference between the two. Hume did not believe it was possible to ground all the moral virtues upon the operation of the moral sentiments. In contrast to Kames, he insisted that some virtues, notably justice, have no foundation in any moral sentiment; rather, they originate *solely* in considerations of public utility. We approve of motives and actions that result in justice because we *reason* they are useful to society. Although over time, we come to develop what might be called a "natural" regard for justice based on its "extensive utility," justice, considered from the standpoint of its origin in reason rather than an innate moral sentiment, remains in this sense an "artificial" virtue.[20]

By contrast, Smith sought to establish a full-fledged theory of moral *sentiments*, which derive the virtues exclusively from certain innate feelings, independent of reason and calculation. Instead of reason seeking to determine what is useful, Smith asks us to *imagine* whether an impartial spectator would sympathize with and approve of our feelings and actions. Smith insists that we can win this approval only if we moderate our passions so that the spectator is able to sympathize with the propriety and merit of our feelings.[21] According to Smith, this exercise in moderation, necessitated by the universal human need for approval, results in the exercise of those virtues that are useful and agreeable to ourselves and to others, but without having to compromise the primacy of the sentiments as the spring of all moral action.

Thus, by grounding his theory of moral sentiments on the imaginative capacity to sympathize with the joys and sorrows of others and to have them, in turn, sympathize with us, Smith avoids the difficulties encountered by Hutcheson and Kames. He does not have to defend the existence of the moral sense as a faculty of sense perception; nor does he derive all the social virtues from the one affection of benevolence, as Hutcheson did. Sympathy, which is rooted in human sociality and the need for the approval of others, points in several different directions. It gives rise to justice, the virtue most needful to society, as well as to prudence, the virtue connected with the care of the self. The moral sentiments are largely, but not exclusively, other-directed; there are certain moral virtues, like prudence, that arise out of self-love with which all human beings can and do sympathize and approve. At the same time, however, Smith reserves the highest praise for benevolence, that virtue that looks to the happiness and well-being of others.

These differences are important to keep in mind as we try to figure out how the moral sense contributes to the formation of character and what kind of character it recommends. For despite the centrality of the moral sense to Jefferson's understanding of human nature, he seldom does more than mention the faculty, and only twice discusses its operation in any detail.[22] Moreover, the discussions occur in two letters separated by more than twenty-five years. In each, Jefferson does no more than sketch the broad outline of his views, and he does so in a way that tends to emphasize the agreement between him and his correspondent.[23] Thus, the more extended analyses provided by the Scots help to fill in some, though by no means all, of the lacunae.

The Operation of the Moral Sense

Although Jefferson had alluded to certain aspects of moral sense philosophy, and had used the term without elaborating in earlier writings and letters,[24] his first discussion of the operation of the moral sense occurred in a letter to his nephew, Peter Carr, written in 1787 while Jefferson was in Paris. In this letter, Jefferson describes the moral sense as a distinct faculty for perceiving right and wrong, analogous to the sense organs. "This sense is as much a part of his [man's] nature as the sense of hearing, seeing, or feeling." And

Jefferson never wavered from this view; for nearly thirty years later, he repeated the analogy, shifting the focus to emphasize that the occasional absence of the moral sense, like the absence of sight or hearing, "is no proof that it is a general characteristic of the species."[25]

But if the moral sense is a distinctive faculty of perception, analogous to the sense organs, what bodily organ is its seat? Jefferson can answer this question only metaphorically: the organ of the moral sense is the "heart." Adopting the voice of the heart in his celebrated letter to Maria Cosway written during this same period, Jefferson has the heart reply to the "head": "when Nature assigned us the same habitation, she gave us over it a divided empire. To you, she allotted the field of science. To me that of morals." It is in the "mechanics of the heart" that generous affections of sympathy, benevolence, gratitude, and justice all find their metaphorical home.

Just as Jefferson remains untroubled by the inability to locate the moral sense in an actual organ of perception, he seems to ignore the other previously mentioned breakdown in this analogy. Whereas we possess fully the capacity to see, to hear, to feel, and so forth, from birth, the moral sense does not operate so automatically. The ability to make moral judgments develops only slowly with practice as we mature, and even then, not always to full capacity. Perhaps this is why, in the very next sentence of his letter to Peter Carr and without any sense of contradiction, he compares the moral sense to the limbs of the body. "The moral sense, or conscience, is as much a part of man as his leg or his arm." And like these bodily appendages, it "may be strengthened by exercise, as may any particular limb of the body."[26] In likening the moral sense to the arms and the legs, Jefferson can drive home the importance of regular exercise and good habits in forming moral character. But he does so at the cost of undermining his earlier analogy with the sense organs.[27]

Yet, despite these difficulties, Jefferson continued to view the moral sense as a distinct faculty of sense perception, the particular task of which is to approve the moral impulses of each individual and to sit in judgment upon the moral actions of others. But how does this "Internal Monitor"[28] know what to approve? Is the approbation of the moral sense automatic, requiring no assistance from the faculties of reason or imagination, or are these faculties also involved? At times, Jefferson seems to deny reason any positive role in moral judgment and action. To Maria Cosway, he insisted, "morals were too essential to the happiness of man, to be risked on the uncertain combinations of the head. She laid their foundation, therefore, in sentiment, and not in science." And when reason does become involved, it is usually to mislead the promptings of the heart. Thus, he concludes by chiding the head, "I do not know that I ever did a good thing on your suggestion, or a dirty one without it."[29] Nor was this an isolated romantic outburst, for Jefferson returns to this point some years later: "The practice of morality being necessary to the well-being of society, he has taken care to impress its precepts so indelibly in our hearts that they shall not be effaced by the subtleties of our brain."[30]

But in the letter to Peter Carr, where Jefferson explicitly discusses the operation of the moral sense, he backs away from this position. Here, he concedes that the moral sense "is submitted in some small degree to the guidance of reason," though he is quick to add, "it is a small stock which is required for this: even a less one than what we call common sense."[31] These must have been something like the "prudential rules"[32] for governing our conduct in society that Jefferson offered to his grandson when he went away from home for the first time. But beyond such prudential advice, nothing more apparently was needed. Indeed, Jefferson worried that too much reliance upon reason could corrupt moral judgment by leading it astray with "artificial rules."[33] The plowman was at least as good a judge, if not a better one, of moral cases than the professor. Acting on this belief, Jefferson advised his nephew and later on another grandson not to waste time studying moral philosophy or metaphysics in college.[34]

At first sight, Jefferson's disparagement of reason in discovering our moral duties may seem odd for the man considered to be the foremost representative of the American Enlightenment. But upon further consideration, Jefferson's position (although excessively polemical) is consistent with Enlightenment assumptions. What Jefferson objects to is not reason per se, but the traditional rationalist argument that the moral and political truths necessary for men living together in society can be known *only* by reason, and in particular, intuitive reason.[35] If this were true, then the bulk of humankind, whose ability to reason was limited, would be dependent upon the wise few for moral knowledge. And, indeed, traditional moral philosophy tended to support aristocratic, or at least nondemocratic, political arrangements for precisely this reason.[36]

Stated positively, Jefferson's distrust of reason alone in discovering our moral duties rests on the premise that a benevolent Creator was not at the same time a "pitiful bungler." Since he had intended men for society, he had equipped each of them with the capacity to know and act on those truths most needful for their common life together. It was the moral sense, with its instinctive feelings of virtue and vice, knowable in principle by all, that was the rightful seat of moral judgment. For Jefferson, human sociality had decidedly republican implications, in morals and in epistemology, no less than in politics.

Having established the primacy of the moral sense, Jefferson can then, like Kames, grant reason a supporting role; though he never takes up the issue systematically, he sometimes gives the impression that reason is necessary only when the moral sense is defective or absent. In these unhappy cases, "appeals to reason and calculation," especially in matters of honesty, may help to supply the defect.[37] Yet it is precisely in these cases that reason seems least effective. Jefferson never explains how, lacking a basic moral sense, rational appeals to "other motives" such as the "love, or the hatred, or rejection of those among whom he lives,"[38]—all of which start from the premise of human sociality and are, in fact, bound up with the operations of the moral sense—can restrain an individual bereft of social impulses.

Yet, despite his tendency to deprecate, and occasionally even to blame, reason for corrupting the moral sense, Jefferson in fact accords reason a more positive role in moral judgment than he is prepared to admit.[39] Consider the extensive comment entered into his copy of Kames's *Essays* on the perfectibility of the moral sense. Responding to Kames's suggestion that the moral sense "admits of great refinements by culture and education,"[40] Jefferson reflects upon the progress made over two millennia in treating prisoners of war:

> This is a remarkable instance of improvement in the moral sense. The putting to death captives in war was a general practice among savage nations. When men became more humanized the captive was indulged with life on condition of holding it in perpetual slavery; a condition exacted on this supposition, that the victor had right to take his life, and consequently to commute it for his services. At this stage of refinement were the Greeks about the time of the Trojan War. At this day, it is perceived we have no right to take the life of an enemy unless where our own preservation renders it necessary. But the ceding his life in commutation for service admits there was no necessity to take it, because you have not done it. And if there was neither necessity nor right to take his life then there is no right to his service in commutation for it. This doctrine is acknowledged by later writers, Montesquieu, Burlamaqui, etc., who yet suppose it just to require a ransom from the captive. One advance further in refinement will relinquish this also. If we have no right to the life of a captive, we have no right to his labor; if none to his labor we have none to his absent property which is but the fruit of that labor. In fact, ransom is but commutation in another form.[41]

Such abstract propositions can never be the work of the moral sense acting alone. It is, according to Kames, reason that clarifies and extends the original moral sentiments, leading to ever more delicate and refined judgment and action. In other words, although abstract reasoning is not critical in the formation of each individual's moral judgments, which seem to require only a "small stock" of reason, the ability of particular individuals to reason abstractly is essential to moral progress and helps to explain why some societies are more morally advanced than others.[42]

Utility, Reason, and the Moral Sense

There is, moreover, a second way in which reason helps to influence moral judgment, though reason in this instance involves the capacity to calculate consequences, rather than reason abstractly. The discussion occurs in Jefferson's most extended treatment of the moral sense, in a letter to Thomas Law in 1814, where he announces that "nature has constituted utility the standard and test of virtue."[43] Commentators have seized on this statement to argue that Jefferson's last and fullest statement on the moral sense seems to contradict his earlier comments and even his discussion of the moral sense in this same letter. For if the standard and test of virtue is now a matter of utilitarian calculation, if virtue now has to do with the "effect" of our actions, what becomes of the moral sense? In earlier letters, Jefferson had seemed to follow the Scottish School in making the approbation of the moral sense the test of virtue, while here, in the letter to Law and in another to John Adams, he shifts over to calculation. Similarly, he had earlier stressed the importance of motive, while here he focuses upon consequences. By invoking utility as the standard of virtue, has Jefferson rendered the moral sense superfluous?[44]

As long as we do not insist upon viewing the moral sense as a faculty that operates without any assistance from reason, a position that Jefferson in his few direct discussions of the moral sense never maintained, the answer is no. So what is he doing? We can better appreciate his intention if we examine the context in which Jefferson introduces utility. In the letter to Law, and in a similar response to Adams, Jefferson is attempting to answer a particular question: if human beings everywhere perceive the same moral sentiments, why do people around the world have such different and even conflicting ideas of right and wrong, justice and injustice, virtue and vice? Jefferson anticipates an imaginary critic who, observing these differences, sensibly believes that, if nature had given us such a sense, impelling us to virtuous actions, and warning us against those which are vicious, then nature would have designated, by some particular ear-marks, the two sets of actions which are, in themselves, the one virtuous, the other vicious. Whereas, we find, in fact, that the same actions are deemed virtuous in one country and vicious in another.[45]

Similarly, in the letter to Adams, Jefferson is trying to refute the idea that the moral sense and justice are not natural to human beings because different societies hold radically different views of virtue and vice, right and wrong.

In both instances, Jefferson introduces utility precisely to defend the existence of the moral sense. His argument is as follows: all human beings, in whatever circumstances, are moved by impulses to duty or justice as well as benevolence; "every human mind feels pleasure in doing good to another." In every society, "the essence of virtue is doing good to others."[46] The difficulty is that under "different circumstances, different habits and regimens," these natural impulses are pulled in different directions, so that "what is good may be one thing in one society, and it's [sic] opposite in another." Although the moral sentiments are natural, they are too weak and diffuse to tell us how to act in particular circumstances. Reason, in the form of utilitarian calculation, directs the original impulses to consider the moral consequences of actions, that is, what will do good to others, under vastly different circumstances.

This is not to say that the opinions different societies form about virtue and vice are all morally equal. The French opinion that adultery is acceptable in aristocratic societies where marriages are arranged to protect property does not contribute to true human happiness.[47] Still, the moral codes that different societies have evolved are probably the best they can do under the circumstances; in any case, it is fallible reason, not the absence of the moral sense, that explains why different societies have different opinions about virtue and happiness. To be sure, Jefferson's reply does not address the contradiction between his earlier assertion that it is the moral sense that determines right and wrong and his insistence here that it is a matter of utility. But in the context, this is not his principal concern. Jefferson is here trying to defend the existence of the moral sense while accounting for the variety of different moral codes in different cultures. Whatever the difficulties, Jefferson introduced utility to defend the moral sense, not to replace it.

As for the switch from motives to consequences in determining what is virtuous, Jefferson might have responded, as Adam Smith did, that although the theory of moral sentiments was, strictly speaking, concerned only with motives, consideration of consequences could be explained as an "irregularity" of the moral sentiment that served a necessary, practical purpose. Because human beings are social, they must be concerned with the effects of their actions upon others, even if this is ultimately not the most important moral question. That we may sometimes do the right thing for the wrong reasons should not be judged too harshly. Conversely, vicious consequences must as a rule be punished because motives are more difficult, if not impossible, to determine, and, in any case, a liberal society cannot punish or reward people for their intentions alone. There are, then, good practical reasons to focus on effects, even if the moral sense theory, strictly speaking, is concerned with motives.[48] At the same time, the virtues remain genuine virtues and are never admirable simply because they achieve good results.

Finally, it is important to keep in mind that Jefferson introduced utility to explain how societies form different opinions about right and wrong based upon different circumstances and cultural traditions. He is not suggesting that utilitarian calculation plays a critical role in the formation of individual moral judgment. While some small degree of prudence and common sense may be necessary, moral imagination and habituation are far more important in shaping individual character.

Imagination and Moral Judgment

In contrast to the "small stock" of reason, imagination plays a larger and more positive role in the operation of the individual moral sense. Writing to his young grandson away from home for the first time, after receiving a letter from the boy's mother confiding her fears about his character, Jefferson explains how his imagination helped him overcome the temptations of youth. When, as a fourteen-year-old also on his own, Jefferson was uncertain how to act, he would ask himself what the most respected and distinguished men he knew would do and "what course in it w[ould] insure me their approbation." Jefferson assures his grandson that "this mode of deciding my conduct tended more to correctness than any reasoning powers I possessed." For young people, in particular, imaginative identification with people of superior moral and intellectual character is more likely than inexperienced reason to lead to a "prudent and steady pursuit of what is right."[49]

Jefferson also recognizes the power of literature to shape the

moral imagination and so mold character. This is why, after advising
Peter Carr not to bother with lectures in moral philosophy, he urges
him to "read good books." For Jefferson, the "entertainments of
fiction" are no less valuable than experience in eliciting "the sympathetic emotions of virtue."[50] When we read good literature, "the spa-
cious field of imagination is thus laid open to our use, and lessons
may be formed to illustrate and carry home to the mind every rule
of moral life."[51] Jefferson is confident that every reader of "feeling
and sentiment" will react with disgust to the villainy of Macbeth,
just as every son or daughter will form "a lively and lasting sense
of filial duty" from reading *King Lear*. Marmontel can excite in the
reader a strong desire to emulate acts of "fidelity" and "generosity," while the fictional writings of Sterne, "form the best course
of morality ever written."[52] Comedy, tragedy, epic poetry, even
the "well-written" romance[53] can excite our virtuous sentiments and
make us feel that we are better people for having read them. And
the more we exercise such dispositions, even in our imagination, the
stronger they become.

Still, it is not clear that Jefferson means to confine the imagination
to sympathetic identification with those whom we admire, either in
real life or in literature. As social creatures, we need the love and
approval of those with whom we live, and whose society is essential
to our happiness and even survival. Thus, in the same letter where
Jefferson tells his young nephew of how he deliberately sought to
win the approval of the most respected characters, he recommends
to the boy a somewhat different imaginative exercise. Whenever the
lad is in doubt about whether an act is right or wrong, he should
imagine how he would act if "all the world" were watching.[54] "When
tempted to do anything in secret," he advised his nephew, "ask your-
self if you would do it in public. If you would not, be sure it is
wrong." Without perhaps realizing it, Jefferson assumes that public-
ity, with its implicit appeal to majority sentiment, is the same as, or
no worse than, sympathetic identification with the best.

This same confusion crops up in the letter to Thomas Law. Here,
Jefferson (mistakenly) remembers Lord Kames as having taught that
moral obligation arises not from "the feeling of a single individual,"
but from the "general feeling in a given case."[55] In other words, Jefferson tends to equate (to a far greater extent than Kames) the approval of the moral sense with the approval of those around us. The
role of the imagination would then be to internalize for the moral
sense the moral sentiments of the majority, not simply of those we
esteem and admire.[56]

The danger here is that by relying so heavily upon what will win the approval of others, Jefferson's version of the moral sense encourages social conformity at the expense of right conduct.[57] For if the "general feeling" of the majority "in a given case" is what merits approval and, hence, determines what is right and wrong, virtuous or vicious, how can anyone ever challenge existing opinions and moral standards? How can Jefferson square such moral majoritarianism with moral reform? These questions take on added meaning when we consider that Jefferson regarded Jesus the greatest moral reformer of all time, and, in his own day, antislavery Southerners found little support for emancipation in the "general feeling" of the people in their states. What the majority approves of is not necessarily right.

It seems likely, then, that Jefferson does not mean to link the approbation of the moral sense with the reigning opinions in every society, but only those societies where the natural moral impulses of the people are encouraged by enlightened practices and benevolent institutions.[58] For although he does not often mention it, he recognizes that corrupt societies, though they cannot annihilate the moral sense, can warp and distort it. Indeed, he considers the effect of slavery on the South in just these terms. Although the "love of justice and love of country"[59] continue to plead the cause of the slaves, Southerners have ceased to feel their own moral impulses. "Nursed, educated, and daily exercised in tyranny,"[60] Southern children have learned to imitate the vices of their parents and to approve the most "boisterous" and haughty passions. Just as the moral sense could be strengthened by proper exercise, so too could it be corrupted by immoral institutions that inflame and distort an otherwise healthy pride. In such circumstances, imaginative identification with those around us in society will not lead to moral action.

Perhaps this is why Jefferson continued to insist upon the necessity of believing in divine rewards and punishments, and not only for those few individuals lacking a moral sense. Imagination could be put to powerful effect in summoning up the terrible vision of an avenging God, exacting retribution for the moral offense of slavery. In language that anticipates Lincoln's warning of divine retribution in his Second Inaugural Address, Jefferson asks:

> And can the liberties of a nation be secure when we have removed their only firm basis, a conviction in the minds of the people that these liberties are the gift of God? That they are not to be violated but with his wrath? Indeed I tremble for my country when I reflect that God is just: that his justice cannot sleep forever: that considering numbers, nature and natural means, only, a

revolution of the wheel of fortune, and exchange of situation, is among possible events: that it may become probable by super- natural interference! The Almighty has no attribute which can take side with us in such a contest.[61]

Yet such warnings, which excite the imagination to reflect upon the awful possibility of divine wrath in order to get us to do what is right, are rare in Jefferson. Although belief in a future state of re- wards and punishments was the only tenet of Christianity not ratio- nally provable upon which he continued to insist,[62] Jefferson tended to emphasize the love, rather than the fear, of God and to view the Diety as a benevolent Creator who had equipped human beings with the capacity to know and act upon what was right.

The Moral Sense and the Role of Habit in Character Formation

In the two letters in which Jefferson discusses the operation of the moral sense in detail, he gives the impression that this faculty func- tions as automatically as do the five senses. The moral sense appears to perceive right and wrong as spontaneously as the eye sees an object placed before it. But in fact, these letters give an incomplete and somewhat misleading picture of how moral character is actually formed. To correct this impression, it is necessary to recall that Jef- ferson compared the moral sense not only to the sense organs, but also to the limbs of the body. And like an arm or a leg, the moral sense requires regular exercise, supplemented by appeals to "other motives," to develop properly. Perhaps nowhere is this clearer than in the letters Jefferson wrote to his daughters, grandchildren, and other family members.[63] In attempting to form their characters, Jef- ferson understood that the moral impulses by themselves are too weak and diffuse to move us to moral action. These sentiments need to be strengthened by regular exercise and affectionate encourage- ment until they become like a second nature. It is the long process of habituation, of acquiring good manners, that ultimately results in the steady disposition to virtue that constitutes our character.[64] Thus, Jefferson advised his nephew, Peter Carr, to take every opportunity to exercise and strengthen his "dispositions to be grateful, to be gen- erous, to be charitable, to be humane, to be true, just, firm, orderly, courageous, etc."[65] It was the habitual practice of these virtues, and not simply the occasional good act, that would bring happiness and win the esteem and approbation of others. Jefferson, as we have seen, takes it for granted that most people, with the proper moral instruction, can learn to admire what is truly virtuous. That the greatest virtues are social, rather than intellectual, only increases the likelihood that this is so.

In his long absences from his daughters, Jefferson regularly appealed to their natural desire for his love and approval in order to encourage them to cultivate pleasing manners and virtuous dispositions. He does not scruple to say what is obvious, but is today too infrequently said out of fear of being considered "manipulative,"[66] namely, that he will love his daughters more as they prove themselves "more worthy" of his love. Jefferson never threatens to withhold his love if the girls disobey or disappoint him. When Mary fails to respond to his letters and entreaties, when Martha stalls in her Latin or falls into adolescent indolence, Jefferson's response is neither angry nor severe. He continues to encourage them, with patience and humor, to exercise their virtuous dispositions so that they will become "valuable to others and happy in [them]selves."[67] Later on, he took the same approach with his grandchildren, promising "the more I perceive you are advancing in your learning and improving in good dispositions, the more I shall love you and the more everybody shall love you."[68] The appeal to "other motives" to reinforce the natural moral sentiments is not confined, as Jefferson elsewhere suggested, to those lacking a moral sense, but is a regular part of moral development.

Thus, the process of character formation turns out to be more complicated than the letters on the moral sense, when taken by themselves, suggest. Although all human beings directly perceive certain moral sentiments of which the moral sense approves, the moral sense by itself is too weak to call forth virtuous conduct. It requires some small assist from reason, not in the form of abstract or speculative thinking, but of experience and common sense. More important still is the role of the imagination, which enables us from youth to put ourselves in the place of others to determine whether they would approve of our motives and acts. Finally, good character does not result from the occasional good act; it is the result of permanent and steady dispositions. Thus, the moral sentiments must be regularly exercised and reinforced by appropriate social rewards, beginning with parental love and later extending to the approbation and esteem of those we admire. In time, the steady "exercise . . . of the moral feelings produces a habit of thinking and acting virtuously."[69]

Moral Sense And Moral Sentiments:
Justice and Benevolence

We come now to the questions of what are the moral feelings or sentiments that move us to virtuous action, and what virtues do they recommend? Are the social virtues activated by benevolence, as Hutcheson argued; or do they arise out of other more compelling principles that the moral sense not only approves, but also obliges, as Kames insisted?[70] Among the students of Jefferson, only Garry Wills has explored this question in any detail, and he is wrong. Wills concludes that Jefferson followed Hutcheson in grounding morality entirely upon benevolence and that benevolence could be enforced by appropriate government action. Wills considers briefly the competing argument, advanced by Kames, that by far the greater part of morality consists in those sentiments of which the moral sense not only approves, such as benevolence, but feels obliged to exercise, in particular, refraining from harming others and keeping our agreements. But because Wills wrongly insists that the impulse to duty is rooted exclusively in self-love, he concludes that Jefferson could not have intended this sentiment to serve as the foundation of morality. This, however, is to misread Jefferson, who did not mean to exclude considerations of self-love from all of morality, but only from morality in the strict sense, as entailing our duties to others. It is, moreover, to misread Kames, who never argued that the sense of duty is founded in self-love alone. The duty to respect agreements and honor engagements seems to partake of both the selfish and the social principles of action; it is midway between benevolence and self-love. And it is massively to distort the political implications of benevolence in Hutcheson's thinking in order to justify the use of public power to enforce Wills's own vision of the good.[71] Yet, in fact, Jefferson seems not to have noticed, or if he noticed, not to have cared, that Hutcheson and Kames differ in their moral psychology. In his eclectic analysis, benevolence and the impulse to duty each give rise to different social virtues. Moreover, Jefferson understands, as Wills does not, that they are not both enforceable by government.

To support his interpretation, Wills focuses on those passages where Jefferson equates the moral sense with the "love of others." Thus, for example, in the letter to Thomas Law, Jefferson asserts that "nature hath implanted in our breasts a love of others, a sense of duty to them, a moral instinct in short, which prompts us irresistibly to feel and succour their distresses."[72] In this instance, the "sense of duty" does seem to refer to the benevolent impulse to relieve the suffering of others. But in other letters, Jefferson makes it clear that the impulse to duty is also related to justice. In a letter to Francis Gilmer, which Wills fails to mention, Jefferson seems to have Kames's argument unambiguously in mind when he observes that because we are social beings, the "sense of justice" must be part of our "natural organization."[73] And to John Adams, Jefferson seems almost to equate the moral sense with justice: "I believe [that justice] is instinct, and innate, that the moral sense is as much a part of our constitution as that of feeling, seeing, or hearing."[74]

What this suggests is that, unlike Hutcheson, but like Kames, Jefferson believed that there are several moral sentiments or "principles of action" that present themselves to the moral sense for its approval. Depending upon the particular context, Jefferson would emphasize one or the other of these sentiments and the social virtue to which each gave rise. Thus, for example, in the letter to Gilmer, where Jefferson is discussing the legitimate scope of political power and what actions government may compel, he focuses solely upon the "sense of justice." Because justice is essential to the preservation of society, it is the one virtue that a liberal republic must enforce. In other letters that concentrate more directly upon morality, and especially in those that examine the relative merits of different moral codes, Jefferson could and did acknowledge the importance and, indeed, the primacy of benevolence.[75]

Justice

In thinking about the origin of justice, Jefferson rejects the Hobbesian notion that justice is merely conventional, that it only comes into being with the establishment of civil society and is whatever the sovereign declares it to be. He criticizes the projected treatise on morals by Destutt de Tracy (whose economic writings he much admired) for adopting "the principles of Hobbes or humiliation to human nature; that the sense of justice is not derived from our natural organization, but founded on convention only."[76]

With Hutcheson and Kames, Jefferson insists that man is by nature social and that part of his endowment as a social creature is a natural sense of justice. Jefferson offers his view in the form of a "syllogism": "Man was created for social intercourse; but social intercourse cannot be maintained without a sense of justice; then man must have been created with a sense of justice."[77] Since this sense of justice belongs to man as a social being, Jefferson would seem to agree with Kames that this principle of action cannot be traced back exclusively to the selfish passions. Justice, understood as the mutual recognition of personal and property rights, does not arise solely out of the selfish desire to have our own rights respected. (And this, even when the rights themselves are grounded on the selfish passions.) Justice also arises out of the realization that, as social beings, we are bound by certain "moral duties which exist between individual and individual in a state of nature, and accompany them into a state of society."[78] Chief among these are honoring engagements, observing compacts, and respecting the equal rights of others. Justice in this sense is natural because it is rooted in the impulsive duty each individual feels to perform those obligations that are necessary to the peace and order of society. At the same time, justice remains an essentially negative virtue, a list of things that we may not do. Indeed, it is precisely because government can force us to fulfill our obligations, and does not leave them to our free will and moral choice, that justice is not the highest virtue. For Jefferson, who here again follows the Scots, the peak of the moral virtues can be found in uncoerced acts of benevolence that take place beyond the reach of government.

Benevolence

Jefferson's belief that we are by nature social beings who depend for our happiness and well-being upon the approval of others means that the most praiseworthy virtue will be that which perfects, rather than merely preserves, us in our dealings with others. For Jefferson, it is the innate "love of others," variously described as the natural impulse to charity, generosity, humanity, and compassion, that moves us to the "most sublime" virtue, benevolence.[79] Benevolence is more noble than justice because it is always freely chosen. Whereas government must enforce "equal and impartial justice" as its "sacred duty,"[80] it cannot demand that its citizens exercise benevolence. The perfection of the moral character must be an act of free will. As such, benevolence is always accompanied by the greatest pleasure and approval. Conversely, the failure to act benevolently may disappoint, but it cannot, like the breach of justice, be punished.[81]

If Jefferson learned from the Scots that benevolence was the "most beautiful" of the virtues, it was not principally from them that he came to appreciate its true meaning and extent. Thus Wills is particularly misguided when he tries to explain what Jefferson means by benevolence with reference to Hutcheson. For Jefferson, the model of true benevolence is to be found in the life and teachings of Christ. Of course, it was not orthodox (Trinitarian) Christianity that Jefferson embraced; this he regarded as mere superstition, invented by unscrupulous priests to gain power and control over the unsuspecting multitude.[82]

Jefferson's discovery of the writings of the English Unitarian Dr. Joseph Priestley helped him to consider religion in a new light.[83] In his two-volume *History of the Corruptions of Christianity* (which Jefferson read sometime after 1793), Priestley argued that Jesus was not the son of God, but merely an exemplary moral reformer to whom God had granted the power to work miracles as a sign of his divine approval. What Christianity taught could be reduced to a few straightforward moral principles concerning our duties to one another. Following Priestley, Jefferson now views Christ as a human being and true Christianity as a moral code knowable by reason and the moral sense alone. Religion merely ratifies those "moral precepts, innate in man, and made a part of his physical constitution, as necessary for a social being."[84] Jefferson misses the irony of his rationalist attempt to persuade Americans that Jesus was only a man in order to prove the naturalness and superiority of sentiment over reason in matters of morality.

What is it that "true religion" teaches, and in what way is it superior to other moral systems? A decade later, and again following Priestley's lead, Jefferson set out to compare the morals of Jesus with those of the ancient moralists he had admired as a youth.[85] Having read Priestley's most recent "treatise" on this subject, favorably comparing Jesus with Socrates, Jefferson confided in a letter to Dr. Benjamin Rush that he, too, had come to regard Jesus' teachings as superior. Not only did Jesus emphasize the duties we owe to one another, rather than the duties we owe to ourselves, but he took a more expansive view of these obligations. When the ancient moralists spoke of our duties to others, they tended to think in terms of patriotism and justice, "but scarcely viewed them [our neighbors and countrymen] as within the circle of Benevolence. Still less have they inculcated peace, charity, and love to our fellow men, or embraced with benevolence the whole family of mankind."[86] It was, then, precisely because Jesus extended our moral obligations beyond justice to benevolence, and benevolence "not only to kindred and friends, to neighbors and countrymen, but to all mankind," that Jefferson considered the "genuine" teachings of Christ as the "most perfect and sublime that [have] ever been taught by man."[87]

Moreover, in contrast to the ancient moralists (as Jefferson now read them), who laid principal stress on the acts, Jesus taught that our motives must be as pure as our acts. "He pushed his scrutinies into the heart of man, erected his tribunal in the region of his thoughts, and purified the waters at the fountainhead."[88] It was this common emphasis upon motive, along with the elevation of benevolence as the highest moral virtue, that encouraged Jefferson to blend the moral doctrines of Christ with those recommended by the Scottish school. From this syncretism, Jefferson could reaffirm his belief that a benevolent Creator had endowed human beings with a faculty that would enable them, once they were instructed by the example of Christ, to acts of benevolence even more extensive than the most utopian of those the Scots had proposed.

What precisely does Christianity, understood as a moral code, require of us as social and moral beings? In answer to this question, Jefferson compiled his forty-page extract of the New Testament,[89] in which he proposed to separate the genuine moral teachings of Jesus from the fraudulent and fantastic accounts of the evangelists. Undaunted by the complexity of the task, Jefferson repeatedly insisted that the genuine teachings of Jesus were as easy to distinguish as "diamonds in a dunghill."[90] In keeping with Jefferson's general view that religion teaches only "the moralities of life and the duties of a social being,"[91] which can be known by reason and the moral sense, he omits all references to "the immaculate conception of Jesus, His deification, the Creation of the world by Him, His miraculous powers, His resurrection and visible ascension, His corporeal presence in the Eucharist, the Trinity, original sin, atonement, regeneration, election, orders of Hierarchy, etc."[92] For Jefferson, the essential teaching of Christianity boils down to the two commandments: to "love our neighbors as ourselves and to do good to all men."[93] In answer to the question, who is our neighbor? Jefferson offers the Parable of the Samaritan, which he commends as "true Benevolence."[94] Elsewhere in the table of contents to his treatise, he includes Luke 14:12–14, which exhorts us to invite to the feast those who can never repay us, subjoining to it the comment, "the merit of disinterested good." And he endorses Luke's view (17:7–10) that we cannot discharge our duties to others simply by fulfilling our legal obligations, adding his own comment, "mere justice no praise." Among other selections Jefferson included without comment are Matthew 5:44, "love your enemies, bless them that curse you, do good to them that hate you, and pray for them that despitefully use you," and the Sermon on the Mount. Although Jefferson made no comment on the latter selection at the time, years later he would express the wish that "all the Christian religions would rally to the Sermon on the Mount, make that the central point of Union in religion, and the stamp of genuine Christianity, since it gives us all the precepts of our duties to one another."[95] As Jefferson abridged them, the Gospels of Jesus contain the "most sublime and benevolent code of morals which has ever been offered to man,"[96] enjoining upon us the duty to relieve the suffering of others and to promote their positive good.

Yet, precisely because the true teachings of Jesus would require the most heroic exertions that are far beyond the natural feelings registered by the moral sense, we are justified in wondering whether such universal benevolence can reasonably be expected of the mass of citizens and whether this is what Jefferson had in mind when he linked the pursuit of happiness with virtue. The question gains force in the kind of liberal republic Jefferson helped to create, where benevolence cannot be compelled by legislation and where the commitment to private property and individual rights runs counter to such selfless virtue. The advice in Matthew 6:25, "Take no heed for your life, what ye shall eat, or what ye shall drink; nor yet for your body, what ye shall put on," or Matthew 19:21, "If thou wilt be perfect, go and sell what thou hast, and give it to the poor, and thou shalt have treasure in heaven," both of which Jefferson included in his digest, would seem well beyond the reach of a democratic society. The problem is not that Jefferson lacks a vision of human excellence but, on the contrary, that at its highest, it may be too exalted and self-denying for a liberal republic.

Jefferson's appropriation of Christian benevolence for his own social and political purposes helps us to appreciate both the strength of his moral vision and the defects to which it almost inevitably gives rise. Although the model of Christian love that Jefferson recommends as the *akmé* of purely "human excellence" remains beyond the reach of most individuals, it does continue to inspire the imagination and to evoke the greatest admiration and esteem whenever, in all its purity and innocence, it appears. Instructed by carefully chosen Gospel stories, the moral sense reserves its highest approbation for those sentiments that inspire voluntary acts of extensive benevolence. Yet, at the same time, there is the danger that such exalted virtue may encourage its own particular form of corruption. The reduction of religion to a mere moral code concerned principally with our obligations in this world may inspire political idealists to use the innate "love of others" for their own ends. Failing to recognize that benevolence is a virtue only when it is uncoerced, and divorcing the practice of virtue from the goal of eternal salvation, such activists may be tempted to remake the world by compelling others to exercise benevolence and compassion. The extensive model of benevolence set forth in the Gospels and endorsed by Jefferson sets no geographic limits to such aspirations.[97]

Nevertheless, after having held up the model of the most extensive philanthropy, Jefferson is perfectly prepared to retreat to the more realistic ground occupied by the Scots. While the Good Samaritan remains the finest example of "true benevolence," Jefferson understood that, for most people, extensive benevolence is usually restricted to a close circle of family and friends. Here again, Jefferson's advice to his daughters, and later to his grandchildren, provides a model for benevolent actions that is both practical in its goals and realistic in its limitations. Although he exhorted his children to take every opportunity to exercise their hearts in benevolence and to "pity and help anything in distress,"[98] he did not urge them to look much beyond home. It was sufficient for his daughters to focus their kind attentions on their families and those immediately around them. "The circle of our nearest connections is the only one in which a faithful and lasting affection can be found. . . . It is therefore the only soil on which it is worth while to bestow much culture."[99]

Accordingly, Jefferson offers sound practical advice for how to conduct themselves with family and friends:

> never be angry with any body, nor speak harm of them, try to let every body's faults be forgotten, as you would wish yours to be; take more pleasure in giving what is best to another than in having it for yourself, and then all the world will love you, and I more than all the world.[100]

The emphasis here is on self-control and on cultivating those pleasing dispositions that will win the approval and admiration of others. It is altogether an agreeable portrait, in which individuals are linked through the natural bonds of affection and goodwill, and each understands that her own happiness is linked to the happiness and well-being of others. Moreover, Jefferson here acknowledged that even within the family, the exercise of these virtuous dispositions would not always be as easy as he sometimes suggested.[101] Although benevolence is not always, or even usually, heroic, it still requires considerable practice and effort to bring the desires into alignment with what is right.

For all but the most liberal minds, the further we move from these intimate attachments, the weaker the impulse to do good. To acquaintances and strangers we owe nothing more than good humor or, failing even that, the "artificial" virtue of politeness. And it is precisely the mark of good humor that it "deprive[s] us of nothing worth a moment's consideration"; it demands nothing more than the sacrifice of "the little conveniences and preferences." No wonder Jefferson can exclaim, "how cheap a price for the goodwill of another."[102] In practice, the biblical proclamation "goodwill toward men" turns out, for most people, most of the time, to be little more than a call to courtesy and good manners.

The Legacy of Jefferson's Moral Vision

It is easy to criticize a moral vision that ranges from the sublime to the quotidian, in which all human beings are simultaneously called to the most extensive benevolence, yet praised for their amiability and mere politeness. Thus, Thomas Pangle and Lorraine Smith Pangle object that Jefferson's moral sense doctrine leaves no room for magnanimity; it seems to cut off at the roots the psychological motivation of the great-souled man, who acts for others not out of any moral sentiment directed toward their well-being, but out of a sense of his own superior nature and what is due him.[103] But magnanimity of this sort cannot reasonably be expected in a liberal republic, founded on the proposition that "all men are created equal." It properly belongs to an earlier, more aristocratic age, like the one Jefferson deliberately set out to overthrow.

At the opposite extreme, Gordon Wood lays bare what some revolutionaries regarded as the residual hierarchical assumptions of benevolence. Although benevolence was intended to replace earlier relations of hierarchy and dependence by uniting people on the basis of so-called natural affections, the obligation of gratitude to which benevolence gives rise masks a lingering inequality and dependence. In the end, benevolence must give way to the more powerful and radical forces of democratic equality.[104]

But what has been the effect of this more radical idea of equality upon the American character? We have moved from Jefferson's faith in the capacity of ordinary men and women to discipline their selfish desires and bring them under the governance of the moral sense to a postmodern doubt about the very possibility of moral judgment. Under this dispensation, we have seen the virtual extinction of politeness and goodwill, even as the voices calling for the public enforcement of benevolence have become more insistent.

As Americans struggle with these problems today, Jefferson's moral vision has much to recommend it. More than any other founder, Jefferson speaks to the republican hope that human beings can act as responsible moral agents. But at the same time, he reminds us that virtue and good character depend upon instruction and practice. Human beings may have a natural instinct for virtue, but this instinct requires training and development before it bears fruit. Moreover, the task of building character is, and in a liberal republic must remain, the responsibility of those "mediating institutions" of civil society. It is not primarily the task of government to build character, though no government can remain indifferent to the need for character. The virtues Jefferson seeks to encourage are especially appropriate to the kind of society he helped to create. His vision of a republic dedicated to equal and impartial justice, while privately seeking, as far as possible, to cultivate goodwill and benevolence as part of what is recognized for our own happiness, does honor to democratic morality.

Notes

This essay will appear as chapter 2 in *Thomas Jefferson and the Formation of American Character*, forthcoming from and copyrighted by the University Press of Kansas; it is included here by permission of the University Press of Kansas.

1. Jefferson to Mary Jefferson Eppes, January 7, 1798, in *The Family Letters of Thomas Jefferson*, Edwin Morris Betts and James Adam Bear Jr., eds. (Columbia: University of Missouri Press, 1996), 152; hereinafter cited as *Family Letters*.

2. For a contemporary examination of the moral sense, see James Q. Wilson, *The Moral Sense* (New York: Free Press, 1993).

3. Jefferson to Peter Carr, August 10, 1787, in *The Writings of Thomas Jefferson*, Andrew A. Lipscomb and Albert E. Bergh, eds., 20 vols. (Washington, DC: Thomas Jefferson Memorial Association, 1904–1905), 6:256–262; hereinafter cited as *Jefferson Writings*.

4. Jefferson to Thomas Law, June 13, 1814, in *Jefferson Writings*, 14:138–144.

5. Jefferson to William Short, October 31, 1819, in *Jefferson Writings*, 15:219–224.

6. See, for example, Aristotle, *Nichomachean Ethics*, T. E. Page, ed. (Cambridge, England: The Loeb Classical Library, [1926] 1962), II.1104b.10–15.

7. Jefferson to Maria Cosway, October 12, 1786, in *Jefferson Writings*, 5:430–448.

8. See Henry Home Kames's criticism of Locke in, *Essays on the Principles of Morality and Natural Religion, 1751* (New York: Garland Publishing, 1976), 2–15; hereinafter cited as *Essays*.

9. Here, it may be useful to distinguish between the claim made by Aristotle that "man is by nature a political animal" *(Politics*, Carnes Lord, trans. [Chicago: University of Chicago Press, 1985], I.1253al–3) and the Scottish assertion that he is by nature social. For Aristotle, man's political nature is linked to his capacity for speech, which in turn rests on his ability to reason and deliberate about the right way to live. Aristotle's emphasis upon reason as the distinctively human faculty points to what is most excellent in human nature. It does not mean that all human beings actually do reason about justice, only that the capacity to reason is

what separates us from the animals. Indeed, since not all human beings possess the capacity for reasoned judgment, the claim that man is by nature political has decidedly aristocratic, or at least nondemocratic, implications.

Moreover, in the *Ethics*, Aristotle argues that the moral virtues are largely the result of habituation. He rejects outright the suggestion that there exists a distinct moral faculty, akin to the sense organs, for perceiving right and wrong. Similarly, he rejects the idea that virtue arises out of the social passions. All passions stand in need of correction so that they achieve a mean between excess and deficiency. No passion can by itself give rise to virtue. Ultimately, it is prudence or practical wisdom that establishes what is right in any given situation. In contrast to the moral sense philosophers, then, the argument that man is by nature political points to the supremacy of practical reason over sentiment, and of habit over impulse, in determining moral virtue.

10. Francis Hutcheson, *Illustrations on the Moral Sense*, Bernard Peach, ed. (Cambridge, MA: Belknap Press of Harvard University Press, 1971), 118–119.

11. *Essays,* 84, 61.

12. Ibid., 85.

13. Ibid., 55.

14. Ibid., 81.

15. In fairness, Hutcheson had not argued in favor of such universal benevolence. But because Kames seeks to ground moral obligation in those sentiments that give rise to universal duty and can be enforced by the state, he rejects benevolence. Indeed, for Kames, it is not clear if, strictly speaking, we have any "duty" to act for the positive good of others at all. Though such actions merit the highest approbation, the neglect of them is not enforceable (ibid., 126–127).

16. Ibid., 87–88.

17. Ibid., 103.

18. Ibid., 112, 133.

19. Aristotle, *Ethics*, II.1103a15–1103b5.

20. David Hume, *A Treatise of Human Nature*, bk. III, pt. II, chap. 1; and David Hume, *An Enquiry concerning the Principles of Morals*, section 3, in *Hume's Moral and Political Philosophy*, Henry D. Aiken, ed. (New York: Hafner Publishing Co., 1972).

21. Adam Smith, *Theory of Moral Sentiments* (Indianapolis, IN: Liberty Classics, 1969), 47–53.

22. Jefferson to Peter Carr, August 10, 1787, and Jefferson to Thomas Law, June 13, 1814, in *Jefferson Writings*, 6:256–262 and 14:138–144.

23. On this latter point, see Michael Zuckert, "Thomas Jefferson on Nature and Natural Rights," in *The Framers and Fundamental Rights*, Robert A. Licht, ed. (Washington, DC: American Enterprise Institute, 1991), 137–169, at 168.

24. See, in particular, his observation that both Native Americans and African American slaves possessed a moral sense, in Thomas Jefferson,

Notes on the State of Virginia, William Peden, ed. (Chapel Hill: University of North Carolina Press, 1955), query 14, 140–149; Jefferson to Robert Skipwith, August 3, 1771, in *Jefferson Writings*, 4:237–240; Jefferson to Peter Carr, August 19, 1785, in *Jefferson Writings*, 5:82–87.

25. Jefferson to Thomas Law, June 13, 1814, in *Jefferson Writings*, 14:138–144; Jefferson to John Adams, October 14, 1816, in *The Adams–Jefferson Letters: The Complete Correspondence between Thomas Jefferson and Abigail and John Adams*, Lester J. Cappon, ed., 2 vols. (Chapel Hill: University of North Carolina Press, 1959), 492, hereinafter cited as *Adams–Jefferson Letters*.

26. Jefferson to Peter Carr, August 10, 1787, in *Jefferson Writings*, 6:256–262.

27. For a fuller discussion of these difficulties, see David Daiches Raphael, *The Moral Sense* (London: Oxford University Press, 1947), 1–14.

28. Jefferson to Martha Jefferson, December 11, 1783, in *Family Letters*, 20–21.

29. Jefferson to Maria Cosway, October 12, 1786, in *Jefferson Writings*, 5:430–448.

30. Jefferson to James Fishback, September 27, 1809, in *Jefferson Writings*, 12:314–316; also Jefferson to Dr. John Manners, June 12, 1817, in *Jefferson Writings*, 15:124–126. But see also Morton White, *The Philosophy of the American Revolution* (New York: Oxford University Press, 1978), who argues that at the time of the Revolution, Jefferson was more of a rationalist in moral matters and that only later did he "abandon" the position of his early insistence that "the moral sense is subordinate to reason" (124–125).

31. Jefferson to Peter Carr, August 10, 1787, in *Jefferson Writings*, 6:256–262. See also Jefferson's "Opinion on the French Treaties," where reason shares equally with the moral sense in its claim to moral knowledge: "Questions of natural right are triable by conformity with the moral sense and reason of man" (April 28, 1793, in *Jefferson Writings*, 3:226–243).

32. Jefferson to Thomas Jefferson Randolph, November 24, 1808, in *Family Letters*, 362–365; also Jefferson to Mary Jefferson Eppes, January 7, 1798, in *Family Letters*, 152.

33. Jefferson to Peter Carr, August 10, 1787, in *Jefferson Writings*, 6:256–262. The contrast with Kames on this point is striking. Where, for the Scotsman, abstract reason helps to refine the original moral impulses and to promote moral improvement, Jefferson, despite his agreement with Kames on the larger point, tends to stress the ways in which reason can lead the heart astray.

34. Jefferson to Peter Carr, August 10, 1787, in *Jefferson Writings*, 6:256–262; Jefferson to Francis Wayles Eppes, June 27, 1821, in *Family Letters*, 439–440.

35. Jefferson to Thomas Law, June 13, 1814, in *Jefferson Writings*, 14:138–144; see also Kames's critique of the modern rationalists, *Essays*, 95–100.

36. See especially Plato, *Republic*, Allan Bloom, trans. (New York: Basic Books, 1968), 544a; Aristotle, *Politics*, III.1268bl.4–9; IV.1239bl.15–20; VII.1328bl. 25–40; Cicero, *On the Commonwealth*, George Holland Smith and Stanley Barney Smith, trans. (Indianapolis, IN: Bobbs-Merrill, 1984), bk.1, xxvii–xxxv.

37. Jefferson to Thomas Law, June 13, 1814, in *Jefferson Writings*, 14:138–144.

38. Ibid.

39. In this regard, see especially, White, *The Philosophy of the American Revolution*, 97–141.

40. *Essays*, 143.

41. Cited in Adrienne Koch, *The Philosophy of Thomas Jefferson* (New York: Columbia University Press, 1943), 18. And see the discussion in Kames, *Essays*, 145–149.

42. This position would, moreover, accord with Jefferson's faith in the natural aristocracy to rule in the interests of the people.

43. Jefferson to Thomas Law, June 13, 1814, in *Jefferson Writings*, 14:138–144.

44. Raphael, *The Moral Sense*, 25n2.

45. Jefferson to Thomas Law, June 13, 1814, in *Jefferson Writings*, 14:138–144.

46. Jefferson to John Adams, October 14, 1816, in *Adams-Jefferson Letters*, 490–493.

47. Jefferson to John Bannister Jr., October 15, 1785, in *Jefferson Writings*, 5:185–188.

48. Smith, *Theory of Moral Sentiments*, 194–199; also Kames, *Essays*, 132–135.

49. Jefferson to Thomas Jefferson Randolph, November 24, 1808, in *Family Letters*, 362–365. To be sure, one must first possess the good judgment to identify those worthy of emulation, but that is not Jefferson's point here. And see Jefferson's letter to Richard Price, February 7, 1788, in *Memoir, Correspondence, and Miscellanies, from the Papers of Thomas Jefferson*, Thomas Jefferson Randolph, ed. (Charlottesville, VA: F. Carr & Co., 1829), 2:290, where Jefferson observes that reason becomes more important in moral judgment as it "grows stronger by time and experience."

50. Jefferson to Robert Skipwith, August 3, 1771, in *Jefferson Writings*, 4:237–240. For some reason, the Pangles do not discuss this important letter and so fault Jefferson for failing to appreciate the role that literature can play in stimulating the moral imagination (Lorraine Smith Pangle and Thomas L. Pangle, *The Learning of Liberty: The Educational Ideas of the American Founders* [Lawrence: University Press of Kansas, 1993], 258–259).

51. Jefferson to Robert Skipwith, August 3, 1771, in *Jefferson Writings*, 4:237–240; unless otherwise noted, all quotations in this section are from this letter. See also Jefferson's Shakespeare entries in *Jefferson's Literary Commonplace Book*, in *The Papers of Thomas Jefferson, Second Series*, Douglas L. Wilson, ed. (Princeton, NJ: Princeton University Press, 1989).

52. Jefferson to Peter Carr, August 10, 1787, in *Jefferson Writings*, 11:256–262.

53. See Jefferson to Nathaniel Burwell, Esq., March 14, 1818, in *Jefferson Writings*, 15:165–168, where Jefferson criticizes popular and trashy novels, aimed at girls, for their tendency to produce, among other things, "a bloated imagination" and "sickly judgment." On the other hand, certain popular works, like *Modern Griselda*, can apparently instruct by the "rule of contraries," that is, showing us how not to behave (Jefferson to Anne Randolph Bankhead, May 26, 1811, in *Family Letters*, 400–401).

54. Jefferson to Peter Carr, August 19, 1785, in *Jefferson Writings*, 5:82–87.

55. Jefferson to Thomas Law, June 13, 1814, in *Jefferson Writings*, 14:138–144. But compare Jefferson's recollection with the discussion in Kames's *Essays*, 77. What Kames is arguing is that we have no moral obligations to which we are not prompted by some natural impulse. All our duties are grounded on our nature. Jefferson shifts Kames's emphasis upon the naturalness of morality to an argument for moral majoritarianism.

56. This is a confusion that runs throughout Jefferson's political thought. As statesman, he, too, tended to confuse the approbation of the wise few with that of his countrymen as a whole, until the distinction was made painfully clear to him. He hoped that the passage of time would erase the distinction, winning him the approval of all.

57. Raphael, *The Moral Sense*, 44–46; Arthur O. Lovejoy, *Reflections on Human Nature* (Baltimore, MD: Johns Hopkins University Press, 1961), lecture 7, esp. 228ff.

58. Consider, for example, Jefferson's reference to the "wise and honest part of mankind" in the "Opinion on the French Treaties," April 28, 1793, in *Jefferson Writings*, 3:226–243.

59. Jefferson to Edward Coles, August 25, 1814, in *The Works of Thomas Jefferson*, Paul Leicester Ford, ed., 10 vols. (New York: G. P. Putnam's Sons, 1904), 11:416–420; hereinafter cited as *Works*.

60. Jefferson, *Notes on the State of Virginia*, query 18, 162; Jefferson to Edward Coles, August 25, 1814, in *Works*, 11:416–420. For the way in which slavery has corrupted the moral sense of the slaves, see *Notes on the State of Virginia*, query 14, 142.

61. Jefferson, *Notes on the State of Virginia*, query 18, 163.

62. Jefferson to Dr. Benjamin Rush, April 21, 1803, in *Jefferson Writings*, 10:379–385.

63. Only Thomas Pangle and Lorraine Smith Pangle have focused on this aspect of moral development in Jefferson; see *The Learning of Liberty*, esp. chap. 13. It is worth noting that Hutcheson and Kames both consider the importance of good habits in developing the moral sense.

64. See especially Martha Jefferson Randolph to Jefferson, November 18, 1808, in *Family Letters*, 359–361. It was this letter that provoked Jefferson's famous advice to his grandson, Thomas Jefferson Randolph, written later that month.

65. Jefferson to Peter Carr, August 10, 1787, in *Jefferson Writings*, 6:256–262.

66. See especially Jan Lewis, "'The Blessings of Domestic Society': Thomas Jefferson's Family and the Transformation of Republican Politics," in *Jeffersonian Legacies*, Peter Onuf, ed. (Charlottesville: University Press of Virginia, 1993), 109–146, at 115.

67. Jefferson to Martha Jefferson, May 21, 1787, in *Family Letters*, 41–42; also, Jefferson to Martha Jefferson, March 6, 1786, and April 7, 1787, in *Family Letters*, 30, 36–37; and Jefferson to Mary Jefferson, April 11, 1790, in *Family Letters*, 52.

68. Jefferson to Anne Cary, Thomas Jefferson, and Ellen Wayles Randolph, March 2, 1802, in *Family Letters*, 218.

69. Jefferson to Robert Skipwith, August 3, 1771, in *Jefferson Writings*, 4:237–240.

70. Despite the importance of the imagination, sympathy, as Hume and Smith understood it, that is, the capacity to enter imaginatively into the joys and sorrows of others and to have them enter imaginatively into ours, does not figure prominently in Jefferson's analysis.

71. Garry Wills, *Inventing America* (Garden City, NY: Doubleday, 1978), esp. 193–206.

72. Jefferson to Thomas Law, June 13, 1814, in *Jefferson Writings*, 14:138–144.

73. Jefferson to Francis Gilmer, June 7, 1816, in *Jefferson Writings*, 15:23–27.

74. Jefferson to John Adams, October 14, 1816, in *Adams-Jefferson Letters*, 490–493; also Jefferson to William Johnson, June 12, 1823, in *Jefferson Writings*, 15:439–452.

75. Jefferson to Dr. Benjamin Rush, April 21, 1803, in *Jefferson Writings*, 10:379–385; Jefferson to Maria Cosway, October 12, 1786, in *Jefferson Writings*, 5:430–448; and Jefferson to P. S. duPont de Nemours, April 24, 1816, in *Works*, 14:487–493.

76. Jefferson to John Adams, October 14, 1816, in *Adams-Jefferson Letters*, 490–493; Jefferson to Francis Gilmer, June 7, 1816, in *Jefferson Writings*, 15:23–27.

77. Jefferson to Francis Gilmer, June 7, 1816, in *Jefferson Writings*, 15:23–27. See also, Jefferson to John Adams, October 14, 1816, in *Adams-Jefferson Letters*, 490–493; and Jefferson to William Johnson, June 12, 1823, in *Jefferson Writings*, 15:439–452. Context is important here, too, as Jefferson is again reacting to the argument that justice is conventional and not developing an argument about the moral sense in general.

78. "Opinion on the French Treaties," April 28, 1793, in *Jefferson Writings*, 3:226–243.

79. Like Hutcheson, Jefferson speaks of benevolence both as a passion that the moral sense perceives and as the virtue that ensues (Raphael, *The Moral Sense*, 22).

80. "Prospectus on Political Economy," enclosed in a letter from Jefferson to Joseph Milligan, April 6, 1816, in *Jefferson Writings*, 14:456–466.

81. See especially the discussions in Kames, *Essays*, 126–127 and 132–133, and in Smith, *Theory of Moral Sentiments*, 155–160.

82. Jefferson to John Adams, July 5, 1814, in *Adams-Jefferson Letters*, 433–434.

83. Paul Conkin, "The Religious Pilgrimage of Thomas Jefferson," in *Jeffersonian Legacies*, 19–49.

84. Jefferson to John Adams, May 5, 1817, in *Adams-Jefferson Letters*, 512; Gordon Wood, *The Radicalism of the American Revolution* (New York: Alfred A. Knopf, 1992), 213–225.

85. Jefferson to Dr. Benjamin Rush, April 21, 1803, in *Jefferson Writings*, 10:379–385; see also Jefferson to Edward Dowse, April 19, 1803, in *Jefferson Writings*, 10:376–378.

86. Jefferson to Dr. Benjamin Rush, April 21, 1803, in *Jefferson Writings*, 10:379–385; see also Jefferson to Edward Dowse, April 19, 1803, in *Jefferson Writings*, 10:376–378.

87. Jefferson to Dr. Benjamin Rush, April 21, 1803, in *Jefferson Writings*, 10:379–385.

88. Ibid.

89. Jefferson actually compiled two digests. The first, which he entitled *The Philosophy of Jesus*, is now lost to us. The second, compiled much later, is the *Life and Morals of Jesus of Nazareth*, which sifts through the same materials, with a few changes. The big difference is that Jefferson offers his selections in four languages.

90. Jefferson to John Adams, October 12, 1813, in *Adams-Jefferson Letters*, 383–386; Jefferson to Francis Adrian Van der Kemp, April 25, 1816, in *Jefferson Writings*, 15:1–3; Jefferson to William Short, October 31, 1819, in *Jefferson Writings*, 15:219–224.

91. Jefferson to Ezra Stiles Ely, June 25, 1819, in *Jefferson Writings*, 15:202–204.

92. Jefferson to William Short, October 31, 1819, in *Jefferson Writings*, 15:219–224.

93. Letter to Ezra Stiles Ely, June 25, 1819, in *Jefferson Writings*, 15:202–204.

94. See the table of contents in, Dickinson W. Adams, ed., *Jefferson's Extracts from the Gospels: The Papers of Thomas Jefferson*, 2d ser. (Princeton, NJ: Princeton University Press, 1983), 59. It is this example that he offers in his discussion of the moral sense with Thomas Law (Jefferson to Thomas Law, June 13, 1814, in *Jefferson Writings*, 14:138–144).

95. Jefferson to George Thacher, January 26, 1824, in *Works*, 12:332–339.

96. Jefferson to John Adams, October 12, 1813, in *Adams-Jefferson Letters*, 383–386.

97. On this point, see Hannah Arendt on the corruptions of the French Revolution in *On Revolution* (New York: Viking Press, 1963), chap. 2, and Jean Bethke Elshtain, *Democracy on Trial* (New York: Basic Books, 1995), 122–123.

98. Jefferson to Martha Jefferson, March 6, 1786, in *Family Letters*, 30; Jefferson to Anne Cary, Thomas Jefferson, and Ellen Wayles Randolph, March 2, 1802, in *Family Letters*, 218.

99. Jefferson to Mary Jefferson Eppes, January 1, 1799, in *Family Letters*, 170; Jefferson to Martha Jefferson Randolph, July 17, 1790, in *Family Letters*, 60–61.

100. Jefferson to Mary Jefferson, April 11, 1790, in *Family Letters*, 52.

101. Jefferson to Martha Jefferson Randolph, July 17, 1970, in *Family Letters*, 61; see also Jefferson to Thomas Jefferson Randolph, November 24, 1808, in *Family Letters*, 362–365.

102. Jefferson to Thomas Jefferson Randolph, November 24, 1808, in *Family Letters*, 362–365.

103. Pangle and Pangle, *The Learning of Liberty*, 262–264.

104. Wood, *Radicalism of the American Revolution*, 224–225.

Index

About the Contributors

Raoul Berger was Charles Warren Senior Fellow in American Legal History at Harvard Law School from 1971–1976 and was professor of law at the University of California, Berkeley, from 1962–1965. Mr. Berger is the author of over 100 articles in legal periodicals as well as seven books in American legal history including *Congress v. the Supreme Court, Impeachment: Some Constitutional Problems, Executive Privilege: A Constitutional Myth,* and *Government by Judiciary.* His most recent book is *The Fourteenth Amendment and the Bill of Rights.*

Colin Bonwick is professor of United States and English history. His books include *English Radicals and the American Revolution* and *The American Revolution.*

Robert K. Faulkner teaches political science at Boston College. He is the author of *The Jurisprudence of John Marshall, Richard Hooker and the Politics of a Christian England,* and *Francis Bacon and the Project of Progress* as well as of various articles on moral and political philosophy and American politics.

Elizabeth Fox-Genovese is the Eleonore Raoul Professor of the Humanities and professor of history at Emory University, where she is also an associate member of the English department. Her publications include *The Origins of Physiocracy: Economic Revolution and Social Order in Eighteenth Century France* and *Within the Plantation Household: Black and White Women of the Old South.* She has published numerous articles on feminist theory and women's history and literature.

Morton J. Frisch is emeritus and adjunct professor of political science at Northern Illinois University. He is coeditor and coauthor of *American Political Thought: The Philosophic Dimension of American Statesmanship*, and his books include *Franklin D. Roosevelt: The Contribution of the New Deal to American Political Thought and Practise* and *Alexander Hamilton and the Political Order: An Interpretation of his Political Thought and Practice*. He has also edited a volume of the *Selected Writings and Speeches of Alexander Hamilton*.

Richard King is reader in American studies at the University of Nottingham. He is the author of *The Party of Eros, A Southern Renaissance*, and most recently *Civil Rights and the Idea of Freedom*. He has also served as chairman of the British Association for American Studies.

Gary L. McDowell is the director of the Institute of United States Studies and professor of American studies at the University of London.

Sharon L. Noble practiced law in California from 1988 to 1991. She is currently a visiting research fellow at the Institute of United States Studies.

Peter J. Parish was the director of the Institute of United States Studies (1983–1992), where he is now professor emeritus and distinguished senior fellow. He is a former chairman of the British Association for American Studies. His books include *The American Civil War* and *Slavery: History and Historians*. He has recently edited the Everyman edition of Abraham Lincoln's *Speeches and Letters*.

J. R. Pole is the Rhodes Professor of American History emeritus at Oxford University. He has served on the Council of the Institute of Early American History and Culture in Williamsburg, Virginia, and is also a fellow of the British Academy. Among his publications are *Abraham Lincoln and the Working Classes of Britain, Political Representation in England and the Origins of the American Republic*, and *Pursuit of Equality in American History*. He is also coeditor of *The Blackwell Encyclopedia of the American Revolution*.

Paul A. Rahe is currently Jay P. Walker Professor of American History at the University of Tulsa. Among his publications is *Republics Ancient and Modern: Classical Republicanism and the American Revolution*.

Robert A. Rutland is professor emeritus of history at the University of Virginia, where he also served as editor-in-chief of *The Papers of James Madison*. He also edited *The Papers of George Mason* and is the author of *The Birth of the Bill of Rights, Ordeal of the Constitution, James Madison: The Founding Father, The Presidency of James Madison*, and *The Democrats: From Jefferson to Carter*. He is currently visiting professor of history at the University of Tulsa.

Jeffrey Leigh Sedgwick is associate professor of political science at the University of Massachusetts. He is author of *Law Enforcement Planning: The Limits of and Economic Analysis* and numerous articles and book chapters on American political thought, criminal justice policy, and the American presidency. He is currently completing a new textbook on the history of American political thought.

James R. Stoner is assistant professor of political science at Louisiana State University and author of *Common Law and Liberal Theory: Coke, Hobbes, and the Origins of American Constitutionalism*.

Howard Temperley is professor emeritus of American studies at the University of East Anglia. His publications include *British Antislavery: 1833–1870, The Journals of Lieutenant Colonel Joseph Gubbins, Introduction to American Studies* (with Malcolm Bradbury), and *White Dreams, Black Africa: The Antislavery Expedition to the Niger, 1841–42*. He has served as editor of the *Journal of American Studies* (1977–1986) and chairman of the British Association of American Studies (1986–1989).

Jean M. Yarbrough is professor and chair of government and legal studies at Bowdoin College. She has published numerous articles in American political thought and is completing a book about Thomas Jefferson and the formation of the American character.

John Zvesper is lecturer in politics at the University of East Anglia and a teaching fellow at the Institute of United States Studies. Among his publications are *Political Philosophy and Rhetoric: A Study of the Origins of American Party Politics* and *Nature and Liberty*.